**The Future of Youth
Violence Prevention**

The Future of Youth Violence Prevention

● ● ● ● ● ● ● ● ● ● ● ● ● ● ● ● ● ● ● ●

A Mixtape for Practice, Policy, and Research

EDITED BY PAUL BOXER AND
RAPHAEL TRAVIS JR.

Rutgers University Press
New Brunswick, Camden, and Newark, New Jersey
London and Oxford

Rutgers University Press is a department of Rutgers, The State University of New Jersey, one of the leading public research universities in the nation. By publishing worldwide, it furthers the University's mission of dedication to excellence in teaching, scholarship, research, and clinical care.

Library of Congress Cataloging-in-Publication Data

Names: Boxer, Paul, editor. | Travis, Raphael, editor.
Title: The future of youth violence prevention : a mixtape for practice, policy, and research / edited by Paul Boxer and Raphael Travis.
Description: New Brunswick, NJ : Rutgers University Press, [2025] | Includes bibliographical references and index.
Identifiers: LCCN 2024010915 | ISBN 9781978833777 (paperback ; alk. paper) | ISBN 9781978833784 (hardcover ; alk. paper) | ISBN 9781978833791 (epub) | ISBN 9781978833814 (pdf)
Subjects: LCSH: Youth and violence. | Violence in adolescence. | Violence—Prevention. | At-risk youth—Services for.
Classification: LCC HQ799.2.V56 F87 2025 | DDC 303.60835—dc23/eng/20240717
LC record available at https://lccn.loc.gov/2024010915

A British Cataloging-in-Publication record for this book is available from the British Library.

This collection copyright © 2025 by Rutgers, The State University of New Jersey
Individual chapters copyright © 2025 in the names of their authors
All rights reserved

No part of this book may be reproduced or utilized in any form or by any means, electronic or mechanical, or by any information storage and retrieval system, without written permission from the publisher. Please contact Rutgers University Press, 106 Somerset Street, New Brunswick, NJ 08901. The only exception to this prohibition is "fair use" as defined by U.S. copyright law.

References to internet websites (URLs) were accurate at the time of writing. Neither the author nor Rutgers University Press is responsible for URLs that may have expired or changed since the manuscript was prepared.

♾ The paper used in this publication meets the requirements of the American National Standard for Information Sciences—Permanence of Paper for Printed Library Materials, ANSI Z39.48-1992.

rutgersuniversitypress.org

To our children, our partners, our friends, our mentors and students,
our mothers, our fathers, our families, our ancestors, our communities.

Contents

Introduction: Youth Violence and the Mixtape
Framework   I
PAUL BOXER AND RAPHAEL TRAVIS JR.

Part I   Foundations

1   Theoretical Foundations of Youth Violence Prevention   9
PAUL BOXER AND ZION CRICHLOW

2   A Life Course Approach to Youth Violence Prevention   19
JOYCE LEE, ELIZABETH BARNERT, AND NEAL HALFON

3   Promoting Competencies and Preventing Violence with
Social-Emotional and Social-Cognitive Programs in Schools   35
KAREN L. BIERMAN AND REBECCA SLOTKIN

4   Anger Control Counseling for Youth Violence Prevention   45
RAYMOND W. NOVACO AND ISAIAS M. CONTRERAS

5   A Socioecological Framework for Youth Violence Prevention:
Treatment in Homes and Communities   55
KATHERINE KELTON AND ASHLI J. SHEIDOW

Part II   Expansions

6   Culturally Responsive Clinical Interventions for Youth Violence   69
STANLEY J. HUEY JR. AND EMILY N. SATINSKY

7   Trauma-Informed Mentoring and Related Approaches   81
MATTHEW HAGLER AND JEAN RHODES

viii • Contents

8 What Does Rap Music Have to Do with Violence Prevention?   93
JALEEL ABDUL-ADIL

9 Entrepreneurship and Vocational Development:
Pathways for Youth Violence Prevention   105
JORJA LEAP

10 Gun Violence in the Black Community:
The Rise of a Credible Messenger   115
SAMSON STYLES

11 Healed People Heal People: Stopping Violence
the Paterson Healing Collective Way   123
LIZA CHOWDHURY

12 Empowering Youth to Become Coproducers of Public Safety:
Implementation of Data-Informed Community Engagement
in Newark, NJ   133
ALEJANDRO GIMENEZ-SANTANA AND JOEL M. CAPLAN

13 Place-Based Prevention for Youth Gun Violence: Analytics
and Application   143
JONATHAN JAY

14 Culturally Rooted Strategies for Youth-Positive Development
among Youth of Color: A Holistic Approach to the Evaluation
of Community-Driven Youth Violence Prevention Programs   155
FIORELLA L. CARLOS CHAVEZ, PETER REJ, AND CHERYL GRILLS

Part III   Extensions

15 Hospital-Based Violence Intervention Programs
for Violently Injured Youth   173
STEPHANIE BONNE

16 Violence Prevention and Safety Promotion in the
LGBTQ+ Community   183
COREY PRACHNIAK

17 Disrupting the Crossover: Using and Improving Child
Welfare Practice as Youth Violence Prevention   193
CLAIRE TERREBONNE

18 Following the Lead of Child Survivors of Domestic Violence:
Toward Peace, Equity, and Wholeness   203
SHENNA MORRIS AND CASEY KEENE

Contents • ix

19 Current Issues and Emerging Needs in Teen Dating
Violence Prevention 215
KATRINA J. DEBNAM

20 Spiritual and Faith-Based Approaches to Preventing
Youth Violence 227
KRISTA R. MEHARI AND DEMETRIUS R. SMITH

21 Reimagining Violence Prevention within Youth Sport:
A Social Justice Approach to Youth Development through Sport 237
JILL KOCHANEK

Part IV Vistas

22 Understanding the Roles of Structural, Interpersonal,
and Intrapersonal Violence in the Lives of Black Girls 249
JANICE JOHNSON DIAS

23 Broadening the Scope of Hospital-Based Programs
to Prevent Youth Gun Violence 261
WILLIAM WICAL AND JOSEPH RICHARDSON JR.

24 The Law Alone Cannot Fix It 271
MARSHA LEVICK

25 Hip Hop Culture and a New Paradigm for Preventing
Violent Experiences among Youth 279
RAPHAEL TRAVIS JR. AND SIERRA MULLAN

26 Rooted Solutions: A Critical Race Perspective
on Violence Prevention for Black Youth 293
NONI K. GAYLORD-HARDEN AND ROBYN D. DOUGLAS

Conclusion: Transcending the Silos: The Mixtape
in Theory and Practice 303
RAPHAEL TRAVIS JR. AND PAUL BOXER

Acknowledgments 307
Notes on Contributors 311
Index 319

**The Future of Youth
Violence Prevention**

Introduction

• •

Youth Violence and the
Mixtape Framework

PAUL BOXER AND
RAPHAEL TRAVIS JR.

"Sooner or later you're gonna have to fight." That's what a twelve-year-old boy said to one of us (PB), years ago, during a group counseling session held at a community center located in a large southern city. The topic of discussion that day was violence—seeing it, encountering it, handling it. As is typical in these sorts of counseling sessions with youth, the conversation had eventually landed on what to do to stay safe and avoid violence. "What can you do if there is someone who wants to fight with you? How do you get out of it?"

The question had spurred a groupwide headshake. You can't get out it, these youth said almost in unison. And the twelve-year-old boy—a Black boy, growing up in this southern city—said to the adult leading the conversation—a white adult, a transplant who grew up in a northeastern suburb—"Sooner or later you're gonna have to fight."

The anecdote illustrates an important disconnect between the vast scholarly literature on preventing youth violence and the lived experiences of youth. On the one hand, we have a large base of research and theory describing the development and expression of aggression and violence among children and adolescents. This work has led to the creation of an array of well-established "best practice" approaches to preventing youth violence—and in turn promoting positive development. At the same time, we have the stark knowledge that no single approach has been shown to be 100 percent effective. And despite meaningful declines across various indicators of youth violence in the United States—including reports of involvement in physical fights (from the Centers for Disease Control and Prevention), reports of violent victimization (from the Bureau of Justice Statistics), and reports of arrests for violent crimes (from the Office of Juvenile Justice and Delinquency Prevention)—youth violence is far from being eliminated.

We also have the slowly emerging reality that much of what we have come to know about youth development and violence prevention is a body of knowledge with some significant gaps and oversights. For example, studies would suggest that Black youth are more likely to be involved in physical fights than are white youth. Yet studies also suggest that Black youth have increased exposure to indicators of poverty and community violence and experience greater academic challenges and the persistent stress of racism. In fact, one recent, large-scale study by J. C. Barnes and Ryan Motz (published in the 2018 volume of *Developmental Psychology*) demonstrated quite convincingly that race—and race alone—is a major driver of harsh school disciplinary responses, and in turn a critical predictor of arrest by early adulthood. Have our decades of research and theory of development and prevention adequately taken race and racism into account? Have our models of youth development and violence, and the extensive datasets upon which those models were built, really addressed the variations of social development and social ecologies—the gulfs between rural and urban upbringing, the powerful impact of early or persistent trauma? And if they haven't, what has been the fallout for our approaches to preventing youth violence? What are we missing, and how can we fill in those gaps?

Cue the Mixtape

In this volume we assert that the future of youth violence prevention demands a blend of traditional and cutting-edge perspectives—a mix of the old and the new. This volume is a platform for the intersection of research and practice in youth violence prevention that recognizes the major accomplishments of the pioneers in the field while spotlighting newer or more off-the-beaten-path approaches. We bring together a respected and diverse group of authors, blending long-standing evidence-based perspectives on the development and prevention of youth violence with fresh, new innovations in theory and methods. The result is a more holistic and multidisciplinary examination of the future of youth violence prevention. What we are offering is a scholarly but pragmatic mixtape of what well-established research and newer pathbreaking strategies have to offer to help prevent youth violence and to promote positive youth development.

The dictionary says that a mixtape is a "compilation of music, typically from multiple sources, recorded onto a medium." Although mixtapes can of course reflect any genre, contemporary mixtapes are commonly associated with Hip Hop culture. There is a rich history and variety in what constitutes a mixtape. Whether homemade or from a DJ or producer, a mixtape often involves pulling together preexisting content from well-established artists and/or adding content from unknown or lesser known artists. It can be a simple compilation, like a playlist, or a more dynamic, integrated, and continuous sequence of songs without abrupt transitions. Sometimes it is more blended with individual songs/tracks, featuring well-known beats, samples, or riffs from older artists combined with live freestyles or recorded raps or voice-overs from newer artists. Sometimes it is completely recontextualized remixed pieces drawing inspiration from other past and current material. To move beyond the playlist and industry dictated content, mixtapes are broadly democratized with current technology. Anyone with a strong sense of the music they like, and access to simple, often free, music applications or recording devices, can create one.

By and large this has not been the case with respect to what might be described as "evidence-based" or "best practice" youth violence prevention programming. The official designation of "evidence-based" or "best practice" largely emanates from a complex combination of scholarly research, tightly controlled practice, and a generous public or private funding stream. Despite the fact that mainstream approaches to preventing youth violence all rest on a shared foundation of common theories and research-based tactics reflecting what Dennis Embry has called the "kernels" of intervention practice, the highest-rated, top-flight programs have not been universally accessible to the youth who might need them. For example, even though several well-regarded programs had been in place for decades by the time of his analysis, in 2008 Peter Greenwood estimated that only about 5 percent of youth in the juvenile justice system received documented research-based intervention services. And while most public K–12 schools now implement some form of social-emotional, character-development-oriented programming designed to prevent aggressive and violent behavior and related behavioral health challenges, we do not know whether all programs are necessarily incorporating the key elements or "kernels" of successful intervention. Yet none of this is to say that children and adolescents in schools and justice settings are not receiving effective services—it might just as well be the case that huge numbers of youth are indeed receiving quality care, just not from "brand-name" or otherwise immediately recognizable programs or strategies.

Surely there is some truth to the idea that youth are indeed receiving some degree of effective service: as noted, juvenile arrests for person crimes and student reports of fighting have been declining. And it is not like the elements of effective youth violence prevention are some closely held secrets. They are in fact quite straightforward—a focus on training and promoting specific behavioral skills related to handling social interactions, engaging and empowering parents and other caregivers to manage youth constructively and consistently, and linking services to the broad array of positive supports in the wider neighborhood and community.

The "kernels" of effective prevention work on youth violence align directly with what decades of research on child and adolescent development have yielded: aggressive and violent behaviors emerge through a blend of specific personal and social-contextual risk factors that maintain through ongoing transactions between youth and their environments. Aggressive or violent youth tend to be irritable, impulsive, and easily triggered into intense emotional reactions. They tend to grow up in stressful, trauma-inducing environments. They frequently experience significant trauma early in development as well as persistently over time. Oftentimes these traumas co-occur with other by-products of stressful conditions including parental hostility, interparental or marital conflict, and neighborhood crime. And these youth tend to inhabit social networks of peers and/or relatives who promote or at least support their problem behavior. Effective interventions work in opposition to all of those sources of risk by improving neighborhood conditions, school climates, and access to supports through social, human, and family services agents; guiding youth into positive and prosocial settings and peer groups; helping caregivers coalesce around supporting their children; and improving behavioral self-regulation.

In theory—and we mean this directly, literally following the theory, which has followed the research—all youth can and should be able to access these sorts of services. Again, the elements of successful intervention are not secret—they are not the product of arcane magic, not subject to highly specific or esoteric instructions. Indeed, when properly understood and recognized, it is possible to implement effective violence prevention ideas in almost any context, with a variety of modes for delivery. A well-assembled mixtape seamlessly produces a brilliant sound by fusing classic tunes with new riffs, older beats with newer melodies, and traditional styles with cutting-edge flourishes. Similarly, a well-conceived and well-executed violence prevention program can mix established theories and strategies with new methods and tactics. A mixtape reflects the personal style of the creator to share with their audience. A violence prevention program can reflect the personal and professional strengths and skills of the creator to address the immediate needs of their community. This is how we democratize access to quality services.

In this book, we mix reports on theory and research with dispatches from the field across a variety of programmatic modalities, settings, and orientations. We challenge our authors—and our readers—to consider brand-new questions in an arena that has been open for inquiry for decades. We asked our authors to prepare chapters for this volume that authentically reflect their engagement with the work—to let their experiences and their passion for their research or practice flow through the text. We bring new voices into the discourse in harmony with those we have heard from for years. In part I (Foundations), we hear from scholars who have been studying mainstream youth violence and prevention strategies and are able to share deep insights from their time developing theory and evaluating evidence-based approaches. In part II (Expansions), we hear from scholars and practitioners working on a variety of new or out-of-the-mainstream approaches to preventing youth violence. In part III (Extensions), we hear from a mix of scholars and practitioners who are working on key emerging issues or increasingly urgent programmatic approaches relevant to mainstream youth violence prevention. In part IV (Vistas), we receive a bird's-eye view on some of the big-picture issues and ideas encompassing the landscape of youth violence prevention. Taken together, this eclectic blend of researchers, clinicians, community interventionists, educators, attorneys, and activists offers a multifaceted, multidisciplinary perspective on how to think about and do youth violence prevention in a manner that sets a conceptual foundation for the development of a broadly based workforce in the field.

Press Play

Welcome to the youth violence prevention mixtape.

Part I

Foundations

Theoretical Foundations of Youth Violence Prevention

● ● ● ● ● ● ● ● ● ● ● ● ●

PAUL BOXER AND ZION CRICHLOW

Overview

Having a strong theoretical foundation is important for any prevention or intervention programming (Institute of Medicine, 1994). A theory represents an extensively researched system of testable ideas intended to explain some phenomenon. This sort of foundation allows for the design of program components that flow from an established body of research. Having a "theory of change"—an informed idea about how kids are impacted by a program—can help push the field forward by making it easier to study the outcomes of the program, easier to communicate any findings to the broader community of scholars and practitioners, and easier to implement the program in different settings over time. For example, cognitive behavioral therapy (CBT), a popular "best practice" approach for treating problems with anger and aggression, relies on the observation that teaching people how to think differently about social situations, and apply new skills for handling intensely negative emotions, will help them avoid engaging in aggressive behavior. CBT is aligned with cognitive behavioral theory, which has established that behavior is at least in part driven by controllable cognitive (mental) processes and that problem behavior can be reduced by engaging those controllable thoughts directly.

One of the reasons a good theory of change is so critical for good practice is that the theory allows for replicability of programs and treatments across settings (e.g., offices, classrooms, community centers), clients (e.g., high school students, juvenile detainees), and, importantly, modalities. A broader view on youth violence prevention requires the consideration of multiple approaches that can include traditional psychotherapies along with arts and music education, youth sports engagement, street outreach, and mentoring. But the challenge for program developers and others wishing to develop the next-generation workforce for youth violence prevention is this: How can theoretical ideas from best-practice, evidence-based approaches to youth violence prevention be infused into the variety of places, and for the variety of people, engaged in the work?

We are two clinically oriented psychologists: PB is an academic clinical psychologist who has been conducting applied research on youth aggression and violence for over two decades, and ZC is a graduate student on the verge of entering clinical psychology doctoral training. Both of us are concerned with finding the best ways to help kids struggling with a variety of challenges, including poverty, violence, discrimination, and justice involvement. In this chapter, we discuss the common theoretical ideas that underlie evidence-based approaches to preventing youth violence and how to identify those ideas in more novel and less well-researched approaches in the field. Our hope is that by identifying these ideas in this context, we can encourage new understanding of, interest in, or commitment to the implementation of evidence-based approaches to preventing youth violence.

What Constitutes Effective Youth Violence Prevention?

Consider this scenario: You are traveling in an area far from your home, you have a headache, and you would like to purchase aspirin. So, you head to a local grocery store and scan the shelves. Now, you have a straightforward choice to make. On the one hand, you might want to pick up a bottle of aspirin produced by a well-known, name-brand company—the kind that advertises on television, the kind you can purchase in just about any store that sells aspirin, perhaps the kind you know and therefore trust. On the other hand, you might want to save a few dollars and instead purchase a bottle of aspirin produced by the grocery store chain where you are shopping—the "generic" aspirin. You have a look at the "active ingredients" listed on the packaging and you discover that they are the same. But this is a grocery store chain you have never visited previously, with a name you don't recognize—can you trust that they got the formula just right? You know, deep down, that the product wouldn't be on the shelves if it weren't safe, proven, field-tested—and it's just *aspirin*, after all—but the name brand is just so familiar, so well-known, and the company has been in business for so long.

Now consider that instead of your own headache, you are considering treatments for headaches and similar pains that might be experienced by youth involved in a large public system of care such as juvenile justice or child welfare. Your decision about which aspirin to purchase in bulk for the system will determine which painkillers can be provided to youth who need it. Now, on the one hand, you might want to conserve costs and thereby select a generic aspirin. But on the other hand, you might be concerned about liability and safety—although you know the generics might be safe, they might not carry the same weight of the brand names. You are making the decision on behalf of the many children who will receive the aspirin, the many families who bring those children for care, the many physicians and nurses who will administer the aspirin, and all of the taxpayers and other funders who will pay for the aspirin. What should you do?

Choosing between a brand-name and generic aspirin might seem like low stakes or small potatoes next to larger issues of preventing youth violence. But the aspirin decision and the consideration of "effective ingredients" is a useful analogy for considering the broader issue. Should programs utilize delivery models that are tried-and-true or fresh and innovative? If tried-and-true is the way to go, what does that mean? Does it refer to a program that has simply been in place for a long time with no obvious failures? Does it mean a program that rests on a body of evidence attesting to its effectiveness? If "fresh and innovative" is a better approach—what does *that* mean? Something, anything different from what was done before? Something that builds on existing programs in a new way? The same dilemma also can apply at the level of service delivery. How should a service provider choose among available methods of intervention? Does the physician pass out the "new and improved" aspirin or the standard form that has been working for years? Does the psychotherapist implement a brand-new therapeutic procedure or the basic model that has been the bedrock of his or her training and practice for years?

In the arena of youth violence prevention and intervention service provision, the basic issue of whether and how to select among intervention models has become complex. At the forefront there now exist dozens of intervention packages and programs that boast strong, lengthy track records of positive outcome evaluations—these are "brand-name" approaches with highly recognizable names and strategies that have been extensively vetted and highly rated by federal, state, and other evaluative authorities such as the U.S. Department of Education or the University of Colorado's Blueprints program (see https://blueprintsprograms.org). These trademarked approaches are promoted on foundations of solid empirical research conducted over periods of years. Yet in the background—and, to an extent, underpinning all the name-brand programs—are a number of theory-driven, field-tested practices that, time and again, have proven to be effective as generic strategies for prevention and intervention (Embry & Biglan, 2008; Welsh et al., 2014). Comprehensive meta-analytic analyses, conducted primarily by Mark Lipsey and his colleagues, have shown that these practices are persistently and robustly effective.

The key factor unifying these two distinct bodies of scholarship—research on the "brand-name" packages on the one hand, and research on the "generic" practices on the other—is that evidence-based approaches to helping children and adolescents grappling with problems related to violence all rest on a shared foundation of theory and empirical research. This applies regardless of whether the approach happens to be a name-brand package or manualized program, or a generic practice strategy. Evidence-based approaches utilize behavioral or cognitive behavioral engagement tactics, involve family members directly to improve relationships and caregiver skills, and connect youth to positive influences in their broader social context (Boxer & Dubow, 2002; Boxer et al., 2005, 2008; Boxer & Frick, 2008a, 2008b; Boxer & Goldstein, 2012; Goldstein et al., 2023; Kemp et al., 2020). Of course, as we are learning more and more in the field, the successful and sustained prevention of youth violence can engage strategies and tactics that move well beyond traditional youth-centered models, even those that typically involve community- and home-based services instead of office-based counseling. For example, hospital-based violence intervention programs, in tandem with a variety of community-based intervention approaches, are becoming popular and better funded. These can include some individual interventions, such as supportive counseling and mentoring, but also systemwide changes in how law enforcement and health care systems manage the victims of violence. Other approaches, such as those that integrate geospatial crime analytics and modifications to community infrastructure, might not engage individual youth at all while they work to impact the broader physical settings and associated setting conditions that attract violence. Still other methods might rely on fairly standard tactics (e.g., group-based interventions or individual counseling) but leverage new themes or pedagogies for reaching youth, such as music education or spiritual integration.

Given that modern youth violence prevention might require professionals or paraprofessionals with multiple skill sets, we think it is important to consider the possibility that any practitioner, at any level, can align practices with best-practice models through careful attention to theoretically coherent philosophies of intervention and change. Best practices are, of course, intervention and prevention approaches supported by meaningful evidence from research and theory. They are not limited to trademarked silos, nor do they reside solely in the experiential wisdom of seasoned practitioners. We acknowledge that the "gold standard" for inferring the effectiveness of an intervention program will likely always be the randomized controlled trial (RCT) that yields both short- and long-term indicators of positive and sustained change. But even the best-designed RCT must rest on theory—and we assert that the theory associated with effective approaches represents a foundational platform from which innovations can be launched.

Contemporary Theory on Youth Violence

Studies on the causes and consequences of violence among youth have been organized around an increasingly robust theoretical framework that has been alternatively referred to as "social-ecological," "developmental-ecological," or "personal-contextual" theory, among other similar terms. The labels all refer to a general consensus that youth development typically occurs through the interaction over time of personal dispositions (genetically or otherwise biologically mediated) and environmental characteristics (static social, physical, and economic conditions along with dynamic social-interactional situations). If this sounds like a familiar refrain, it certainly is. Human development is often cast as the product of the well-known "nature" and "nurture" dichotomy—our individual traits (our genotypes) interact with our unique environmental circumstances in utero and beyond to make us who we are (our phenotype). So the idea that youth violence emerges in this manner—or the idea that youth outcomes from violent victimization are determined in this manner—is not new.

Human behavior is of course complex and multifaceted. But the violence prevention professional often will be faced with a more straightforward question: Is this tactic helpful or not? For example, coping styles (how a youth handles stress) might be constructive (e.g., listening to music to distract, exercising to reduce tension) or destructive (e.g., aggressive acting out, isolation); neighborhoods might be health-promoting (e.g., safe and walkable spaces, well-kept parks) or health-risking (e.g., heavy crime, urban blight). The basic, theory-driven assertion from developmental research on aggression and violence and how to manage those behaviors is this: what youth *do* is the product of what they *think* and how they *feel*; and these thoughts, feelings, and actions come from their internal tendencies, what they have seen around them, and what they are immediately experiencing.

By way of illustration, consider the now-classic experiment conducted by Albert Bandura in the sixties (Bandura et al., 1961). This study, often referred to in the popular discourse as the "Bobo doll" study, involved two groups of children. One group of children was assigned randomly to watch an adult model walk around a room filled with toys, with no particular engagement with any of the toys. Another group of children was assigned randomly instead to watch the same adult enter the same room filled with the same toys, with a key difference: in this condition, the adult began playing very aggressively with a Bobo doll—a large inflatable clown that could be punched and kicked and would still right itself. What Bandura discovered was that the children who watched the adult aggress against the Bobo doll were more likely to do so themselves during a subsequent free-play session in comparison to the children who had not viewed such aggression. Applying our more contemporary developmental-ecological framework to the Bobo doll situation, it should be understood that seeing an adult beat up a toy is only one factor that might lead a child to act in the same manner. What else would increase the likelihood that a child behaves aggressively in that scenario?

The first set of influences likely to place the Bobo doll at risk is *personal*—they relate to the innate characteristics of the child. Research studies have shown that in terms of personal characteristics or internal dispositions, youth at risk for aggression and violence tend to be irritable, impulsive, callous, narcissistic, hostile, anger-prone, and other traits that are typically associated with negative emotional and cognitive states.

The second set of influences that would increase the likelihood of a youth beating on the poor Bobo doll is *contextual*—the characteristics of the youth's past and present social environment. A wide variety of social experiences have been associated with involvement in problem behaviors, including exposure to aggression and violence in the home, school, media, and community; victimization in any form and by any perpetrator; rejection or neglect by peers; and neighborhoods marked by social and physical disorder. These social experiences can exert impacts over the short term as well as over long periods of time, as has been shown through the highly influential Adverse Childhood Experiences (ACE) study (Felitti et al., 1998).

The third set of influences that increase risk of harm to the Bobo doll also is contextual, but in the more immediate sense—these influences are *situational*. Whereas the influences described in the preceding paragraph might be understood as broad socializing conditions, shaping outcomes gradually over time, situational influences are direct stimulators of behavior. These influences can run the gamut from provocation to conflict to trauma to intense stress and, of course, to any number of adverse situations.

So the child who might be considered *most likely* to attack the Bobo doll in Bandura's paradigm is a child who is intensely angry or otherwise irritable and hostile, who has been exposed to family, school, media, and neighborhood violence, and who just experienced a traumatic and stressful loss. This sort of "laundry list" approach to adding up risk factors is fairly common in studies of development and is essential to designing appropriate prevention and intervention programming. Yet these factors are still not enough to produce aggression. We still need a conceptual bridge between those risk factors and a behavioral response: coping.

Coping with some stressful or otherwise challenging situation is a process that involves cognitive, emotional, and/or behavioral steps taken to blunt or eliminate the stressor itself, or the psychological distress caused by the stressor. For example, a student who receives a failing grade on an exam, and becomes very distressed by this event, might do a number of things to cope with this distress. To deal with the stressor itself—the failing grade—the student might decide to study harder, appeal the grade, advocate for adequate resources, request extra help from the teacher, or change habits to study more effectively at home. Alternatively, the student might decide that the class is too hard and stop trying or argue aggressively with the teacher. To deal with the distress—caused by the failing grade—the student might listen to some music, go for a walk, or spend time with friends. Then again, the student might smoke a cigarette, get into a physical altercation, or go for a too-fast joyride.

Coping styles—how youth habitually tend to cope with stress and stressful situations—are learned behaviors or behavioral sequences that involve thought, feeling, and action (Boxer & Sloan-Power, 2013; Dubow & Rubinlicht, 2011). Some coping tactics (often termed "positive coping"), such as constructive problem solving and appropriate emotion regulation, can result in improved adjustment and better adaptation. Other coping tactics ("negative coping"), such as avoidance or withdrawal, can lead to worse adjustment and maladaptation. Coping tactics are best understood within the larger contexts of their use—for example, a coping tactic used by youth living in dangerous urban environments would have different results for youth living in relatively safe suburban environments. After all, coping efforts are responses to situational challenges—and thus how a youth responds to such challenges, whether momentary or chronic, represents to a meaningful extent how successfully a child adapts to his or her broader environment.

It can be difficult to isolate the impact of one particular factor on youth outcomes or disentangle the complex interplay of dispositional and contextual forces driving violent behavior. Yet this is the task of interventionists charged with providing prevention or treatment services to youth. Coping is a bridge connecting personal, contextual, and situational difficulties to outcomes, but to promote better adjustment the interventionist must attempt to take into account the multiple ways in which all of those influences might interact.

Theorizing on children's development and mental health has led to descriptive categorizations of dispositional, contextual, and situational factors and how they might interface with children's effortful behaviors and outcomes. For example, for most youth, growing up in poverty or struggling with cognitive impairment is associated with some form of adverse outcome—those challenges are risk factors. On the other hand, for most youth, more education or supportive caregivers leads to better outcomes. Therefore, one basic starting point for the interventionist, whether formulating an individual treatment plan or designing a whole-school prevention program, is to develop an approach to *reducing risk* and *increasing promotive factors* in the target youth or population.

Whereas risk factors increase negative outcomes and promotive factors increase positive outcomes, vulnerability factors amplify the impact of risk and protective factors reduce the impact of risk. For example, prior experiences with trauma might lead some children to react even more strongly and negatively to subsequent traumatic exposures—in that case, a history of trauma represents vulnerability. Alternatively, experiences with trauma might lead some children to develop effective coping resources for handling traumatic stress—in that case, coping resources represent protection. Thus, after considering the presence of risk and promotive factors, an interventionist should discern the relevance of any sources of vulnerability and protection.

The starting point of any successful intervention is the theoretical framework upon which it is based. The present and future of youth violence prevention have been and will continue to be multidisciplinary and multimodal. But foundational ideas about the causes and persistence of youth violence—personal, contextual, and situational sources of risk, and the internal psychological processes that in turn lead to aggressive and violent responses—are multidisciplinary as well. Youth violence prevention programming should endeavor to stay close to these thoroughly researched theoretical concepts.

References

Bandura, A., Ross, D., & Ross, S. A. (1961). Transmission of aggression through imitation of aggressive models. *Journal of Abnormal and Social Psychology, 63,* 575–582.

Boxer, P., & Dubow, E. F. (2002). A social-cognitive information-processing model for school-based aggression reduction and prevention programs: Issues for research and practice. *Applied & Preventive Psychology, 10,* 177–192.

Boxer, P., & Frick, P. J. (2008a). Treating conduct disorder, aggression, and antisocial behavior in children and adolescents: An integrated view. In R. Steele, M. Roberts, & T. D. Elkin (Eds.), *Handbook of evidence-based therapies for children and adolescents* (pp. 241–259). Sage.

Boxer, P., & Frick, P. J. (2008b). Treatment of violent offenders. In R. D. Hoge, N. G. Guerra, & P. Boxer (Eds.), *Treating the juvenile offender* (pp. 147–170). Guilford.

Boxer, P., & Goldstein, S. E. (2012). Treating juvenile offenders: Best practices and emerging critical issues. In E. Grigorenko (Ed.), *Handbook of juvenile forensic psychology and psychiatry* (pp. 323–340). Springer.

Boxer, P., Goldstein, S. E., Musher-Eizenman, D., Dubow, E. F., & Heretick, D. (2005). Developmental issues in the prevention of school aggression from the social-cognitive perspective. *Journal of Primary Prevention, 26,* 383–400.

Boxer, P., & Sloan-Power, E. (2013). Coping with violence: A comprehensive framework and implications for understanding resilience. *Trauma, Violence, & Abuse, 14*, 209–221.

Boxer, P., Terranova, A. M., Savoy, S. C., & Goldstein, S. E. (2008). Developmental issues in the prevention of aggression and violence in school. In T. Miller (Ed.), *School violence and primary prevention* (pp. 277–294). Springer.

Dubow, E. F., & Rubinlicht, M. (2011). Coping. In B. B. Brown & M. Prinstein (Eds.), *Encyclopedia of adolescence* (pp. 109–118). Academic Press.

Embry, D. D., & Biglan, A. (2008). Evidence-based kernels: Fundamental units of behavioral influence. *Clinical Child and Family Psychology Review, 11*, 75–113.

Felitti, V. J., Anda, R. F., Nordenberg, D., Williamson, D. F., Spitz, A. M., Edwards, V., Koss, M. P., & Marks, J. S. (1998). Relationship of childhood abuse and household dysfunction to many of the leading causes of death in adults: The Adverse Childhood Experiences (ACE) Study. *American Journal of Preventive Medicine, 14*, 245–258.

Goldstein, S. E., Terranova, A., Savoy, S. C., Bradley, S., Park, J., & Boxer, P. (2023). Developmental issues in the prevention of aggression and violence in school. In T. Miller (Ed.), *School violence and primary prevention* (2nd ed., pp. 65–99). Springer.

Institute of Medicine. (1994). *Reducing risks for mental disorders: Frontiers for preventive intervention research.* National Academy Press.

Kemp, E. C., Boxer, P., & Frick, P. J. (2020). Treating conduct problems, aggression, and antisocial behavior in children and adolescents. In R. G. Steele & M. C. Roberts (Eds.), *Handbook of evidence-based therapies for children and adolescents* (pp. 203–218). Springer.

Welsh, B. C., Rocque, M., & Greenwood, P. W. (2014). Translating research into evidence-based practice in juvenile justice: Brand-name programs, meta-analysis, and key issues. *Journal of Experimental Criminology, 10*, 207–225.

A Life Course Approach to Youth Violence Prevention

• • • • • • • • • • • • •

JOYCE LEE, ELIZABETH BARNERT,
AND NEAL HALFON

Overview

Youth violence is a serious threat to the health and development of children and can dramatically impact their life course trajectories. It is preventable, but doing so requires a thorough understanding of the complex pathways that lead to it. Children displaying aggressive or violent behavior should be viewed not as perpetrators of criminal behavior but as children in distress, who should be supported as such. Many pathways leading to youth violence have roots in the early years, during sensitive periods of physiological and psychological development. These pathways are influenced not just by individual characteristics but also by the family, community, and societal environments in which each child lives. Interventions designed to prevent the genesis of youth violence must consider these environments and may benefit from adopting a life course approach. Life course interventions are strategically timed, developmentally appropriate, multilevel, family-centered, antiracist, and codesigned using processes that include service providers, families, community stakeholders, and the youth themselves. They aim to improve each young person's lifelong trajectory, accepting that health and well-being are the product of dynamically intertwined processes. Incorporating life course principles into preventive interventions may increase their effectiveness leading to a reduction in youth violence, at individual and societal levels. Here, we present the impact of youth violence on the life course, the life course health development (LCHD) research framework as it applies to youth violence prevention, and implications to guide future work.

Personal Introductions

EB: I am a youth justice researcher and clinician who provides care to youth detained in the U.S. juvenile legal system; I have realized that the ripple effects of the cycles of violence in the lives of children and adolescents are all too apparent. The preventability of youth violence and the opportunity to reduce the suffering of the children I care for as a clinician and on a global scale as a public health professor motivate me to elevate the topic of youth violence prevention as an essential priority for improving health across the life course.

JL: As a medical student, I am studying clinical manifestations of diseases and their treatments, but most importantly I am learning how health is never the product of one, individual choice but the result of many factors at play—like youth violence, access to food, neighborhood safety, and health literacy. It is humbling to witness people's strength in the face of violence, and I believe that there is a responsibility to work preventatively toward a healthier future for the generations to come.

NH: As a senior clinician, researcher, social innovation entrepreneur, and educator I have spent my career attempting to use science as way of discovering new ways forward and innovation as a way of prototyping how those scientific insights can be translated into social change. My clinical career began taking care of young people in the child welfare system who often "graduated" into the juvenile legal system because their developmental needs were unaddressed and appropriate developmental supports were unavailable to them.

Impact of Youth Violence on Life Course

Youth violence, increasingly recognized not only as a major social challenge but as a major public health problem, has lasting effects into adulthood. We define "youth violence," per the Centers for Disease Control and Prevention (CDC), as "the intentional use of physical force or power to threaten or harm others by young people ages 10–24" (CDC, 2022). Applying a life course framework for elucidating the dimensions of youth violence can illuminate targets for prevention.

Key rationale for why life course principles are important in youth violence research are as follows. First, studying the life paths of young people who engage in violence reveals that many of the contributing factors may have taken place years before (Office of the Surgeon General et al., 2010). Examining early childhood pathways and how to disrupt early contributors can be key to overcoming the precipitating events and experiences that lead to youth violence. Second, because exposure to violence perpetuates youth violent behavior, prevention entails understanding the risk factors for violence exposure (Freire-Vargas, 2018). Frequent violence exposure contributes to the persistent threat of violence and toxic levels of stress in childhood that can impact young people's health into adulthood (Graham-Bermann & Seng, 2005; Johnson et al., 2013; Moffitt & Klaus-Grawe Think, 2013; Wood et al., 2002). Persistent toxic stress can undermine health trajectories, leading to mental health and substance use disorders, premature death, and the exacerbation of medical conditions later in life, raising risks of asthma, heart disease, and cancer, among more, in adults with childhood exposure to adversity (Felitti et al., 1998; Shonkoff et al., 2009; Wright et al., 2004). Exposure to violence has also been linked to a higher likelihood of engaging in unhealthy behaviors such as smoking and substance use (McNutt et al., 2002). Using life course principles to prevent youth violence can thus have implications for lifelong health.

Furthermore, violence has complex manifestations with widespread influence beyond the individual. Violence can originate in patterns of inequality and racism and be transmitted through intergenerational patterns of community underinvestment and neglect (Black et al., 2010; Cordero et al., 2012). Children who witness violence repeatedly may form a violent learned response to challenges that is passed on across generations. Reports of violence in the media are commonplace and accessible even to young children. Because higher levels of violence are associated with social turbulence and economic uncertainty, youth violence is expected to increase because of climate change, war, and increasing political and cultural polarization in many countries (United Nations, 2020). Thus, violence prevention cannot be addressed simply as an isolated problem of "bad behavior" but rather must be tackled as a social challenge deeply interwoven with widespread societal and life course impact that is likely to intensify in the coming decades. Life course principles provide a tool for disentangling the complexity of youth violence.

Summary and Highlights of Life Course Interventions as Applied to Youth Violence

Introduction to the Life Course Health Development (LCHD) Framework

Our team at UCLA has worked on an LCHD framework to better understand how health and well-being develop over a person's life (Halfon et al., 2014; Halfon & Hochstein, 2002). The Life Course Intervention Research Framework applies life course principles to the development of carefully designed interventions (Russ, Hotez, Berghaus, Verbiest, et al., 2022a). Application of the Life Course Intervention Research Framework to youth violence prevention holds promise for best practices that can not only move health trajectories back on track but also optimize them (Russ, Hotez, Berghaus, Verbiest, et al., 2022a).

Health and Youth Violence from the Health Development Perspective

Health and well-being result from complex relational interactions between biology, behaviors, and social ecological conditions (Halfon & Forrest, 2017). The early years appear critical for healthy development and adaptation, when many of our neurophysiological processes and ways of relating to other people become established (Kessel et al., 2013; Lo et al., 2015; Perry et al., 2016; Tierney & Nelson, 2009). When children grow up with parents who experience material and social disadvantage; are stressed for time, resources, and services; and are challenged to provide adequate nurturing environments in the context of high levels of family discord, they are more likely to exhibit early unhealthy relationship patterns and to engage in youth violence (Sitnick et al., 2017). Exposure to violence at an early age is developmentally harmful, and factors including family dynamics, violence preventing community norms, and cultural practices that promote resilience can enable successful adaptation to stress and benefit health trajectories (American Academy of Pediatrics, 2009). It is not only characteristics of the children themselves that predispose them to later violent behavior, but also qualities of their family, community, cultural environments, and developmental processes that weave these forces together.

Thus, preventative methods that focus on children alone instead of a whole of society response will be shortsighted. To this end, the Life Course Intervention Research Network (LCIRN) Node on Youth Justice provides guidance to conceptualize collaborative interventions to prevent youth violence.

The LCIRN and Its Relationship to the LCHD Framework

The LCIRN is a national network of over a hundred researchers, service providers, community representatives, and thought leaders (Russ, Hotez, Berghaus, Hoover, et al., 2022) that has identified twelve qualities of life course interventions that hold the best promise of improving life course health trajectories for children and families (Russ, Hotez, Berghaus, Verbiest, et al., 2022). In Table 2.1

Table 2.1

Application of the Twelve Characteristics of Life Course Interventions to Youth Violence Prevention

Characteristic	Description	Application to Youth Violence Prevention
Developmentally focused	Tailored to the child's developmental stage	Prevention focus is appropriate for child's developmental age. For example, focus on positive, reciprocal, nurturing healthy relationships in the early years rather than a sole emphasis on early discipline. Intervention could aim to improve emotional self-regulation in early childhood as a step on the pathway to self-control and resilience.
Strategically timed	Targets a critical or sensitive period of development	Prevention interventions maximized at times of transition such as the early years, school entry, high school entry, workforce entry.
Longitudinally focused	Improves health reserves and resilience early in life; will contribute to prevention of problems later on	Universal prevention strategies focused on topics such as supporting healthy relationships, emotional regulation development, resilience development. Interventions are repeated and reinforced in later years.
Multi-level or holistic	Improves multiple aspects of the child's developmental ecosystem	Interventions consider, respond to, and target risk factors like bullying and exposure to firearms for youth violence at child, family, community, and societal levels.
Strengths-based	Identifies and incorporates child, youth, family, and community strengths	Family members who exhibit healthy relational and conflict resolution skills can contribute to early skills building interventions. Community resources can be harnessed to provide alternatives to activities with higher risks of violence and target issues like food insecurity that contribute to toxic stress.
Optimization focused	Aims to achieve optimal health trajectories, not simply treat problems	Interventions support development of empathy and maximally prosocial behaviors not just violence prevention. Interventions support not only targeting risks but also better contributing to health. For example, interventions do not just remove children from violent homes but also provide supportive resources and education that model healthy behaviors and conflict resolution.

(continued)

Table 2.1
(continued)

Characteristic	Description	Application to Youth Violence Prevention
Equity focused	Designed to help the most disadvantaged whose circumstances and contexts may warrant different levels of intervention	Prevention intervention considers and addresses factors across child's whole developmental ecosystem. Children, families, and communities with multiple risks will need broader more intensive interventions than those with fewer risks.
Family centered	Recognizes and supports the unique role of families as incubators of early child development	Interventions engage families and incorporate family context. They address family processes, relationships, and governance. Interventions target family level risks— including family conflict resolution strategies, decision-making, monitoring and supervision of children—and reinforce healthy strategies such as proactive community engagement in violence prevention efforts.
Antiracist	Incorporates anti-racist principles and considers potential role of racism Interventions are antibiased, trauma-informed, and culturally grounded.	Interventions to prevent violence look for the possibility of and address lived experiences of racism at all levels. This may include incorporation of critical ethnography, in-depth interviewing, indigenous knowledge, and understanding of power relationships. Interventions should consider historic and communal as well as individual trauma.
Vertically, horizontally, and longitudinally integrated	Integrated with existing services and programs	Youth violence prevention interventions are developed from a systems perspective, integrated across domains of biological, behavioral, and social function; across services and programs; and across life stages and even generations.
Collaboratively codesigned	Designed by stakeholders (individuals, families, and communities) and professionals working together	Individuals and communities that have been impacted by high levels of violence participate as equal partners with professionals in creating and implementing interventions to prevent youth violence.

Table 2.1
(*continued*)

Characteristic	Description	Application to Youth Violence Prevention
Address emerging health development capabilities	Supports and enables processes leading to development of capacities for positive health	Interventions support the adoption and reinforcement of healthy behaviors and coping strategies—including social skills training, pro-social behaviors, self-regulation, and violence de-escalation. Interventions can also promote well-being, including through emphases on school attendance, food security, and access to health care

SOURCE: Russ, Hotez, Berghaus, Verbiest, et al., 2022a and b.

we apply these characteristics to a consideration of interventions for youth violence prevention.

The LCHD Framework views health development as an active process (Halfon et al., 2014; Halfon & Hochstein, 2002) in multiple dimensions (time, place) and at multiple levels (individual, family, society) and phases (preconception, peri-conception, early childhood, adolescence; Halfon et al., 2014). By recognizing the dynamic complexity of health trajectories, the Life Course Intervention Research Framework (Russ, Hotez, Berghaus, Hoover, et al., 2022) is designed to guide researchers studying interventions to improve lifelong health. Specifically, interventions for youth violence prevention that draw from the Life Course Intervention Research Framework hold potential for improvement of lifelong health.

Qualities of a Life Course Intervention for Youth Violence Prevention

The twelve characteristics of life course interventions provide a starting point for researchers who wish to incorporate life course principles into their youth violence prevention interventions (Russ, Hotez, Berghaus, Hoover, et al., 2022). Too often, traditional approaches have relied on identification of early signs of behavioral problems, with secondary prevention via remediation programs and responses to "first offenses." A life course view suggests that this approach represents "too little too late." Instead, there is an opportunity to address risks earlier, before problem behaviors occur. These interventions require an understanding of the biological, psychological, individual, family, and community processes that can predispose children to later develop violent behaviors.

Identifying effective interventions to disrupt these processes and shift them in ways that are supportive of optimal developmental trajectories is an essential goal for research, practice, and policy. For example, the Nurse-Family Partnership (NFP), a program of home visits by nurses for low-income mothers and their children, has demonstrated that even prenatal interventions can prevent violence years later (Kitzman et al., 1997; Kitzman et al., 2019; Olds et al., 1998). Even small changes early in life can potentially disrupt entire chains of risk.

Many processes targeted by violence prevention interventions are relational, operate at the level of the family, and target enhanced family function (American Academy of Pediatrics, 2009; Feinberg et al., 2022; Hoover et al., 2022). Family support contributes to resilience in individuals (Jaffee, 2007; Lytle et al., 2011), enabling them to adapt successfully to stress and prevent violence (American Academy of Pediatrics, 2009). Interventions that appreciate early exposure to positive, protective factors by building resilience in the home via parenting behaviors, cognitive stimulation, and emotional support—as opposed to risk-based approaches—can be strategic for the prevention of youth violence (American Academy of Pediatrics, 2009). Importantly, youth may often be exposed to violence in the home. To have a measurable impact, prevention of exposure to domestic violence requires interventions designed to stop adult violent behaviors and/or remove adult perpetuators from the home. Developing *family-centered* interventions that build resilience is a priority for preventing and mitigating the effects of youth violence.

Similarly, the LCHD perspective entails an understanding of how health development emerges as a result of a dynamic interplay of nested environments, including biologic, behavioral, social, and economic contexts (Halfon & Hochstein, 2002). For example, factors like access to food—a social and economic issue—contribute to physiological growth and development, and the amount of exposure to air pollution—a biological and structural dilemma—affects asthma exacerbations. Similarly, during different stages in life, relative influences of nested communities change: family has a greater effect on young children, while neighborhood and peers become more important with age (Halfon & Hochstein, 2002). By appreciating and incorporating the changing influences of family and neighborhood environment, the life course qualities of being *developmentally focused*, *strategically timed*, and *multilevel* give a framework for interventions that appropriately respond to changing nested communities.

Disparities often develop because of health insults experienced early in the life course whose effects compound over time. Minoritized groups are more likely to experience structural violence, resulting from social structures that put individuals and populations in harm's way (Farmer et al., 2006) and may be more exposed to violent experiences compared to dominant racial and ethnic groups. Communities of color and families living in low-income areas are more subject to certain types of violence exposure (Prevention Institute, 2011; Sumner et al., 2015), making this a health equity issue. For example, structural forces contribute to excess availability of firearms, which disproportionally harm marginalized groups, particularly Black boys and young men, through an excess of firearm homicide fatalities and exposure to firearm violence (Bottiani et al., 2021). Involvement in the racially unjust carceral system further perpetuates cycles of youth violence.

Additionally, some kinds of violence like police brutality are concentrated in marginalized communities, further exacerbating health inequities due to violence (Alang et al., 2017; Alang et al., 2021; DeVylder et al., 2020). These factors can trigger cascades of intergencrational violence. Children exposed to violence may become the adult perpetrators of violence that expose the next generation to developmentally harmful cues. Disproportionate experiences of violence in marginalized communities compound preexisting intersectional inequities in part because such experiences of violence may become normalized, setting marginalized groups up to suffer devastating consequences, like depression, anxiety, and death, disproportionately in comparison to peers. Thus, preventing youth violence as well as all types of violence exposure can support health equity.

An equity-focused and antiracism lens to law enforcement can prevent the types of violent encounters that instigate police brutality and excessive force among marginalized communities. In other words, using the life course intervention principles of being *equity focused* and *antiracist* can strategically address the intersectional nature of violence with health inequities and guide effective interventions. In brief, youth violence prevention necessitates prioritizing the eradication of disparities by using a life course perspective.

Where Are We Going?

Leading Paradigm

A paradigm shift is required: rather than being viewed solely as perpetuators of delinquent behavior, children who display violence are in distress and should be supported as such. The conceptualization of children with troubled behavior as needing help facilitates fairer and more effective prevention methods. The United States is in great need of innovative approaches to address youth violence upstream (Travis et al., 2019). In a nation with devastating mass-casualty school shootings by adolescents and frequent rights violations in a punitive and racist carceral system that exacerbates youth violence (Barnert et al., 2017), new strategies are needed urgently. One such strategy is to apply the LCHD framework to interventions designed to prevent youth violence and actively promote optimal environments for young children and families.

As an example of how LCHD principles have a real impact, let us consider Canada's approach to children who interface with law enforcement, where a holistic, nonpunitive approach to youth justice—in place of the criminal legal system for children younger than twelve years of age—follows key concepts of child development (Barnert et al., 2022a). In understanding children's disruptive behavior as a symptom of distress, indicative of a health development challenge or unmet need, Canada's youth justice minimum age law allows for supportive interventions outside of the judicial system. Such interventions appropriately prevent the escalation of disruptive behaviors and future criminal legal system involvement, promoting healthy lives instead of the perpetuation of violence (Barnert et al., 2022b). Canada's minimum age law signifies a paradigm shift in which youth violence prevention via a punitive response is recognized as developmentally inappropriate, indicating the need for a life course paradigm that moves youth violence prevention away from criminal proceedings and into supports that nurture children's healthy trajectories.

Future Research Areas

The LCHD model highlights the need for interventions that are *multilevel* and *wholly integrated* across different levels and sectors of social organization—from individual to society. There is an imperative to better understand how we can build strong and supportive family relationships and resilience via parental involvement as an important facet of preventing youth violence (Brady et al., 2008). The NFP and the Incredible Years Program provide good examples where interventions focused on both parents and children foster social competence and reduce conduct problems in children (Menting et al., 2013; Olds, 2006; Olds et al., 1988; Webster-Stratton, 2001). Understanding what families and children need to thrive—ways to encourage family harmony, address conflict, and respond to external stressors—is an important research gap (Walsh, 2015).

Similarly, communities need support in efforts to reduce rates of youth violence, especially in schools, the primary stable environment for most children outside of their families. Examples of community engagement strategies implementing life course research include programs to eradicate bullying, foster stable mentoring relationships with caring adults, build leadership programs for meaningful youth participation (Oliver et al., 2006), and fortify collaboration with health departments to promote healthy and safe neighborhoods. These efforts represent the life course qualities of *addressing emerging health development capabilities* and being *optimization-focused*, thus aligning with goals to reduce community violence.

We also need to better understand what facilitates youth violence at a societal level. For example, racism—structural and internalized—increases risk for violence. Greater attention at the societal level to adopting *antiracist* approaches, an LCHD principle, could have a powerful impact on youth violence prevention. Additionally, given that one of the largest contributors to youth violence is access to firearms, an example of a life course priority is engaging school systems in collaborative research to implement interventions aimed at reducing access and exposure to firearms (Price & Khubchandani, 2019). Personal, family, and community strengths can be built on through strategies designed to reduce contributors to toxic stress, such as food insecurity, and to support positive factors in the child's developmental ecosystem. These positive factors include safe and secure relationships, strong family ties, peaceful neighborhoods, cohesive communities, financial stability, food security, and reliable health care. These efforts would be *strengths-based* and could readily incorporate *collaborative codesign* in which youth, families, and professionals work together to design, test, and implement intervention strategies aimed at fostering these positive qualities in children's lives. Life course principles can properly realize the complexity of forces at work that propagate youth violence.

Youth Violence Prevention in Training and Practice

Professionals working with youth would benefit from special training in trauma-informed care, in life course influences on youth violence, and in intervention research to promote collaborative processes to implement and learn from intervention science. Life course interventions to address youth violence prevention can expand from traditional settings like health care facilities, schools, detention centers, and community youth centers to a wider range of community-based settings, like local parks, recreation facilities, sports leagues, libraries, and places of worship, contributing to and integrating with existing programs in a manner that honors each group's beliefs and traditions.

Conclusion

Ultimately, youth violence is not a simple behavioral issue affecting an isolated individual child. Its prevention requires life course health development principles that address the complexity of the origins, manifestations, and impacts of youth violence. Each of the twelve characteristics of the life course intervention research framework contributes to a more holistic developmental conceptualization of youth violence that shapes the timing of critical targets for prevention. Applying LCHD principles to youth violence prevention can have significant, tangible effects on improving the lives of children, now and for generations to come. Youth violence should not be a norm. Despite disturbing trends, we must persist and step up intervention efforts. Children deserve to feel safe in their homes, their neighborhoods, and their schools—they deserve to have healthy lives. The life course framework provides guidance to identify targets for effective interventions.

Acknowledgments

This project is supported by the Health Resources and Services Administration of the U.S. Department of Health and Human Services (HHS) under award UA6MC32492, the Life Course Intervention Research Network. Dr. Barnert's time is also supported by the National Institutes of Health (NIH) National Institute on Drug Abuse (NIDA) (K23DA045747). The information, content, and/or conclusions are those of the authors and should not be construed as the official position or policy of, nor should any endorsements be inferred by HRSA, HHS, or the U.S. government.

References

Abrams, L. S., Godoy, S. M., Bath, E. P., & Barnert, E. S. (2020). Collaborative responses to commercial sexual exploitation as a model of smart decarceration. *Social Work, 65*(4), 387–396.

Alang, S., McAlpine, D., McClain, M., & Hardeman, R. (2021). Police brutality, medical mistrust and unmet need for medical care. *Preventive Medicine Reports, 22*, 101361.

Alang, S., McAlpine, D., McCreedy, E., & Hardeman, R. (2017). Police brutality and Black health: Setting the agenda for public health scholars. *American Journal of Public Health, 107*(5), 662–665.

American Academy of Pediatrics. (2009). Role of the pediatrician in youth violence prevention. *Pediatrics, 124*(1), 393–402.

Barnert, E. S., Abrams, L., Maxson, C., Gase, L., Soung, P., Carroll, P., & Bath, E. (2017). Setting a minimum age for juvenile justice jurisdiction in California. *International Journal of Prisoner Health, 13*(1), 49–56.

Barnert, E. S., Gallagher, D., Lei, H., & Abrams, L. S. (2022a). Applying a health development lens to Canada's youth justice minimum age law. *Pediatrics, 149*(Suppl. 5).

Barnert, E. S., Gallagher, D., Lei, H., & Abrams, L. S. (2022b). Implementation of Canada's youth justice minimum age of 12: Implications for children in Canada and globally. *Journal of Public Health Policy. 43*(3):379-390.

Bath, E. P., Godoy, S. M., Perris, G. E., Morris, T. C., Hayes, M. D., Bagot, K., . . . Tolou-Shams, M. (2021). Perspectives of girls and young women affected by commercial sexual exploitation: mHealth as a tool to increase engagement in care. *Journal of Health Care for the Poor and Underserved, 32*(2 Suppl.), 128–147.

Black, D. S., Sussman, S., & Unger, J. B. (2010). A further look at the intergenerational transmission of violence: Witnessing interparental violence in emerging adulthood. *Journal of Interpersonal Violence, 25*(6), 1022–1042.

Bottiani, J. H., Camacho, D. A., Lindstrom Johnson, S., & Bradshaw, C. P. (2021). Annual research review: Youth firearm violence disparities in the United States and implications for prevention. *Journal of Child Psychol. Psychiatry, 62*(5), 563–579.

Brady, S. S., Gorman-Smith, D., Henry, D. B., & Tolan, P. H. (2008). Adaptive coping reduces the impact of community violence exposure on violent behavior among African American and Latino male adolescents. *Journal of Abnormal Child Psychology, 36*(1), 105–115.

Centers for Disease Control and Prevention. (2022, May 31). *Preventing youth violence.* https://www.cdc.gov/violenceprevention/youthviolence/fastfact.html

Cordero, M. I., Poirier, G. L., Marquez, C., Veenit, V., Fontana, X., Salehi, B., . . . Sandi, C. (2012). Evidence for biological roots in the transgenerational transmission of intimate partner violence. *Translational Psychiatry, 2*, e106.

DeVylder, J., Fedina, L., & Link, B. (2020). Impact of police violence on mental health: A theoretical framework. *American Journal of Public Health*, *110*(11), 1704–1710.

Farmer, P. E., Nizeye, B., Stulac, S., & Keshavjee, S. (2006). Structural violence and clinical medicine. *PLOS Medicine*, *3*(10), e449.

Feinberg, M., Hotez, E., Roy, K., Ledford, C. J. W., Lewin, A. B., Perez-Brena, N., . . . Berge, J. M. (2022). Family health development: A theoretical framework. *Pediatrics*, *149*(Suppl. 5), e2021053509I.

Felitti, V. J., Anda, R. F., Nordenberg, D., Williamson, D. F., Spitz, A. M., Edwards, V., . . . Marks, J. S. (1998). Relationship of childhood abuse and household dysfunction to many of the leading causes of death in adults. The Adverse Childhood Experiences (ACE) Study. *American Journal of Preventive Medicine*, *14*(4), 245–258.

Freire-Vargas, L. (2018). Violence as a public health crisis. *AMA Journal of Ethics*, *20*(1), 25–28.

Godoy, S. M., Abrams, L. S., Barnert, E. S., Kelly, M. A., & Bath, E. P. (2020). Fierce autonomy: How girls and young women impacted by commercial sexual exploitation perceive health and exercise agency in health care decision-making. *Qualitative Health Research*, *30*(9), 1326–1337.

Graham-Bermann, S. A., & Seng, J. (2005). Violence exposure and traumatic stress symptoms as additional predictors of health problems in high-risk children. *Journal of Pediatrics*, *146*(3), 349–354.

Halfon, N., & Forrest, C. B. (2017). The emerging theoretical framework of life course health development. In N. Halfon, C. B. Forrest, R. M. Lerner, & E. M. Faustman (Eds.), *Handbook of life course health development* (pp.19–43). Springer.

Halfon, N., & Hochstein, M. (2002). Life course health development: An integrated framework for developing health, policy, and research. *Milbank Quarterly*, *80*(3), 433–479.

Halfon, N., Larson, K., Lu, M., Tullis, E., & Russ, S. (2014). Lifecourse health development: Past, present and future. *Maternal and Child Health Journal*, *18*(2), 344–365.

Hoover, C., Ware, A., Serano, A., & Verbiest, S. (2022). Engaging families in life course intervention research: An essential step in advancing equity. *Pediatrics*, *149*(Suppl. 5), e2021053509G.

Jaffee, S. R. (2007). Sensitive, stimulating caregiving predicts cognitive and behavioral resilience in neurodevelopmentally at-risk infants. *Development and Psychopathology*, *19*(3), 631–647.

Johnson, S. B., Riley, A. W., Granger, D. A., & Riis, J. (2013). The science of early life toxic stress for pediatric practice and advocacy. *Pediatrics*, *131*(2), 319–327.

Kessel, E. M., Huselid, R. F., Decicco, J. M., & Dennis, T. A. (2013). Neurophysiological processing of emotion and parenting interact to predict inhibited behavior: An affective-motivational framework. *Frontiers in Human Neuroscience*, *7*, 326.

Kitzman, H., Olds, D. L., Henderson, C. R., Jr., Hanks, C., Cole, R., Tatelbaum, R., . . . Barnard, K. (1997). Effect of prenatal and infancy home visitation by nurses on pregnancy outcomes, childhood injuries, and repeated childbearing: A randomized controlled trial. *JAMA*, *278*(8), 644–652.

Kitzman, H., Olds, D. L., Knudtson, M. D., Cole, R., Anson, E., Smith, J. A., . . . Conti, G. (2019). Prenatal and infancy nurse home visiting and 18-year outcomes of a randomized trial. *Pediatrics*, *144*(6), e20183876.

Lo, S. L., Schroder, H. S., Moran, T. P., Durbin, C. E., & Moser, J. S. (2015). Neurophysiological evidence of an association between cognitive control and defensive reactivity processes in young children. *Developmental Cognitive Neuroscience, 15,* 35–47.

Lytle, L. R., Oliva, G. A., Ostrove, J. M., & Cassady, C. (2011). Building resilience in adolescence: The influences of individual, family, school, and community perspectives and practices. In D. H. Zand & K. J. Pierce (Eds.), *Resilience in deaf children: Adaptation through emerging adulthood* (pp. 251–277). Springer.

McNutt, L.-A., Carlson, B. E., Persaud, M., & Postmus, J. (2002). Cumulative abuse experiences, physical health and health behaviors. *Annals of Epidemiology, 12*(2), 123–130.

Menting, A. T. A., Orobio de Castro, B., & Matthys, W. (2013). Effectiveness of the Incredible Years parent training to modify disruptive and prosocial child behavior: A meta-analytic review. *Clinical Psychology Review, 33*(8), 901–913.

Moffitt, T. E., & Klaus-Grawe Think, T. (2013). Childhood exposure to violence and lifelong health: Clinical intervention science and stress-biology research join forces. *Development and Psychopathology, 25*(4, Pt. 2), 1619–1634.

Office of the Surgeon General, National Center for Injury Prevention and Control, National Institute of Mental Health, & Center for Mental Health Services. (2010). *Youth violence: A report of the Surgeon General.* U.S. Office of the Surgeon General.

Olds, D. L. (2006). The Nurse-Family Partnership: An evidence-based preventive intervention. *Infant Mental Health Journal, 27*(1), 5–25.

Olds, D., Henderson, C. R., Jr., Cole, R., Eckenrode, J., Kitzman, H., Luckey, D., . . . Powers, J. (1998). Long-term effects of nurse home visitation on children's criminal and antisocial behavior: 15-year follow-up of a randomized controlled trial. *JAMA, 280*(14), 1238–1244.

Olds, D. L., Henderson, C. R., Jr., Tatelbaum, R., & Chamberlin, R. (1988). Improving the life-course development of socially disadvantaged mothers: A randomized trial of nurse home visitation. *American Journal of Public Health, 78*(11), 1436–1445.

Oliver, K. G., Collin, P., Burns, J. & Nicholas, J. (2006). Building resilience in young people through meaningful participation. *Australian e-Journal for the Advancement of Mental Health 5*(1), 1–7.

Ozer, E. J. (2016). Youth-led participatory action research: Developmental and equity perspectives. In S. S. Horn, M. D. Ruck, & L. S. Liben (Eds.), *Advances in child development and behavior* (Vol. 50, pp. 189–207). JAI.

Ozer, E. J., Abraczinskas, M., Duarte, C., Mathur, R., Ballard, P. J., Gibbs, L., . . . Afifi, R. (2020). Youth participatory approaches and health equity: Conceptualization and integrative review. *American Journal of Community Psychology, 66*(3–4), 267–278.

Perry, N. B., Swingler, M. M., Calkins, S. D., & Bell, M. A. (2016). Neurophysiological correlates of attention behavior in early infancy: Implications for emotion regulation during early childhood. *Journal of Experimental Child Psychology, 142,* 245–261.

Prevention Institute. (2011). *Fact sheet: Violence and health equity.* Retrieved from https://www.preventioninstitute.org/sites/default/files/publications/Violence.HealthEquity.Overview.pdf

Price, J. H., & Khubchandani, J. (2019). School firearm violence prevention practices and policies: Functional or folly? *Violence and Gender, 6*(3), 154–167.

Russ, S. A., Hotez, E., Berghaus, M., Hoover, C., Verbiest, S., Schor, E. L., & Halfon, N. (2022a). Building a life course intervention research framework. *Pediatrics, 149*(Suppl. 5), e2021053509E

Russ, S. A., Hotez, E., Berghaus, M., Verbiest, S., Hoover, C., Schor, E. L., & Halfon, N. (2022b). What makes an intervention a life course intervention? *Pediatrics, 149*(Suppl. 5), e2021053509D.

Shonkoff, J. P., Boyce, W. T., & McEwen, B. S. (2009). Neuroscience, molecular biology, and the childhood roots of health disparities: Building a new framework for health promotion and disease prevention. *JAMA, 301*(21), 2252–2259.

Shrimali, B. P., Luginbuhl, J., Malin, C., Flournoy, R., & Siegel, A. (2014). The Building Blocks Collaborative: Advancing a life course approach to health equity through multi-sector collaboration. *Maternal and Child Health Journal, 18*(2), 373–379.

Sitnick, S. L., Shaw, D. S., Weaver, C. M., Shelleby, E. C., Choe, D. E., Reuben, J. D., . . . Taraban, L. (2017). Early childhood predictors of severe youth violence in low-income male adolescents. *Child Development, 88*(1), 27–40.

Sumner, S. A., Mercy, J. A., Dahlberg, L. L., Hillis, S. D., Klevens, J., & Houry, D. (2015). Violence in the United States: Status, challenges, and opportunities. *JAMA, 314*(5), 478–488.

Tierney, A. L., & Nelson, C. A., III. (2009). Brain development and the role of experience in the early years. *Zero to Three, 30*(2), 9–13.

Travis, R., Gann, E., Crooke, A. H. D., & Jenkins, S. M. (2019). Hip hop, empowerment, and therapeutic beat-making: Potential solutions for summer learning loss, depression, and anxiety in youth. *Journal of Human Behavior in the Social Environment, 29*(6), 744–765.

United Nations. (2020). *A new era of conflict and violence.*

Walsh, F. (2015). *Strengthening family resilience* (3rd ed.). Guilford.

Webster-Stratton, C. (2001). The incredible years: Parents, teachers, and children training series. *Residential Treatment for Children and Youth, 18*(3), 31–45.

Wood, J., Foy, D. W., Layne, C., Pynoos, R., & James, C. B. (2002). An examination of the relationships between violence exposure, posttraumatic stress symptomatology, and delinquent activity. *Journal of Aggression, Maltreatment & Trauma, 6*(1), 127–147.

Wright, R. J., Mitchell, H., Visness, C. M., Cohen, S., Stout, J., Evans, R., & Gold, D. R. (2004). Community violence and asthma morbidity: The Inner-City Asthma Study. *American Journal of Public Health, 94*(4), 625–632.

3

Promoting Competencies and Preventing Violence with Social-Emotional and Social-Cognitive Programs in Schools

● ● ● ● ● ● ● ● ● ● ● ● ●

KAREN L. BIERMAN AND
REBECCA SLOTKIN

Overview

Schools represent a critically important context influencing the socialization of aggression. In this chapter, we describe the different facets of school experiences that influence the development of aggressive behavior. These include the quality of relationships and interactions students have with teachers and peers at school, the characteristics of the students who compose the school population and are assigned to various classrooms, and the way that problematic behaviors are managed by teachers and handled administratively. School experiences affect the way students feel, the way they think about their teachers and peers, and the way they act. Positive school experiences support empathic, moral, and self-controlled behavior, whereas negative school experiences increase alienation and hostile responding.

We then review empirical evidence documenting the impact of school-based social-emotional learning (SEL) and social-cognitive programs on the school influences that affect aggressive behavior, with a focus on the formative preschool and elementary school years. We review the findings from model intervention studies that document the potential individual and social benefits of these programs when they are integrated into school practice and implemented with fidelity. Finally, we consider the future challenges and next steps needed to build on the promise schools offer to reduce youth violence.

Summary and Highlights

This chapter focuses on patterns of elevated aggressive behavior that emerge in childhood and get worse as children get older, culminating in serious antisocial and violent actions in later adolescence and early adulthood. Young children who are exposed to adversity during early childhood, especially persistent experiences with inconsistent and harsh punishment, often learn to use defiant and aggressive behaviors to protect themselves and avoid unwanted demands and restrictions (Dishion & Patterson, 2006; Stormshak et al., 2000). At school entry, frequent physical aggression signals high risk for future violent behavior in later adolescence, along with risk for substance abuse, criminal activities, and domestic abuse. Progression to these negative outcomes is not predetermined, however. The transition into school is especially important for children with elevated risk factors because it offers a new set of socializing influences that can reroute aggressive tendencies and habitual responses (or amplify them).

Negative Developmental Progressions in School Contexts

Children who enter school exhibiting high rates of aggression (fighting, temper outbursts, rule-breaking behaviors) can set off a cascade of negative events that worsen their poor social adjustment (Dodge et al., 2008). Disruptive, aggressive rule-breaking behavior leads to rebuke and dislike by peers and teachers along with punishments such as removal of privileges and isolation from others. Negative treatment by teachers and peers fuels feelings of anger, frustration, and emotional distress, making problem behaviors worse rather than better. Peer dislike also reduces opportunities for positive peer interactions that might strengthen prosocial attitudes. So aggressive children form affiliations with other aggressive students, which supports increases in problem behaviors, further reduces positive teacher and peer support, and amplifies feelings of persecution, discontent, and disengagement (Powers et al., 2013).

Children who engage in high rates of aggression are more likely to experience this kind of negative developmental cascade when they attend underresourced schools that serve many students with academic and behavioral needs and when teachers and school administrators rely on punitive and exclusionary discipline practices (Sanders et al., 2020). In the United States, schools typically are organized by neighborhood in ways that tend to segregate marginalized segments of the population. Schools often struggle to provide appropriate levels of instructional and behavioral support when they serve a high proportion of at-risk students. When the school administration is not up to the task, teachers and other school staff become highly stressed and demoralized, and poor management results in a peer context in which aggressive behaviors are normalized and tolerated (Hoglund et al., 2015). Without school-based interventions and supports, children displaying high levels of aggression are likely to become more alienated and disengaged from school over time, increasing defiant rule-breaking and antisocial behaviors into adolescence. The transition to the larger, less structured context of middle school along with the physical and social changes associated with puberty also contribute to increases in truancy, covert antisocial activity (i.e., lying, stealing, vandalism), emerging substance use, and risky sexual activity, as well as aggressive and violent behaviors (Loeber & Burke, 2011).

The good news is that schools have the potential to provide positive developmental supports that can divert aggressive children from this negative developmental cascade. Schools can adopt programs that have proven effective at promoting growth in the skills children need to control aggression and form positive relationships. Administrators and teachers can receive professional development support that helps them manage problem behaviors in positive ways, strengthening support for social-emotional skill development and appropriate behavior. Proven programs can also create more positive social climates that nurture engagement and reduce risk for all students (see reviews by Durlak et al., 2011; Schonert-Reichl & Weissberg, 2015). In the next section, we review research documenting the school programming that supports student well-being and reduces antisocial development.

Best Practices

Research documents the power of school-based SEL and social-cognitive interventions to promote the social and emotional skills that produce long-term improvements in student well-being and reduce violence. These include the skills for friendship-making, the ability to understand and empathize with others' feelings and to talk about and manage one's own feelings, the self-regulation skills that help children control impulses and follow rules, and the problem-solving skills that support the peaceful resolution of conflicts. School-based programs with documented efficacy exist at different levels of focus. These include programs designed for schoolwide or classroom-wide implementation (universal or tier 1 programs designed to benefit all students) and more intensive programs for children at elevated risk (targeted or tier 2/3 programs to benefit students exhibiting high rates of aggression). As illustrated by the examples we provide below, different programs vary in the degree to which they emphasize the emotional skills that support self-control (often labeled SEL programs) relative to the thinking skills that support effective decision making and social interaction (often labeled social-cognitive programs). Social-emotional and social-cognitive skills overlap considerably. In discussing specific programs, we refer to SEL as a general umbrella term that includes social-cognitive programs.

As a first step, these programs introduce skill concepts using stories, discussions, and role-play activities to convey the basic ideas and behaviors that represent exemplars of the skill. Next, they provide students with multiple opportunities to practice the skills and receive feedback. Teachers are provided with lesson plans and receive professional coaching to help them support student growth and well-being throughout the day. School-based SEL programming is most effective when it involves a whole school commitment that integrates tier 1 universal (classroom-based) and tier 2/3 targeted (small-group, individual) levels of intervention. For overviews of SEL approaches, see Bierman et al. (2016) and Schonert-Reichl and Weissberg (2015).

Universal (Tier 1) Classroom-Level Programs

Universal SEL programs typically involve a curriculum of lessons taught by classroom teachers, along with coaching in teaching practices that foster a positive classroom climate. The goal is to promote the social-emotional competencies and behavioral adjustment of all students and to create classroom norms that support these skills schoolwide. A good example of an evidence-based universal SEL program is the Promoting Alternative Thinking Strategies (PATHS) curriculum (see Greenberg et al., 2011; Kusche et al., 2011). PATHS provides sequential lesson plans at each elementary school grade level. PATHS uses routines and posters to help children remember and use the target skills, including feeling face cards to help children identify their own and others' emotions, and a traffic light poster to guide them in the steps of self-control and problem solving. Teachers and other school staff remind children to use the problem-solving steps when conflicts arise: (1) stop, calm down, and define the problem (red light); (2) discuss possible solutions (yellow light); and (3) make a plan, try it out, and evaluate if the problem is solved (green light).

Multiple studies have shown that school-based SEL programs like PATHS effectively promote social-emotional competencies and reduce aggression (see Durlak et al., 2011; Wilson & Lipsey, 2007). These include programs such as Caring School Community, Positive Action, Resolving Conflicts Creatively Program, Responsive Classroom, Second Step, Social Decision Making/Problem Solving Program, and Steps to Respect (Schonert-Reichl & Weissberg, 2015). Readers can find information about these and other evidence-based SEL programs at websites for the Collaborative for Social, Emotional, and Academic Learning (CASEL; https://pg.casel.org) and Blueprints for Healthy Child Development (https://www.blueprintsprograms.org).

Targeted (Tier 2/3) Programs

Targeted (tier 2/3) small-group or individualized SEL programs have demonstrated positive impact for students who exhibit high rates of aggressive-disruptive behavior. These programs complement the universal programs and provide intensive practice in social-emotional competencies, especially the skills that help children manage strong emotions and resolve conflicts peacefully.

Coping Power is one evidence-based tier 2 program designed for aggressive elementary school students (Lochman & Wells, 2004). It includes small-group sessions for children focused on friendship skills, strategies for managing anger and reducing hostile thoughts, and social problem solving. A parallel set of sessions help parents manage behaviors in positive ways at home (e.g., clear expectations, specific praise, stress management, communication, nonpunitive discipline strategies). Coping Power reduces student aggression, promotes social adjustment, and can be implemented effectively by school counselors (Lochman et al., 2019).

A second example is the Fast Track Friendship Group program for elementary students (Bierman et al., 2017). Small-group sessions introduce skill concepts using stories, discussions, and role-play activities and give students a chance to practice the skills during games and cooperative challenges. The program begins with basic skills for communication, emotion knowledge, and self-control and then progresses to the more complex skills of conflict resolution and stress management. Parents and teachers receive handouts about the skills and how to help children at home and school. School counselors, teachers, and paraeducators can be trained to deliver Friendship Group at school and effectively reduce student aggressive and disruptive behavior, while also promoting social competence and improving peer, teacher, and parent relationships (see Bierman et al., 2023). Readers can find information about additional school-based tier 2 programs documented to reduce aggression, including Check-in, Check-out, Incredible Years, First Steps to Success, and others, at the What Works Clearinghouse (https://ies.ed.gov/ncee/wwc/).

Integrated, Multicomponent Programs

Schools can have the most positive effects on aggressive behaviors by integrating universal (tier 1) and targeted (tier 2/3) school-based SEL programs and coordinating them with parent-focused interventions. Several model programs demonstrate the value of this integrated approach (see Bruhn et al., 2014, for a review.) One model program, Fast Track, shows the potential long-term benefits of multicomponent interventions when they are sustained over the elementary and secondary school years. Fast Track started in 1990 and worked with students who entered elementary school showing high rates of aggressive behaviors in four diverse U.S. communities (Conduct Problems Prevention Research Group [CPPRG], 2019). The intervention included classroom SEL (the PATHS Curriculum), along with Friendship Group and parent group sessions and individualized home visits during elementary school. Youth and families got extended care tailored to their level of need through the transition to high school. Follow-up assessments in early adulthood showed that Fast Track intervention recipients had lower levels of problem behaviors, mental health difficulties, and criminal activity compared to similar youth in the comparison group (CPPRG, 2019). These findings show the potential power of coordinated and sustained multicomponent SEL programing to promote competencies and reduce risk for antisocial behavior among children who show high rates of aggression in their early years. The big challenge is moving from these kinds of model programs supported with research funding to sustainable school-based programming.

Where Are We Going?

An important next step in this area is to find ways to scale up evidence-based programs and deliver them in cost-effective ways across the country and in other regions of the world. To be most effective, SEL programming must be implemented with high fidelity on a schoolwide basis. Barriers to schoolwide program adoption include developing the necessary school system infrastructure and staffing, attaining the buy-in of school leadership and teaching staff, and creating data systems and communication supports to manage program delivery, coordination, and evaluation (George et al., 2018). There is also a need for ongoing research to identify program adjustments that can reduce school costs and burdens without reducing program benefits (see Lochman et al., 2019).

Promising advances have been made in identifying school team structures that support high-fidelity and sustained multicomponent SEL programming

(George et al., 2018). A recent study found that teams that included school personnel and community mental health experts using the Interconnected Systems Framework were effective at expanding school capacity to offer multitiered SEL and mental health programming (Weist et al., 2022). At the national level, CASEL provides guidelines and training programs to support school districts in their efforts to implement schoolwide SEL programming and to help policymakers interested in supporting statewide SEL scaffolds (Dermody & Dusenbury, 2022).

Multitiered SEL programming requires that schools include screening systems to monitor child risk and need for services. Regular screening of student behavioral adjustment and well-being also provides a basis for program evaluation and continuous program improvement. Exemplars of effective schoolwide data management systems are emerging (Weist et al., 2022), but more research is needed to identify optimal systems that match student needs to appropriate levels of intervention without raising concerns regarding inappropriate and potentially iatrogenic labeling of students.

In addition, ongoing program development is needed to ensure culturally responsive programming. Evidence-based programs have documented efficacy in the schools and populations where they were tested but may not have generalizable benefits. Adaptations may be required to ensure that programs are sensitive to and effective for diverse groups of students. Rather than customizing SEL for separate groups, the major push in this area is to ensure equity in SEL programming, addressing the range of student cultures and experiences and confronting the systemic issues that impact students from underrepresented and marginalized groups (Ramirez et al., 2021).

Finally, it is critical to recognize that school-based SEL programming is only one approach to addressing youth aggression. It must be accompanied by additional efforts to address the broader aspects of the social and school contexts that influence violence. In the school context, rigid and punitive disciplinary strategies must be replaced with positive behavior management strategies. School practices sometimes involve aggregating students exhibiting disruptive and aggressive behavior into restrictive classroom or school programs in order to provide intensive behavior management support. While well-intentioned, these restrictive aggregation practices often have unintended negative effects that contribute to decreases in student school engagement, increases in problem behaviors, and reductions in academic attainment (Powers et al., 2016). Aggregating students with aggressive behavior problems for small-group SEL intervention is generally effective when well-structured, evidence-based programs are implemented by well-trained facilitators who proficiently manage group dynamics (Weiss et al., 2005). However, youth with very high levels of aggressive behavior remain at elevated risk for experiencing negative peer responses during intervention sessions (Ho et al., 2023; Lavallee et al., 2005) and may benefit more from individual than from small-group intervention (Lochman et al., 2019). At the broader level of social policy and governance, efforts to reduce structural inequities and opportunity gaps are critical, including changes to the structural inequities evident in school funding and school quality.

In summary, school-based SEL is one essential part of a larger set of violence prevention strategies. We have a strong research base documenting the effectiveness of this approach and the potential benefits to children and society of widespread use. The challenge ahead is to continue efforts to refine programming and tackle the hurdles associated with scaling up high-quality and sustained implementation.

Acknowledgments

This chapter was supported in part by the Institute of Education Sciences (grant R305A150488) and the National Institute of Child Health and Human Development (grant HD046064). The views expressed in this article are ours and do not necessarily represent the granting agencies. The authors report no conflicts of interest.

References

Bierman, K. L., Greenberg, M. T., & Abenavoli, R. (2016). *Promoting social and emotional learning in preschool: Programs and practices that work*. Edna Bennet Pierce Prevention Research Center, Pennsylvania State University. https://www.prevention.psu.edu/uploads/files/rwjf437157-SELPreschool.pdf

Bierman, K. L., Greenberg, M. T., Coie, J. D., Dodge, K. A., Lochman, J. E., & McMahon, R. J. (2017). *Social and emotional skills training for children: The Fast Track Friendship Group Manual*. Guilford.

Bierman, K. L., Welsh, J. A., Hall, C. M., Jacobson, L. N., Lee, D. L., & Jones, D. E. (2023). Efficacy of the Fast Track Friendship Group Program for peer-rejected children: A randomized-controlled trial. *Journal of Clinical Child and Adolescent Psychology, 52*, 763–779.

Bruhn, A. L., Lane, K. L., & Hirsch, S. E. (2014). A review of tier 2 interventions conducted within multitiered models of behavioral prevention. *Journal of Emotional and Behavioral Disorders, 22*, 171–189.

Conduct Problems Prevention Research Group (CPPRG). (2019). *The Fast Track Program for children a risk: Preventing antisocial behavior*. Guilford.

Dermody, C. M., & Dusenbury, L. (2022). *Supporting evidence-based SEL programs: What state policymakers can do*. Edna Bennett Pierce Prevention Research Center, Pennsylvania State University.

Dishion, T. J., & Patterson, G. R. (2006). The development and ecology of antisocial behavior in children and adolescents. In D. Cicchetti & D. J. Cohen (Eds.), *Developmental psychopathology: Risk, disorder, and adaptation* (pp. 503–541). John Wiley.

Dodge, K. A., Greenberg, M. T., Malone, P. S., & Conduct Problems Prevention Research Group (CPPRG). (2008). Testing an idealized dynamic cascade model of the development of serious violence in adolescence. *Child Development, 79,* 1907–1927.

Durlak, J. A., Weissberg, R. P., Dymnicki, A. B., Taylor, R. D., & Schellinger, K. B. (2011). The impact of enhancing students' social and emotional learning: A meta-analysis of school-based universal interventions. *Child Development, 82,* 405–432.

Dusenbury, L., & Weissberg, R. P. (2017). *Social emotional learning in elementary school: Preparation for success.* Edna Bennett Pierce Prevention Research Center, Pennsylvania State University. https://www.prevention.psu.edu/uploads/files/rwjf436221-SELElemSchl.pdf

George, H. P., Cox, K. E., Minch, D., & Sandomierski, T. (2018). District practices associated with successful SWPBIS implementation. *Behavioral Disorders, 43,* 393–406.

Greenberg, M. T., Kusche, C. A., & Conduct Problems Prevention Research Group (CPPRG). (2011). *Grade level PATHS (Grades 3–4).* Channing-Bete.

Ho, L. C., Bierman, K. L., Jacobson, L. N., Welsh, J. A., Hall, C. M., & Lee, D. L. (2023). Linking intervention experiences to child outcomes in a school-based social skills training program. *Psychology in the Schools, 60,* 1855–1876.

Hoglund, W. L. G., Klingle, K. E., & Hosan, E. (2015). Classroom risks and resources: Teacher burnout, classroom quality and children's adjustment in high needs elementary schools. *Journal of School Psychology, 53,* 337–357.

Kusche, C. A., Greenberg, M. T., & Conduct Problems Prevention Research Group (CPPRG). (2011). *Grade level PATHS (Grades 1–2).* Channing-Bete.

Lavallee, K. L., Bierman, K. L., Nix, R. L., & Conduct Problems Prevention Research Group (CPPRG). (2005). The impact of first-grade "friendship group" experiences on child social outcomes in the Fast Track Program. *Journal of Abnormal Child Psychology, 33,* 307–324.

Lochman, J. E., Boxmeyer, C. L., Kassing, F. L., Powell, N. P., & Stromeyer, S. L. (2019). Cognitive behavioral intervention for youth at risk for conduct problems: Future directions. *Journal of Clinical Child and Adolescent Psychology, 48,* 799–810.

Lochman, J. E., & Wells, K. C. (2004). The Coping Power Program for preadolescent boys and their parents: Outcome effects at the 1-year follow-up. *Journal of Consulting and Clinical Psychology, 72,* 571–578.

Loeber, R., & Burke, J. D. (2011). Developmental pathways in juvenile externalizing and internalizing problems. *Journal of Research on Adolescence, 21,* 34–46.

Powers, C. J., Bierman, K. L., & Coffman, D. (2016). Restrictive educational placements for students with early-starting conduct problems: Associations with high-school non-completion and adolescent maladjustment. *Journal of Child Psychology and Psychiatry, 57,* 899–908.

Powers, C. J., Bierman, K. L., & Conduct Problems Prevention Research Group (CPPRG). (2013). The multifaceted impact of peer relations on aggressive-disruptive behavior in early elementary school. *Developmental Psychology, 49,* 1174–1186.

Ramirez, T., Brush, K., Raisch, N., Bailey, R., & Jones, S. M. (2021). Equity in social emotional learning programs: A content analysis of equitable practices in PreK 5 SEL programs. *Frontiers in Education.* https://doi.org/10.3389/feduc.2021.679467

Sanders, M. T., Bierman, K. L., & Heinrichs, B. S. (2020). Longitudinal associations linking elementary and middle school contexts with student aggression in early adolescence. *Journal of Abnormal Child Psychology, 48*, 1569–1580.

Schonert-Reichl, K. A., & Weissberg, R. P. (2015). Social and emotional learning: Children. In T. P. Gullotta & M. Bloom (Eds.), *Encyclopedia of primary prevention and health promotion: Part II* (2nd ed., pp. 936–949). Springer.

Stormshak, E. A., Bierman, K. L., McMahon, R. J., & Lengua, L. J. (2000). Parenting practices and child disruptive behavior problems in early elementary school. *Journal of Clinical Child Psychology, 29*, 17–29.

Weiss, B., Caron, A., Ball, S., Tapp, J., Johnson, M., & Weisz, J. R. (2005). Iatrogenic effects of group treatment for antisocial youth. *Journal of Consulting and Clinical Psychology, 73*, 1036–1044.

Weist, M. D., Splett, J. W., Halliday, C. A., Gage, N. A., Seaman, M. A., Perkins, K. A., Perales, K., Miller, E., Collins, D., & DiStefano, C. (2022). A randomized controlled trial on the interconnected systems framework for school mental health and PBIS: Focus on proximal variables and school discipline. *Journal of School Psychology, 94*, 49–65.

Wilson, S. J., & Lipsey, M. W. (2007). School-based interventions for aggressive and disruptive behavior: Update of a meta-analysis. *American Journal of Preventive Medicine, 33*, S130–S143.

Anger Control Counseling for Youth Violence Prevention

●●●●●●●●●●●●●

RAYMOND W. NOVACO AND
ISAIAS M. CONTRERAS

Overview: Authors' Backgrounds

Ray Novaco began as a clinical psychologist with an internship that focused on adolescents and their parents. In his early extensions of the anger control treatment that he pioneered, he worked with juvenile probation officers, with county social service staff dealing with family violence, and with school psychologists in junior high schools in conducting anger management sessions. Much of his research on anger has been conducted in high-security forensic psychiatric facilities and with military service members. He continues to work with the Orange County Family Justice Center, where he has contributed to its programs for children and for parents.

Isaias Contreras double-majored as an undergraduate in psychology and criminology. He has long been interested in studying why some people are violent and others are not. He began working with Dr. Novaco as an undergraduate research assistant on domestic violence projects. His honors thesis on anger rumination and forgiveness was his entry into the anger/aggression field, in which he continues to engage. His doctoral research concerns law enforcement officers and their experiences with job stress, anger, and burnout, through which he aims to improve the well-being of officers and the citizens whom they serve.

Summary and Highlights

Youth Violence and Anger as Public Health Problems

Youth violence is widely recognized as a serious social problem in many countries, and the World Health Organization has identified it as a global public health problem. Viewing violence through a public health lens is advantageous for understanding the multifactorial causes of violence and providing a framework for how to situate anger treatment programs, which aim to provide harm reduction not only to the victims of violent behavior but also to the chronically angry person. Although violence can occur in the absence of anger and the occurrence of anger need not be followed by violence, anger does impel violent behavior, particularly when its intensity and duration override efforts at self-control.

Violence perpetration and victimization have had heightened significance for students and schools, particularly in the wake of tragedies at Marjory Stoneman Douglas High School (Florida), perpetrated by an expelled student, at Oxford High School (Michigan), perpetrated by an enrolled student, and at Robb Elementary School (Texas), perpetrated by a former student. These were revenge-seeking episodes with many fatalities. In 2019, 8.7 percent of high school students did not go to school because of safety concerns, 7.4 percent were threatened or injured with a weapon at school, and 19.5 percent were bullied in some way (Centers for Disease Control and Prevention, 2019). Violence against teachers and staff is also a problem. A meta-analysis of twenty-four studies indicated that 20 to 75 percent of teachers were victimized by a student within the past two years (Longobardi et al., 2019). Such victimizations are plausibly the result of anger-driven retaliation motives.

Problematic anger has received epidemiological attention. A U.S. national sample (over 34,000 people) interviewed by Okuda et al. (2015) found a 7.8 percent rate of problematic anger. They called for screening and early intervention, especially for young adults, as anger interferes with work, school, and relationships. From a harm-inducing standpoint, anger that is too frequent, high in intensity, and prolonged has adverse consequences for whomever an angry person might target, but also for the chronically angry person's psychological and physical well-being. Dysregulated anger can be a product of traumatic exposure to violence and then become a key activator of PTSD-related violent behavior. Youth who are incarcerated have high rates of PTSD along with other psychiatric disorders that extend after their initial detainment (cf. Duron et al., 2022).

The Importance of Anger Control

Anger control has been cherished since classical philosophers grappled with the regulation of inner life and the enhancement of virtue. Anger is the prototype of the classic view of emotions as "passions" that seize the personality, disturb judgment, alter bodily conditions, and imperil behavior. Nevertheless, anger is a primary emotion having adaptive functions linked to survival mechanisms. Although there are sociocultural variations in its expression, anger can mobilize psychological resources, energize behaviors for corrective action, and facilitate perseverance. Anger serves as a guardian to self-esteem, operates as a means of communicating negative sentiment, potentiates the ability to redress grievances, and boosts determination to overcome obstacles to our happiness and aspirations. Recognizing how anger functions is crucial to bear in mind when seeking to engage someone in an anger control intervention, as both youth and adults are reluctant to relinquish the protection that they believe anger provides.

Social gatekeepers—parents, school principals, employers, police officers, and judges—are not charmed by the mastery-toned elements of anger but rather are sensitized to and unsettled by images of anger as eruptive, unbridled, savage, venous, burning, and consuming. They know that violent behavior is often activated by anger. Gatekeepers must keep in mind, though, that the instrumental value of anger and aggression can make for their intractability and that many youths who have anger regulatory difficulties are beset with hardships. Children and adolescents whose lives are replete with avenues of friction, such as bleak family finances, chaotic social relationships, failures in school, and conflict at home, are short in countervailing resources for inhibiting aggression, and anger easily becomes a default response. Beyond anger's violence-engendering faculty, it also detracts from good judgment, the establishment of prosocial core relationships, school and work performance, and physical well-being.

Anger has particular relevance for juvenile offenders. In large-scale studies performed in California, Massachusetts, and Virginia, anger assessed upon intake to a correctional facility was subsequently associated with assaults on staff and on youth inmates as well as other misconduct. These studies controlled for personal background and mental health variables, including the psychiatric care provided within the institution. Anger, self-reported by incarcerated juvenile offenders, is predictive of their violent and nonviolent institutional offending, ascertained by official records data and by the juveniles' own self-reporting of their behavior (cf. Kelly et al., 2019). Moreover, youth who have a history of violent offending are more likely to reoffend if they have a long duration pattern of anger (Acland & Cavanagh, 2023).

Transmission of Anger and Violence through Social Media

Nearly all adolescents in developed countries use the internet regularly. A study conducted across twenty-nine countries found that 45 percent of adolescents reported being online almost *constantly* (Boer et al., 2020). While the ability to connect with people, share information, and discuss ideas has enormous societal benefits, social media is a double-edged sword that can also fuel anger and propel violence when used inappropriately.

Because emotion-laden content is intrinsically more engaging than other content, social media algorithms can preference and promote controversial content to drive online activity. On Twitter, negative messages spread faster than positive ones. Anger is more contagious than joy, and anger is also more likely than joy to spread to individuals with weaker social ties. While most social media sites are moderated, some unmoderated spaces contain blatantly hateful or violent messages (Weimann & Masri, 2023).

Social media can also create and maintain echo chambers—online spaces that limit exposure to opposing viewpoints and promote like-minded thinking. Adolescents who feel alienated or aggrieved can self-select into online groups that reinforce alienation and resentment, amplifying the potential for anger to foment and fester. Social media sites can also illustrate and propel violence and be a zone for victimization in broadcasting and perpetuating bullying, cyberbullying, dating violence, and even suicide. The anonymity provided by the internet can embolden users to vent their anger and display aggression. Longitudinal studies have found that cybervictimization predicts cyberaggression and anger rumination in a vicious cycle.

Rumination, Revenge, Violent Fantasy

Repetitive dwelling on anger experiences is an important marker of dysregulated anger. A common motivation among perpetrators of school violence is vengeance. In the U.S. Secret Service Analysis of Plots Against Schools, which analyzed sixty-seven reported and averted plots against schools between 2006 and 2018, the most frequently identified motive among plotters (45 percent of cases) was having grievances with classmates, romantic partners, and/or staff. Communications about retaliatory plans were made in 94 percent of those cases (U.S. Secret Service, 2021), as it was in the now infamous 2022 Uvalde, Texas, episode. Resentment and revenge plots are likely cultivated over long periods of angry rumination about perceived injustices. Eric Harris, one of the infamous Columbine High School attackers, stated, "If you could see all the anger I've stored over the past four [expletive] years . . . you made me what I am" (Harris & Klebold, 1999).

Many manifestations of violence in school settings involve anger that has incubated over time, infused with revenge seeking. Anger associated with intergroup conflict, small-scale personal disputes, and shooting rampage episodes has plausibly been prolonged and amplified in brooding about aversive experiences and thoughts of retaliation. Vengeful thinking can also entail imagined violence, which a number of scientific studies with psychiatric patients have found to be associated with their future violent behavior. Revenge-oriented anger rumination has high relevance for violence risk assessment; however, detecting it requires clinical skills.

Psychotherapeutic Intervention for Anger

An extensive range of studies with children, adolescents, and adults show the efficacy of psychological therapies for problematic anger. This has been found in many meta-analyses (reviews that combine and synthesize the results of numerous studies). One by Sukhodolsky et al. (2004) specifically focused on cognitive behavioral therapy (CBT) for anger-related problems in children and adolescents. It involved fifty-one CBT treatment versus control comparisons. Across several meta-analyses, the CBT approach to the treatment of anger has a medium to strong effect size—which roughly means that 75 percent of those in the CBT treatment group improve more than those in the control conditions. Meta-analyses on various types of anger treatments, including school-based programs and psychiatric hospitals, have found small to medium effect sizes, which reflects about 65 percent higher gains for those in the treatment condition.

Anger control treatment for youth was most fully developed by Eva Feindler with institutionalized adolescents (cf. Feindler & Ecton, 1986). Since Feindler's important work, only a few controlled studies have concerned justice-involved youth. One is the Goldstein et al. (2018) study of a Juvenile Justice Anger Management treatment for girls conducted in several residential facilities in New Jersey and Pennsylvania. Their program involved psychoeducation about anger and aggression, cognitive restructuring of how anger-provoking events are perceived and experienced, identifying physiological cues and triggers of anger, skill-building sessions for managing arousal and preventive aggression, and generalizing skills for future use. All of these components actually have been part of CBT anger treatment since its inception. Goldstein and her colleagues though designed the treatment to be responsive to the therapeutic needs of girls, who are more inclined toward "relational" or indirect aggression, have higher psychological disorder comorbidity than boys in the justice system, and are more likely to aggress against staff. Their sixteen-session, eight-week program, when compared to a treatment-as-usual condition, resulted in significantly reduced anger, physical aggression, and indirect aggression.

Among various extensions of CBT for anger has been giving it a "mindfulness" focus. A systematic review of mindfulness-based interventions for adolescents' mental health problems supports their efficacy (Kostova et al., 2019).

Best Practices

Anger is part of the confluence of multilevel risk factors affecting violent behavior—such as low empathy, impulsivity, poor parental supervision, family violence exposure, and negative attitudes. The major causes of someone's violent behavior may not be anger dysregulation, and in such cases an anger treatment would not be the appropriate intervention. When violence happens without an obvious display of anger, the relevance of anger should not be dismissed. Violence-driving anger experiences may be distant from the violent act, such as when someone has been mistreated, ruminates in anger about grievances, then later enacts a "cool" vengeance.

Anger is comingled with various forms of psychological distress or psychopathology. Among adolescents prone to violence, anger commonly co-occurs with depression. Several studies, though, have shown that anger accounts for the relationship between depression and aggressive behavior (e.g., Gresham et al., 2016). Also, youth exposed to physical or sexual abuse and those involved in the justice system tend to have high rates of PTSD (Duron et al., 2022). Dysregulated anger is a key part of PTSD and its association with violent behavior. Anger is also a main feature of psychopathological conditions of paranoia and emotional instability in personality disorders.

The implementation of therapeutic interventions for anger best proceeds from a case formulation that is grounded in a thorough assessment of the nature of the anger problem and the associated psychological impairments. Far too many implementations of "anger management" in correctional settings and in schools are not based on a proficient case formulation and are all too often delivered as group-based psychoeducational programs. One must ascertain to what extent anger is a problem for the person, what sets of factors contribute to the anger control difficulties, what should be the foci or targets of treatment, and how the therapeutic process should unfold.

What determines whether anger is problematic? This can be gauged by *reactivity* (frequency of onset and how easily anger is triggered), *intensity* (how strongly anger is activated or engaged), *duration* (persistence of anger arousal), and *mode of expression* (aggressive or avoidant behavior). Treatment aims to minimize these problematic dimensions of anger to reduce the costs of anger. The concept of "anger costs" is pivotal here. People having anger control problems, regardless of their age, will engage in treatment when they begin to see that the costs of staying the same are higher than the costs of trying to be different. Those costs can be assessed through a supportive interview that aims to learn the person's (1) awareness of anger pattern features, (2) degree of investment in anger habits, and (3) degree troubled by the personal and social products of the anger reactions. Heightening recognition of anger costs is part of the anger treatment "preparatory phase" to facilitate treatment engagement, which is fully described in Taylor and Novaco (2005).

Detaching someone from his or her anger/aggression routines smartly proceeds from recognition of the functions served by them, both manifest and latent, and providing ample support and psychological safety. High anger people in forensic settings (prisons and highly secure psychiatric hospitals) can present with a hard exterior, but they can be psychologically fragile—especially those having histories of recurrent abuse or trauma, for whom abandonment and rejection are significant life themes. Anger and aggression, as character armor, can mask felt vulnerability, which can be exacerbated by punitive actions of social systems, including schools. Anger can be an entrenched mode of reactance to stressful or aversive experiences. Chronically angry people are reluctant to surrender the anger-aggression system that they have found useful to engage because they discount the costs of its engagement.

There are a number of standardized anger assessment instruments that have demonstrated validity with youth populations. Among them is the Novaco Anger Scale (NAS; Novaco, 2003), which is designed to measure anger disposition with forty-eight items on the Cognitive, Arousal, and Behavioral subscales (each with four thematic subsets), plus a separate Anger Regulation scale. The NAS was uniquely designed to provide for case formulation, through identifying aspects of anger for treatment targeting. For example, in the Cognitive subscale, there are "justification," "rumination," "suspicion," and "hostile attitude" subsets. However, the NAS may be too long to administer and interpret for screening purposes. In that case, there is a simplified anger screening tool, the seven-item Dimensions of Anger Reactions (DAR-R) that Novaco developed, which has received strong validation in a number of studies (cf. Kannis-Dymand et al., 2019). Such screening tools have "cutting scores" or thresholds for gauging whether anger is a problem.

Because psychotherapeutic interventions for anger have largely been CBT approaches to enhance self-control, building client self-monitoring skills is a fundamental step in being able to control anger. A superb anger self-monitoring tool with high value for youth is Feindler's Hassle Log, which identifies anger triggers, setting events, appraisals, range of responses, and self-evaluation. A case illustration of her assessment approach with a thirteen-year-old girl is in Feindler and Engel (2011).

To facilitate engagement in treatment, the therapist or counselor must provide for the safety, patience, and psychological space for reflection, exploration, and choice. In screening for anger problems or providing therapeutic care, a practitioner should acknowledge the legitimacy of a client's feelings, as anger is not violence. Building trust in the therapeutic relationship is pivotal. Improved self-regulation hinges on education about anger and discovery of one's "anger signature." Giving attention to the anger *intensity* has high value because most people recognize that when they become very angry, they often do something that they later regret.

Attending to anger rumination as a violence risk factor is also important. In looking to prevent violent behavior, teachers, counselors, and administrators who encounter students (or staff) showing signs of anger should ascertain whether there is perseverative thinking about adverse experiences and listen for ruminative content. To be sure, there have been enough "lessons learned" from infamous cases to red-flag someone's communicated plans for revenge against staff or students. Even when retaliation is not being contemplated, anger rumination can detract from a student's well-being beyond what might be attributed to depression.

There are various CBT-based anger therapies, one of which is Novaco's "stress inoculation" approach, within which anger provocation is simulated by therapeutically paced progressive exposure to anger incidents created in imaginal visualization and in role play, based on a hierarchy of anger incidents produced by the collaborative work of client and therapist. This graduated, hierarchical exposure is the basis for the "inoculation" metaphor. This approach involves a number of key components: client education about anger, building self-monitoring skills, arousal reduction techniques, cognitive restructuring of anger experiences, training new behaviors as modeled and rehearsed with the therapist, and practicing the cognitive, arousal regulatory, and behavioral coping skills while visualizing and role playing progressively more intense anger-arousing scenes from the personal hierarchies. Conceptual and empirical background on this approach can be found in the Taylor and Novaco (2005) book. Various simplified CBT-based anger management interventions that rely on the psychoeducational, cognitive restructuring, and problem-solving skill components have been implemented in studies conducted in school settings and shown to be efficacious.

Where Are We Going?

Some promising avenues for effective treatments of anger include forgiveness therapy, mindfulness-based CBT, and transdiagnostic therapy for emotional disorders. Case examples of a CBT mindfulness treatment of anger can be found in Clark (2020) and of a transdiagnostic treatment protocol for anger in Grossman and Ehrenreich-May (2020), which may be better for youths who present with other forms of emotional malaise, such as anxiety and depression.

Regarding future research, there is considerable opportunity for development of digital technology for anger assessment and treatment. The evidence for the value of e-mental health for justice-involved youth is promising, but such work is thin regarding anger (Grove et al., 2021), but an online psychoeducational anger management program by Braeuer et al. (2022) displayed good results. A virtual-reality-based treatment of anger may also be on the horizon, as this mode of therapy has had effectiveness in PTSD treatment for combat veterans and for the treatment of psychosis.

References

Acland, E. L., & Cavanagh, C. (2023). Anger, violence, and recidivism in justice system involved youth. *Justice Quarterly, 40*, 241–262.

Boer, M., Van Den Eijnden, R. J., Boniel-Nissim, M., Wong, S. L., Inchley, J. C., Badura, P., . . . Stevens, G. W. (2020). Adolescents' intense and problematic social media use and their well-being in 29 countries. *Journal of Adolescent Health, 66*(6), S89–S99.

Braeuer, K., Noble, N., & Yi, S. (2022). The efficacy of an online anger management program for justice-involved youth. *Journal of Addictions & Offender Counseling, 43*, 26–37.

Centers for Disease Control and Prevention. (2019). *Youth risk behavior survey: Data summary and trends report 2009–2019*. U.S. Department of Health and Human Services.

Clark, L. B. (2020). Utilizing mindfulness based CBT to address anger and aggression in middle schools. *Journal of Child and Adolescent Counseling, 6*, 97–109.

Duron, J. F., Williams-Butler, A., Mattson, P., & Boxer, P. (2022). Trauma exposure and mental health needs among adolescents involved with the juvenile justice system. *Journal of Interpersonal Violence, 37*(17–18). https://doi.org/10.1177 /08862605211016358.

Feindler, E. L., & Ecton, R. B. (1986). *Adolescent anger control: Cognitive-behavioral techniques*. Pergamon Press.

Feindler, E. L., & Engel, E. C. (2011). Assessment and intervention for adolescents with anger and aggression difficulties in school settings. *Psychology in the Schools, 48*, 243–253.

Goldstein, N. E., Giallella, C. L., Haney-Caron, E., Peterson, L., Serico, J., Kemp, K., . . . Lochman, J. (2018). Juvenile Justice Anger Management (JJAM) treatment for girls: Results of a randomized controlled trial. *Psychological Services, 15*, 386–397.

Gresham, D., Melvin, G. A., & Gullone, E. (2016). The role of anger in the relationship between internalising symptoms and aggression in adolescents. *Journal of Child and Family Studies, 25*, 2674–2682.

Grossman, R. A., & Ehrenreich-May, J. (2020). Using the unified protocol for transdiagnostic treatment of emotional disorders with youth exhibiting anger and irritability. *Cognitive and Behavioral Practice, 27*, 184–201.

Grove, L., King, C. M., Bomysoad, R., Vasquez, L., & Kois, L. E. (2021). Technology for assessment and treatment of justice-involved youth: A systematic literature review. *Law and Human Behavior, 45*, 413–426.

Harris, E., & Klebold, D. (1999). *Transcript of the Columbine "Basement Tapes."* https://schoolshooters.info/sites/default/files/columbine_basement_tapes_1.0.pdf

Kannis-Dymand, L., Salguero, M., Cejudo, J. R., & Novaco, R. W. (2019). Dimensions of Anger Reactions-Revised (DAR-R): Validation in Australia and Spain. *Journal of Clinical Psychology, 75,* 1233–1248.

Kelly, E., Novaco, R. W., & Cauffman, E. (2019). Anger and depression among male juvenile offenders: Predictors of violent and non-violent offending during adjustment to incarceration. *Journal of Consulting and Clinical Psychology, 87,* 693–705.

Kostova, Z., Levin, L., Lorberg, B., & Ziedonis, D. (2019). Mindfulness-based interventions for adolescents with mental health conditions: A systematic review of the research literature. *Journal of Child and Family Studies, 28,* 2633–2649.

Longobardi, C., Badenes-Ribera, L., Fabris, M. A., Martinez, A., & McMahon, S. D. (2019). Prevalence of student violence against teachers: A meta-analysis. *Psychology of Violence, 9,* 596–610.

Novaco, R. W. (2003). *The Novaco Anger Scale and Provocation Inventory.* Western Psychological Services.

Okuda, M., Picazo, J., Olfson, M., Hasin, D. S., Liu, S. M., Bernardi, S., & Blanco, C. (2015). Prevalence and correlates of anger in the community: Results from a national survey. *CNS Spectrums, 20,* 130–139.

Sukhodolsky, D. G., Kassinove, H., & Gorman, B. S. (2004). Cognitive-behavioral therapy for anger in children and adolescents: A meta-analysis. *Aggression and Violent Behavior, 9,* 247–269.

Taylor, J. L., & Novaco, R. W. (2005). *Anger treatment for people with developmental disabilities.* John Wiley.

U.S. Secret Service. (2021). *Averting school violence: A U.S. secret service analysis of plots against schools.* U.S. Department of Homeland Security.

Weimann, G., & Masri, N. (2023). Research note: Spreading hate on TikTok. *Studies in Conflict and Terrorism, 46,* 752–765.

A Socioecological Framework for Youth Violence Prevention

• • • • • • • • • • • • •

Treatment in Homes and Communities

KATHERINE KELTON
AND ASHLI J. SHEIDOW

Overview

What tends to be labeled as disruptive behavior (e.g., aggression, property destruction, truancy, stealing) and attributed to individual or family issues might actually be adaptive behavior that has lost its context. Disruptive behaviors are deeply connected within and across historical, sociocultural contexts and include intersecting identities. When disruptive behaviors are misunderstood, the risk for institutional involvement, cyclical and intergenerational wounds, and violence increases. While treatments for intense and persistent youth violence (i.e., youth with legal system involvement) often use a socioecological framework, their availability is sparse and research-to-practice gaps remain.

Behaviors Do Not Exist in a Vacuum

The first author, Dr. Katherine Kelton, is a white, Mexican American, cisgender woman who grew up in a neighborhood nicknamed the Land of Entrapment, a play on New Mexico's motto, the Land of Enchantment, due to high poverty and crime rates. While she was in elementary school, homicide was the second leading cause of death for kids under ten in Albuquerque (Centers for Disease Control and Prevention, 2004). As in many minoritized and poor communities, legal or institutional involvement of her neighborhood's youth could be traced back to the wounds from adverse childhood experiences (ACEs), such as sexual or physical abuse, emotional neglect, food insecurity, and homelessness. ACEs impact the development of people's abilities to understand and manage thoughts, feelings, and behaviors. Consequently, considering ACEs is critical to understanding causes of disruptive behaviors (Dunn et al., 2018). Further, ACEs are often embedded in larger contexts, driven by sociocultural and systemic inequities not necessarily visible or tangible, like laws or policies.

Treatments must be relevant to the contexts where they are implemented and accommodate how cross-system dynamics (e.g., culture, current/historical events/policies) influence interpersonal, psychological, and biological factors associated with violence. Effective clinician-driven treatments require a balance between acknowledging and addressing systemic issues versus individual behaviors as necessary for change. Along these lines, Bronfenbrenner's (1979) socioecological model is a "how-to" framework for identifying drivers of youth violence and informing treatments for youth violence (see Figure 5.1). The field could benefit from more clinicians and clinician-researchers with lived experiences and recognition that appropriate vulnerability and self-disclosure within practice and research are not always the antithesis to professionalism. There are no hard-and-fast guidelines for self-disclosure in research or practice (Henretty & Levitt, 2010). While some self-disclosure can be ineffective (e.g., sharing information for self-serving reasons or when disclosure distracts from the intervention), self-disclosure can center a professional's values and beliefs about (and thus help balance) power dynamics, strengthen rapport, and empower others. Consequently, a segment of Dr. Kelton's personal journey demonstrates the complexity of viewing youth violence from a socioecological lens and informs how treatments must utilize such a view.

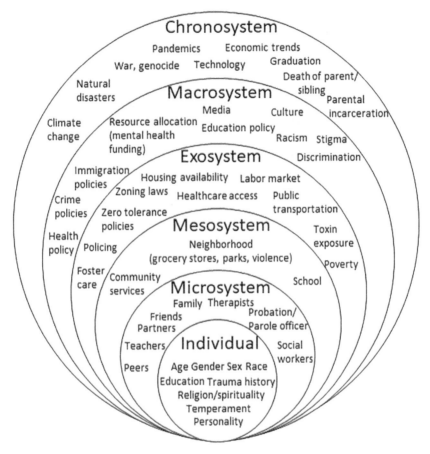

FIGURE 5.1 Example of the socioecological model of youth violence.

Dr. Kelton's Journey: A Personal Account through the Socioecological Model

My first romantic relationship with a Latinx teen named Carlos (pseudonym) was a formative experience and a driving force to pursue my doctorate. As the socioecological model suggests, however, our lived experiences are not purely our own—they are shared. The aspects of my life I choose to write about here are the same others are actively living, trying to forget, or healing through, and this privilege must be acknowledged. To extend power to peoples who have been silenced or unheard, excerpts from one of Carlos's rap songs summarize each level of the socioecological model.[1] Some language is location- or context-specific, but the experiences are universal: being born into a network of factors that increase the likelihood of adversity exposure and violent behavior patterns.

The socioecological model's first level contains individual factors that impact the likelihood of becoming a victim or perpetrator of youth violence. Factors can be based on identity (gender, age, race, education), personal history (e.g., diagnoses, trauma history), or biology (e.g., temperament, personality). Carlos experienced ACEs like physical and sexual violence, food and housing insecurity, and poverty. Such trauma may shape one's ability to accurately predict risk, resulting in interpreting neutral or harmless social interactions as threatening, or manifesting as concentration difficulties from conditioning to vigilantly scan the environment for threats.

> *It's too late, I'm on the wrong road, the wrong road . . .*
> *I'm sick of drama, I'm hurtin' bad*
> *and always gotta' worry that*
> *I might get popped, I might get shot*

The model's second level—the microsystem—describes a person's close social network (e.g., family, friends, partners, and teachers). Carlos's family had a strong gang affiliation, and because children learn behavioral patterns through social learning via modeling (observational learning) and reinforcement (Ford & Blaustein, 2013), he learned many needs could be met through aggression. Therefore, Carlos interpreted seemingly harmless situations as threatening, responding with defiant and escalating behavior. Very quickly, an in-class reminder to pay attention could turn to name-calling and spiral into storming out or throwing a chair.

> *I chose this path, no turning back*
> *I f-cked things up, I'm learning that, but the demons inside me lurkin man*
> *I had a crackhead mom and a worthless dad,*
> *and I'd talk to God but I am sure He's mad*
> *that I didn't stop when I had the chance*
> *I chose to bang and have a blast*
> *Sittin' in the lane where shit happens fast*

The third level, the mesosystem, includes settings and environments where the individual lives and where their relationships occur. Carlos attended one of the poorest schools, where unmet behavioral expectations were responded to with punitive and exclusionary discipline. "Zero tolerance" policies prescribe mandatory consequences for a range of behaviors, from firearm or drug possession to "disruptive" behaviors like tardiness or vandalism. Carlos often received detention for eating in class, without any exploration from school staff as to why this was repetitive behavior. Instead of learning that Carlos saved his lunch to ration food throughout the day because of living in a food-insecure home, school policies labeled Carlos as a "bad kid." Often called the *school-to-prison pipeline*, zero tolerance policies actually result in higher rates of misbehavior, dropout, and legal system contact (American Psychological Association [APA] Zero Tolerance Task Force, 2008; Bailey, 2017). Carlos actively straddled contexts: one of ongoing threat, where many of his behaviors were adaptive, and where these "survival tactics" were punished, in turn undermining social-emotional learning opportunities.

Tell me how to change because I do not know
I stay strugglin' in the game, I'm a lost soul
That's why you always see me blazin' it,
even though I try, it seems like I ain't changin' shit

Fourth, the exosystem level represents settings or people indirectly influencing the individual. For example, policies making people with drug-related felonies ineligible for services (e.g., public housing, food assistance; Golembeski & Fullilove, 2005) in part resulted in Carlos living with his grandmother instead of his mother. Environments also can increase exposure to ACEs. For example, after a family member attempted to murder a notorious drug dealer, Carlos and others were forced into hiding for months. Even though I wasn't directly involved in the gang's activities, such experiences impacted me, and I wasn't safe from attacks from Carlos's family or rival gangs. It wasn't until I left New Mexico for graduate school that I stopped automatically sweating and clenching my jaw when seeing certain colors or symbols on baseball hats associated with gang membership.

In these streets, it's do or die
I am trying not to lose my mind
I done seen too many homies commit suicide
And who would cry if I did the same and jumped off a bridge
how could my momma' live knowin' that she lost a kid
I try to do the positive
but I only do the opposite
And one day I know I'll have to pay the consequence
They say that God forgives but I don't think he'd forgive me for all I did
like poppin' a clip and makin' a body drop from that hollow tip

The fifth level, the macrosystem, includes formal and informal policies and cultural norms. These can generate and maintain disparities, including conditions where ACEs are more likely. For example, zero tolerance policies disproportionately impact Black and Latinx youth (APA, 2008) and trace back to laws like the 1986 Anti-Drug Abuse Act. Compared to white students, Black students are 3.2 times more likely to be suspended or expelled, and Latinx students are 1.3 times more likely (U.S. Government Accountability Office, 2018). Biases, prejudices, and stereotypes impact the interpretation of behavior and application of harsher punishments (Henry et al., 2021; Owens & McLanahan, 2020; Riddle & Sinclair, 2019). Such automatic associations are influenced by other levels of the socioecological model, including media portrayals of Black and Latinx youth as "criminals" or "dangerous." My telling a teacher "you can't tell me what to do" would be labeled, at most, as "acting disrespectfully," due to my whiteness and gender. For Carlos, a male with dark skin, this would be labeled as "threatening," at minimum. Carlos dropped out of school around tenth grade.

> *I'm a loc motherf-cker, Lord I need help*
> *I haven't cried in a while, guess I'm heartless now*
> *Look at me then, and look at me now*
> *There's so much shit I been through, when it comes to pain I wear the crown*
> *You say you been through what I been through*
> *but my shoes don't even fit you*

The broadest system is at the sixth level—time. The chronosystem helps us understand the timing of events influencing youth behavior. It includes major transitions (e.g., parental incarceration, multigenerational gang affiliations) and external events (e.g., natural disasters, pandemics). Carlos's risk factors for being both a victim and a perpetrator of violence were tied to a series of historical and contemporary events. Zero tolerance policies are rooted in the historical context of racial and civil rights issues. The impact of these events today highlights how deeply held racial fears and anxieties translate into racially coded crime-related issues (National Research Council, 2014).

> *I been a loc ever since the day of my birth*
> *and there is no changin' unless I'm underneath the dirt*
> *I'm dead inside, so I gotta see you hurt*

Our response to disruptive behaviors and youth violence should be connected to our understanding of how systems interact to impact development. Too often, however, these contexts are overlooked or dismissed. While research suggests gang membership is motivated by individual factors like financial gain and social inclusion, it also is a means of protection from further victimization (Keels, 2022). For Carlos, joining a gang was his way to avoid victimization. For me, becoming associated with Carlos's gang was a problem-solving strategy to gain protection from sexual violence, which I had previously experienced by another gang member. We often ignore these contexts and blame the individual, labeling gang members as "bad" or young girls like me as "stupid." As a reaction to these labels, punitive and exclusionary discipline is used, despite evidence indicating punishment is less effective than other responses.

Treatment Approaches

Ultimately, we know that youth violence is developed and maintained within a socioecological context, but many treatment approaches do not leverage this deep academic and experiential knowledge base. Risk and protective factors at each socioecological level are potential points of intervention, but most are difficult to target when youth are detained in criminal or legal facilities or placed in residential hospitals outside of their context. "Light touch" treatments, such as psychoeducational groups or cognitive behavioral therapy-only protocols, where the clinician does not see the full perspective of the family (McCart & Sheidow, 2016), are unlikely to sustain impact on deeply rooted and long-experienced contextual factors. Targeting risk factors in the absence of leveraging strengths is unlikely to result in engaged participants. Further, youth and families who need services the most may not benefit from typical outpatient clinic services due to systemic biases, financial burdens, caregiving and work needs, transportation issues, and other barriers.

Treatments taking a true socioecological and strengths-based approach are proven to work for targeting intense youth violence (i.e., youth with legal system involvement; Sheidow et al., 2021). Empirically supported treatments are those rigorously tested through science, rather than based on personal opinions about what works. Proven treatments that work for intense youth violence are ones that are home-based and conceptualize such violence from a socioecological stance. Tailored interventions are then planned and adapted for the family's context. Although these empirically supported treatments are relatively brief, they are intensive and more comprehensive than traditional therapies. For example, multisystemic therapy (MST; Henggeler et al., 2009) lasts three to five months but includes multiple weekly contacts with the family and others (e.g., school, juvenile legal system) to target multiple domains (family, individual, peer, school, community). The MST treatment team (i.e., two to four full-time, master's-level clinicians and master's/doctoral supervisor) provides individualized crisis support twenty-four hours a day, seven days a week, so each clinician works with only four to six families. Similarly, functional family therapy (FFT; Alexander et al., 2000) is three to four months long and aims to replace ineffective patterns of family behavior with new ones through treatment phases: engagement, motivation, relational assessment, behavior change, and generalization. Additionally, Treatment Foster Care Oregon (TFCO; Chamberlain, 2003) simultaneously targets multiple domains (individual, family, peer, school); youth initially live with specially trained foster parents for six to nine months, while a family therapist works with guardians and an individual therapist works with the youth. Youth also receive mentoring and skill building to improve problem solving, school/work functioning, and prosocial activities.

Unlike many, these treatments' foundation of research has focused on "real-world" effectiveness, with studies generally being inclusive (e.g., not excluding for co-occurring mental health or substance use) and using "real-world" clinicians employed in community-based organizations rather than employees of the treatment developer or university clinic (Sheidow et al., 2021). When we provide sociological treatments to youth and families that don't fit their context, we reinforce the idea that treatment wasn't designed with them in mind, furthering the distrust in our treatment system of marginalized youth and their families.

Crucial implementation issues exist with home- and community-based socioecological treatments for intense youth violence. Treatment fidelity and quality assurance are essential (see McCart & Sheidow, 2016). Without fidelity, expected outcomes may not be achieved, and there is little evidence of maintaining fidelity in the absence of strong ongoing quality assurance systems (e.g., Smith-Boydston et al., 2014). While MST, TFCO, and FFT could be effective and socioecologically adaptive to varied contexts, they require significant support and resources to implement, creating additional barriers for the underresourced communities that need them most. Being home-based is a unique implementation barrier. Travel time for clinicians to reach the outskirts of town where Carlos and Dr. Kelton lived or for Carlos to take the forty-minute city bus ride after school to access services would require considerable planning and a substantial budget combined with lower caseloads than is typical outside of MST, TFCO, and FFT. Solutions to such challenges can be addressed at various socioecological levels, ranging from problem solving in session with families to increasing public funding for behavioral health services. At the microsystem level, it is unlikely Carlos's grandmother could have attended weekly sessions while caring for other children. The home-based services and problem solving these treatments use would be essential to solve this. Other factors like culture might shape acceptability of treatment and impact participation. For example, some empirically supported manuals include harmful phrasing like "put your thoughts on trial to test the evidence supporting them" or potentially dangerous examples, like teaching assertive communication skills that generate danger with police. This suggests the importance of diversifying the people who design and implement treatments.

The socioecological lens can be crucial to treatment success. In the empirically supported approaches, clinicians use research and educational expertise about behavior to leverage lived expertise of youth and guardian(s). As equal experts within a team, they map out the socioecological factors driving the youth's behavior, identify barriers to treatment and implement solutions (e.g., home-based delivery, flexible hours), as well as create strategies that would sustainably work within the family's ecology.

Elevating Diversity and Resiliency

Valuing diversity, equity, and inclusion is a necessary but insufficient condition to improve the science of youth violence. According to the APA (2022), 81 percent of the psychology workforce self-identified as white. Clinicians need to keep in mind how these factors shape treatment implementation and research. Greater investment in training for historically marginalized individuals and those with unconventional experiences is necessary to transform norms and establish new knowledge. Deconstruction of our current method for evaluating scientific merit of research studies and different methodologies is needed to shift funding streams to increase the likelihood programs will be integrated and sustained in communities with limited resources.

Community-based participatory research (CBPR) could be an essential methodology in addressing youth violence and improving the application of socioecological treatments. In CBPR, researchers partner directly with community shareholders beginning with the community prioritizing research topics and combining knowledge with action to improve outcomes. Youth could be engaged independently or collectively with adult community members in cocreating study materials and program infrastructure. A CBPR study with Latinx families created a youth development program that lowered school violence and sustained effects on community violence (Oscós-Sánchez et al., 2021). These programs were socioecologically tailored because the cocreators understood firsthand the context of program recipients. CBPR methods approach from a standpoint of cultural humility, where researchers and clinicians let go of the belief that they bring something to others that is "missing." CBPR draws upon existing community strengths and resilience, a much-needed paradigm shift. Youth and those raising them are better reinforced when they know their lives can be more than an avoidance of negative events and when there is opportunity for a life worth living, something beyond mere survival. CBPR could inform new treatment development, improve existing practices and refine established treatments, and inform implementation strategies in settings or populations where established treatments have not yet been rigorously tested.

Decision Making about Services

Context and factors that drive behavior are central to socioecological treatment. Finances, however, are often the key determinant for services, creating a paradox that those who would benefit most from socioecological treatments are least likely to have access. On a broader level, states and communities should create non-siloed funding streams (e.g., clinical services being separated from public safety funding) for full implementation of complex, socioecological treatments that will be sustainable. While expensive at the outset, such an investment will pay for itself by reducing service costs in other public sectors (e.g., detentions, victim costs) and will offer benefits beyond the individual (e.g., family, peers, intergenerational). For example, every dollar spent on TFCO returns $3.15 in averted criminal and child welfare costs (Saldana et al., 2019). Some states are moving to shut down youth detention facilities; for example, California Senate Bill 823 closed the Division of Juvenile Justice and shifted funding to county trauma-informed facilities providing evidence-based treatments. We need to continue to move away from the prison-industrial complex that has benefitted from incarcerating youth. The socioecological factors that drive youth violence persist, and we have the responsibility to catch up with the need for socioecological services.

Acknowledgments

This publication was supported by the National Institute on Drug Abuse of the National Institutes of Health (NIH) under award numbers R01DA041434 and R01DA041425. The content is solely the responsibility of the authors and does not necessarily represent the official views of the NIH.

Note

1 The song lyric excerpts are reprinted with the permission of the artist.

References

Alexander, J. F., Pugh, C., Parsons, B. F., & Sexton, T. (Eds.). (2000). *Functional family therapy* (Bk. 3, vol. 2). In D. S. Elliott (Series Ed.), *Blueprints for violence prevention*. Boulder: Institute of Behavioral Science, Regents of the University of Colorado.

American Psychological Association. (2022). *Demographics of U.S. psychology workforce* [Interactive data tool]. Retrieved May 18, 2024, from https://www-apa-org.ezp.slu.edu/workforce/data-tools/demographics

American Psychological Association Zero Tolerance Task Force. (2008). Are zero-tolerance policies effective in the schools? An evidentiary review and recommendations. *American Psychologist, 63*(9), 852–862.

Bailey, J. (2017). From "zero-tolerance" to "safe and accepting": Surveillance and equality in the evolution of Ontario's education law and policy. *Education & Law Journal, 26*(2), 147–180.

Bronfenbrenner, U. (1979). *The ecology of human development: Experiments by nature and design.* Harvard University Press.

Centers for Disease Control and Prevention. (2004). *Web-Based Injury Statistics Query and Reporting System (WISQARS)*. https://wisqars.cdc.gov/data/lcd/home

Chamberlain, P. (2003). The Oregon multidimensional treatment foster care model: Features, outcomes, and progress in dissemination. *Cognitive and Behavioral Practice, 10*(4), 303–312.

Dunn, E. C., Nishimi, K., Gomez, S. H., Powers, A., & Bradley, B. (2018). Developmental timing of trauma exposure and emotion dysregulation in adulthood: Are there sensitive periods when trauma is most harmful? *Journal of Affective Disorder, 227*, 869–877.

Ford, J. D., & Blaustein, M. E. (2013). Systemic self-regulation: A framework for trauma-informed services in residential juvenile justice programs. *Journal of Family Violence, 28*(7), 665–677.

Golembeski, C., & Fullilove, R. (2005). Criminal (in)justice in the city and its associated health consequences. *American Journal of Public Health, 95*(10), 1701–1706.

Henggeler, S. W., Schoenwald, S. K., Borduin, C. M., Rowland, M. D., & Cunningham, P. B. (2009). *Multisystemic therapy for antisocial behavior in children and adolescents* (2nd ed.). Guilford.

Henretty, J. R., & Levitt, H. M. (2010). The role of therapist self-disclosure in psychotherapy: A qualitative review. *Clinical Psychology Review, 30*(1), 63–77.

Henry, K. K., Catagnus, R. M., Griffith, A. K., & Garcia, Y. A. (2021). Ending the school-to-prison pipeline: Perception and experience with zero-tolerance policies and interventions to address racial inequality. *Behavior Analysis in Practice, 15*(4), 1254–1263.

Juvenile Justice Realignment Bill of 2020. S.B. 823, chap. 337. https://leginfo .legislature.ca.gov/faces/billTextClient.xhtml?bill_id=201920200SB823.

Keels, M. (2022). Developmental and ecological perspective on the intergenerational transmission of trauma and violence. *Daedalus, 151*(1), 67–83.

McCart, M. R., & Sheidow, A. J. (2016). Evidence-based psychosocial treatments for adolescents with disruptive behavior. *Journal of Clinical Child and Adolescent Psychology, 45*(5), 529–563.

National Research Council. (2014). *The growth of incarceration in the United States: Exploring causes and consequences*. National Academies Press.

Oscós-Sánchez, M. Á., Lesser, J., Oscós-Flores, L. D., Pineda, D., Araujo, Y., Franklin, B., Hernández, J. A., Hernández, S., & Vidales, A. (2021). The effects of two community-based participatory action research programs on violence outside of and in school among adolescents and young adults in a Latino community. *Journal of Adolescent Health, 68*(2), 370–377.

Owens, J., & McLanahan, S. S. (2020). Unpacking the drivers of racial disparities in school suspension and expulsion. *Social Forces, 98*(4), 1548–1577.

Riddle, T., & Sinclair, S. (2019). Racial disparities in school-based disciplinary actions are associated with county-level rates of racial bias. *PNAS, 116*(17), 8255–8260.

Saldana, L., Campbell, M., Leve, L., & Chamberlain, P. (2019). Long-term economic benefit of Treatment Foster Care Oregon (TFCO) for adolescent females referred to congregate care for delinquency. *Child Welfare, 97*(5), 179–195.

Sheidow, A. J., McCart, M. R., & Drazdowski, T. K. (2021). Family-based treatments for disruptive behavior problems in children and adolescents: An updated review of rigorous studies (2014–April 2020). *Journal of Marital and Family Therapy, 48*, 56–82.

Smith-Boydston, J. M., Holtzman, R. J., & Roberts, M. C. (2014). Transportability of multisystemic therapy to community settings: Can a program sustain outcomes without MST services oversight? *Child & Youth Care Forum, 43*(5), 593–605.

U.S. Government Accountability Office. (2018). *K–12 education: Discipline disparities for Black students, boys, and students with disabilities* (Pub. No. 18-258). https://www.gao.gov/assets/gao-18-258.pdf

Part 2

Expansions

● ● ● ● ● ● ● ● ● ● ● ● ●

Culturally Responsive Clinical Interventions for Youth Violence

• • • • • • • • • • • • •

STANLEY J. HUEY JR. AND
EMILY N. SATINSKY

Overview

Youth violence is a public health issue in the United States. Such violence—including fighting, bullying, gang-related aggression, and threats or use of weapons—has broad-reaching financial and societal consequences (Dowd, 1998). Youth exposed to school and neighborhood violence experience poorer academic performance and higher rates of depression, anxiety, substance use, and delinquent behaviors (Fowler et al., 2009; Margolin & Gordis, 2000). Furthermore, youth violence is linked to morbidity and mortality. In fact, in 2020, firearm-related injuries surpassed motor vehicle crashes as the leading cause of death among children and adolescents (Goldstick et al., 2022). Even if initial violence exposure is nonfatal, violent injury increases risk of subsequent homicide (Caputo et al., 2012; Rowhani-Rahbar et al., 2015). These patterns operate in an aggressive cycle, whereby youth chronically exposed to violence are nearly thirty-two times more likely to exhibit patterns of chronic violent behaviors themselves (Spano et al., 2010).

Given structural inequities in the United States, ethnic/racial minority youth are at particularly high risk of injury and death due to violence (Centers for Disease Control and Prevention, 2008). Violence hotspots are disproportionately localized to neighborhoods exposed to other environmental risk factors (Farrington & Loeber, 2000), including inner-city areas with high concentrations of low-income, ethnic/racial minority families. Over half of children and adolescents arrested for violent crimes belong to an ethnic/racial minority group (Office of Juvenile Justice and Delinquency Prevention, 2022), and firearm homicide rates are about ten times higher among Black youth compared to white and Asian American youth (Fowler et al., 2017). Given disparities in youth violence, it makes theoretical sense for prevention interventions to incorporate the norms, values, and cultural traditions of the target population (Resnicow et al., 2000).

One of us (SJH) has personal motivations for pursuing research in this area, particularly as it relates to communities of color. Like that of many Black Americans, my family life was impacted and shaped by criminal justice involvement and violence. My younger brother had significant behavioral, mental health, and substance use problems in his youth and adulthood, cycled through the criminal justice and public mental health systems, and spent much of his life in contexts where violence reigned. His life ended violently as well—a few years ago he died of suicide while incarcerated. Although I do not blame our public mental health system, I have wondered if he would still be with us if the system had been more responsive to my family's needs.

So for the past twenty or so years, I have engaged in research collaborations to address questions concerning intervention efficacy and cultural responsiveness, with a particular focus on mitigating violence, antisocial behavior, and criminal justice involvement for youth of color. This chapter summarizes some of the lessons learned in doing and reviewing violence mitigation research. We briefly summarize literature on the effectiveness of youth violence prevention interventions and culturally tailored youth interventions (i.e., interventions developed or adapted to address cultural needs and preferences). We also highlight limitations in the evidence, discuss best practices, and consider how we can move forward.

Although much of the research addresses primary prevention, this chapter focuses on intervening with youth already involved in antisocial or violent behavior and those at higher risk given past behaviors (i.e., secondary and tertiary prevention). The emphasis is on youth of color, given their overrepresentation in statistics on violence exposure, and given that they are the primary targets of cultural tailoring efforts. Finally, the chapter's scope is limited to individual-, group-, and family-based approaches in comparison with school- or community-wide interventions.

Summary and Highlights

Effectiveness of Youth Violence Interventions

In this section, we summarize evidence on the effectiveness of youth violence prevention interventions. We focus primarily on approaches replicated in two or more randomized clinical trials. Of note, although we report violence-related outcomes when possible, many studies do not assess reductions in violence.

For youth with mild to moderate disruptive behaviors, including fighting and other acts of aggression, the pool of effective interventions is deep and wide. Parent-Child Interaction Therapy (PCIT), Brief Strategic Family Therapy (BSFT), the Incredible Years program, and Lochman's Coping Power intervention are just a few of the approaches with strong support, and each appears to be effective with youth of color (Huey & Polo, 2008; Pina et al., 2019). Although effective interventions tend to be parent- and family-based, programs that focus exclusively on individual skills training (i.e., *without* parent or family involvement) are also well supported.

Support is also strong for a handful of interventions geared toward youth in the juvenile justice and social welfare systems, including treatments for serious and chronic offenders. Topping the list is multisystemic therapy (MST), a family-based intervention that integrates intensive individual, family, and community-based support (Fagan & Catalano, 2012). A research synthesis of MST studies supports its effectiveness in reducing delinquent behaviors, particularly among youth under the age of fifteen (van der Stouwe et al., 2014). Follow-up studies show that criminal offending is significantly lower for MST participants than control participants nearly twenty years later and that MST is equally effective for Black and white youth (Sawyer & Borduin, 2011).

The picture is mixed but mostly disappointing when it comes to interventions for gang-involved youth and young adults. In a synthesis of thirty-eight studies of gang-focused treatments (Huey et al., 2016), we found that intervention led to significant but small reductions in gang involvement, yet *no effects were found for antisocial behavior.* A follow-up analysis showed even more concerning results. About 20 percent of interventions reported at least one adverse effect. In other words, some studies showed that antisocial behavior (e.g., institutional misconduct, illegal activities) actually worsened for those who received the gang-focused intervention (Rubenson et al., 2020). These adverse effects were more likely in interventions that included law enforcement officers on the intervention team. This suggests that law enforcement involvement in interventions could either increase crime detection or inspire reactance by participants toward authority figures. Despite this disappointing finding, a handful of gang-focused interventions show promise (Huey et al., 2016). For example, Valdez et al. (2013) tested whether an adapted version of BSFT worked for gang-affiliated, drug/alcohol-using Mexican American adolescents. Although no effects were found for gang involvement, BSFT led to greater reductions in conduct problems compared to the control group. Another intervention, Functional Family Therapy (FFT), demonstrated significantly lower rates of recidivism among Black and Latinx youth at high risk of gang membership, although this finding did not hold up for youth at lower risk (Thornberry et al., 2018). The latter finding is encouraging given evidence that gang membership can reduce the effectiveness of well-supported delinquency interventions (Boxer, 2011; Boxer et al., 2015).

Unfortunately, the evidence gap is greatest when it comes to interventions for youth with the highest risk of violence-related mortality: hospitalized violence victims and youth with firearm-related offenses. In an ongoing review, we summarized results from six studies testing whether hospital-based violence interventions (HBVIs) reduced recidivism in youth admitted to emergency departments for violence assault injury (Huey et al., 2023). Intervention involved some combination of case management, skills training, and adult mentoring, and all studies included predominantly Black male victims. None of the studies showed reductions in violence-related rehospitalization, although one study showed a reduction in self-reported reinjury (Huey et al., 2023). Furthermore, at the individual intervention level, we know almost nothing about how to reduce youth gun violence. Although firearm-related injury is now the leading cause of death among youth (Goldstick et al., 2022), and despite heightened rates of firearm homicide among ethnic/racial minority adolescents (Fowler et al., 2017), intervention research in this area has solely focused on primary prevention or community- and policy-level strategies (Bottiani et al., 2021).

Existing studies on youth violence prevention interventions paint a mixed picture of their effectiveness for violence-related outcomes. While the evidence for interventions aimed at youth with mild to moderate disruptive behaviors is consistently strong, findings are weaker or absent for interventions targeting youth at higher risk of violence (e.g., gang-involved and firearms-involved youth).

Cultural Tailoring of Youth Violence Interventions: Benefits and Challenges

Next we address whether violence prevention interventions are more effective when tailored to address the cultural contexts of targeted youth. Given racial disparities in violence vulnerability *and* mental health care access, scholars and practitioners highlight the relevance of designing interventions that are sensitive and responsive to cultural factors. Exploring the value of culturally tailored interventions is particularly important given the historical exclusion of ethnically diverse participants from research studies that laid the groundwork for established evidence-based interventions (Jones et al., 2018).

At first glance, current research seems to support the use of cultural tailoring when doing violence prevention work with youth of color. For example, reviews show that most treatment outcome studies that address youth antisocial behavior and violence include culturally tailored interventions (Gillespie & Huey, 2015; Pina et al., 2019), and research shows that culturally tailored interventions for youth of color lead to greater reductions in problem behaviors compared to no treatment or "usual services" (Huey & Jones, 2013). On closer inspection, however, more rigorous research—that is, studies that compare culturally tailored and generic versions of the same core treatment—casts doubt on the benefit of cultural tailoring above and beyond standard evidence-based treatment. Of the two published studies that provide a strong test of the benefits of culturally adapted treatment for youth of color, both found that standard treatment was just as effective as culturally adapted treatment at reducing conduct problems in Latinx youth (McCabe & Yeh, 2009; Szapocznik et al., 1986). This evidence challenges the notion that cultural tailoring is critical to increasing intervention effectiveness.

One study in particular highlights the potential pitfalls of cultural tailoring. Kliewer et al. (2011) assigned predominantly Black seventh grade students in a high-violence neighborhood to one of three conditions: (1) a control condition in which they wrote about a nonemotional topic, (2) a standard expressive writing condition in which they wrote about experiencing or witnessing violence, or (3) an enhanced, culturally tailored version of the same expressive writing condition. Building on the oral tradition valued in African American culture, students in the enhanced condition had the option to write stories, skits, songs, or poetry about experiencing or witnessing violence. Unexpectedly, the culturally tailored intervention was less effective than standard expressive writing at reducing teacher-rated youth aggression. The authors speculated that youth in the adapted condition may have focused too much on generating a creative product rather than delving into their personal experiences and feelings about violence (Kliewer et al., 2011). In this case, cultural tailoring could have inadvertently diluted a core intervention component.

Key gaps remain in our understanding of where and when adaptations are appropriate to optimize benefits of youth violence prevention interventions (Park et al., 2023). We must continue our search for strategies to engage ethnic/minority youth in violence prevention interventions, both through a concerted examination of the active ingredients that uniquely benefit youth of color and by valuing cultural humility in the implementation of evidence-based interventions.

Best Practices

As outlined above, a range of strategies may be effective in reducing youth violence outcomes; however, no one approach has consistently integrated cultural adaptations to mitigate outcomes above and beyond standard treatment. Considering the mixed state of the evidence, we offer a nuanced view on how to think about cultural tailoring when developing and implementing violence prevention interventions for youth of color.

Consider Family-Based Interventions

Our first recommendation is to consider family- and parent-based approaches when engaging in youth violence prevention efforts. Our primary rationale is empirical. Many effective interventions for youth of color with disruptive/aggressive behaviors are parent- or family-focused (Pina et al., 2019). As noted earlier, BSFT, FFT, and MST are perhaps the most prominent family-based treatments, and each has a strong base of empirical support. However, there are also conceptual reasons for embracing family-based interventions. Given cultural differences in worldviews, family-based treatments might be particularly effective for youth of color because they allow providers to consider the youth's implicit cultural context (Huey & Polo, 2008). In particular, family-based approaches may bolster treatment efforts by minimizing family inhibition against mental health services and mobilizing family members as natural resources (Tharp, 1991). In preparing to implement family-based interventions, training efforts might consider building practitioners' cultural competence with regard to family customs and practices.

The recommendation comes with one major caveat. Despite the impressive track record, it is unclear whether family-based treatments are superior to individual treatments that include the same content (Huey & Polo, 2008). In a series of studies, Szapocznik and colleagues found that conjoint BSFT that included multiple family members was no more effective than "one-person" BSFT that covered the same material but included only the youth (Szapocznik et al., 1983; Szapocznik et al., 1986). To our knowledge, no studies have tested directly whether the "family" component of FFT and MST accounts for intervention effects.

Tailor as Needed, but Maintain Fidelity by Minimizing Dilution of "Active Ingredients"

A parallel recommendation, or perhaps more a cautionary note, is to balance the impulse to modify with the need for treatment fidelity. Cultural tailoring is the norm for clinicians who work with ethnically diverse populations, and most believe they are well prepared to deal with cultural issues in clinical contexts (Hamp et al., 2016; Huey et al., 2014). Unfortunately, the elements of *effective* cultural tailoring are still a mystery to clinical scientists, with evidence suggesting that tailoring is potentially a double-edged sword (Huey et al., 2014). In other words, cultural tailoring can help at times and hinder at others.

One argument for why cultural tailoring might misfire and paradoxically impede treatment progress relates to treatment fidelity. Some of our published work highlights the importance of maintaining treatment fidelity when intervening with ethnic minority youth (Gillespie et al., 2017; Huey et al., 2000). Unfortunately, cultural tailoring can at times water down core treatment elements that drive positive change. In particular, cultural tailoring that interferes with or replaces these elements might lead to inefficiencies that compromise treatment fidelity and outcomes (Huey et al., 2014). Kliewer et al. (2011) made just this argument regarding their culturally adapted writing intervention for violence-exposed youth.

Despite mixed support for cultural tailoring of youth violence prevention, it remains normative among clinicians. More research is needed to investigate how cultural tailoring is practiced by real-world violence interventionists and which tailoring strategies lead to optimal outcomes for ethnic minority youth (Huey et al., 2014). In the meantime, clinicians should recognize the benefits *and* risks of culturally tailored practice and thoughtfully navigate the tension between cultural tailoring and ensuring fidelity to core treatment elements (Castro et al., 2010).

Adopt a Flexible Model That Accommodates Cultural Diversity

Our final recommendation addresses culturally salient risks and strengths by incorporating methods to individualize treatment (Huey & Polo, 2008; Jones et al., 2018). Two exemplars of this approach are MST for serious and chronic juvenile offenders (Henggeler et al., 1998) and the Incredible Years intervention for disruptive youth (Leitjen et al., 2015; Reid et al., 2001). Neither is explicitly branded as culturally tailored, but both are flexible enough to account for individual differences that might be culturally based. However, the models differ in how cultural factors are accommodated.

In MST, therapists assess the "fit" of the problem behavior within the youth's larger social-ecological context (Bronfenbrenner, 1979). This "fit" assessment informs the selection and use of evidence-based strategies to alter individual, family, and contextual factors that contribute to the problem behavior (Henggeler et al., 1998). The individualized treatment plan and intervention across multiple contexts (e.g., home, school, community) allow MST to flexibly address differences that exist across family units. Through this unique tailoring approach, MST incorporates cultural strengths of diverse families (e.g., extended kinship networks in African American families). Indeed, one of the nine principles guiding MST strategies requires clinicians to identify and build on individual and family strengths. This context sensitivity may explain why

MST has a strong track record with African American youth in juvenile justice settings (Borduin et al., 1995).

The Incredible Years program is a parenting intervention consisting of eight to fifteen group sessions led by a trained facilitator (Reid et al., 2001). Parents watch videotaped scenes of common parenting situations, learn behavior management skills (e.g., praising, limit setting), discuss scenarios and skills with other parents, and role-play learned skills. Although the content provided to families is "generic," cultural sensitivity is fostered implicitly. First, parents identify individual goals for their children and formulate strategies that will help reach those goals. Second, the facilitator and group members actively support parental goals—they initiate discussion on how identified goals and strategies connect with the parent's own upbringing and why they believe certain strategies will benefit their child. Thus, diverse parental values, linked to cultural or other contextual factors, can easily be accommodated without requiring the creation of culturally distinct curricula (Reid et al., 2001). Several studies show that the Incredible Years program is effective at reducing disruptive behavior for ethnic minority youth in the United States and the Netherlands (Leitjen et al., 2015; Reid et al., 2001).

Fortunately, flexible models of this sort may be more common than believed. Several effective youth prevention programs accommodate individual and cultural differences by encouraging participants to select their own goals and situational examples (Bruhn et al., 2016; Reid et al., 2001). In this way, implicit cultural sensitivity may be built into the fabric of many youth violence prevention interventions.

Given mixed evidence on the value of cultural tailoring, it is imperative that we continue studying the contexts in which adaptations are recommended. Meanwhile, we offer three broad suggestions above for optimizing intervention outcomes with youth of color. First, we advocate for consideration of family-based approaches that recognize youths' implicit cultural environments. Second, we urge clinicians to maintain fidelity to core treatment elements, particularly when incorporating culturally relevant components into their practice. And finally, we recommend individualized treatment approaches that fit the sociocultural environments of youth and their families. Although macro-level and community-based interventions that address structural and systemic contributors to violence are beyond the scope of this chapter, they are an important complement to individual-, group-, and family-based approaches.

Where Are We Going?

Moving forward, we need high-quality research to inform violence prevention intervention for youth of color. Arguably the greatest need is for rigorous intervention research focused on youth at the highest risk of violence, including gang-involved youth, youth with firearm-related offenses, and hospitalized violence victims. Although they make up the majority of youth homicide victims (Fowler et al., 2017), there are no well-supported interventions for these youth.

While these research efforts are ongoing, we also see value in investigating the potential of peer-based intervention approaches. Association with deviant peers is one of the strongest contributors to youth antisocial behavior (Calkins & Keane, 2009), but peers are rarely utilized as core intervention agents in youth violence mitigation research. For example, of the more than thirty youth gang intervention studies summarized in a recent review, none included peer-led training as a primary intervention component (Huey et al., 2016). Similarly, none of the six treatments described in our review of HBVIs included peers as central intervention agents (Huey et al., 2023). Notably, peer-led interventions are increasingly common in the substance use prevention and autism treatment literatures, and effects are generally positive (MacArthur et al., 2015; Zhang & Wheeler, 2011). Moving forward, intervention efforts should consider drawing on peer relationships to better mitigate violence-related outcomes.

References

Borduin, C. M., Mann, B. J., Cone, L. T., Henggeler, S. W., Fucci, B. R., Blaske, D. M., & Williams, R. A. (1995). Multisystemic treatment of serious juvenile offenders: Long-term prevention of criminality and violence. *Journal of Consulting and Clinical Psychology, 63*(4), 569–578.

Bottiani, J. H., Camacho, D. A., Lindstrom Johnson, S., & Bradshaw, C. P. (2021). Annual research review: Youth firearm violence disparities in the United States and implications for prevention. *Journal of Child Psychology and Psychiatry, 62*(5), 563–579.

Boxer, P. (2011). Negative peer involvement in multisystemic therapy for the treatment of youth problem behavior: Exploring outcome and process variables in "real-world" practice. *Journal of Clinical Child & Adolescent Psychology, 40*(6), 848–854.

Boxer, P., Kubik, J., Ostermann, M., & Weysey, B. (2015). Gang involvement moderates the effectiveness of evidence-based intervention for justice-involved youth. *Children and Youth Services Review, 52*, 26–33.

Bronfenbrenner, U. (1979). *The ecology of human development: Experiments by nature and design.* Harvard University Press.

Bruhn, A. L., McDaniel, S. C., Fernando, J., & Troughton, L. (2016). Goal-setting interventions for students with behavior problems: A systematic review. *Behavioral Disorders, 41*(2), 107–1211.

Calkins, S. D., & Keane, S. P. (2009). Developmental origins of early antisocial behavior. *Development and Psychopathology, 21*(4), 1095–1109.

Caputo, N. D., Shields, C. P., Ochoa, C., Matarlo, J., Leber, M., Madlinger, R., & Waseem, M. (2012). Violent and fatal youth trauma: Is there a missed opportunity? *Western Journal of Emergency Medicine, 13*(2), 146–150.

Castro, F. G., Barrera, M., Jr., & Holleran Steiker, L. K. (2010). Issues and challenges in the design of culturally-adapted evidence-based interventions. *Annual Review of Clinical Psychology, 6*, 213–239.

Centers for Disease Control and Prevention. (2008). *Youth Risk Behavior Survey.* http://www.cdc.gov/injury/wisqars/index.html

Dowd, M. D. (1998). Consequences of violence. Premature death, violence recidivism, and violent criminality. *Pediatric Clinics of North America, 45,* 333–340.

Fagan, A. A., & Catalano, R. F. (2012). What works in youth violence prevention: A review of the literature. *Research on Social Work Practice, 23*(2), 141–156.

Farrington, D. P., & Loeber, R. (2000). Epidemiology of youth violence. *Child and Adolescent Psychiatry Clinics of North America, 9,* 733–748.

Fowler, K. A., Dahlberg, L. L., Haileyesus, T., Gutierrez, C., & Bacon, S. (2017). Childhood firearm injuries in the United States. *Pediatrics, 140*(1). https://doi.org /10.1542/peds/2016-3486

Fowler, P. J., Tompsett, C. J., Braciszewski, J. M., Jacques-Tiura, J. J., & Baltes, B. B. (2009). Community violence: A meta-analysis on the effects of exposure and mental health outcomes of children and adolescents. *Development and Psychopathology, 21,* 227–259.

Gillespie, M. L., & Huey, S. J., Jr. (2015). *Psychotherapy for ethnic minorities with conduct problems: A meta-analysis.* Paper presented at the 123rd annual meeting of the American Psychological Association, Toronto.

Gillespie, M., Huey, S. J., Jr., & Cunningham, P. (2017). Predictive validity of an observer-rated adherence protocol for multisystemic therapy with juvenile drug offenders. *Journal of Substance Abuse Treatment, 76,* 1–10.

Goldstick, J. E., Cunningham, R. M., & Carter, P. M. (2022). Current causes of death in children and adolescents in the United States. *New England Journal of Medicine, 386*(20), 1955–1956.

Hamp, A., Stamm, K., Lin, L., & Christidis, P. (2016). *2015 APA survey of psychology health service providers.* http://www.apa.org/workforce/publications/15-health -service-providers/index.aspx

Henggeler, S. W., Schoenwald, S. K., Borduin, C. M., Rowland, D. M., & Cunningham, P. B. (1998). *Multisystemic treatment of antisocial behavior in children and adolescents.* Guilford.

Huey, S. J., Jr., Henggeler, S. W., Brondino, M. J., & Pickrel, S. G. (2000). Mechanisms of change in multisystemic therapy: Reducing delinquent behavior through therapist adherence, and improved family and peer functioning. *Journal of Consulting and Clinical Psychology, 68*(3), 451–467.

Huey, S. J., Jr., & Jones, E. O. (2013). Improving treatment engagement and psychotherapy outcomes for culturally diverse youth and families. In F. A. Paniagua & A. M. Yamada (Eds.), *Handbook of multicultural mental health* (2nd ed., pp. 427–444). Elsevier.

Huey, S. J., Jr., Lewine, G., & Rubenson, M. P. (2016). A brief review and meta-analysis of gang intervention trials in North America. In C. L. Maxson & F. A. Esbensen (Eds.), *Gang transitions and transformations in an international context* (pp. 217–233). Springer.

Huey, S. J., Jr., Li, Y., Jang, J., Konovalov, H., Chang, T., & Galbraith, K. (2023). *Effects of hospital-based violence interventions: Review and meta-analysis.* Manuscript in preparation.

Huey, S. J., Jr., & Polo, A. J. (2008). Evidence-based psychosocial treatments for ethnic minority youth. *Journal of Clinical Child & Adolescent Psychology, 27*(1), 262–301.

Huey, S. J., Jr., Tilley, J. L., Jones, E. O., & Smith, C. A. (2014). The contribution of cultural competence to evidence-based care for ethnically diverse populations. *Annual Review of Clinical Psychology, 10,* 305–338.

Jones, E., Huey, S. J., Jr., & Rubenson, M. P. (2018). Cultural competence in therapy with African Americans. In C. L. Frisby & W. T. O'Donohue (Eds.), *Cultural competence in applied psychology: An evaluation of current status and future directions* (pp. 557–573). Springer.

Kliewer, W., Lepore, S. J., Farrell, A. D., Allison, K. W., Meyer, A. L., Sullivan, T. N., & Greene, A. Y. (2011). A school-based expressive writing intervention for at-risk urban adolescents' aggressive behavior and emotional lability. *Journal of Clinical Child & Adolescent Psychology, 40*(5), 693–705.

Leitjen, P., Raaijmakers, M. A. J., Orobio de Castro, B., van den Ban, E., & Matthys, W. (2015). Effectiveness of the Incredible Years parenting program for families with socioeconomically disadvantaged and ethnic minority backgrounds. *Journal of Clinical Child & Adolescent Psychology, 46*, 59–73. https://doi.org/10.1080/15374416.2015.1038823

MacArthur, G. J., Harrison, S., Caldwell, D. M., Hickman, M., & Campbell, R. (2015). Peer-led interventions to prevent tobacco, alcohol and/or drug use among young people aged 11–21 years: A systematic review and meta-analysis. *Addiction, 111*, 391–407.

Margolin, G., & Gordis, E. B. (2000). The effects of family and community violence on children. *Annual Reviews in Psychology, 51*, 445–479.

McCabe, K., & Yeh, M. (2009). Parent-child interaction therapy for Mexican Americans: A randomized clinical trial. *Journal of Clinical Child & Adolescent Psychology, 38*, 753–759.

Office of Juvenile Justice and Delinquency Prevention. (2022). *OJJDP Statistical Briefing Book.* https://www.ojjdp.gov/ojstatbb/crime/qa05104.asp?qaDate=2020

Park, A. L., Rith-Najarian, L. R., Saifan, D., Gellatly, R., Huey, S. J., & Chorpita, B. F. (2023). Strategies for incorporating culture into psychosocial interventions for youth of color. *Evidence-Based Practice in Child and Adolescent Mental Health, 8*, 181–193. https://doi.org/10.1080/23794925.2022.2025629

Pina, A. A., Polo, A. J., & Huey, S. J. (2019). Evidence-based psychosocial interventions for ethnic minority youth: The 10-year update. *Journal of Clinical Child & Adolescent Psychology, 48*(2), 179–202.

Reid, M. J., Webster-Stratton, C., & Beauchaine, T. P. (2001). Parent training in Head Start: A comparison of program response among African American, Asian American, Caucasian, and Hispanic mothers. *Prevention Science, 2*(4), 209–227.

Resnicow, K., Soler, R., Braithwaite, R. L., Ahluwalia, J. S., & Butler, J. (2000). Cultural sensitivity in substance use prevention. *Journal of Community Psychology, 28*, 271–290.

Rowhani-Rahbar, A., Zatzick, D., Wang, J., Mills, B. M., Simonetti, J. A., Fan, M. D., & Rivara, F. P. (2015). Firearm-related hospitalization and risk for subsequent violent injury, death, or crime perpetration: A cohort study. *Annals of Internal Medicine, 162*(7), 492–500.

Rubenson, M., Galbraith, K., & Huey, S. J., Jr. (2020). Understanding adverse effects in gang-focused interventions: A critical review. In C. Melde & F. Weerman (Eds.), *Gangs in the era of internet and social media* (pp. 271–290). Springer.

Sawyer, A. M., & Borduin, C. M. (2011). Effects of multisystemic therapy through midlife: A 21.9-year follow-up to a randomized clinical trial with serious and violent juvenile offenders. *Journal of Consulting and Clinical Psychology, 79*(5), 643–652.

Spano, R., Rivera, C., & Bolland, J. M. (2010). Are chronic exposure to violence and chronic violent behavior closely related developmental processes during adolescence? *Criminal Justice and Behavior, 31*, 1160–1179.

Szapocznik, J., Kurtines, W. M., Foote, F. H., Perez-Vidal, A., & Hervis, O. (1983). Conjoint versus one-person family therapy: Some evidence for the effectiveness of conducting family therapy through one person. *Journal of Consulting and Clinical Psychology, 51*(6), 889–899.

Szapocznik, J., Rio, A., Perez-Vidal, A., Kurtines, W., Hervis, O., & Satisteban, D. (1986). Bicultural Effectiveness Training (BET): An experimental test of an intervention modality for families experiencing intergenerational-intercultural conflict. *Hispanic Journal of Behavioral Sciences, 8,* 303–330.

Tharp, R. G. (1991). Cultural diversity and treatment of children. *Journal of Consulting and Clinical Psychology, 59*(6), 799–812.

Thornberry, T. P., Kearley, B., Gottfredson, D. C., Slothower, M. P., Devlin, D. N., & Fader, J. J. (2018). Reducing crime among youth at risk for gang involvement. *Criminology & Public Policy, 17*(4), 953–989.

Valdez, A., Cepeda, A., Parrish, D., Horowitz, R., & Kaplan, C. (2013). An adapted brief strategic family therapy for gang-affiliated Mexican American adolescents. *Research on Social Work Practice, 23*(4), 383–396.

van der Stouwe, T., Asscher, J. J., Stams, G. J. J. M., Devoic, M., & van der Laan, P. (2014). The effectiveness of multisystemic therapy (MST): A meta-analysis. *Clinical Psychology Review, 34*(6), 468–481.

Zhang, J., & Wheeler, J. J. (2011). A meta-analysis of peer-mediated interventions for young children with autism spectrum disorders. *Education and Training in Autism and Developmental Disabilities, 46*(1), 62–77.

Trauma-Informed Mentoring and Related Approaches

• • • • • • • • • • • • •

MATTHEW HAGLER AND
JEAN RHODES

Overview

Mentoring programs facilitate relationships between "at-risk" youth and caring, nonparent adults, hoping to promote positive youth development while reducing risk for negative outcomes, such as violence and mental health problems. For decades, mentoring researchers and practitioners have expressed the belief that the relationship itself is the "active ingredient" of mentoring and that positive outcomes will naturally unfold as a close mentor-youth bond is cultivated. Some have even argued that structured approaches, like providing mentors with skills trainings, manuals, or program curricula, distract from relationship formation. Reflecting this belief, only half of mentoring programs in the United States use any kind of guide or curriculum, and most programs provide mentors with just a few hours of training before matching them with youth (Garringer et al., 2017).

These widespread practices imply that adults do not need special skills to be mentors and that just showing up with good intentions is enough to make a difference. This idea is broadly appealing and, if true, would make mentoring an incredibly efficient intervention! If mentors really do not need special skills, programs can quickly recruit and assign them to youth with minimal investment of time and money. Under this premise, mentoring programs have significantly expanded over the past three decades (serving an estimated 4.5 million youth each year), fueled by significant governmental funding. In particular, mentoring has become a key component of the Department of Justice's strategic plan to address youth violence, with over $100 million of annual funding allocated to mentoring programs focused on violence and delinquency prevention (Fernandes-Alcantara, 2018).

Unfortunately, the "just showing up" philosophy has led the field to prioritize *quantity* (of mentors recruited and youth served) over *quality* (of mentor training and supervision), resulting in some disappointing statistics. On average, mentoring programs have very small positive effects on youths' mental health, behavior, and academic performance (Raposa et al., 2019), especially compared to other prevention-based programs like wilderness adventure therapies and social-emotional learning (Gutman & Schoon, 2015). Alarmingly, about 40 percent of mentor-mentee matches end prematurely because relationships failed to take root and grow (Kupersmidt et al., 2017).

In this chapter, we propose that there is more to mentoring than "just showing up" because many youth enter programs with significant trauma. By "trauma," we mean direct exposure to violence, such as physical, sexual, and verbal abuse as well as other adverse childhood experiences (ACEs) that disrupt children's sense of safety and security, such as deaths of close family members and having caregivers with serious mental health, substance use, and/or legal problems. Research has found that ACEs often lead to serious mental health problems during childhood, adolescence, and adulthood, including depression, anxiety, suicidality, posttraumatic stress, and substance use (Kalmakis & Chandler, 2015). Concerningly, exposure to ACEs, especially abuse, is also linked to higher levels of aggression and likelihood of committing violent crimes, creating a dangerous cycle of violence (Mumford et al., 2019). Almost two-thirds of the U.S. population has experienced at least one ACE, and a quarter have experienced three or more (Merrick et al., 2018). Youth referred to mentoring programs tend to come from backgrounds that place them at even higher risk for experiencing ACEs (Jarjoura et al., 2018).

As clinical psychologists, both authors have worked directly with trauma-exposed youth. We have experienced—firsthand—the challenge of breaking through the walls youth have erected—out of necessity—to protect themselves, and we have made many mistakes in the process. Unintentional missteps, such as canceled appointments, lapses in attention, and offhand comments, can trigger trauma responses and abruptly derail relationships. Serving trauma-exposed youth requires consistency, patience, and attunement—skills that must be honed through training and practice.

Despite our critiques, we believe that mentoring can play an important role in helping youth recover from trauma and other mental health difficulties. Yet we also believe that mentors *do* need special skills to work effectively with the trauma-exposed youth and that these skills can be learned through training in trauma-informed care. As the name implies, trauma-informed programs assume that anyone and everyone may have trauma histories and services are designed to promote healing and decrease the likelihood of further harm. Core principles of trauma-informed care include trustworthiness (establishing and fulfilling clear expectations), choice and collaboration (shared decision making), and empowerment (through choice, collaboration, and skill-building; Huckshorn & LeBel, 2013). Although many mentoring programs express similar values, they often do so without a clear, articulated connection to trauma-informed care. In this chapter, we expand our rationale for trauma-informed mentoring, discuss exemplary and aspirational program practices, and identify recommended next steps.

Summary and Highlights

First, we examine the typical backgrounds of youth enrolling in mentoring programs, which provides strong rationale for trauma-informed approaches. A recent survey of programs across the United States (Jarjoura et al., 2018) found that, among participating mentees,

- 69 percent lived in single-parent homes
- 70 percent were racial minorities
- 85 percent faced significant financial adversity
- 18 percent had a family member in jail or prison

These background characteristics are all risk factors that increase the likelihood of experiencing adverse childhood events and trauma (Lieberman et al., 2011). In terms of presenting issues, the same survey found that, among mentees,

- 52 percent had major academic difficulties (failing a class, frequent absences)
- 46 percent had significant mental health problems
- 19 percent had serious behavioral problems (substance use, violence)

These are all issues that can be caused or made worse by trauma exposure, and they are much more prevalent among mentees compared to national averages

(Lieberman et al., 2011). Together, these figures suggest that a significant proportion—probably a large majority—of youth in mentoring programs have trauma histories.

With such vulnerable young people enrolling in programs, you would expect mentors to receive a lot of training, right? Not necessarily. In a national survey of mentoring programs across the United States, most programs reported that their volunteers received less than two hours of training before they started meeting with youth (Garringer et al., 2017). As meetings continue, program staff attempt to oversee matches but typically carry huge caseloads, making it difficult to provide meaningful supervision except during urgent crises. We already noted that almost 40 percent of mentoring relationships result in early, unplanned endings. Adding to this concern, premature endings are more common for youth with trauma-related risk factors, such as poverty, foster care involvement, parental incarceration, and aggressive behavior (Kupersmidt et al., 2017). When interviewed, mentors who experienced early endings expressed feeling unprepared and overwhelmed by the severity of youths' needs (Spencer, 2007). One mentor stated, "I realized how very difficult it is to have any kind of intimate relationship . . . with someone that is vulnerable like that. . . . It's such a big responsibility."

As you might expect, longer-lasting mentoring relationships tend to be more impactful. But short-lived matches not just are ineffective but can be *harmful* (Zilberstein & Spencer, 2017). For example, in a landmark study that ignited ethical concerns in the field, youth with abuse histories were more likely to experience early relationship endings, and early endings led to *decreased* self-esteem and *increased* alcohol use (Grossman & Rhodes, 2002). These findings make sense from a trauma-informed perspective. Trauma-exposed youth tend to be more sensitive to rejection in relationships, and an abrupt, unplanned ending could worsen trauma-related symptoms and make youth less likely to seek out relationships the future. We believe that mentoring programs should operate under similar ethical standards as other human services, particularly the core principle of "do no harm" (Rhodes et al., 2009). To meet this standard, programs must better understand and address trauma.

Exemplary and Aspirational Program Practices

Next, we discuss how mentoring programs can integrate trauma-informed practices. First, we identify universal practices of trauma-informed care that should be implemented in all mentoring programs, regardless of focus. Second, we review exemplary practices of specialized mentoring programs designed to addressing trauma and prevent violence. Finally, we conclude the chapter with a discussion of recommended next steps for research, practice, and policy.

Universal Trauma-Informed Mentoring Practices

All mentoring programs, even those less "clinical" in focus such as academic and career mentoring, should assume that many mentees (not to mention mentors, program staff, and mentees' caregivers) may have trauma histories that impact program engagement and relationship formation. Although a comprehensive review of trauma-informed practices is beyond our scope (see Huckshorn & LeBel, 2013), we highlight four key strategies.

1. Mentoring programs should screen all participating youth for trauma exposure and trauma-related symptoms. As routine practice, programs should include questionnaires on trauma exposure and symptoms in enrollment packets (see Eklund et al., 2018, for a review of questionnaires). To increase caregivers' and youths' willingness to disclose, programs should also describe how this sensitive information will be used. For example, trauma screens can help staff make more effective matches by assigning youth with significant trauma histories to experienced mentors. Screening data can also help programs identify youth who need referrals for specialized services (see point 4, below).

2. All mentors should complete evidence-based training on trauma-informed care. One exemplary training program is Attachment, Regulation, and Competency (ARC), which was designed for youth-serving workers without formal clinical training, such as teachers, day care workers, and after-school program staff (Fehrenbach et al., 2022). ARC training includes psychoeducation about trauma, key practices for forming relationships with trauma-exposed youth, and basic coping skills to teach youth. ARC requires twelve group-based, hour-long training sessions, although providers may begin meeting with youth after four to six sessions while completing the rest. ARC offers "train-the-trainer" courses, which would allow mentoring program staff to become certified instructors and then provide "in-house" training to mentors. Despite the time investment required, ARC may help programs retain mentors over time. For example, one study found that ARC training reduced turnover of child welfare caseworkers by 66 percent because caseworkers felt more effective and less burnt out (Glisson et al., 2006).

3. Mentors should have regular, meaningful supervision from professional staff. The form and scope of supervision will depend on the nature of the program, but all mentors should have regular contact with experienced program staff, roughly corresponding to the frequency they see youth. In particular, supervisors should monitor relationships for signs of early termination and then provide "at-risk

matches" with more intensive support to prevent this damaging outcome.

4 Mentors and supervising staff should regularly consult with professionals with advanced clinical training, such as social workers, who can provide guidance when youth exhibit clinically significant symptoms. Even with high-quality training like ARC, mentoring programs should be aware of their limitations and provide referrals to professional services when necessary. Often, youth can continue in a mentoring program in conjunction with professional services. Ideally, program staff should form working relationships with local agencies and develop streamlined procedures for referral and care coordination.

Mentoring Programs for Trauma-Exposed Youth

Next, we turn to specialized mentoring programs designed for youth at elevated risk for trauma exposure and for committing violence, such as youth in foster care and those living high-crime communities. We highlight three key practices from two exemplary programs: Fostering Healthy Futures and Choose to Change.

1 Programs targeting trauma-exposed youth should engage in stringent mentor screening and selection. Research shows that mentors from helping professions (like teachers and health care providers) and those with previous experience working with youth tend to form longer and more impactful relationships with higher-risk mentees (Raposa et al., 2019). For this reason, programs serving trauma-exposed youth should prioritize recruiting mentors with necessary qualifications and experience. For example, Fostering Health Futures, a program for youth in foster care, exclusively uses mentors who are graduate students in psychology or social work (Taussig et al., 2021). Choose to Change, a program for adolescents from low-income, high-crime communities, recruits full-time, paid mentors who share similar backgrounds to mentees and have previous experience working with youth (University of Chicago Crime and Education Labs, 2020).

2 Targeted mentoring programs should have more intensive and routine supervision (not just as-needed consultation) with mental health professionals. Fostering Healthy Futures and Choose to Change both have master's- and/or doctoral-level clinical supervisors who regularly meet and consult with mentors.

3 Targeted mentoring programs should integrate skills-based curricula that address trauma-related difficulties and risk for violence. Fostering Healthy Futures and Choose to Change both integrate mentoring with therapeutic skills groups based on principles of cognitive

behavioral therapy (CBT). In both programs, CBT groups are led by professional clinicians while mentors assist and participate alongside youth. Mentors also meet with mentees individually, outside of group sessions, to help them practice and apply skills in "real-life" settings, such as at school, at home, and in the community (Taussig et al., 2021; University of Chicago Crime and Education Labs, 2020).

Program evaluations, which compare youth who participated in a program to peers who did not, suggest that both of these programs significantly reduced youths' trauma-related difficulties, especially risk for violence. During the seven years after the program ended, youth who participated in Fostering Healthy Futures were 15 to 30 percent less likely to commit violent crimes (Taussig et al., 2021). Although long-term evaluations of Choose to Change are not yet available, participating youth had 48 percent fewer violent crime arrests and 42 percent fewer total arrests at the end of the program (University of Chicago Crime and Education Labs, 2020).

Where Are We Going?

Fortunately, many mentoring researchers and practitioners have recently expressed commitment to trauma-informed care, although there is much work left to do. Next, we discuss considerations for future research, policy, and practice.

Costs and Benefits of Implementing Trauma-Informed Practices

Perhaps most daunting, programs will require financial resources to implement recommended trauma-informed practices (screening, training, supervision, and consultation). Practitioners and researchers (hopefully in close partnership) will need to develop convincing proposals to governmental, philanthropic, and private funders. Initially, the investment in trauma-informed practices will be significant, although it may be reduced over time. For example, having staff certified as ARC trainers would enable programs to provide in-house trainings to incoming cohorts of mentors. Adequate mentor training and screening may promote mentor retention, reducing expenses related to recruiting and training new mentors. If programs have difficulty recruiting mentors willing to make the time commitment, they might consider ways to increase incentives. For example, Fostering Healthy Futures recruits graduate students, providing them with professional development and course credit. Choose to Change employs mentors as full-time, paid paraprofessionals (a term used for care providers without advanced degrees or training). Although it may seem counterintuitive, paying mentors in effective programs like Choose to Change, which decreases youth delinquency and violence, ultimately saves money by reducing need for (more expensive) professional providers and costs incurred through criminal justice involvement.

Other recommended changes, such as trauma screening and coordinating care with local mental health agencies, have less explicit financial costs but will require time and effort by program staff. Programs will need to understand that commitment to trauma-informed care might initially result in fewer youth served, although capacity can be scaled up with time. As programs weigh the costs of adopting these changes, they should consider the larger return on investment of more effective interventions and better outcomes.

Integrating Mentoring and Evidence-Based Trauma Treatment

At this time, specialized mentoring programs for trauma-exposed youth appear to be confined to a few urban centers. This reflects a broader pattern of "mental health care deserts," which are regions (often rural) with very limited mental health services (Livingston & Green, 2022). Expanding specialized programs beyond major cities will require support from funders, advocacy organizations, and university-community partnerships. Alternatively, nonspecialized mentoring programs, which are widespread even in many rural regions (Garringer et al., 2017), can explore ways to integrate mentoring with services that are available. One idea is for programs to embed mentors within existing agencies, such as community mental health centers, to support youth engaged in trauma treatment (McQuillin et al., 2022). Trauma-focused therapies for children and adolescents are more effective when caregivers are involved, partly because caregivers help youth practice therapeutic skills between sessions (Brown et al., 2020). Yet some youth, like those in foster care, may lack consistent caregiver relationships, or caregivers may lack the capacity to participate regularly due to their own mental health challenges, inflexible work schedules, or other factors.

In our proposed model, mentors embedded in mental health agencies would be assigned to youth with barriers to caregiver involvement. Mentors would participate in "caregiver" sessions and meet with youth between sessions to facilitate real-life skills practice. Mentors may be able to engage with caregivers more flexibly than professional providers to deliver some session content. If in-person mental health services are not available in very remote or underserved areas, a similar model may be achieved by engaging mentors and youth in telehealth service via videoconferencing, which has become increasingly accessible and effective (Freitag et al., 2022).

Embedding mentors in formal mental health services may require practitioners and policymakers to tackle legal issues related to credentialing, billing, and documenting services (see McQuillin et al., 2022). Some states, such as Massachusetts, have passed legislation and practice guidelines for "therapeutic mentors" who work among clinical settings and youth populations (Children's Behavioral Health Initiative, 2015). Beyond addressing legal issues, formalized therapeutic mentoring could help programs attract service-oriented mentors and elicit more sustained commitments, and therapeutic mentoring programs could become accessible entry points into the human services field by providing professional credentials such as supervised clinical experience, certifications, and college credits. Further development and expansion of therapeutic mentoring will require advocacy and legislation at local, state, and national levels.

Measuring and Understanding Change

Finally, mentoring researchers and practitioners need to better understand the "active ingredients" of trauma-informed mentoring. In other words, we need to know when, why, and how changes occur through mentoring (Rhodes et al., 2006). After reviewing fifty-seven evaluations of school-based mentoring programs, McQuillin and colleagues (2020) reported that just 46 percent of programs contained *any* discussion of activities that occurred between mentors and youth and only 7 percent measured activities in a systematic way. When designing programs, researcher-practitioner teams must develop and test theories of change—that is, the changes expected to occur within the program to bring about the intended outcome. For example, if a program's goal is to reduce youths' aggressive behavior by building emotional regulation skills, a program evaluation should measure how much mentor-youth dyads practiced emotional regulation skills, how well youth learned and used emotional regulation skills in real life, and youths' level of aggression before, during, and after the program.

Conclusions

We end this chapter how we started—expressing cautious optimism for the promise of trauma-informed mentoring. We have argued that all mentoring programs must adopt some universal practices of trauma-informed care, such as screening youth for trauma and providing mentors with training, supervision, and consultation, which will result in higher-quality mentoring relationships, even in programs that do not explicitly target trauma symptoms and violence prevention. Additionally, we described existing and aspirational practices for integrating mentoring with trauma-focused psychological interventions. Although we recognize that our recommendations require significant time, money, and effort, we believe they will help to alleviate personal and social burdens of untreated trauma.

Acknowledgments

Dr. Rhodes would like to acknowledge support from MENTOR: The National Mentoring Partnership.

References

Brown, E. J., Cohen, J. A., & Mannarino, A. P. (2020). Trauma-focused cognitive-behavioral therapy: The role of caregivers. *Journal of Affective Disorders, 277,* 39–45. https://doi.org/10.1016/j.jad.2020.07.123

Children's Behavioral Health Initiative. (2015). *Therapeutic Mentoring Practice Guidelines.* MassHealth.

Eklund, K., Rossen, E., Koriakin, T., Chafouleas, S. M., & Resnick, C. (2018). A systematic review of trauma screening measures for children and adolescents. *School Psychology Quarterly, 33*(1), 30–42. https://doi.org/10.1037/spq0000244

Fehrenbach, T., Sax, R. M., Urban, T. H., Simon-Roper, L., Novacek, J., Aaby, D. A., & Hodgdon, H. B. (2022). Trauma treatment for youth in community-based settings: Implementing the Attachment, Regulation, and Competency (ARC) framework. *Journal of Child and Family Studies, 31,* 434–446. https://doi.org/10.1007/s10826-021-02096-x

Fernandes-Alcantara, A. L. (2018). *Vulnerable youth: Federal mentoring programs and issues.* Congressional Research Services.

Freitag, G. F., Urcuyo, A. E., & Comer, J. S. (2022). Moving beyond the clinic. *Advances in Psychiatry and Behavioral Health, 2*(1), 141–153. https://doi.org/10.1016/j.ypsc.2022.06.004

Garringer, M., McQuillin, S., & McDaniel, H. (2017). *Examining youth mentoring services across America: Findings from the 2016 National Mentoring Program Survey.* MENTOR.

Glisson, C., Dukes, D., & Green, P. (2006). The effects of the ARC organizational intervention on caseworker turnover, climate, and culture in children's service systems. *Child Abuse & Neglect, 30*(8), 855–880. https://doi.org/10.1016/j.chiabu.2005.12.010

Grossman, J. B., & Rhodes, J. E. (2002). The test of time: Predictors and effects of duration in youth mentoring relationships. *American Journal of Community Psychology, 30*(2), 199–219. https://doi.org/10.1023/A:1014680827552

Gutman, L. M., & Schoon, I. (2015). Preventive interventions for children and adolescents. *European Psychologist, 20,* 231–241. https://doi.org/10.1027/1016-9040/a000232

Huckshorn, K., & LeBel, J. L. (2013). Trauma-informed care. In K. R. Yeager, D. L. Cutler, D. Svendsen, & G. M. Sills (Eds.), *Modern community mental health: An interdisciplinary approach* (pp. 62–83). Oxford University Press.

Jarjoura, G. R., Tanyu, M., Forbush, J., Herrera, C., & Keller, T. E. (2018). *Evaluation of the mentoring enhancement demonstration program: Technical report.* American Institute for Research.

Kalmakis, K. A., & Chandler, G. E. (2015). Health consequences of adverse childhood experiences: A systematic review. *Journal of the American Association of Nurse Practitioners, 8*(27), 457–465. https://doi.org/10.1002/2327-6924.12215

Kupersmidt, J. B., Rhodes, J. E., Stump, K. N., & Stelter, R. L. (2017). Mentoring program practices as predictors of match longevity. *Journal of Community Psychology, 45,* 630–645. https://doi.org/10.1002/jcop.21883

Lieberman, A. F., Chu, A., Van Horn, P., & Harris, W. W. (2011). Trauma in early childhood: Empirical evidence and clinical implications. *Development and Psychopathology, 23,* 297–410. https://doi.org/10.1017/S0954579411000137

Livingston, K., & Green, M. (2022). *America's mental health care deserts: Where is it hard to access care?* ABC News.

McQuillin, S. D., Hagler, M. A., Werntz, A., & Rhodes, J. E. (2022). Paraprofessional youth mentoring: A framework for integrating youth mentoring with helping institutions and professions. *American Journal of Community Psychology, 69*(1–2), 201–220. https://doi.org/10.1002/ajcp.12546

McQuillin, S. D., Lyons, M. D., Clayton, R. J., & Anderson, J. R. (2020). Assessing the impact of school-based mentoring: Common problems and solutions associated with evaluating nonprescriptive youth development programs. *Applied Developmental Science, 24*, 215–229. https://doi.org/10.1080/10888691.2018.1454837

Merrick, M. T., Ford, D. C., Ports, K. A., & Guinn, A. S. (2018). Prevalence of adverse childhood experiences from the 2011–2014 Behavioral Risk Factor Surveillance System in 23 states. *JAMA Pediatrics, 172*(11), 1038–1044. https://doi.org/10.1001/jamapediatrics.2018.2537

Mumford, E. A., Taylor, B. G., Berg, M., Liu, W., & Miesfeld, N. (2019). The social anatomy of adverse childhood experiences and aggression in a representative sample of young adults in the U.S. *Child Abuse and Neglect, 88*, 15–27. https://doi.org/10.1016/j.chiabu.2018.10.016

Raposa, E. B., Rhodes, J. E., Stams, G. J. J. M., Card, N., Burton, S., Schwartz, S. E. O., Sykes, L. A. Y., Kanchewa, S. S., Kupersmidt, J. B., & Hussain, S. B. (2019). The effects of youth mentoring programs: A meta-analysis of outcome studies. *Journal of Youth and Adolescence, 48*(3), 423–443. https://doi.org/10.1007/s10964-019-00982-8

Rhodes, J. E., Liang, B., & Spencer, R. (2009). First do no harm: Ethical principles for youth mentoring relationships. *Professional Psychology: Research and Practice, 40*(5), 452–458. https://doi.org/10.1037/a0015073

Rhodes, J. E., Spencer, R., Keller, T. E., Liang, B., & Noam, G. (2006). A model for the influence of mentoring relationships on youth development. *Journal of Community Psychology, 34*(6), 691–707. https://doi.org/10.1002/jcop.20124

Spencer, R. (2007). "It's not what I expected": Mentoring relationship failures. *Journal of Adolescent Research, 22*(4), 331–354. https://doi.org/https://doi.org/10.1177/0743558407301915

Taussig, H. N., Dmitrieva, J., Garrido, E. F., Cooley, J. L., & Crites, E. (2021). Fostering Healthy Futures preventive intervention for children in foster care: Long-term delinquency outcomes from a randomized controlled trial. *Prevention Science, 22*(8), 1120–1133. https://doi.org/10.1007/s11121-021-01235-6

University of Chicago Crime and Education Labs. (2020). *Choose to change: Your mind, your game.* Chicago Urban Labs.

Zilberstein, K., & Spencer, R. (2017). Breaking bad: An attachment perspective on youth mentoring relationship closures. *Child and Family Social Work, 22*, 67–76. https://doi.org/10.1111/cfs.12197

8

What Does Rap Music Have to Do with Violence Prevention?

● ● ● ● ● ● ● ● ● ● ● ● ●

JALEEL ABDUL-ADIL

Overview: *What* Is This Noise?

What does rap music have to do with violence prevention—as opposed to provocation? I was *curious* the first time that I heard rap music. As a fifth-grader in rural Florida, I heard "Rapper's Delight" featured in a special radio spot on the only traditional "Black" radio station in our area. Everyone excitedly came into our middle school the next day trying to make sense of the creative combination of a funky beat we knew very well from the group Chic's hit song "Good Times" and the catchy rhymes we never heard before by some people—called "rappers"—who were talking on a record. What was this new song and sound, and what may be the future impact on us and society?

I *cringed* the second time that I heard rap music. As a third-year student who had just transferred from the majority-white Florida State University to the majority-Black Howard University, I was trying to absorb all the enormous—and positive—changes in campus cultural context when I heard the apparently "harsh" lyrics laid out by a multitude of modern rap artists ranging from Rakim to N.W.A. As someone who was raised on—and still preferred—the smooth sounds of Motown and the funk of Parliament, I was taken aback by the rapid-fire rhymes and gritty (often profane) depictions in rap music and rising Hip Hop culture. Who were these artists, and why did this nonmainstream musical genre have the "ears" (and also cultural trends in language, fashion, etc.) of my fellow students—especially those from New York and the related northeastern regions but increasingly encompassing growing constituents from Miami to Chicago to Los Angeles and around the country?

I was *inspired* the third time that I heard rap music. As a first-year graduate student in clinical psychology at DePaul University, I typically volunteered to take on the most difficult assignments in classrooms and communities that targeted serving the highest risk and most systemically oppressed ethnic "minority" youth and families in Chicago. In facing the daunting task of translating mainstream mental health research and practice into tangible and culturally relevant psychosocial programs that would best serve these African American and Latinx youth, I stumbled upon the potent combination of powerful positive lyrics from Public Enemy as the soundtrack to the searing social commentary depicted in Spike Lee's hit movie *Do the Right Thing*. Listening to Chuck D's intensive urging to "Fight the Power" against the backdrop of Lee's cinematic depiction of urban oppression (poverty, police brutality, racial conflict, etc.), I wondered aloud whether someone (namely me) could somehow capture this contingent of "conscious" (prosocial) rappers as a component of an innovative approach to prevention and intervention. This innovative approach could potentially reduce community violence and other health disparities that adversely impacted ethnic minority youth and families with the highest psychosocial needs and lowest available resources who were attracted to this burgeoning musical genre. Naively (and perhaps foolishly), I have pursued this career course ever since.

Actually . . . *Bring* the Noise!

Rap music and Hip Hop culture have certainly experienced a long, complicated evolution to their current places in contemporary culture. Once mainly marginalized as "ghetto music" among mainstream music critics while paradoxically demonstrating enormous crossover commercial appeal across wide sectors of U.S. society, rap music and Hip Hop culture are now undeniably recognized as the dominant musical genre in America whether referring to commercial sales (e.g., highest selling music genre in the United States) or cultural influences (e.g., pervasive presence across popular culture in sports, movies, television, fashion, etc.). Moreover, rap/Hip Hop has expanded internationally to include multilingual rap sounds and localized Hip Hop scenes that are currently thriving in multiple countries throughout the world (e.g., Canada, England, Brazil, Germany, Morocco, France, Nigeria, South Africa, Japan, India, Korea, Albania, Sweden, etc.).

Paradoxically (and unfortunately), rap/Hip Hop seems to still be struggling to gain traction in the fickle frameworks of mainstream academic research and practice on youth violence prevention. While it has become fashionable to offer begrudged recognition of this rap/Hip Hop phenomenon in certain college courses or entertain some limited discussions of practical psychosocial applications of rap/Hip Hop content toward youth wellness, established violence prevention programs appear to continue to neglect—and often even actively reject—the opportunity to tap the potential beneficial elements of this immensely popular (albeit controversial) art form. Furthermore, the continued racism, sexism, classism, oppression, as well as many other sensitive sociopolitical issues that are often described and depicted in intense uncensored rap songs may uniquely create hesitancy or even *refusal* among mainstream mental health providers to explore or embrace beneficial aspects of rap/Hip Hop.

A few promising breakthroughs, however, have emerged in recent years related to the prosocial use of rap music and Hip Hop culture as a means of enhancing the appeal and impact of violence prevention and other psychosocial issues. For example, pioneering efforts of scholars such as Don Elligan, Edgar Tyson, Raphael Travis, Alonzo DeCarlo, and Adia Winfrey paralleled my own work with Rod Watts in providing initial demonstrations of the practical positive applications of properly employing rap/Hip Hop within structured psychosocial youth programs. More recently, another wave of work by similarly rap-oriented scholars illustrates sustained attention among some practitioners toward potential programmatic resources and supplements available by rap/Hip Hop integration that can improve the appeal and relevance of traditional psychosocial approaches (Adjapong & Levy, 2021; Afuape & Kerry Oldham, 2022; Levy et al., 2021; Washington, 2018).

Rap-Based Best Practice Paradigms: A "Sample" from Hip Hop H.E.A.L.S.!

In addition to the aforementioned rap-based models and related resources, my current program, called Hip Hop H.E.A.L.S.! (H3), is an example of potential future benefits of rap-based violence prevention models.

"Started from the Bottom . . ."

H3 is derived from my original work with rap-based violence prevention called the Young Warriors (YW). The initiative provided school-based mental health program to adolescent youth who suffered chronic exposure to, and involvement with, multiple forms of interpersonal violence, including domestic, community, school, and gang types. The YW program began during my "inspiration" phase mentioned before as an attempt to provide motivating and culturally relevant messages to enhance traditional evidence-based social skills programming that had limited effects with low-income ethnic minority youth who were my program participants. The key elements of the YW program consisted of the following:

- *ethnic/gender identity affirmation* to promote healthy self-concept, combat racial stigma, and instill healthy masculinity/femininity/androgyny notions;
- *sociopolitical education* to promote individual and collective activism toward social, political, and economic, and institutional factors contributing to current urban crises
- *behavioral health* to promote mental, physical, and emotional well-being related to risk and resilience factors impacting daily lives of participating youth

Although there remains no magic pill to make violence disappear overnight, preliminary formative evaluation results suggested that these rap-oriented programs indeed could capture attention and periodically change behavior, even among youth with chronic behavioral difficulties and intensive gang activities in high-rise projects and among historically oppressed communities.

". . . Now We're Here!"

Building on that YW content and experience, I subsequently developed the H3 program as an expanded and (ideally) improved version of rap-based violence prevention. I serve as cofounder/codirector of the Urban Youth Trauma Center (UYTC) at the University of Illinois at Chicago (UIC), which was established in 2009. Led by myself and UYTC cofounder/codirector Liza Suarez, our UYTC team first developed a culturally sensitive and trauma-informed violence prevention model for urban youth and communities of color by adapting and integrating two leading research-based approaches promoted by top federal agencies: (1) the Centers for Disease Control and Prevention (CDC) socioecological model of violence prevention and intervention (CDC, 2009) and (2) the Substance Abuse and Mental Health Services Administration (SAMHSA) trauma-informed care model (SAMHSA, 2014) adopted by key provider networks including the National Child Traumatic Stress Network (NCTSN, n.d.). Key components of UYTC's integrated trauma-informed violence prevention model included both the CDC's evidence-based violence prevention strategies (e.g., social-cognition and supportive relationships across individual, family, community, and society levels) as well as SAMHSA's trauma-informed services shift from "what is wrong with you" to "what happened to you" (and some practitioners even include additional novel elements like "what's good about you" to promote even further healing).

Following positive preliminary feedback on this core UYTC curriculum, I subsequently "rebooted" and revised the original YW program to reflect the recent rigorous violence prevention research, the emergence of trauma-informed care (a term that didn't exist during the original YW program development), and more contemporary—and controversial—rap music trends. This new program was renamed "Hip Hop H.E.A.L.S.! (Helping Everyone Achieve Liberation and Success)" (i.e., H3) to reflect this updated emphasis on the health and healing of urban youth through strategic and intentional uses of rap music and Hip Hop culture as part of this manualized model's innovative approach to violence prevention.

Key H3 program elements that derived from the UYTC evidence-based framework to guide employing strategically selected rap music videos to both engage and educate youth on violence prevention practices included the following:

- culturally sensitive media content (selecting artists, messages, and experiences among rap/Hip Hop that affirm intersectional identities and experiences of youth participants, such as selecting a prosocial/conscious African American female rap artist or African American female adolescent groups, like Rapsody, whose song "Power" identifies both positive and negative examples of perceived power in youths' lives while promoting the former)
- critical consciousness and media literacy (pros and cons of violence in urban contexts depicted in rap songs such as "justifiable self-defense vs. avoidable and unreasonable aggression," comparisons and contrasts of several types of "conscious" and "gangsta" [antisocial] rap, etc.)
- peer-to-peer support (e.g., restorative justice circle formats, provider-facilitated debates and discussions on plausibility and application of specific violence prevention strategies displayed in rap/Hip Hop as related to their own local daily contexts, encouragement of new prosocial friendships or changed norms among existing relationships around shared rap/Hip Hop interests, etc.)
- community-based activity linkages (e.g., rap-related after-school programs and extracurricular activities that supplement H3 activities or provide alternatives to antisocial activities, etc.)

These efforts and experiences certainly suggest that current researchers and practitioners should continuously strive to (re)consider identifying and incorporating carefully selected elements of conscious and gangsta rap/Hip Hop that

98 • Jaleel Abdul-Adil

can be used prosocially to enhance the appeal and impact of traditional violence prevention programs.

Reflecting Forward?

A brief "sample" of H3 program developments and experiences during this integration of evidence-based research and youth-oriented rap/Hip Hop may offer lessons learned from research reflections toward moving forward in future directions with violence prevention. For example, H3 experiences and observations confirmed the immense benefits of systematically incorporating rap music into established evidence-based violence prevention research to enhance engagement and impact with youth programming. In addition, these types of innovative rap/Hip Hop-based approaches that systematically integrate rigorous research into their standard operations will be further strengthened by proper recognition and resources from mainstream funding agencies. Both evidence-based science and community-based service have respective merits as well as synergistic integration, and I look forward to a future era of systemic iterative research-to-practice cycle that formally combines the best rap/Hip Hop-based musical innovations with the most rigorous empirically validated violence prevention curricula.

In addition, H3 illustrated a clear example of the pressing need to continue keeping our "ears to the street" (a timeless adage and ongoing task) in identifying, assessing, and incorporating the fluid and often tricky trends in contemporary rap music. The H3 program uses the intentionally broad distinctions of conscious rap and gangsta rap (antisocial behavior) as a starting point for unpacking the layered complexities and messages of selected rap songs to determine the best uses of the lyrics, beats, backstories (e.g., artists' lived experiences and/or professional motifs), imagery (music videos, etc.), internet interviews (podcasts, YouTube, etc.), and other rap/Hip Hop cultural components that contribute to violence prevention principles. Moreover, H3 embraces blended songs that contain relative ratios of both conscious and gangsta genre elements within the same track. I do, however, strongly caution anyone considering or using rap-based programs today (much more so than during the classical "Afrocentric" and "pro-Black" empowerment era of the early 1990s) to first acquire sufficient training on contemporary rap/Hip Hop content *before* attempting programming to avoid provider and/or youth confusion and maximize accurate messaging.

Although we "old schoolers" can certainly choose to limit ourselves to lamenting the perceived lapses of this new generation of rap/Hip Hop compared to our romanticized bygone eras, we may be much more helpful to today's youth to engage them in respectful and motivational violence-related critical conversations. Many of our most oppressed and violent youth are merely reflecting and reacting to the harsh social, political, and economic conditions that compose their daily structural inequalities including poverty, dilapidated education offerings, health disparities, domestic and community violence, police brutality, mass incarceration (preschool-to-prison pipeline), and so on that were all created or tolerated by us adults. Of course, that is no excuse for them—nor for us.

Who's Got Next?

Although certain advances in innovation and adaptation with rap-oriented programs have occurred to date, violence prevention practitioners in general and rap-oriented programmers in particular face a number of remaining research tasks and related questions to fully harness the healing power of rap/Hip Hop in violence prevention. The urgency of this work is evident in the recent 30 percent rise in U.S. homicide rates reported by the CDC during 2019–2020 that disproportionately involved low-income ethnic minority youth and communities (CDC, 2021). This high-risk minority youth constituency is also the very same one that is most responsive to modern rap music and, consequently, the most in need of rap-based violence prevention programs.

Expanded Focus?

Based on what has—and has not—been done in bridging the gap between mainstream violence prevention models and innovative rap/Hip Hop service programs right now, a few key priorities appear viable as a focused task list to "keep it movin'" toward more effective rap-based violence prevention with contemporary youth. First of all, an expanded scope of focus and activity should be embraced by violence prevention practitioners in response to ongoing societal events. Although we definitely have an overwhelming number of complex issues already under professional discussion, we cannot ignore emergent trends that impact violence prevention and intervention:

- the status and dynamics of entrenched problems (e.g., gangs, guns, etc.) as well as burgeoning burdens (e.g., cyberbullying, mass shootings, etc.)
- programs for marginalized high-risk populations (e.g., immigrants, refugees, undocumented residents, etc.)
- digital technology, telehealth, and other novel service delivery mechanisms (smartphone apps, computer software, and social media platforms including YouTube, Twitter, TikTok)
- acute and ongoing impacts of the COVID-19 crises and its aftermath (e.g., educational setbacks especially due to the "digital

divide" of remote schooling for impoverished families without sufficient computer resources and high-speed connectivity, health care inequalities exacerbating existing disparities including access and effectiveness; mental health challenges of isolation, alienation, depression, etc.)

An ongoing examination of related rap/Hip Hop content on these issues may provide both insight and engagement from contemporary youth on the motivational songs, important artists, and real-time events that can best inform our respective violence prevention program strategies.

Evidence-Informed Approach

While H3 and other programs may remain under rigorous preliminary empirical development through ongoing implementation piloting and formative outcome evaluation of both the manualized youth curriculum and provider training components, our violence prevention field must also immediately address the ongoing chasm of research-to-community gaps in creative ways. According to the CDC statistics, there was a nearly 30 percent increase in youth gun violence between 2019 and 2020—such that gun violence has become the leading cause of death for U.S. youth up to age nineteen (Goldstick et al., 2022). This tragic violence also often disproportionately devastates urban ethnic minority youth in neighborhoods already experiencing chronic adversity—such as in Chicago, where 79 percent of homicide or nonfatal shooting victims were African American and 15 percent were Latinx (Chicago Mayor's Office of Violence Reduction, 2022).

One helpful tactic to respond to these current crises may be embracing the nouveau practice of using evidence-informed best practices (use the best available research and practice knowledge) as opposed to exclusively waiting for a multiyear emergence of some possible fully formed "gold-standard" evidence-based model (rigorously evaluated and randomized, producing statistically significant effects). While a plethora of evidence-based rap-oriented programs may remain the ultimate goal and "dream scenario," we passively decline our professional input on this current crisis since alternative rapid research mechanisms are available and appropriate for this public health emergency (e.g., action and community-based participatory research models). One day in the future we may have finally earned the luxury of awaiting the results of multiyear experimental randomization trials and sophisticated multiple regression statistical analyses for hip hop–integrated strategies. We can, however, immediately begin building on existing knowledge about incorporating the use of modern rap music and related Hip Hop culture as well as trauma-informed care to improve and expand current youth violence prevention and intervention efforts.

Youth Co-creation

Finally—and perhaps most importantly—violence prevention programs that feature rap/Hip Hop must more actively collaborate with the targeted youth and communities themselves in the design, delivery, and evaluation of these rap-based models toward having true evidence of impact. For example, the formally organized involvement of youth, community-based providers, and even parents/caretakers (who during this time have now either been significantly exposed to or even grown up on rap/Hip Hop music themselves) in collaboratively selecting and adapting the proposed violence prevention strategies, musical selections, evaluation measures, data analyses, and public findings disseminations appears most consistent with the rap/Hip Hop ethos of "keepin' it real."

Moreover, potential grassroots program partners such as street violence interrupters like Cure Violence (Buggs et al., 2022) offer additional complementary mechanisms for reinforcing rap-related prevention efforts (e.g., training interrupters in rap-oriented conversations to supplement their de-escalation techniques). These types of collaborative efforts appear most suited to ensuring youth engagement and empowerment, culturally relevant content alignment, and sustainable community support as a means of continuing to try to capture and capitalize on this fast-moving musical genre.

A Final Raised Fist

As I commented in the opening section, I vividly remember Chuck D and other Afrocentric rappers raising the fist in protest over thirty years ago as rap/Hip Hop ascended into national visibility, and I still see those same symbolic salutes in response to both systemic violence (Black Lives Matter movement in response to police brutality) as well as internalized oppression ("Peace in the 'Hood" marches in response to gang and gun violence).

We have certainly seen an extensive array of rap-related events over the past thirty years that have either apparently prevented (the pro-Black era) or glorified violence (the infamous Death Row Records era)—or both (the current era including recent examples like Nipsey Hussle's inspirational yet tragically short transformation). A consistent factor across these decades, however, has been the undeniable and increasing influence of this rap/Hip Hop phenomenon on youth audiences. Consequently, we are well past time to get grimy and do this painstaking work of addressing violence prevention by rolling up our sleeves and getting busy building more innovative and effective violence prevention programs—especially ones that feature rap/Hip Hop.

So what should we do when we hear rap music *today?* Should we criticize this music as calls for more chaos or embrace it as chants for much-needed change? The choice—and chance—of making a positive difference in the lives of youth is up to us.

References

Abdul-Adil, J., & Suárez, L. M. (2022). The Urban Youth Trauma Center: A trauma-informed continuum for addressing community violence among youth. *Community Mental Health Journal, 58*(2), 334–342.

Adjapong, E., & Levy, I. (2021). Hip-hop can heal: Addressing mental health through hip-hop in the urban classroom. *New Educator, 17*(3), 242–263.

Afuape, T., & Kerry Oldham, S. (2022). Beyond "solidarity" with Black Lives Matter: Drawing on liberation psychology and transformative justice to address institutional and community violence in young Black lives. *Journal of Family Therapy, 44*(1), 20–43.

Buggs, S. A., Webster, D. W., & Crifasi, C. K. (2022). Using synthetic control methodology to estimate effects of a Cure Violence intervention in Baltimore, Maryland. *Injury Prevention, 28*(1), 61–67.

Centers for Disease Control and Prevention. (2009). *Violence prevention—The social-ecological model: A framework for prevention.* https://www.cdc.gov/violenceprevention/publichealthissue/social-ecologicalmodel.html

Centers for Disease Control and Prevention. (2021, October 6). *New CDC/NCHS data confirm largest one-year increase in U.S. homicide rate in 2020.* https://www.cdc.gov/nchs/pressroom/nchs_press_releases/2021/202110.htm (accessed May 24, 2024).

Chicago Mayor's Office of Violence Reduction. (2022). *Violence reduction dashboard.* https://www.chicago.gov/city/en/sites/vrd/home.html

DeCarlo, A., & Hockman, E. (2003). Rap therapy: A group work intervention method for urban adolescents. *Social Work with Groups, 26*(3), 45–60.

Elligan, D. (2004). *Rap therapy: A practical guide for communicating with youth and young adults through rap music.* Kensington Books.

Goldstick, J. E., Cunningham, R. M., & Carter, P. M. (2022). Current causes of death in children and adolescents in the United States. *New England Journal of Medicine, 386*(20), 1955–1956.

Levy, I. P., Hess, C. W., Elber, A., & Hayden, L. (2021). A community-based intervention: A hip hop framework toward decolonizing counseling spaces. *Journal of Creativity in Mental Health, 16*(2), 212–230.

National Child Traumatic Stress Network. (n.d.). *Who we are.* https://www.nctsn.org/treatments-and-practices/trauma-treatments

Substance Abuse and Mental Health Services Administration. (2014). *SAMHSA's concept of trauma and guidance for a trauma-informed approach.* https://store.samhsa.gov/sites/default/files/d7/priv/sma14-4884.pdf

Travis, R. (2016). *The healing power of hip hop.* Praeger.

Tyson, E. H. (2002). Hip hop therapy: An exploratory study of a rap music intervention with at risk and delinquent youth. *Journal of Poetry Therapy, 15*(3), 131–144.

Washington, A. R. (2018). Integrating hip-hop culture and rap music into social justice counseling with Black males. *Journal of Counseling & Development, 96*(1), 97–105.

Watts, R. J., & Abdul-Adil, J. K. (2018). Promoting critical consciousness in young, African-American men. In R. J. Watts & R. J. Jagers (Eds.), *Manhood development in urban African-American communities* (pp. 63–86). Routledge.

Watts, R. J., Abdul-Adil, J. K., & Pratt, T. (2002). Enhancing critical consciousness in young African American men: A psychoeducational approach. *Psychology of Men & Masculinity, 3*(1), 41–50.

Entrepreneurship and Vocational Development

• • • • • • • • • • • • •

Pathways for Youth Violence Prevention

JORJA LEAP

In the first half of our history, we were job-centric. Our goal was to find employers willing to hire felons. We discovered that the task at hand was not to train homies so that they'd be "ready" for employment, but to help homies so that they'd be healed . . . to live. They know how to survive but, as a homie told me once, "I don't know how to live." The outsider view thinks our population is deficient. They aren't. They just have been carrying more than most and are wounded and broken by it. A healing community where people feel safe and

> seen, allows our folks to flourish. Now,
> they can be employed almost anywhere.
> This is the power of community, the
> power of beloved belonging.
>
> **—FATHER GREG BOYLE**

Overview

For anyone working to prevent youth violence in Los Angeles and in similar metropolitan settings, the challenge of gangs is impossible to ignore. Throughout my career, first as a social worker then as a community-based researcher, gangs and youth violence were always central to my efforts. When I began working with gang-involved youth in Watts, I heard about a Catholic priest in East Los Angeles who was trying to replace gang violence with meaningful employment. I immediately knew I had to find out more. In 1988, I met Father Greg Boyle, whose initial youth-based effort—Jobs for a Future—ultimately became the clarion call of anyone interested in connecting youth violence prevention with vocational development. He first partnered with community businesses in Boyle Heights, enlisting them to hire at-risk and gang-involved youth. However, his efforts soon shifted into something more entrepreneurial. In 1992, Father Greg acquired an abandoned bakery, restarting the business while offering training for future bakers, and Homeboy Industries (HBI) was born. From these beginnings, Homeboy expanded into a multimillion-dollar nonprofit with multiple social enterprises that employ formerly system-involved youth and adults and help to fund HBI. "G"—as Father Greg is known throughout Los Angeles—became a visible champion of integrating entrepreneurship and vocational development as a crucial strategy in preventing youth violence, embodied in the early mission statement of HBI: "Nothing stops a bullet like a job."

Homeboy's mission and its programs flourished as an answer to the epidemic of gang violence that ensnared youth in Los Angeles County. As the program outgrew its original Boyle Heights headquarters and moved to a larger, more central location, it was time to figure out if Homeboy's program was truly effective. Twenty years after meeting G, in 2008, I undertook the first evaluation of HBI.

This wasn't an easy proposition. Father Greg and the Homeboy leadership staff weren't open to any study that involved experimental methodology. There would be no random assignment of trainees to control or intervention groupings. They didn't want to have to choose between offering services to some and denying services to others. Luckily, their conditions matched my own research philosophy. I've never been convinced that RCT methodology could adequately capture the effective work taking place on the ground. Guided by a commitment to community-based participatory research and designing innovative measures, our methods were acceptable to HBI, documenting the transformation of Homeboy clients without sacrificing anyone's needs. The five-year mixed-methods evaluation charted the trajectories of a hundred youth and turned up several promising findings, including a recidivism rate half the national average. This meant that only one-third of the Homeboy program participants returned to prison, while nationally two-thirds of youth and young adults returned.

Summary and Highlights

The wellspring of valuable material at HBI emerged from in-depth interviews and ethnographic observations, offering important lessons for all programs serving vulnerable populations.

Doing Good and Doing Well: The Importance of Ongoing Innovation

What began as a local grassroots effort has now grown into a model focused on helping at-risk and gang-involved youth and adults become prosocial, contributing members of society through job training, placement, education, wraparound services, and kinship in a healing community. Many individuals have found their way to HBI for good reason—its programs are vital to those wanting to end their involvement with violence and to rejoin their families and communities. As HBI and its social enterprises grew, G and his leadership team realized that their businesses could both offer vocational development and provide revenue to support their mission. In 2022, this entrepreneurial model literally paid off! HBI social enterprises brought in over $6 million that year—accounting for approximately 20 percent of overall revenues.

Jobs Alone Aren't Enough to Ensure Violence Prevention

Even with early entrepreneurial success, G noted a disturbing trend. Although HBI successfully trained and employed individuals within its businesses, youth were still susceptible to the lure of gangs. G saw that vocational development had to be paired with services to deal with trauma and help youth form new identities. Youth needed support services just as badly as they needed jobs; it was up to places like Homeboy to provide both. Today, HBI offers a range of services, from substance abuse prevention and intervention to mental health services and trauma-focused case management. As Steve Delgado, a Homeboy executive team member, explains, "Healing is the thread that runs through everything we do."

Integrating Vocational Development and Healing

Shanley Rhodes, HBI director of career pathways, relates, "We try to ask youth, what do you want to do with the rest of your amazing life?" The mixture of vocational development, entrepreneurship, and healing informs every aspect of Homeboy's efforts, focusing on kinship, personal strengths, mental and physical wellness, and personal agency. A former gang member turned case manager, Gabriel, offers an example: "You don't just tell youth they should show up on time. You have to connect being on time with purpose. People learn to show up on time if they feel purposeful. This always leads back to healing and giving each youth a sense of their own strength." The healing evoked in Gabriel's words includes health services in the broadest sense. HBI's wraparound approach helps individuals deal with trauma as well as everyday struggles with issues such as housing and raising children. With a holistic approach, Homeboy guides each individual's pathway of transformation.

Vocational Development Is Multifaceted

Father Greg and his executive team realized that HBI trainees were often too young to definitively know exactly what pathway they'd want to follow. In response, Homeboy provided the opportunity for youth to explore their interests and plan their futures. While exploring, youth complete high school at the Homeboy Learning Works Charter School. At the same time, the Homeboy Youth Reentry Center offers four pathways:

- job readiness education and employment in Homeboy businesses
- job readiness education and placement in nonprofits or businesses
- charter school education, college prep, and enrollment
- Homeboy Art Academy and participation in the creative economy

The fourth option—the Homeboy Art Academy—is the most recent addition. The academy grew out of Homeboy artist Fabian Debora's vision of the creative economy as a pathway to both education and work, offering employment in artists' studios and with partner agencies. The academy has space for painting, computers for digital media, and a recording studio. Raul, a trainee raised in a gang-connected family, described the impact of HBI's youth programming: "Homeboy helped me get my birth certificate and my high school diploma. Homeboy helped me with a lot of stuff. My family told me I was nothing... but Homeboy taught me I could love myself. I'm learning I can be an artist—I can paint. I want to teach art to others. It's a way we can all heal."

How and Where Is the Best Work Getting Done?

Some violence prevention programs simply declare they are best practices, while others describe empirically supported best practices that are often detached from the daily implementation of highly successful programming. Some programs don't receive the "best practices" label or the even loftier "evidence-based practices" seal of approval but nevertheless serve youth and their communities effectively. So how and where is the best work getting done? The answers to this question have meaning for national efforts surrounding youth violence prevention, vocational development, and entrepreneurship. The promising practices and foundational impacts demonstrated by HBI include their focus on building individual identity, creating a community of kinship, and ultimately being guided by the integration of healing and service provision. What's been learned at HBI is reinforced by effective work being conducted at other community-based youth violence prevention programs throughout the country.

Serve the "Whole Youth" with Diverse Programming

One of the earliest and most successful of such programs is located far from Los Angeles, in Chelsea, Massachusetts: Roca (see https://rocainc.org). Founded in 1988, Roca, which means "rock" in Spanish, supports high-risk youth aged seventeen to twenty-four to complete high school while offering job training and placement. However, in a philosophy close to Homeboy's, Roca focuses beyond vocational development to problems youth face, including gang involvement, violent behavior, teenage motherhood, and school dropout. Always growing, they operate the Roca Impact Institute and their sites now reach as far as Baltimore. Additionally, Roca is now engaged in the nation's largest Pay for Success project—the Massachusetts Juvenile Justice Pay for Success Initiative—offering services to system-involved youth.

Involvement of Community Is Critical to Youth Vocational Development and Violence Prevention

Homeboy emphasizes a community of "kinship." As Father Greg explains, "There is no them and us, there is only us." For youth employed at Homeboy social enterprises, community members support their labors and their businesses. "I love seeing the Homeboy stand at farmers' markets," one Los Angeles screenwriter enthused, "I love to support the Homeboy mission." The LAPD chief of police has held breakfast meetings for his nine deputy chiefs at the Homegirl Café, explaining, "We need to show we care about youth trying to change their lives." Additionally, community volunteers tutor youth and teach classes ranging from yoga to financial planning. This melding of entrepreneurship and community involvement is integral to the Homeboy model.

Similar to Homeboy, Youth Uprising (YU; https://youthuprising.org), a nonprofit organization founded in 2005 in East Oakland, concentrates on building the identity and self-sufficiency of the youth it serves. Its mission of youth leadership development is based on three core activities: a social enterprise hub, job training program, and community entrepreneurship. YU has established businesses that train youth in skills transferrable to other settings. Right now, there are two social enterprises: Corners Café & Catering and YU Green, each with managers who began as trainees. This social enterprise hub provides culinary and management training while generating revenue for the nonprofit. In turn, YU Green offers landscaping services to more than fifty-five properties throughout Oakland. Along with these efforts, YU is currently working to create a hub of community entrepreneurship—growing a small business owner support system in East Oakland. Always, YU engages community members as volunteers, as clients, and as supporters of these efforts.

Any Effective Program Creates a Community among Youth with the Same Experience

What so many youth shared with my team at UCLA was their belief that they'd found a "home" at HBI. They also expressed surprise at being able to work alongside rival gang members: "It's hard to hate someone when you're baking bread together," said Hector, a young adult who'd been involved with gangs from the age of ten. This is emblematic of the community of kinship HBI fosters. Although early gang research indicated that similar efforts might build gang ties, our research revealed that the kinship Homeboy practiced broke down gang identities and replaced these with a Homeboy identity. As Miguel, a trainee, explained, "The gang told me who they wanted me to be. But Homeboy helped me to find out who I really was."

Where Are We Going?

My experiences studying HBI and learning about similar programs such as Roca and Youth Uprising have yielded some "lessons learned" about how to move the field forward.

Research Must Be More Participatory with Innovative Methodology

Research around violence prevention and vocational development has largely been evaluative and focused on experimental methodology. My years at Homeboy showed that researchers should be more deeply embedded in communities, working with residents, including youth, as our partners. Additionally, the definition of successful outcomes must be expanded. Just as Father Greg discovered simply training youth and placing them in jobs wasn't enough, research must move beyond traditional indicators to consider issues such as employment engagement, ongoing training, trauma-informed services, education, and finally youth identification with their roles as entrepreneurs—building their identities alongside a sense of agency. While we continue to chart recidivism at Homeboy, we've also viewed engagement with one's children, reconciliation with family, sustained physical health, completion of high school/GED, and self-reports of well-being as meaningful indicators of success.

Communities are constantly changing. Correspondingly, strategies connecting youth violence prevention to vocational development and entrepreneurship must evolve. Over three decades ago when I worked in Watts, the community was predominantly Black; today it is majority Latinx. The need for youth violence prevention endures, but the population and its requirements have changed, a reminder that community needs change. Both programming and social enterprises at HBI have responded to changes in the LA landscape. What was once perceived as a "Mexican gang intervention program" based in Boyle Heights has organically enlarged its cultural practices. Our HBI research has revealed an organization whose programming continues to reflect the diversity of Los Angeles—serving BIPOC and LGBTQ+ individuals. Additionally, Homeboy has been nimble in responding to social needs. Their newest social enterprise, Feed HOPE, arose in response to the COVID-19 pandemic—with the Café and Bakery joining forces to produce and deliver prepackaged meals to vulnerable individuals and families.

Similarly, Roca has recognized the changing needs of the communities it serves. To guide its organization, Roca developed a Theory of Change in 2005, seventeen years after its founding. From 2005 through 2011, Roca reshaped its Theory of Change three times, integrating emerging cultural needs to fine-tune its model. Roca refined its focus with increased outreach to diverse refugee populations including Bosnian, Somali, Moroccan, and Sudanese families settling in Chelsea. As with HBI, this process was driven by Roca's sensitivity to changing community and social dynamics.

Legislation and Social Policies Are the Missing Element in the Future Evolution of Youth Vocational Development

Often, policymakers haven't recognized the interrelationship between youth violence prevention and vocational development. However, the landscape has begun to change. The Biden administration launched the Community Violence Intervention (CVI) initiative in April 2021, with investments in evidence-based and trauma-informed approaches to youth violence prevention. Concurrently, the Department of Justice supports this interrelationship through its Comprehensive Youth Violence Prevention and Reductions Program, Young Adult Reentry Partnership, and Workforce Innovation and Opportunity Act programs. State-based efforts in this direction include, for example, the California Board of State and Community Corrections (BSCC) funding nonprofits including Homeboy through its Violence Intervention and Prevention (Cal-VIP) program, with financial support for youth vocational development. However, more can be done; the following section offers guidance for future legislation and policymaking.

There Should Be Dedicated Public Funding and Incentives for Youth Vocational Development and Entrepreneurship

Law enforcement consistently receives a dedicated budget line item. Vocational development and youth violence prevention merit an equally necessary, dedicated line item. Policymakers can also seek philanthropic matching funds for vocational development services building public-private partnerships that are sustainable over time. Accountability is key, but nonprofits should *not* be required to carve out part of their budgets for evaluation; many struggle to deliver services on shoestring budgets without an extra financial burden. Instead, all public funding should require and fund evaluation.

However, policymaking involves more than fund allocation. Private employers should receive special subsidies and/or tax breaks for employing the "hard to hire"—at-risk or system-involved youth. Employment shouldn't be automatic but can instead depend on youth completing vocational training and life skills programs offered by organizations like Homeboy, Roca, and Youth Uprising.

Legislation should endeavor to remove obstacles to youth employment while continuing to fund vocational development, and key legislation that has been enacted should be reinforced. Required reporting of criminal history poses an obstacle to youth employment that is finally being addressed. For instance, in January 2018 California's Fair Chance Act, which prohibits employers from asking job applicants about prior criminal convictions, went into effect. In turn, thirty-seven states and over 150 cities and counties have adopted similar legislation, and fifteen states and twenty-two cities and countries have extended these policies. At the federal level, the Fair Chance to Compete for Jobs Act went into effect as part of the National Defense Authorization Act in December 2021.

Additionally, California has enacted legislation to remove obstacles to youth employment *specifically* tying this legislation to funding for vocational development and education. At the federal level, the Workforce Innovation and Opportunity Act of 2014 (WIOA) is the principal law helping economically vulnerable youth access employment, education, training, and support services. The U.S. Department of Labor also sponsors youth-related workforce programs such as YouthBuild and Reentry Employment Opportunities (REO). These efforts represent replicable examples of legislation funding and supporting youth vocational development and violence prevention.

While professional training is important, what ultimately matters is the attitude and values of individuals who work with youth. When I met Father Greg, I told him I wasn't a Catholic and was not a fan of organized religion. He laughed and said, "I don't care what you are. Do you want to help these kids?" His words resonated; being a social worker didn't matter as much as my commitment to youth and their communities. But commitment isn't a job requirement. Often, probation departments oversee vocational development services. But the ranks of those who work with vulnerable youth must be diversified. Social workers and human service professionals are crucial to this effort. So are individuals who have been system involved. One approach with successful outcomes for HBI, Roca, and Youth Uprising involves employing individuals with lived experience to lead entrepreneurship and vocational development. What's optimal is a combination of both professionals and what Watts grassroots leader Elder Mike Cummings refers to as "people with a PhD in the street." Beyond the values and attitudes of *who* is working with youth, there are key concepts guiding *what* they need to know.

There Is No Typical Youth

Youth aren't a monolithic population requiring a one-size-fits-all approach to vocational development; instead, they possess varied backgrounds, ages, and genders. For example, much of what's been written about youth completely ignores girls and women, let alone nonbinary individuals. Recognizing this, HBI continuously expands services to address diversity. One of their social enterprises, the Homegirl Café, was specifically geared to supporting girls and women. More recently, they have created classes and mental health services to meet the needs of nonbinary youth.

Understanding and investing in youth vocational development and entrepreneurship serves multiple purposes. Certainly, as I've been writing this, places like HBI, Youth Uprising, and Roca continue to offer both hope and meaningful violence prevention strategies. They play a crucial role in sustaining public safety. Beyond that, they build economic stability and personal agency. Finally, they lift up individuals whose talents and abilities serve their communities and our society. In the end, all of this works to transform the lives of youth and ensure violence is extinguished forever.

References

California Workforce Development Board. (2021, October). *AB 1111: Breaking Barriers to Employment Initiative.* Cwddb.ca.gov. https://cwdb.ca.gov/wp-content/uploads/sites/43/2021/10/AB-1111-Interim Report_ACCESSIBLE.pdf

Janisch, K. (2021, October 26). *California ban the box law: Enhanced enforcement.* https://www.govdocs.com/california-ban-the-box-law-enhanced-enforcement/

JD Supra. (2022, February 7). *AB 628: Breaking Barriers to Employment Initiative.* https://www.jdsupra.com/legalnews/ab-628-breaking-barriers-to-employment-2790162/

Leap, J. (2012). *Jumped in: What gangs taught me about violence, drugs, love and redemption.* Beacon.

Leap, J., Franke, T., Christie, C., & Bonis, S. (2010). Nothing stops a bullet like a job. In J.S. Hoffman, L. Knox, & R. Cohen (Eds.), *Beyond suppression: Global perspectives on youth violence* (pp. 127–138). Praeger.

National Network for Youth. (n.d.). *Connecting Youth to Jobs Act of 2021.* https://nn4youth.org/connecting-youth-to-jobs-act-of-2021/

U.S. Department of Labor. (n.d.-a). *About youth services.* https://www.dol.gov/agencies/eta/youth/about

U.S. Department of Labor. (n.d.-b). *Workplace Innovation and Opportunity Act.* https://www.dol.gov/agencies/eta/wioa

White House. (2021, April 7). *Fact sheet: More details on the Biden-Harris administration's investments in community violence interventions.* https://www.whitehouse.gov/briefing-room/statements-releases/2021/04/07/fact-sheet-more-details-on-the-biden-harris-administrations-investments-in-community-violence-interventions/

Gun Violence in the Black Community

• • • • • • • • • • • • •

The Rise of a Credible Messenger

SAMSON STYLES

Overview

I have witnessed gun violence up close and personal on a level that will bring a unique perspective to the issue. I'm a survivor. On July 4, 1988, I was shot five times by two gunmen in Brooklyn, New York. It was during a time when the city of New York was experiencing an average of two thousand murders a year. A period when crack cocaine was dominating the inner cities of Black America on a national level. A time when walking down the street and seeing yellow crime scene tape barricading a lifeless body with smoke ascending from its flesh was a normal occurrence.

    I wasn't only a victim of gun violence; I was once a perpetrator as well. Committing armed robberies on drug dealers was my profession during the crack epidemic, and it held many consequences. For example, an attempt on my mother's life was made, and I almost lost my life due to that destructive lifestyle. While in prison, I started looking at the causes, effects, and solutions to gun violence that exist in the Black community. When I exited Fort Dix Federal Correctional Facility in 2004, I changed my life around and became an award-winning broadcast journalist. I've reconciled with the person who shot me and made amends with people I also hurt in the past. And now I will give you the raw truth from my experiences and research on the gun violence that permeates Black communities.

Environment/School

In my early years I grew up in a well-to-do diverse community called Park Slope, Brooklyn. I grew up seeing almost every nationality living on my block. I had a Chinese next-door neighbor, a Puerto Rican babysitter, Italians who taught me how to play stickball. Our neighborhood looked like the United Nations. I didn't see much violence, only an occasional fight here and there. I went to the esteemed PS 321 public school. That was in the 1970s, and today that school is still held in high regard for academics with test scores far above the state average. My peers would congratulate me with praise for getting top grades and almost always delivering the correct answer when participating in class. It was cool to run errands for the teacher. It was encouraged to sit in the front of the class and raise your hand and participate. Friendly academic competition spread among us students. From kindergarten up until the third grade, being academically competitive and astute was all I knew.

Soft and Friendly versus Hard and Distrustful

I was just one month shy of turning nine years old when my family moved from Park Slope to the low-income and notorious Pink Houses housing development farther east in Brooklyn. Unlike the diverse and mostly peaceful setting I was used to, Pink Houses was approximately 85 percent Black and 15 percent Puerto Rican and had only one white family living there that I knew of. It was a heavily populated and densely concentrated neighborhood. There were twenty-two buildings with at least sixty-four families living in each. It was people stacked on top of people. Most families there were on public assistance ("welfare") and living in poverty. My family wasn't on welfare, but we were far from being middle class.

It was a culture shock. I went from Park Slope's relatively peaceful environment to one filled with violence. The alcohol and drug abuse, missing fathers, and gangs were foreign to me before migrating to Pink Houses. The kids were very aware of their surroundings and seemed as if they were always watching over their back. Their demeanor was hardened and distrustful. Being gullible in this part of town was obsolete. The soft and friendly character I possessed in Park Slope wouldn't serve me well in Pink Houses.

The neighborhood was filled with a criminal element. It wasn't frowned upon if you were known as a thief, pimp, prostitute, or marijuana or cocaine dealer. It was normal for one of the neighborhood thieves to knock on your door trying to sell you things ranging from fresh meat that was stolen from the local supermarket at 50 percent off to name-brand clothes that a booster lifted from one of the major department stores. You were even able to buy government food stamps from someone at half price. The area was so impoverished that the general mindset was survive and thrive by any means necessary. After spending the summer in my new environment, I quickly learned the ways of the land. I became fascinated with my new neighborhood and adapted quickly to the lifestyle.

When school started, I had to adjust again. Unlike Park Slope's PS 321, sitting in front of the class and participating wasn't cool. In my new school, PS 224, my peers would respect me if I was disorderly and quick-tempered. Those who could fight and fought frequently were applauded. Students who had to repeat a grade were glorified, and those who had to repeat the same grade twice were like gods. This conflicted with everything that my parents and the neighborhood of Park Slope taught me. I became confused, but I learned how to balance getting good grades while developing a quick temper. I also learned how to fight quickly. I got pretty good at it.

By the time I reached junior high school, I learned how to pick pockets, and at eleven years of age my run-ins with police and arrest record began.

What You See Is What You Do

Pink Houses was similar to most of the low-income public housing developments around the country. To qualify for entry your income had to be at the poverty level. Most of the women were on government assistance and couldn't receive their benefits if they had a man living in the home (the additional income would disqualify them from eligibility). Out of the 1,408 families living in Pink Houses at the time, I could count on one hand the amount of people I knew who grew up with a father in their home. There was a famous incident with young elephants in South Africa without any mature males around: they became quick-tempered and started attacking all the rhinoceros in the area. The scientists and rangers studying and caring for these elephants then brought in mature male elephants. Shortly afterward, the young elephants stopped killing the rhinos and became more even tempered. They followed the elder elephants' lead and learned to live in harmony instead of being destructive (Raspberry, 1999).

In my experience I have seen that the same is true with young boys without mature wise men to emulate. We became disorderly and destructive. The question asked to me has been, "You had a father in the house. How did you become disruptive?" Well, I quickly fell into the norm of my environment. I didn't look up to my father as a role model. He didn't have a grand personality that was respected throughout my neighborhood. My father was an introvert and very much kept to himself. I wanted to fit in to prevent myself from being bullied and getting taken advantage of. I was also fascinated with the edgy lifestyle that was made to look glamorous. This "ghetto glamorous" façade permeates the mindset of underserved Black communities nationally. Seeing someone become a doctor, lawyer, journalist, accountant, real estate developer, or successful entrepreneur isn't likely in these communities. Success often looks instead like someone making fast money by doing something illegal and getting local notoriety and then seeing their demise shortly after when they go to prison or are killed. The alternative success we might see is someone getting a city or state job making fifty thousand dollars annually. They are making enough to pay their rent with no problem but aren't making enough to buy a house and leave the neighborhood. We also might see the occasional entertainer or sports figure make it out and be successful, which is rare. There are only so many Mike Tysons, Jay-Zs, or Dwyane Wades populating these neighborhoods. What you often see is what you often emulate.

Community Policing

Before Edward Byrne (a Queens, New York, police officer) was killed while on duty protecting a witness ready to testify against Lorenzo "Fat Cat" Nichols's drug organization, community policing showed a major presence in these socioeconomically deprived communities. Police used to walk the beat and knew most everyone by name. They knew who the troublemakers were. They were familiar with the families living in the community and would use discretion while dealing with issues. For instance, if Jo had a weapon on him and Officer John knew that Jo was usually well behaved and a good kid, Officer John would take the weapon from Jo, and walk him upstairs to have a talk with him and his parents to see why he needed to carry the weapon. He might have been bullied or may have started taking a turn for the worse by hanging with the wrong people. The officer would have gotten a feel for Jo's situation and could act accordingly. Officer John wouldn't have acted quickly to arrest Jo and give him a felony for weapon possession.

In this prior model of community policing there was mutual respect and less of a disconnect between the police and the community, which led to less violence because of the familiarity that the police had with the community. But after Byrne's murder and following changes in the way America was viewing crime, the police formed task forces across the nation and started taking a more militarized approach. This resulted in an influx of law enforcement officers unfamiliar with the people, culture, and neighborhood who took a more biased approach to policing. From my observation, this led to less community policing and more violence.

The Crack Era

Crime and violence have always permeated underserved impoverished Black communities. The lack of resources helps promote that "survive by any means necessary, dog eat dog" mindset. In 1984 the minimum wage was $3.35 an hour. The median income was $26,430. Working a minimum-wage full-time job at that time would have brought in $6,968 a year. And that's not counting the taxes being taken and the money spent to travel to and from work. You would basically be running on a hamster wheel exhausting yourself while getting nowhere. The realization of this type of poverty was a lot to bear, and many people self-medicated by using alcohol, marijuana, acid, angel dust, or just about anything cheap they could get their hands on to get high. Some of the street hustlers who stole, picked pockets, snatched gold chains, snatched pocketbooks, or committed armed robberies were able to buy the more expensive cocaine to get high. They were often glorified as they sniffed the white powder through a straw out of a rolled hundred-dollar bill. I was in high school at this time and had a part-time job working at McDonald's for minimum wage. I would bring home $67 a week and would practically be broke by the time I received my paycheck. This reality was the norm for many from communities like mine, and then this wonder drug called crack hit the scene, leading to the crack epidemic. Crack is cocaine that is heated up with baking soda and water to form a hard, rocky substance that can only be smoked. This drug flooded the streets of underserved communities, and within a flash many people were using or selling crack. I watched beautiful, promising women who were beacons of light in my neighborhood become crack-addicted, malnourished prostitutes. I saw law-abiding city workers become jobless thieves. I witnessed morally upstanding, churchgoing young men turn into violent crack dealers. The crack epidemic had widespread devastating impacts on Black communities around the United States (Fryer et al., 2013), and I witnessed it firsthand. I stopped going to school and became a full-time dealer myself. To survive as a good crack hustler, I had to obtain guns for protection. I built a crew to help sell my drugs and to protect my territory. I also started performing armed robberies on drug dealers. It wasn't only the greed that led me to do these armed robberies; I also wanted to intimidate others and to prevent other dealers from infringing on my territory. I became desensitized to the grief and struggles that crack had caused and was only interested in the profits.

The violent movie *Scarface*, starring Al Pacino, about a Cuban immigrant becoming an American cocaine drug lord by means of violence, became the idealized script for most of the profiteers. Gun violence skyrocketed throughout impoverished neighborhoods across the nation. Mass incarceration, fatherless homes, caskets, and despair followed (Evans et al., 2022). And despite the destruction and long prison sentences that were handed out to some of what America would call "the most violent drug dealers," they were often glorified by our society.

Prison/Rites of Passage

I couldn't imagine what a parent feels when they get a call from the police precinct saying, "Your child has been arrested for robbery. They are too young to go to a juvenile detention, so you must come and pick him up." My life of crime started when I entered sixth grade. I was eleven years old and enjoyed the attention the teenagers were getting for what we called "getting money." I'd gotten good at picking pockets and had become well-known locally with the teenagers in my neighborhood. When I turned twelve and a half, I went away to a juvenile detention center to serve eighteen months for robbery and truancy.

I was fourteen when I returned home and received a mini "hero's welcome." The girls wanted me to be their boyfriend because of my reputation, and the older teenagers and young adults treated me with a lot of respect. My eighteen months in detention became a badge of honor. Some of the older boys told me that juvenile detention was the first step and how I had to be prepared to survive in adult prison. Besides my mother and father there wasn't one person who warned me of the true pitfalls and detriments that came with living the way I was living. All I received was tips on how to navigate properly through prison when my number came up. Statistics said that around that time one in three Black men would go to jail or prison in their lifetime (Bonczar & Beck, 1997). The rate increased to as much as one in two in 2004, before declining to about one in six by 2016 (Roehrkasse & Wildeman, 2022). When I first entered prison in 1994 to serve two to four years on a gun possession charge, I already knew how to survive and thrive in that environment. I was released after three years, and I experienced the same welcome home that I received as a juvenile.

The statistics also say one person in three returns to prison within three years of being released, and as much as 68 percent are re-arrested following release from federal prison (Yukhnenko et al., 2020). On the third year of being free I found myself back in prison on a drug charge, and this time I served a little over four years. Once again, I was celebrated when I was released and glorified for my reputation. The so-called rites of passage and glorification of this destructive lifestyle helped gun violence and related violent crimes to permeate underserved Black communities.

A Credible Messenger

On my last journey to prison, I participated in a "Scared Straight" type of program at Fort Dix. Prison officials brought in youth heading down the wrong path who were already in juvenile correctional facilities. We spoke to them candidly about the poor decisions we made as adults and the detrimental impact it had on our lives. The youth were receptive and attentive because we were relatable and credible. When they looked at us and heard our stories, they were able to reflect on their own lives and see themselves in us. They appeared to trust what we said and take our word as gospel. At that moment I knew that when I was released I would continue to talk to youth at every chance.

I was released on June 15, 2004, and in October of that year I started filming a documentary on women street fighters from Brownsville, Brooklyn (one of the areas I grew up in), who fought in an underground fight club. That documentary, *Brooklyn Girl Fight Club*, helped launch my career in journalism and landed me a job at Black Entertainment Television as a broadcast journalist. It was there that I realized how important being a credible messenger was. I covered stories that reflected the social ills in underserved communities of color and was able to relate on a different level because of my past life experiences. I connected with the police when interviewing them about police brutality and helped some of them understand the mindset of the people who occupy the communities that they were serving. I connected with the politicians when talking about programs that can help with reentry and how to decrease recidivism. I was able to connect when talking to trauma unit specialists who operated on gunshot victims because of my experience of being shot five times. I was able to connect with mothers who lost their children to gun violence and sympathize with their pain because of what I experienced, especially during the crack era. I was able to connect with the teachers I interviewed about the peer pressure many youth face and the resources needed for them to reach their full potential, using my own past for reference.

Today I'm no longer at Black Entertainment Television. My wife and I started our own independent TV/film production company, JayCity Enterprise LLC. Our latest documentary, *killing beef: Gun Violence in the Black Community*, has won multiple awards including Best Documentary at the 2018 Newark International Film Festival. *killing beef* was also chosen by Rutgers University's Center for Gun Violence Research to be used as a teaching tool for students, community workshops, and faculty researchers. I often speak to youth in detention centers and alternative-to-incarceration programs about my experiences with gun violence to help encourage them to make better decisions. Sometimes I bring one of the guys who shot me to show youth what real reconciliation and redemption look like in person. Overall, I believe the impact that I have as a credible messenger is like being the cure to a disease, preventing it from spreading. I have coined and often deploy the phrase: "I used to be the virus, and now I'm the vaccine."

References

Bonczar, T.P., & Beck, A.J. (1997). *Lifetime Likelihood of Going to State or Federal Prison*. Bureau of Justice Statistics Bulletin, NCJ 160092. Washington DC: U.S. Department of Justice.

Evans, W. N., Garthwaite, C., & Moore, T. J. (2022). Guns and violence: The enduring impact of crack cocaine markets on young Black males. *Journal of Public Economics, 206*, 104581.

Fryer, R. G., Jr., Heaton, P. S., Levitt, S. D., & Murphy, K. M. (2013). Measuring crack cocaine and its impact. *Economic Inquiry, 51*, 1651–1681.

Raspberry, W. (1999, March 5). The elephants' tale. *Washington Post.* https://www.washingtonpost.com/archive/opinions/1999/03/05/the-elephants-tale/808019f9-5004-4426-96db-c9441134ca11/

Roehrkasse, A.F., & Wildeman, C. (2022). Lifetime risk of imprisonment in the United States remains high and starkly unequal. *Science Advances, 8,* eabo3395.

Yukhnenko, D., Sridhar, S., & Fazel, S. (2020). A systematic review of criminal recidivism rates worldwide: 3-year update. *Wellcome Open Research, 4,* 28.

Healed People Heal People

• • • • • • • • • • • • •

Stopping Violence the Paterson Healing Collective Way

LIZA CHOWDHURY

Overview

As a survivor of childhood trauma who grew up in a working-class community, I understood early on the impact of the posttraumatic stress that puts youth in survival mode. Living in a neighborhood contending with poverty as well as a lack of both adequate housing and education quickly prepares you to grow up earlier than you have to. Parents are too busy working and trying to meet the financial demands of families, and children are often trying to navigate the pressure of youth along with having fewer opportunities than their more affluent peers. Knowing this, I always wanted to work with youth and find ways to create opportunities to support a brighter future for the next generation of youth. In my first job as a juvenile probation officer, I met so many youth who were intelligent and full of life but had so many barriers both at home and outside the home. During my last two years as a probation officer, I remember feeling a great deal of grief because I was losing so many youth to gun violence. It was heartbreaking to hear about a young person I worked with for over a year lose their life at such a young age. After completing my PhD I knew I wanted to find ways to create resources that provided mental health, mentorship, and financial support to families and their children so we could address violence from a broader public health perspective. The youth I worked with didn't need cages—they needed healing. This belief led me to reach out to activists in the community who understood my own healing journey and shared my passion to stop violence, help youth, and create a better community in Paterson, New Jersey.

In 2020, the world shut down due to the COVID-19 pandemic. Our health systems were dealing with overwhelming pressure because of the crisis. At the same time, an epidemic was also rising. In 2020, cities around the United States saw an increase in gun violence. Paterson was no stranger to violence, but like in most cities, the pandemic and the rise in violence required several resources and intentional actions to help prevent further harm. In 2019, Reimagining Justice Inc. (RJ) and St. Joseph's University Medical hospital (St. Joe's) had already been in discussions to create a partnership to address the needs of victims of violence who came through the hospital emergency room (ER). The New Jersey Attorney General's office released an innovative request for proposal to create nine hospital-based violence intervention programs (HVIPs) to utilize community-based public safety tactics, victim services, and a public health approach to reduce retaliatory gun violence. The RJ/St. Joe's partnership submitted a proposal to create Passaic County's first HVIP to address the several victims of street violence who arrive at the ER for services throughout the year. The program was entitled the Paterson Healing Collective (PHC), and the team consisted of community activists, credible messengers, hospital staff, case managers, and mental health support and victim support specialists. Under my direction and the partnership of St. Joseph's ER and administrative staff, PHC utilized evidence-based best practices to design a community-based violence intervention program that can help address the needs of participants holistically. State funding for the program was announced in February 2020, immediately before the world shut down in March.

Despite the pressures, the PHC launched in October 2020. Since then, the program has been able to address the needs of 180 gunshot victims and reduce retaliatory violence. Services include mentoring, high-risk outreach, community walks, HVIP, survivor-of-violence support meetings, and a violence intervention roundtable. This chapter describes the efforts of the PHC and the lessons we have learned along the way.

New Jersey's Third Largest City (Paterson)

With nearly 150,000 residents, Paterson is New Jersey's third most populous city and has one of the lowest per-capita income levels in the state. Nearly 24 percent of residents live in poverty (almost three times the state average), including about 38 percent of children under eighteen (ADCNJ, 2022). The population primarily consists of people of color and racial/ethnic minorities: 63 percent are Hispanic or Latinx (of any race), and 24 percent are Black or African American (U.S. Census Bureau, 2023). Significant communities of Middle Eastern and Southeast Asian descent live in Paterson as well. Many Patersonians face structural and socioeconomic barriers such as lack of economic opportunity, limited safe and affordable housing, difficulties accessing transportation and health care, as well as food insecurity and linguistic isolation. According to a 2017 study, renters in Paterson spend approximately 44 percent of their income on rent, in comparison to the 30 percent typically recommended by the U.S. Department of Housing and Urban Development, among others (Belsky et al., 2005). In neighboring Passaic City, residents spend over 50 percent of their income on rent.

These sociodemographic factors have contributed to a public health crisis of violence in Paterson, which is deemed safer than only 14 percent of all U.S. cities, with a rate of violence four times higher than the New Jersey average: 9.43 violent crimes per 1,000 residents (compared to 2.03 for the whole state; www.neighborhoodscout.com). Gun-related violence is extremely prevalent in Paterson. Between the months of January and December 2021, the PHC recorded 136 shooting victims in Paterson treated by St. Joseph's University Medical Center. In 2021, the month of May saw the most shooting victims with 26, followed by March with 20 shooting victims and June with 18 shooting victims. These data underscored the great need for a community-based violence intervention program. Our program has been acknowledged by community members and community-based partners as an organization driving positive change. Most recently we were spotlighted in a New Jersey News 12 segment and on NorthJersey.com, which highlighted the lack of resources in Paterson and the work that PHC has been doing to alleviate the needs that communities most impacted by violence face.

Addressing Violence as a Public Health Problem

In Paterson, the city deals with an array of issues related to violence such as housing insecurity, unemployment, lack of culturally responsive mental health wellness options, food insecurity, systemic racism, and poverty. In order to support survivors of violence, the PHC utilizes case management and collaborations with community partners to help address client needs and mediate community-based conflict. The PHC has created an ecosystem for community-based public safety that responds to the cultural needs of communities of color. Historically, most victims of violence in Paterson are Black and Brown—and so our program is administered by residents from those communities.

The community-based violence intervention (CVI) and prevention strategies utilized by the PHC are evidence-based, community-driven approaches to addressing violence. There are several different models in the field of CVI strategies, with well-known examples such as Cure Violence and Advance Peace (Butts et al., 2015; Corburn et al., 2022). CVI strategies create a community-wide ecosystem of public safety in part by employing and training nontraditional leaders (credible messengers) who themselves might have been impacted by violence. Fuller and Goodman (2020) emphasized how lived experiences of community members help develop meaningful relationships with justice-involved youth. Research from the Credible Messenger Justice Center (2022) demonstrated that community-based models utilize comprehensive strategies to improve outcomes for justice-involved youth and adults by creating more support systems outside of probation and parole. Indeed, the credibility of these individuals in their neighborhoods and the wider community helps them develop relationships that they can then leverage to resolve conflicts utilizing mediation, refer residents to critical mental health or social service resources, and create critical connections among other community agents such as the police and the health care community.

Another promising community-based approach to violence is the HVIP model. HVIPs are multidisciplinary programs built on equitable partnerships between hospitals and community partners. The PHC, like other HVIPs, responds to gunshot victims at bedside in the ER's trauma bay. These opportunities allow community-based interventionists to directly provide victim services, medical advocacy, safety planning, and continued support in the community upon hospital release. HVIP offers trauma-informed care to patients injured by violence, many of whom are victims of color, all in the service of reducing risk of retaliation and reinjury (Bell et al., 2018). Chong and colleagues (2015) found that HVIPs are cost-effective for preventing future firearm-related injury.

These efforts all utilize relationship building, employing folks closest to the problem who can give us more accurate and authentic solutions, and investing in livable wages to help build infrastructure to create a strategy that is complementary to traditional law enforcement approaches addressing violence. Hiring credible messengers as well as culturally competent case managers and mental health staff, offering discretionary funds to address emergent needs such as relocation after a violent incident or to pay out a debt owed in a street-related conflict, and providing proper resources to support these programs, such as training, technical assistance, funding for overhead costs, research, and sustainable funding opportunities, are all elements needed for these programs to be successful.

The Movement to Expand CVI Work in New Jersey

It is important to emphasize that CVI has always existed in Black and Brown communities. Prior to government investment and buy-in to CVI, nontraditional leaders had always been involved with mediating violence. For example, the Hoe Avenue peace meeting in the Bronx in 1971 led to a peace treaty and truce among more than forty rival gangs and was inspired by a community organizer and forward-thinking gang leaders committed to ending community violence. Along similar lines, the Watts Truce in 1992 involved credible messengers organizing and using community relationships to arrange a peace treaty between the Bloods and Crips gangs of Los Angeles. In 2015, Paterson experienced a similar mediation led by the community. Yet without resources and funding these movements are difficult to sustain because they depend on volunteers and the labor of community members without political buy-in. In New Jersey, although there were several organizations operating in many cities working relentlessly to stop local violence, they lacked the support needed to help these programs grow. In 2014, Newark's mayor, Ras Baraka, utilized his political platform to incorporate his vision for supporting CVI efforts. The result was the Newark Community Street Team (NCST), under the leadership of the Aqeela Sherrills, a nationally recognized expert in the arena of CVI who had helped to facilitate the Watts Truce. NCST was New Jersey's first example of a CVI program backed and financially supported by local government. They were able to reduce violence in their focal areas and since then have been an integral part of the Newark public safety ecosystem (Leap et al., 2020; NCST, 2022).

The PHC developed much of its early framework from NCST and other established CVI programs around the country. Currently, the state of New Jersey supports CVI efforts as a result of the work of leaders around the state such as the NJ Violence Intervention and Prevention Coalition, which was created in 2021 to support statewide CVI efforts to advocate for more support and sustainability for grassroots organizations to get funding support for violence intervention efforts. In 2022, the Biden administration also confirmed their support for CVI efforts as a result of national organizations advocating for support around the country. Although law enforcement has traditionally been the response that is largely talked about with respect to reducing violent crime, the advocacy of grassroots minority-led organizations has pushed CVI work into the national discourse around effective solutions.

Survivor-Centered Work

The PHC has built multiple relationships across communities impacted by violence. When the program first launched, it was very important for us to be present and felt in the community. The first community outreach was done at nine o'clock in the evening in the city's first ward—a sector of the city that had recently experienced several incidents of violence. The program reached out to community leaders in the area to let them know that the group wanted to come by to talk to youth. The PHC team asked about twenty young men in the area how many were victims of violence—thirteen raised their hands. This showed the team the dire need for services to support this community. Since then, PHC has utilized the voices of credible messengers on the team who were also victims of violence to share their stories with community members so they could relate. The team also consistently followed up in communities after someone passed or if there were acts of gun violence to offer victim services and show the community care. This consistency and outreach helped to foster community buy-in.

Arriving at the bedside of a survivor after a shooting is a key moment for PHC to stop retaliations. Due to the vulnerability of victims of violence, this moment is a teachable moment that PHC staff uses to help deescalate the situation and create a conversation around what support the survivor needs once they are released. The team also provides medical advocacy, helps with follow-up medical care, and supports with relocation and other victim services. Benefits are available for victims through New Jersey's Victims of Crime Compensation Office (VCCO), but many times they are accessed through the prosecutor's office. Due to the lack of trust with institutions due to systemic harm, Black, Brown, and immigrant communities do not always access these services. PHC has been able to increase access to VCCO benefits for the community because of our relationships and perceived legitimacy. Black and Brown victims of violence are sometimes seen as perpetrators and not given the same level of empathy as are their white counterparts, and this makes the experience of accessing health care follow-up or victim services unpleasant. PHC found that being the intermediary agency to help victims navigate and access services allows the community to feel seen and supported.

Since PHC launched, we have helped victims of violence reduce their inclination to retaliate because the program was able to provide mediation with the opposite side, help the victim with relocation, advocate for resources, and provide mental health and mentoring services to support the client so they make decisions that can help them deviate away from their thoughts about revenge. We also were able to employ five survivors of violence from different parts of the community that had conflict. This was not an easy process because all of the men did not feel comfortable being around others who might have harmed their neighborhood. However, we were able to provide support through healing circles, training, and mentorship so that the survivors could connect with the mission of the program and its efforts to reduce violence.

One key strength of PHC is that it not only helps survivors but also utilizes the voices of survivors to change the narrative around street violence. There have been several efforts to publicize the importance of understanding the impact of trauma, grief, and poverty to reeducate the community around the popularized belief that street violence is due to "bad people." Since PHC launched, we have led a massive campaign to promote healing and humanize the impact of violence. Since 2020, the community has supported our efforts to raise awareness around gun violence and change the narratives regarding people and places that are dehumanized by calling them "gang members" or "hot spots."

Since the hiring of young survivors of the program to conduct outreach, the program has been able to conduct mediations, engage youth from different neighborhoods in the conversations around peace, and engage hard-to-reach youth into healing-centered services. Most recently, we graduated twenty young men and women from different parts of the community that were in conflict; all twenty had lost friends or family members to violence or had been shot themselves. The group received programming aimed at improving mental health and workforce readiness, and participants were engaged in discussions centered around how to make Paterson safer. However, we will need consistent follow-ups and opportunities for economic support to sustain efforts at maintaining peace.

What Is Needed for the Paterson Healing Collective to Thrive?

One of the most difficult aspects of running a grassroots organization to address violence effectively is economic sustainability. PHC relies on the good will of politicians to allocate funding through grants. These are competitive grants that are open to the public, and there is no guarantee that our program will receive the funding. Further, there is a notable lack of funding specifically to support administrative staff with development, grant writing, and research. In grassroots organizations like PHC, staff members work out in the community intervening in violence but are also responsible for supporting activities with grant writing and drafting budget reports. Staff thus wear multiple hats and have a fluctuating workload. In addition to this, staff deal with a great deal of vicarious trauma, and there is often a great need for their own therapeutic support. Staff are from the community or still reside in the community, so they also are still exposed to violence or are directly impacted by the victimization of community members. Therefore, there is a need for investment in wraparound services for support staff so that they can avoid burnout. Funding also should be expanded to allow for discretionary costs such as relocation or food insecurity

130 • Liza Chowdhury

to support clients as well as more investment in staff salaries and fringe benefits to avoid high turnover. Safe spaces for programming and housing opportunities for clients are also needed. Finally, funding needs to be allocated to help build the capacity of organizations like PHC to hire staff who can help manage budgets, conduct research, raise funds, and write grants. Ideally, CVI would be part of yearly municipal budgets like any other first responder service.

Conclusion

In conclusion, CVI efforts like the PHC need to exist in the popular discourse around how to end violence. Incarceration and overpolicing can help the issue temporarily, and the United States invests a great deal in the carceral and policing infrastructure in communities impacted by violence. However, the same areas that have a high rate of incarceration and large policing efforts continue to suffer from violence. Using a public health, restorative, and community approach allows stakeholders to examine the root causes of local violence. For programs like ours to continue to help, they need to be supported. We have been successful in directly engaging over 180 victims of gun violence and thousands of community members through outreach activities because the program has been consistent in emphasizing the importance of *healing*. The program shows that perhaps the only way to eradicate violence is by making the community whole again by investing in its people and supporting their healing journey. We in the PHC have shown that hurt people might hurt people, but healed people can also heal people. It is time to sustain healing!

References

Advocates for Children of New Jersey. (2022). *Paterson Kids Count 2022: A city profile of child well-being.* Newark, NJ: Advocates for Children of New Jersey.

Bell, T. M., Gilyan, D., Moore, B. A., Martin, J., Ogbemudia, B., McLaughlin, B. E., Moore, R., Simons, C. J., & Zarzaur, B. L. (2018). Long-term evaluation of a hospital-based violence intervention program using a regional health information exchange. *Journal of Trauma and Acute Care Surgery, 84,* 175–182.

Belsky, E. S., Goodman, J., & Drew, R. (2005). *Measuring the nation's rental housing affordability problems.* Joint Center for Housing Studies, Harvard University.

Butts, J. A., Roman, C. G., Bostwick, L., & Porter, J. R. (2015). Cure violence: A public health model to reduce gun violence. *Annual Review of Public Health, 36,* 39–53.

Chong, V. E., Smith, R., Garcia, A., Lee, W. S., Ashley, L., Marks, A., Liu, T. H., & Victorino, G. P. (2015). Hospital-centered violence intervention programs: A cost-effectiveness analysis. *American Journal of Surgery, 209,* 597–603.

Corburn, J., Boggan, D., Muttaqi, K., Vaughn, S., Houston, J., Thibodeaux, J., & Muhammad, B. (2022). Advancing urban peace: Preventing gun violence and healing traumatized youth. *Youth Justice, 22,* 272–289.

Credible Messenger Justice Center. (2022). *A gathering movement: Credible Messenger mentoring across the US*. Credible Messenger Justice Center.

Fuller, C., & Goodman, H. (2020). The answer is in the community: Credible messengers and justice system involved youth. *Social Work with Groups, 43*, 70–74.

Leap, J., Lompa, K., Thantu, M., & Gouche, W. (2020). *Newark Community Street Team Narrative Evaluation*. Los Angeles: UCLA Social Justice Research Partnership.

Neighborhood Scout (2023). *Neighborhood Scout Security Gauge*. Accessed May 18, 2024: https://www.neighborhoodscout.com/nj/paterson/crime.

Newark Community Street Team. (2022). *Impact Report June 2021-July 2022*. Newark, NJ: Newark Community Street Team.

U.S. Census Bureau. (2023). *QuickFacts Paterson City, New Jersey*. Washington, DC: U.S. Census Bureau.

Empowering Youth to Become Coproducers of Public Safety

● ● ● ● ● ● ● ● ● ● ● ● ●

Implementation of Data-Informed Community Engagement in Newark, NJ

ALEJANDRO GIMENEZ-SANTANA
AND JOEL M. CAPLAN

Overview

Across the country, policing has come under intense scrutiny following the killing of George Floyd during his arrest on May 25, 2020. The events that followed ignited protests and calls for extensive police reforms across the United States and around the globe. Demands included ending and correcting systemic racism and more substantial and equitable investments in communities that will reduce crime while strengthening communities. Police often agree that it is not their job to address some of the underlying social conditions that give rise to expressions of criminal behavior (Gimenez-Santana et al., 2022). As noted by Meares (2017, p. 1365), "It is unfair to expect the police to solve what is fundamentally a social safety net problem with the crude tools of crime fighting simply because they are available twenty-four hours a day." Meanwhile, community activists have long demanded an expansion of civic engagement programs that involve the public in programs enhancing community safety and wellness (see Skogan, 2006). This is now happening in Newark, New Jersey, a city with a long history of challenges in the arena of public safety and race relations.

Newark has a history of repeated calls for police reform. Among the most indelible in recent memory is the "long, hot summer" of 1967, when two police officers detained and brutally beat John Smith while bystanders and community members looked on in horror at the unfolding scene. The riots that followed caused about $10 million in damages and reduced entire blocks of Newark's Central Ward to charred ruins, some of which remain vacant grass-covered lots (Rojas & Atkinson, 2017). The scars of this civil rights conflict had long-lasting consequences for a city that descended into decades of intergenerational poverty, social and structural decay, and crime. Today, Newark is racially segregated. According to the integration-segregation index, which measures the relationship between citywide and neighborhood diversity, Newark is more segregated than Detroit, Los Angeles, and Pittsburgh (Silver, 2015).

In May 2011, the U.S. Department of Justice (DOJ) began a preliminary inquiry after receiving serious allegations of civil rights violations by the Newark Police Division (NPD), including excessive use of force, unwarranted stops, and discriminatory police actions (Chillar, 2022). Following an initial investigation, a May 2014 DOJ findings report alleged the NPD had been engaged in unlawful policing practices, particularly against Newark's Black population. According to this report, Blacks accounted for 54 percent of the residents in 2010 but were associated with 85 percent of all pedestrian stops and 79 percent of arrests during that year (U.S. DOJ, 2014). The NPD entered a consent decree with the DOJ in 2016 and has since implemented new policies and practices regarding stops, searches, arrests, training, and disciplinary procedures for all officers (Chillar, 2022).

Newark has set foot in a new era in which community groups and police are working together toward an "ecosystem of multistakeholder collaboration" (see Rengifo & Avila, 2022). This coproduction model of data-informed community engagement (DICE) is coordinated by the Newark Public Safety Collaborative (NPSC) and other local organizations. The NPSC facilitates active engagements by a myriad of city agencies and community organizations, each focusing on specific tasks that align with their unique missions, like homelessness, mental health, and youth programs, and their overlap with pressing public safety issues. This chapter discusses a crime reduction program launched by the NPSC in 2020 that has quickly gained national prominence (see Barrett & McWhirter, 2023; National Institute of Justice, 2023; Newark Opportunity Youth Network [NOYN], 2021) and can now serve as a new model or framework for community collaboration around youth violence prevention. This program also engaged "opportunity youth," young people sixteen to twenty-one years old who attended Newark's LEAD Charter School, to add actionable insights to NPSC's data-informed effort.

The Newark Public Safety Collaborative

NPSC offers an alternative to traditional community policing models, which rely on police-centric responses to crime problems. NPSC demonstrates the coproduction of public safety by multiple community stakeholders as a solution to crime problems. Most community policing efforts of the past share a common characteristic: the leading role of police agencies having control over both the message and the data that inform public safety priorities. These priorities, however, do not necessarily align with community expectations. The novelty brought by the NPSC is the coproduction of public safety by multiple community organizations, local government, and police working together toward a mutually agreed "production" of community safety. The result is DICE, an innovative public safety model with data and analytics at the core of a collaborative effort in which organizations with diverse priorities and objectives can achieve results that would not be attainable had these organizations acted alone.

Established in 2018, the NPSC was formed to foster community participation in public safety. To date, NPSC has brought together over forty different local stakeholders, including community-based organizations, government agencies, law enforcement, businesses and corporations, and developers. It is a diverse group of local stakeholders with varying experiences, expertise, and capacities, thereby enabling multiple simultaneous responses to different crime problems. In this context, groups that advocate for community-based public safety programs like the NCST and the Newark Anti-Violence Coalition work collaboratively alongside local corporations like Prudential Financial, RBH group, and New Jersey's local utility company, PSE&G. These responses are ignited by access to data and analytics, but the solutions are driven by individual efforts among all partner organizations who share the common objective of improving public safety in Newark.

The NPSC applies the DICE model to diagnose crime problems and develop place-based strategies to disrupt risk narratives in a coordinated manner. DICE builds on past successes of problem-oriented policing (Clarke, 2002; Goldstein, 1990) and risk-based policing (Kennedy et al., 2018) and incorporates elements of civic engagement to mobilize local resources where they are needed most. Risk Terrain Modeling (RTM; Caplan et al., 2012; Caplan et al., 2015; Caplan & Kennedy, 2016) analysis is used to diagnose the underlying conditions that give rise to crime patterns. RTM is grounded in research evidence and is based on the premise that criminal behavior is influenced by the physical environment's effects on human behaviors. Technically, RTM identifies the risks that come from features of a landscape and models how these colocate to create unique behavior settings for crime (Caplan et al., 2012). Practically, RTM analysis offers the advantage of identifying not only *where* crime is concentrated but also *why* these incidents are more prone to occur in some places. This is critical for problem solving and related activities because it provides key insights from multiple perspectives that unlock risk narratives explaining why crimes cluster in some places and not others. The observations generated by the RTM analysis set the table for a multistakeholder discussion on programs and activities that actively engage community participants in ways to reduce and prevent violence and crime.

Democratizing data and analytics is a key element of the DICE model. In the past, access to data and other public safety information was traditionally reserved for the police and some academic circles. By making data and analytics (and related technologies) more transparent and accessible, community stakeholders are empowered to engage in public safety programming because empirical evidence justifies their needs and helps to coordinate their efforts.

Data-Informed Community Engagement

NPSC's DICE approach to public safety opens the door to non-police-centric responses to crime problems that put the focus of crime prevention on places and not merely people. Through DICE, local community stakeholders collaboratively engage in problem-solving activities that yield realistic programs and strategies directed at improving and sustaining public safety by making spaces safer. As noted in a report by Cities United (2020), "It is important to identify community-involved solutions and strategies that can interrupt the cycle of violence and dismantle systems of inequity." Using a participatory-action research approach, DICE ensures that community organizations receive equal access to data and analytics, thereby empowering them to maximize their own resources and become coproducers of community safety. The result is a sustainable multistakeholder strategy, informed by data and analytics, capable of responding to the most pressing crime problems. Key aspects of the strategic framework of the NPSC have been the sustainability of the group's efforts, the consistency in delivering analytics and insights, and the complementarity of proposed actions to community organizations' ongoing missions and activities.

The NPSC has coordinated multiple DICE crime prevention efforts over the past four years (see https://newarkcollaborative.org/projects). These campaigns have focused on mitigating the risk of robberies near ATMs, improving lighting conditions in high-risk areas, and engaging domestic violence service providers in a collective effort to improve service delivery. These and other efforts have yielded positive results in reducing crime as a result of increased participation and collaboration of community agencies, youth programs, businesses, and local government representatives (Gimenez-Santana et al., 2022). With DICE, NPSC has positioned itself as a critical player in Newark's efforts to reimagine public safety (see NOYN, 2021). And the NPSC is spearheading new ways to involve young residents in the process.

Empowering Youth to Become Coproducers of Public Safety

Newark experienced a steady increase in the number of motor vehicle thefts (MVTs). Nearly half of all MVTs were associated with individuals leaving their cars running unattended. The NPD has repeatedly warned the public about the risks associated with leaving cars idling unattended. NPSC facilitated a DICE campaign to reduce MVTs in Newark.

NPSC data analysts used RTM to diagnose the location patterns for MVT due to car idling (see Figure 12.1). All crime data for auto theft incidents were obtained directly from the NPD. Then, fifty features of the city landscape were reviewed for accuracy before being utilized as potential "risk factor" inputs for RTM analysis. Past research has found the following place features to be spatially associated with an increased risk for auto theft: abandoned buildings (Xu & Griffiths, 2017), parks (Groff & McCord, 2012), schools (Roncek & Faggiani, 1985), parking lots (Suresh & Tewksbury, 2013), gas stations (Bernasco & Block, 2011), ATMs (Holt & Spencer, 2005), clubs and bars (Sypion-Dutkowska & Leitner, 2017), public housing (Griffiths & Tita, 2009), liquor stores (Gorman et al., 2001), retail stores (McCord et al., 2007), sports facilities (Eck et al., 2007), vacant lots (Kinney et al., 2008), hotels (Sypion-Dutkowska & Leitner, 2017), and train and light rail stations (Cozens et al., 2004). These and other physical and structural elements of the Newark landscape were analyzed.

The following physical and structural elements of the Newark landscape were found to influence settings that have an increased likelihood of MVT incidents: bodegas, restaurants, abandoned buildings, and vacant lots. This information and its accompanying analytical outputs (maps and tables) were then shared at NPSC's community stakeholders meeting to develop a coordinated

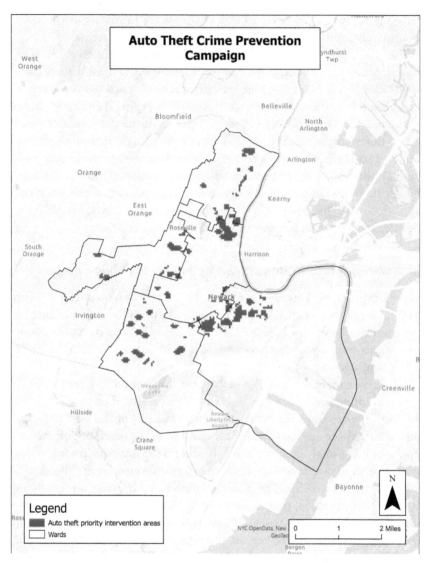

FIGURE 12.1 Newark Public Safety Collaborative (NPSC) auto theft crime prevention campaign in the city of Newark, NJ. Map produced by NPSC analysts with data provided by the Newark Police Division.

response to Newark's ongoing auto theft problem. During the meeting, several people validated the situational context for crime presented by drivers leaving their cars running to keep their vehicles warm when grabbing something quickly at a nearby store. A data-informed risk narrative was formed that connected with local perceptions and lived experiences. Drivers may attempt quick errands to bodegas for coffee or food on their way to or from work, and delivery drivers leave their cars running to pick up food orders from restaurants. At nearby abandoned buildings and vacant lots, motivated offenders search for potential victims with unattended idling cars. There was consensus among NPSC partners that increasing awareness of the various risks associated with car idling at particular businesses in the highest-risk areas could be an effective strategy to significantly reduce this MVT.

The proposed intervention was an educational campaign and poster competition that engaged schools and other community organizations to increase awareness of the risks associated with leaving cars unattended. Residents had a vested interest in the prevention programming and outcome. The winning poster by a six-year-old student was incorporated into a flyer and shared by NPSC's partner organizations at specific locations at increased risk for auto theft victimization (Gimenez-Santana et al., 2022). Between 2020 and 2021, over ten community organizations actively participated in this DICE campaign by distributing flyers at designated high-risk locations for auto theft. The result was a 40 percent decrease in the number of auto thefts in all target areas.

Data and analytics that informed the MVT educational campaign were subsequently shared at a meeting with Newark youth attending NOYN's LEAD Charter School in Newark's West Ward. NPSC staff discussed the current DICE strategy of disseminating flyers in designated areas to increase awareness of the risks of leaving cars running unattended. The response from the students was critical to the evolution of this intervention strategy, which they considered as suboptimal modes of communicating with the city's younger population. In their opinion, young people regularly discard flyers because they are perceived as a marketing instrument. Instead, LEAD students proposed a digital campaign using social media platforms like TikTok, Instagram, and YouTube as a more effective communication strategy to increase awareness and encourage youth to participate in local public safety programming. As a result, a participating LEAD instructor proposed a competition led by students who will work in groups to develop a social media campaign to increase awareness of the risk of leaving cars running unattended. It will be geared to updated risk narratives strengthened by the addition of youth perspectives and their lived experiences. In collaboration with NOYN, the NPSC will incorporate the winning social media video in its MVT prevention campaign throughout the city.

Conclusion

Historically, collaborations between the police and the community have relied on police-centric responses to crime problems that limited community groups' abilities to participate directly in these efforts in any coordinated way (Gimenez-Santana et al., 2022). Creating a sustainable working relationship between community residents of all ages and the police requires a problem-solving process that empowers all participants with data and actionable analytics. Successful collaborations, such as the MVT campaign, are achieved when problem-oriented conversations are data-informed and locally driven.

Prior to the NPSC, Newark community organizations and residents lacked direct and comprehensive access to neighborhood-specific data and analytics to identify priorities informing their programs and activities. Police had a monopoly on data, analysts, and related technologies and human resources. Additionally, there were no mechanisms for police to share the burden of crime prevention in structured and repeatable ways, so crime problems often received primarily law enforcement responses. As noted by a Newark community leader, "NPSC has opened the door to unprecedented access to the information that we need to justify the need for more programs and investment in our community." Community demands for more transparency, inclusion, and negotiation power in decision-making processes require including affected voices to be part of a broader conversation on public safety (Fainstein, 2014).

Amid widespread calls to reimagine public safety, Newark has positioned itself as a leader at the center of a growing movement that calls for more social justice, more equitable distributions of resources, and better policing (NJ Urban Mayor's Press, 2022). DICE via the NPSC offers a model of reform that prevents crime, strengthens communities, and makes police-community relations resolute and resilient. By democratizing access to data and analytics, community groups fully engage in problem-solving activities in effective and sustainable ways. Collectively, local stakeholders coordinate and maximize existing resources and expertise. The result is better public safety.

References

Barrett, J., & McWhirter, C. (2023, February 2). Tyre Nichols case prompts questions about police tactics in crime hot spots. Cities such as Newark and Dallas are trying new ways to involve communities. *Wall Street Journal*. https://www.wsj.com/articles/tyre-nichols-case-prompts-questions-about-police-tactics-in-crime-hot-spots-11675311579?mod=business_minor_pos4

Bernasco, W., & Block, R. (2011). Robberies in Chicago: A block-level analysis of the influence of crime generators, crime attractors, and offender anchor points. *Journal of Research in Crime and Delinquency, 48*(1), 33–57.

Caplan, J. M., & Kennedy, L. W. (2016). *Risk Terrain Modeling: Crime prediction and risk reduction*. University of California Press.

Caplan, J. M., Kennedy, L. W., Barnum, J. D., & Piza, E. L. (2015). Risk Terrain Modeling for spatial risk assessment. *Cityscape, 17*(1), 7–16.

Caplan, J. M., Kennedy, L. W., & Piza, E. L. (2012). Joint utility of event-dependent and environmental crime analysis techniques for violent crime forecasting. *Crime Delinquency, 59*, 243–270. https://doi.org/10.1177/0011128712461901

Chillar, V. F. (2022). The racial divide at micro places: A pre/post analysis of the effects of the Newark consent decree on field inquiries (2015–2017). *Journal of Research in Crime and Delinquency, 59*(2), 240–276.

Cities United. (2020). *Reimagining public safety: Moving to safe, healthy & hopeful communities.* https://cdn.citiesunited.org/files/Cities%20United%20Reimagining%20Public%20Safety_Call%20To%20Action%20(2)843bfcb2-c665-4657-ae9c-af4099331b4a.pdf

Clarke, R. V. (2002). *Problem-oriented policing and the potential contribution of criminology.* U.S. Department of Justice, National Institute of Justice.

Cozens, P., Neale, R., Hillier, D., & Whitaker, J. (2004). Tackling crime and fear of crime while waiting at Britain's railway stations. *Journal of Public Transportation, 7,* 23-41.

Crawford, A. (2017). Research co-production and knowledge mobilisation in policing. In J. Knutsson & L. Tompson (Eds.), *Advances in evidence-based policing* (pp. 195–213). Routledge.

Eck, J. E., Clarke, R. V., & Guerrette, R. T. (2007). Risky facilities: Crime concentration in homogenous sets of establishments and facilities. *Crime Prevention Studies, 21,* 225–264.

Fainstein, S. S. (2014). The just city. *International Journal of Urban Sciences, 18*(1), 1–18.

Gimenez-Santana, A., Caplan, J. M., & Kennedy, L. W. (2022). Data-informed community engagement: The Newark public safety collaborative. In E. L. Piza & B. C. Welsh (Eds.), *The globalization of evidence-based policing: Innovations in bridging the research-practice divide* (pp. 191–205). Routledge.

Goldstein, H. (1990). *Problem-oriented policing.* McGraw-Hill.

Gorman, D. M., Speer, P. W., Gruenewald, P. J., & Labouvie, E. W. (2001). Spatial dynamics of alcohol availability, neighborhood structure and violent crime. *Journal of Studies on Alcohol, 62*(5), 628–636.

Griffiths, E., & Tita, G. (2009). Homicide in and around public housing: Is public housing a hotbed, a magnet, or a generator of violence for the surrounding community? *Social Problems, 56*(3), 474–493.

Groff, E., & McCord, E. S. (2012). The role of neighborhood parks as crime generators. *Security Journal, 25*(1), 1–24.

Holt, T., & Spencer, J. (2005). A Little Yellow Box: The Targeting of Automatic Teller Machines as a Strategy in Reducing Street Robbery. Crime Prevention and Community *Safety, 7,* 15–28.

Kennedy, L. W., Caplan, J., & Piza, E. (2015). *Conjunctive analysis report: 2012 motor vehicle theft in Colorado Springs.* https://www.rutgerscps.org/uploads/2/7/3/7/27370595/cspd_conjanalysis.pdf

Kennedy, L. W., Caplan, J. M., & Piza, E. L. (2018). *Risk-based policing: Evidence-based crime prevention with big data and spatial analytics.* University of California Press.

Kennedy, L. W., & Van Brunschot, E. G. (2009). *The risk in crime.* Rowman & Littlefield.

Kinney, J. B., Brantingham, P. L., Wuschke, K., Kirk, M. G., & Brantingham, P. J. (2008). Crime attractors, generators, and detractors: Land use and urban crime opportunities. *Built Environment, 34*(1), 62–74.

McCord, E. S., Ratcliffe, J. H., Garcia, R. M., & Taylor, R. B. (2007). Nonresidential Crime Attractors and Generators Elevate Perceived Neighborhood Crime and Incivilities. *Journal of Research in Crime and Delinquency, 44*(3), 295–320.

Meares, T. L. (2017). The path forward: Improving the dynamics of community-police relationships to achieve effective law enforcement policies. *Columbia Law Review, 117*(5), 1355–1368.

National Institute of Justice. (2023). *Risk Terrain Modeling: Term of the month, January 2023.* https://nij.ojp.gov/term-month#9spp8g

Newark Opportunity Youth Network. (2021). *Reimagining public safety in Newark.* https://static1.squarespace.com/static/5f31746071617a7025df2436/t/61a910eaa0702149631f46a4/1638469868452/Newark_digital_version_final+%282%29.pdf

NJ Urban Mayor's Press. (2022). *Urban Mayors Policy Center.* https://digitalcommons.kean.edu/cgi/viewcontent.cgi?article=1001&context=urban-mayors

Piza, E. L., & Carter, J. G. (2018). Predicting initiator and near repeat events in spatiotemporal crime patterns: An analysis of residential burglary and motor vehicle theft. *Justice Quarterly, 35*(5), 842–870.

Rengifo, A., & Avila, L. (2022). *The future of public safety: Exploring the power & possibility of Newark's reimagined public safety ecosystem.* EJUSA.

Rojas, R., & Atkinson, K. (2017, July 11). Five days of unrest that shaped, and haunted, Newark. *New York Times.*

Roncek, D. W., & Faggiani, D. (1985). High schools and crime: A replication. *Sociological Quarterly, 26*(4), 491–505.

Silver, N. (2015, May 1). The most diverse cities are often the most segregated. *FiveThirtyEight.*

Skogan, W. G. (2006). *Police and community in Chicago: A tale of three cities.* Oxford University Press.

Suresh, G., & Tewksbury, R. (2013). Locations of motor vehicle theft and recovery. *American Journal of Criminal Justice, 38*(2), 200–215.

Sypion-Dutkowska, N., & Leitner, M. (2017). Land use influencing the spatial distribution of urban crime: A case study of Szczecin, Poland. *ISPRS International Journal of Geo-Information, 6*(3), 74.

U.S. Department of Justice. (2014). *Newark Police Department investigation and agreement principal fact sheet.* https://www.justice.gov/sites/default/files/crt/legacy/2014/07/22/newark_findings_7-22-14.pdf

Xu, J., & Griffiths, E. (2018). Shooting on the street: Measuring the spatial influence of physical features on gun violence in a bounded street network. *Journal of Quantitative Criminology, 33,* 237–253.

13

Place-Based Prevention for Youth Gun Violence

● ● ● ● ● ● ● ● ● ● ● ● ●

Analytics and Application

JONATHAN JAY

Overview

I stood on a street corner in Toledo, Ohio, on an unseasonably mild morning in November 2022. I was facing a vacant lot. Like many U.S. cities, especially across the Rust Belt, Toledo has lost population since its manufacturing heyday. With less demand for housing, buildings that fall into disrepair are eventually demolished, leaving behind a patchwork of empty spaces. Vacant lots often become overgrown with weeds, attracting discarded food wrappers, cigarette packages, and other trash. Researchers have found that neighbors' pulses quicken when they pass these unkempt spaces (South et al., 2015). This sort of physical disorder makes residents feel unsafe and conveys that their neighborhoods—and, by extension, the residents themselves—don't matter (Teixeira, 2015).

But this vacant lot in Toledo was atypical. It was a smooth, uninterrupted expanse of green, from the sidewalk to the ends of the property. Its edges, where the grass met the sidewalk, were so exactingly trimmed as to create a perfectly straight separation between lawn and pavement. The turf maintenance didn't remind me of well-tended suburban lawns; it brought to mind Fenway Park.

This lot marked one boundary of a six-block area receiving investments from a local coalition and its partners. The historically Black neighborhood of Junction is one of Toledo's oldest; it contained a thriving business district until the 1960s, before "urban renewal" infrastructure projects cut the neighborhood off from downtown and turned its commercial hub into a traffic artery. Since then, much of Junction has struggled. In addition to abandoned properties, Junction is one of the neighborhoods in Toledo most impacted by gun violence, a problem that has roughly doubled in the city over the past five years.

The coalition hoped that restoring housing over these six blocks would help revitalize Junction. I toured the site with Shantaé Brownlee, a senior official at the Lucas County Land Bank, a coalition partner that obtains the rights to abandoned properties and finds ways to put them back into use. If successful, Ms. Brownlee explained, refreshing this six-block area would expand a stretch of safe and stable housing that already existed in Junction, including the section where she happened to live. She envisioned capping the project with a sign that would proudly announce, "Welcome to Junction." From there, the pilot would be replicated elsewhere in the city. From what I could see, these efforts were paying off. Could neighborhood investments like this one help curb the city's gun violence epidemic?

Seeking New Solutions on Youth Firearm Violence

Interpersonal gun violence is a public health crisis, particularly for youth. Across the United States, gunshot wounds are now the leading cause of death for children and teens (Lee et al., 2022). Homicides constitute most of those deaths. Firearm homicides have risen across all ages since 2004 (Rees et al., 2022), but the COVID-19 pandemic triggered an unprecedented spike that has disproportionately affected youth (Iantorno et al., 2022). This spike has further exacerbated the vast racial and ethnic disparities that concentrate firearm victimization and violence exposure among Black and Latinx youth (Martin et al., 2022; Pino et al., 2022).

Youth who use violence against others typically display a variety of risk factors, including substance use, carrying weapons, and previous exposure to violence as a victim or witness (Carter et al., 2017). The core of violence prevention work involves offering services, such as counseling and job training, to individuals who display those risk factors. There is also a need, however, for large-scale strategies that can prevent youth from reaching high-risk status in the first place. Place-based interventions are a critical component.

Physical Spaces and Youth Safety

Young people are highly cognizant of the condition of neighborhood spaces. They commonly express concerns about physical safety around abandoned buildings and other deteriorated properties, explaining that these spaces impair health because they are used for selling and consuming drugs, sexual violence, and other interpersonal violence (Mmari et al., 2014; Teixeira, 2015). Concerns about physical safety meaningfully constrain young people's activities: youth alter their routes to avoid exposure to drug markets and other social disorder (Culyba et al., 2021) and try to travel in groups with friends (Teitelman, 2006), but they often simply stay home. Children display worse school attendance when their routes to school require walking through violent areas (Burdick-Will et al., 2019).

Unsafe physical conditions also increase young people's risk of victimization. In an innovative study, researchers in Philadelphia identified the time and place where youth homicide victims (ages thirteen to twenty) were killed, then matched each victim with another young person from Philadelphia who was not victimized and served as a control (Culyba et al., 2016). Under this case-control design, differences in the physical environment at the homicide location, compared to the location of the control individual at the time of the homicide, can be considered risk or protective factors. The researchers found that homicides were more likely in areas that lacked signs of investment and maintenance, such as parks, public transit, and well-kept vacant lots.

Finally, physical deterioration conveys to youth the value (or lack thereof) that society assigns to their community's public spaces. Boarded-up houses make youth think that "no one cares" (Teixeira, 2015). Compared to some other social inequities, the condition of public spaces is highly visible. In my own work in Boston, youth have regularly cited the built environment as a primary dimension along which their communities are denied access to resources—while passing through wealthier neighborhoods, they can readily see the differences in resources like lawns, tree cover, and park space.

Young people can also tell that these inequities are linked with race. U.S. cities are racially segregated by design, carrying the imprint of policies and practices such as redlining, block busting, urban renewal, and gentrification. Williams and Collins (2001) called segregation a "fundamental cause" of racial disparities because it enables the concentration of health- and safety-promoting resources, such as well-maintained physical infrastructure, in the places where white residents can access them, while public and private entities disinvest from the places where residents of color live (Williams & Collins, 2001).

Place and Prevention

The link between built environment and youth safety creates a unique opportunity for violence interventions. One landmark study was a cluster randomized trial in Philadelphia, where researchers sampled 541 vacant lots and randomly assigned some to receive a "clean and green" intervention (Branas et al., 2018). Cleaning and greening involved removing trash and weeds, then installing grass, a few trees, and a simple wooden fence. In other words, dangerous eyesores became simple green spaces. After eighteen months, the researchers found that gun assaults had declined by 12 percent at the intervention lots and by 29 percent at the intervention lots in neighborhoods with high poverty. The research team, which included embedded ethnographers, found no evidence that violence had moved elsewhere. Another study, from Flint, Michigan, had similar findings (Heinze et al., 2018).

These studies have spurred growing interest in place-based violence interventions. I have examined large-scale programs to demolish abandoned buildings in Rochester, New York (Jay, de Jong, et al., 2022), and Detroit, Michigan (Jay et al., 2019). Each study found reductions in gun violence in the area immediately surrounding a demolition (in Rochester) and in neighborhoods receiving at least a handful of demolitions (in Detroit). While demolitions can remove a hazardous building entirely, it is preferable to avoid property abandonment and deterioration before they reach that point. South and colleagues found that a grant program, providing low-income homeowners funds to repair the condition of their homes, was associated with a 26 percent reduction in homicides on blocks that received the funds, compared to others that were eligible but not selected for funding (South et al., 2021).

Why do these interventions work? A leading explanation is that when neighborhood spaces feel safer, they actually become safer. In Flint, researchers found that poorly maintained parcels increased residents' fear of crime, which in turn caused greater mental distress (Burt et al., 2022). Similarly, the Philadelphia greening experiment found that residents living near intervention lots felt safer in their neighborhoods (Branas et al., 2018) and that the intervention reduced depression among nearby residents (South et al., 2018), This finding is consistent with "busy streets theory," which holds that improving public spaces encourages community members to use those spaces, fostering positive social engagement and thereby deterring violence (Aiyer et al., 2015). Risky behaviors might also be discouraged by visual signals that a space is cared for (Keizer et al., 2008).

These physical improvements may also counteract the patterns of disinvestment that have concentrated unsafe environmental conditions in communities of color. For instance, the "tree equity" agenda aims to bring high levels of tree canopy to every urban neighborhood, prioritizing those that display the deepest imprints of institutional racism. With colleagues, I found that, given the association between tree canopy and gun violence, closing the tree canopy gap between neighborhoods could help reduce gun violence disparities (Jay, Kondo, et al., 2022).

Place-based violence interventions, therefore, can be understood as part of broader local efforts to begin repairing the damage from racially discriminatory policymaking. An additional strength of these environmental approaches, from a racial justice perspective, is that they offer an alternative to violence responses (place-based or otherwise) that increase exposure to policing. Police encounters are associated with adverse health effects (Sewell & Jefferson, 2016; Theall et al., 2022), particularly for youth of color (Jackson et al., 2020; McFarland et al., 2019), a group that is disproportionately targeted by aggressive policing tactics.

Adopting Place-Based Strategies

Place-based interventions, therefore, can address major concerns that youth express about physical maintenance, violence, and institutional racism. Studies on the effectiveness of place-based interventions have typically measured all-age violence, not youth-specific outcomes, but there is every reason to believe that place-based interventions work to prevent youth violence. Indeed, given the strong links between youth violence and physical spaces, we might expect even a greater effect among youth than among adults.

To adopt place-based interventions, communities must find champions for this approach. Some practitioners and policymakers may be skeptical. Decades of treating law enforcement as the default response to community violence have reinforced punitive, "crime-fighting" mindsets. However, many others are primed to adopt place-based strategies. In my experience, officials working on transportation, buildings, parks, and other infrastructure-related functions quickly grasp the case for improving safety through environmental upgrades. Community organizations have often been clamoring for local government to take up their concerns about unsafe conditions that hinder their use of public spaces. Cities can draw on existing budgets for physical maintenance and infrastructure improvements.

A key step in getting started with place-based violence intervention is diagnosing the key environmental factors contributing to community violence, both community-wide and at the highest-need locations. Community consultation should be the backbone of this needs assessment process. For instance, in one project, researchers convened groups of South Los Angeles adolescents and adults to analyze safety issues, using a method called participatory mapping (Douglas, 2020). Participants marked up oversized maps with the places and routes where they felt safe and unsafe. They noted that tobacco shops were creating safety problems. The researchers conducted a larger-scale quantitative analysis that confirmed this association. A community coalition used all these data to advocate successfully for a regulatory change that banned tobacco shops from vulnerable locations (Subica et al., 2018).

Algorithmic Assistance

My group at Boston University has developed an analytical tool called Shape-Up. (We chose this name to remind users that safety can be improved without overhauling physical spaces: in barber shops, a shape-up is not a new haircut but a quick service to renew the clean edges of the previous cut.)

Shape-Up helps community members and decision makers understand environmental patterns driving gun violence on a citywide level and identify the locations that might benefit most from place-based interventions. The algorithm ingests a variety of types of data, taking advantage of recent advances in machine learning. The main innovation of Shape-Up has been the use of high-resolution aerial imagery. High-resolution photographs, taken by satellites or planes, can capture data about urban environments that can help predict where gun violence will occur (Jay, 2020) and how the effects of place-based interventions will vary between locations (Jay, de Jong, et al., 2022). This analysis involves converting each image—usually the overhead view of a city block—into a simpler vector of data that can be fed into prediction models alongside other variables.

Image analysis opens new directions for understanding the relationship between gun violence patterns and the physical environment. Among existing approaches, one popular strategy is to obtain the locations of prespecified environmental features, such as liquor stores and pawnshops, that are believed to generate or attract criminal activity (Caplan et al., 2011). One downside is that those location data are not always readily available (Muggy et al., 2022). Alternatively, researchers can generate their own data through trained observers (Furr-Holden, 2008), in person or virtually, with tools such as Google Street View (Mooney et al., 2017), collecting rich information about a range of influences, including street parking, loitering, and trash collection. A downside is that even virtual audits are labor-intensive and thus challenging to conduct on a large scale.

By contrast, aerial image analysis is fast—our image data extraction takes less than an hour for an entire city—and can uncover unexpected influences. The first step of a Shape-Up analysis is visual analysis, in which we model gun violence solely as a function of imagery data. We can then visualize for partners, using photographs representing high-, medium-, and low-risk scenes, the patterns that the algorithm has detected. These pictures often elicit nods from stakeholders as they recognize the most-impacted landscapes in their community, whether it's blocks of dense row housing, cracked sidewalks, or wide thoroughfares. They might not have considered specifying these factors in a more traditional model, and the photographs can prompt useful discussions among stakeholders.

In the next stage of Shape-Up analysis, we can layer additional data sources, through consultation with local partners. For instance, racialized economic segregation is the strongest known predictor of gun violence at the neighborhood level (Jay, Kondo, et al., 2022; Krieger et al., 2017); we have incorporated it using a simple measure called the "index of concentration at the extremes," for race and poverty. After accounting for urban form and segregation measures, we then can add location data, like liquor stores, with less worry that we will over-interpret their importance (e.g., because they are concentrated in the commercial hubs of structurally deprived neighborhoods; Jay, 2020; Muggy et al., 2022).

The output is a Shape-Up score for every city block, representing the environmental risk level for gun violence. These scores can be used to generate priority lists and finely grained maps to help guide intervention strategies. So far, we have used Shape-Up to generate scores for gun violence only across all ages, not specifically youth; but in tests we have found that Shape-Up predicts youth gun violence particularly well.

Shape-Up in the Field

With seed funding from the Everytown for Gun Safety Prize, we have built upon our initial design and tested new versions of the tool with community partners in three cities, Albany, Portland, and Toledo.

In Albany, New York, we partnered with city building officials. They had identified more than two dozen abandoned houses that were ready for demolition but lacked the budget to demolish every house right away. These houses were dispersed across three neighborhoods, all historically redlined and impacted by gun violence and property abandonment. We generated Shape-Up scores for each property. City officials hosted community meetings for each neighborhood, where they presented the Shape-Up scores, along with other information that residents could use to vote for which buildings to demolish. In two neighborhoods, residents' votes aligned closely, though not exactly, with the scores. In the third, the residents declined the demolitions, doubting that this step would enhance livability. The city chose its demolition sites based on the results. This experience helped validate our scoring approach but also taught us that what appears to be a technically "correct" intervention may not be appropriate from the perspective of those who know the neighborhood best.

Partnering in Portland, Oregon, has forced the algorithm to generate insights in a new type of physical setting. Portland has little abandonment, but its infrastructure becomes noticeably unfriendly to pedestrians as one moves from downtown to East Portland, where community violence is concentrated (Riddle, 2022). Interventionists told us that a common gun violence scenario occurs when individuals with ongoing disputes spot one another's vehicles at locations such as gas stations and nightclubs. This insight aligned with Shape-Up's visual analysis, which highlighted major roadways, large parking lots, and other automobile-centric spaces as the highest-risk landscapes. According to busy streets theory, changes that make East Portland spaces more walkable are likely to make them safer from violence; indeed, a recent traffic calming program was credited with curbing one Portland neighborhood's gun violence (Riddle, 2022). One way that Portland has used Shape-Up scores is to incorporate them into a metric for prioritizing pedestrian-friendly infrastructure projects.

Our work in Toledo has provided opportunities to incorporate new data sources. First, we have worked with both community organizations and violence interventionists (known as "interrupters") to collect data on a risk of interest to the model—along the lines of liquor stores and pawnshops in prior work—based on local knowledge, rather than prima facie guesses that might yield spurious results. Second, we are using a trove of data that the Lucas County Land Bank collected by sending out scores of volunteers and temporary employees to record the physical condition of every parcel in the city. These comprehensive, ground-level observations are especially valuable to Shape-Up because they complement the information the algorithm can glean from overhead imagery. The city is already moving ahead with vacant property remediation, but Shape-Up could help identify priority locations and garner additional resources.

Shape-Up encourages new ways of thinking about gun violence. One of these moments came recently in Toledo. I was presenting to meeting of stakeholders from Junction, the neighborhood I had walked earlier with Shantaé Brownlee and her Land Bank colleagues. My slides showed environmental upgrades alongside other community-based strategies, including the highly promising "interrupter" model of street outreach and conflict mediation that Toledo has adopted. As always, I highlighted the value of built environment improvements to address legacies of disinvestment and halt cycles of gun violence. Ms. Brownlee jumped into the conversation, neatly distilling this idea: "We're our own kind of interrupters," she said.

References

Aiyer, S. M., Zimmerman, M. A., Morrel-Samuels, S., & Reischl, T. M. (2015). From Broken windows to busy streets: A community empowerment perspective. *Health Education and Behavior, 42*, 137–147. https://doi.org/10.1177/1090198114558590

Branas, C. C., South, E., Kondo, M. C., Hohl, B. C., Bourgois, P., Wiebe, D. J., & MacDonald, J. M. (2018). Citywide cluster randomized trial to restore blighted vacant land and its effects on violence, crime, and fear. *Proceedings of the National Academy of Sciences of the United States of America, 115*(12), 2946–2951. https://doi .org/10.1073/pnas.1718503115

Buggs, S. A., Webster, D. W., & Crifasi, C. K. (2020). Using synthetic control methodology to estimate effects of a cure violence intervention in Baltimore, Maryland. *Injury Prevention.* https://doi.org/10.1136/injuryprev-2020-044056

Burdick-Will, J., Stein, M. L., & Grigg, J. (2019). Danger on the way to school: Exposure to violent crime, public transportation, and absenteeism. *Sociological Science, 6*, 118–142. https://doi.org/10.15195/V6.A5

Burt, C. J., Kondo, M. C., Hohl, B. C., Gong, C. H., Bushman, G., Wixom, C., South, E. C., Cunningham, R. M., Carter, P. M., Branas, C. C., & Zimmerman, M. A. (2022). Community greening, fear of crime, and mental health outcomes. *American Journal of Community Psychology, 69*, 46–58. https://doi.org/10.1002 /ajcp.12544

Caplan, J. M., Kennedy, L. W., & Miller, J. (2011). Risk Terrain Modeling: Brokering criminological theory and GIS methods for crime forecasting. *Justice Quarterly, 28*(2), 361–381. https://doi.org/10.1080/07418825.2010.486037

Carter, P. M., Cook, L. J., Macy, M. L., Zonfrillo, M. R., Stanley, R. M., Chamberlain, J. M., Fein, J. A., Alpern, E. R., & Cunningham, R. M. (2017). Individual and neighborhood characteristics of children seeking emergency department care for firearm injuries within the PECARN network. *Academic Emergency Medicine, 24*(7), 803–813. https://doi.org/10.1111/acem.13200

Culyba, A. J., Branas, C. C., Guo, W., Miller, E., Ginsburg, K. R., & Wiebe, D. J. (2021). Route choices and adolescent–adult connections in mitigating exposure to environmental risk factors during daily activities. *Journal of Interpersonal Violence, 36*(15–16), NP8852–NP8878. https://doi.org/10.1177/0886260519846859

Culyba, A. J., Jacoby, S. F., Richmond, T. S., Fein, J. A., Hohl, B. C., & Branas, C. C. (2016). Modifiable neighborhood features associated with adolescent homicide. *JAMA Pediatrics, 170*(5), 473–480. https://doi.org/10.1001/jamapediatrics.2015 .4697

Douglas, J. A. (2020). Using participatory mapping to diagnose upstream determinants of health and prescribe downstream policy-based interventions. *Preventing Chronic Disease, 17*, E138. https://doi.org/10.5888/PCD17.200123

Furr-Holden, C. D. M. (2008). *The NIfETy method for environmental assessment of neighborhood-level indicators of violence, alcohol, and other drug exposure.* https:// doi.org/10.1016/j.cortex.2009.08.003.Predictive

Heinze, J. E., Krusky-Morey, A., Vagi, K. J., Reischl, T. M., Franzen, S., Pruett, N. K., Cunningham, R. M., & Zimmerman, M. A. (2018). Busy streets theory: The effects of community-engaged greening on violence. *American Journal of Community Psychology, 62*, 101–109. https://doi.org/10.1002/ajcp.12270

Iantorno, S. E., Swendiman, R. A., Bucher, B. T., & Russell, K. W. (2022). Surge in pediatric firearm injuries presenting to US children's hospitals during the COVID-19 pandemic. *JAMA Pediatrics.* https://doi.org/10.1001/jamapediatrics.2022.4881

Jackson, D. B., Testa, A., Vaughn, M. G., & Semenza, D. C. (2020). Police stops and sleep behaviors among at-risk youth. *Sleep Health.* https://doi.org/10.1016/j.sleh .2020.02.006

Jay, J. (2020). Alcohol outlets and firearm violence: A place-based case-control study using satellite imagery and machine learning. *Injury Prevention*, *26*(1), 61–66. https://doi.org/10.1136/injuryprev-2019-043248

Jay, J., de Jong, J., Jimenez, M. P., Nguyen, Q., & Goldstick, J. (2022). Effects of demolishing abandoned buildings on firearm violence: A moderation analysis using aerial imagery and deep learning. *Injury Prevention*, *28*(3), 249–255. https://doi.org/10.1136/injuryprev-2021-044412

Jay, J., Kondo, M. C., Lyons, V. H., Gause, E., & South, E. C. (2022). Neighborhood segregation, tree cover and firearm violence in 6 U.S. cities, 2015–2020. *Preventive Medicine*, *165*, 107256. https://doi.org/10.1016/j.ypmed.2022.107256

Jay, J., Miratrix, L. W., Branas, C. C., Zimmerman, M. A., & Hemenway, D. (2019). Urban building demolitions, firearm violence and drug crime. *Journal of Behavioral Medicine*, *42*(4), 626–634. https://doi.org/10.1007/s10865-019-00031-6

Keizer, K., Lindenberg, S., & Steg, L. (2008). The spreading of disorder. *Science*, *322*(5908), 1681–1685. https://doi.org/10.1126/science.1161405

Krieger, N., Feldman, J. M., Waterman, P. D., Chen, J. T., Coull, B. A., & Hemenway, D. (2017). Local residential segregation matters: Stronger association of census tract compared to conventional city-level measures with fatal and non-fatal assaults (total and firearm related), using the index of concentration at the extremes (ICE) for racial, economic, and racialized economic segregation, Massachusetts (US), 1995–2010. *Journal of Urban Health*, *94*, 244–258. https://doi.org/10.1007/s11524-016-0116-z

Lee, L. K., Douglas, K., & Hemenway, D. (2022). Crossing lines—A change in the leading cause of death among U.S. children. *New England Journal of Medicine*, *386*, 1485–1487. https://doi.org/10.1056/NEJMP2200169

Martin, R., Rajan, S., Shareef, F., Xie, K., Allen, K., Zimmerman, M., & Jay, J. (2022). Racial disparities in child exposure to firearm violence before and during COVID-19. *American Journal of Preventive Medicine*. https://doi.org/10.1016/j.amepre.2022.02.007

McFarland, M. J., Geller, A., & McFarland, C. (2019). Police contact and health among urban adolescents: The role of perceived injustice. *Social Science and Medicine*, *238*, 112487. https://doi.org/10.1016/j.socscimed.2019.112487

Mesh, A. (2021, August 18). Portland safety officials believe an algorithm can pinpoint the city's most dangerous places and make them safer. *Willamette Week*. https://www.wweek.com/news/courts/2021/08/18/portland-safety-officials-believe-an-algorithm-can-pinpoint-the-citys-most-dangerous-places-and-make-them-safer/

Mmari, K., Lantos, H., Brahmbhatt, H., Delany-Moretlwe, S., Lou, C., Acharya, R., & Sangowawa, A. (2014). How adolescents perceive their communities: A qualitative study that explores the relationship between health and the physical environment. *BMC Public Health*, *14*(1). https://doi.org/10.1186/1471-2458-14-349

Mooney, S. J., Bader, M. D. M., Lovasi, G. S., Teitler, J. O., Koenen, K. C., Aiello, A. E., Galea, S., Goldmann, E., Sheehan, D. M., & Rundle, A. G. (2017). Street audits to measure neighborhood disorder: Virtual or in-person? *American Journal of Epidemiology*, *186*(3), 265–273. https://doi.org/10.1093/aje/kwx004

Muggy, L., Griswold, M., Eloundou, F., & Sean, N. (2022). Accounting for socioeconomic context in quantifying the attractive and repellent influence of built environment on firearms violence in multiple cities. *Journal of Quantitative Criminology*, *40*, 1–32. https://doi.org/10.1007/s10940-022-09560-x

Pino, E. C., Gebo, E., Dugan, E., & Jay, J. (2022). Trends in violent penetrating injuries during the first year of the COVID-19 pandemic. *JAMA Network Open, 5*(2), e2145708. https://doi.org/10.1001/jamanetworkopen.2021.45708

Rees, C. A., Monuteaux, M. C., Steidley, I., Mannix, R., Lee, L. K., Barrett, J. T., & Fleegler, E. W. (2022). Trends and disparities in firearm fatalities in the United States, 1990–2021. *JAMA Network Open, 5*(11), e2244221. https://doi.org/10.1001/jamanetworkopen.2022.44221

Riddle, K. (2022, April 13). How one Oregon community reduced gun violence by 60%. *NPR.* https://www.npr.org/2022/04/13/1092522408/one-community-s-creative-strategy-to-reduce-gun-violence

Sewell, A. A., & Jefferson, K. A. (2016). Collateral damage: The health effects of invasive police encounters in New York City. *Journal of Urban Health, 93*(Suppl. 1), 42–67. https://doi.org/10.1007/s11524-015-0016-7

South, E. C., Hohl, B. C., Kondo, M. C., MacDonald, J. M., & Branas, C. C. (2018). Effect of greening vacant land on mental health of community-dwelling adults. *JAMA Network Open, 1*(3), e180298. https://doi.org/10.1001/jamanetworkopen.2018.0298

South, E. C., Kondo, M. C., Cheney, R. A., & Branas, C. C. (2015). Neighborhood blight, stress, and health: A walking trial of urban greening and ambulatory heart rate. *American Journal of Public Health, 105*(5), 909–913. https://doi.org/10.2105/AJPH.2014.302526

South, E. C., Macdonald, J., & Reina, V. (2021). Association between structural housing repairs for low-income homeowners and neighborhood crime. *JAMA Network Open, 4*(7), 1–12. https://doi.org/10.1001/jamanetworkopen.2021.17067

Subica, A. M., Douglas, J. A., Kepple, N. J., Villanueva, S., & Grills, C. T. (2018). The geography of crime and violence surrounding tobacco shops, medical marijuana dispensaries, and off-sale alcohol outlets in a large, urban low-income community of color. *Preventive Medicine, 108*, 8–16. https://doi.org/10.1016/j.ypmed.2017.12.020

Teitelman, A. (2010). Youth strategies for staying safe and coping. *Journal of Community Psychology, 38*(7), 874–885. https://doi.org/10.1002/jcop.20402

Teixeira, S. (2015). It seems like no one cares: Participatory photo mapping to understand youth perspectives on property vacancy. *Journal of Adolescent Research, 30*(3), 390–414. https://doi.org/10.1177/0743558414547098

Theall, K. P., Francois, S., Bell, C. N., Anderson, A., Chae, D., & Laveist, T. A. (2022). Neighborhood police encounters, health, and violence in a southern city. *Health Affairs, 41*(2), 228–236. https://doi.org/10.1377/hlthaff.2021.01428

Williams, D. R., & Collins, C. (2001). Racial residential segregation: A fundamental cause of racial disparities in health. *Public Health Reports, 116*(5), 404–416. https://doi.org/10.1016/S0033-3549(04)50068-7

Culturally Rooted Strategies for Youth-Positive Development among Youth of Color

• • • • • • • • • • • • •

A Holistic Approach to the Evaluation of Community-Driven Youth Violence Prevention Programs

FIORELLA L. CARLOS CHAVEZ,
PETER REJ, AND CHERYL GRILLS

Overview

Youth violence prevention (YVP) practitioners often implement prevention and early intervention (PEI) strategies rooted in evidence-based practices (EBPs).

Yet disparities related to rates and impacts of youth violence remain, most deeply affecting unserved, underserved, and inappropriately served communities of color. EBPs fail to mitigate risk factors for youth violence when they neglect to consider culture, lived experience, and historical and current community contexts. Although evaluation of effectiveness is a standard expectation of PEI efforts, the extent to which evaluation privileges unique cultural and contextual factors is typically minimal, if present at all.

For more than thirty years, Imoyase Community Support Services in Los Angeles and the Psychology Applied Research Center at Loyola Marymount University (PARC) have conducted program evaluation and action research to validate community-defined evidence practices (CDEPs), which are alternative and/or complementary strategies to EBPs. We have also supported systems and policy change associated with child welfare, mental health disparities, community safety, education, and juvenile justice for more than seventy-five communities across the country. Imoyase and PARC recognize the challenges of conducting valid, reliable evaluations that consider culture, context, history, social justice, and equity and are considered credible evidence. The challenge is to define and measure effectiveness in ways that honor communities' values and priorities. The default approach in academia is to measure effectiveness using the standard metrics of Western-centric mental health care, but is this an appropriate goal? Our mission is to address this issue. We provide evaluation and technical support that is participatory, collaborative, and culturally aligned with communities. We engage with community members in the development of CDEPs, which offer culturally anchored interventions that reflect a community's values, practices, histories, and lived experiences.

To move beyond community-based participatory research (CBPR; Minkler & Wallerstein, 2008), we coined community-based participatory practice (CBPP; Grills et al., 2018). CBPP means the work is rooted in mutual understanding and collective action. It can promote communication, equity, and trust among communities, external stake holders, and researchers (Grills et al., 2018) and achieve shared ownership of interventions and their evaluation.

Many on our team know firsthand the limitations of employing EBPs in communities in which they have not been adequately validated. We also know that tribal, racial, and ethnic groups have increasingly demanded research in which their values, traditions, and worldviews drive program design, development, and implementation (Grills et al., 2023). This approach invites community members to participate in vital decision-making processes and increases the likelihood of concrete benefits for the community (Hartwig et al., 2006). For example, with respect to youth violence within African American communities, the multigenerational history of enslavement, anti-Blackness, and ongoing interpersonal and structural racism must factor into any conceptualization of the causes of youth violence, strategies to address them, and metrics to evaluate program effectiveness. The mere act of community engagement prioritizes community agency to investigate its own circumstances (Stevens & Hall, 1998).

We believe our hard-earned lessons can aid future thinking about the development and evaluation of YVP. We share an overview of processes and experiences from one cross-site, mixed-methods evaluation of a positive youth development (PYD) strategy in Los Angeles County called Ready to Rise (R2R). The findings from the R2R evaluation demonstrate the value of employing CDEPs and highlight the value of community participation. Finally, we reflect on which practices should be considered when implementing culturally and community-affirming strategies in YVP.

Summary and Highlights

Errors of Perception and Understanding

Too often, people attribute the root causes of youth violence to individual deficits, family background, or group disadvantages. One may wonder, "If only youth were better at school, or if only they had more money, better parents, more resources, a different neighborhood, maybe they wouldn't experience or engage with so much violence." Assigning blame does not solve youth violence. People assume that without economic, family, or community deficits, young people would flourish in U.S. society. But understanding youth violence from this perspective translates to PEI strategies focused narrowly on "at-risk" youth. This view (Gottfredson, 1997) dismisses the historical and current structural forces that seed violence.

In Search of a Better Understanding

Youth development is impacted by family, peers, and community institutions, such as schools. Young lives are also shaped by broader sociopolitical and macro-level institutions, including lawmaking bodies and government agencies (Bronfenbrenner, 1979). What is often neglected is that youth are critically impacted by the history that has shaped their current socioeconomic and racial circumstances. Consider, for example, sixteen-year-old Damon. Damon has had repeated encounters with law enforcement due to gang-related fights. We need to determine the drivers of Damon's behavior (e.g., poor communication skills, inability to modulate anger, poor self-regulation, moral depravity, ineffective parenting, inadequate life skills, cognitive or behavioral deficits.) But should we also consider possible historical and environmental causes of Damon's behavior? These causes could be, for example, generations of racial oppression, community disinvestment, underresourced schools, inadequate housing, lack of recreational opportunities, racial bias in policing, lack of employment opportunities, and a tattered community social safety net. There is no simple answer

Better Practices

We cannot endorse a single set of "best" practices. Interventions must be tailored to time, place, and culture. Nonetheless, "better" practices warrant consideration. Better practices include those that (1) are designed in collaboration with community members, (2) operate according to values of equity and justice, and (3) prioritize and conform to a community's cultural and contextual needs, values, histories, and goals.

CBPP and Culture

CDEP development and evaluation is committed to a praxis of listening, engaging, and empowering community. While some researchers adopt principles of CBPR in their work, we advocate for a broader application of community participation called community-based participatory practice (CBPP), which determines needs, defines problems, and shapes. Among other things, community engagement includes meetings with faith communities, collaboration with local organizations, and town-hall-style meetings that connect leaders and service providers with community members.

The jury is out regarding the extent to which interventions that do not meaningfully engage with the focal population have any lasting impact or long-term sustainability (Smith, 2021). At worst, they can lead the field to believe that a problem has been meaningfully addressed (when it has not). Consider for example, Payne's (2008) discussion in *So Much Reform, So Little Change* of the superficial change (e.g., more teachers) rather than substantive school reforms (e.g., teacher quality, increased school budgets, implicit bias training, etc.). A momentary improvement in test scores, attendance, or school violence is quickly replaced with a return to preexisting markers of poor school functioning.

Understanding cultural features and dimensions can be challenging. Ask anyone who has incorporated cultural factors into their work. It can be challenging to articulate core values, beliefs, and perceptions and to identify relevant, beneficial cultural experiences. With communities of color and LGBTQ+ communities across California, we developed a conceptual tool to aid identification and discussion of visible and invisible dimensions of culture—the culture cube (Abe et al., 2018; see Figure 14.1).

The culture cube is one way to make the invisible visible in aid to program design and evaluation. It can be used to articulate (1) how culture shapes the project, (2) how cultural issues guide evaluation questions, methods, and selection of outcomes, and (3) how indigenous epistemological frameworks

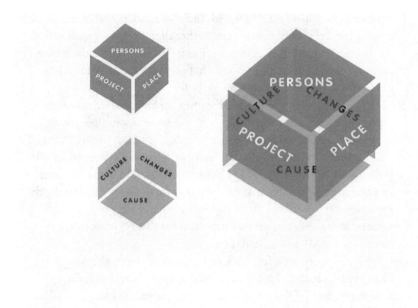

FIGURE 14.1 The culture cube.

shape interventions and evaluations. It is intentionally simple and easy to use within a participatory ethos by following the explanations and examples provided in the Abe et al. (2018) publication.

CBPP in Action

We think of CBPP as a continuously iterative process with six broad steps.

> *Step 1: Engage community.* Community engagement can include outreach, consultation, collaboration, and shared leadership (Epstein et al., 2018). First, it means deciding the scope of engagement and establishing trust and rapport with community members. It requires trust between community institutions, researchers, and/or policymakers (Grills et al., 2018).
>
> *Step 2: Review.* Review existing literature, including (1) reports from funders and community groups, (2) community history texts, (3) data from local police departments, schools, and health agencies, (4) information gleaned from ethnic studies and critical race theory, (5) news media accounts of community priorities, needs, and actions, and (6) government policies, guidelines, and recommended practices.
>
> *Step 3: Develop.* Develop an initial draft of the program or evaluation. One goal is to balance insights from scientific sources with community relevance (i.e., synthesis rather than assimilation). Another goal is to

balance community priorities with those of funders and other relevant external stakeholders. Specifically, rather than exclusively following the funders' agenda, ask community members to explain their most pressing needs, their definition of change, and what benchmarks of change look like from their vantage point.

Step 4: Pilot and feedback. Pilot testing must include individuals who are representative of the focal group (e.g., multiracial, multiple ethnic groups), including mixed-race individuals (e.g., Afro-Latinx [African and Latino/a/x descent], Blasian [African and Asian descent], and/or individuals from the LGBTQ+ population). Community feedback can be sought in multiple ways, including focus groups and in-depth interviews and feedback from an institutional review board that understands CBPP, culture, and context for diverse populations (see Brown et al., 2010; Grills et al., 2018)

Step 5: Revise. Incorporate feedback to (1) improve the methodology, (2) change phrases and expressions to make them more culturally congruent, and (3) share with community members and stakeholders for final approval.

Step 6: Implement and iterate. Involve the community in the ongoing implementation of the intervention and evaluation. Based on findings and community input, calibrate the project's focus, including methodology, duration, and theoretical approach.

CBPP in Ready to Rise (R2R): An Example from Our Work

We employed CBPP in an evaluation of the R2R initiative. R2R is a partnership among the Los Angeles County Probation Department (LACPD) and two private grant-making organizations committed to the growth of a countywide PYD system grounded in culturally responsive, community-based strategies (i.e., CDEPs). LACPD's primary goal is to prevent and reduce youth involvement in the justice system. R2R's priority is to serve marginalized youth of color, including youth who are gang-involved, homeless, or in or transitioning out of foster care or who identify as LGBTQ+. Such youth are at a disproportionate risk for justice system involvement and grapple with a host of trauma-related outcomes (Branson et al., 2017; Espelage et al., 2018; Kaya et al., 2022; Kosciw et al., 2014; Prince et al., 2019; Van Leeuwen et al., 2004).

As the evaluation partner in this initiative, we *engaged the community* (CBPP Step 1) with in-person and virtual site visits (due to COVID-19) as well as formal and informal discussions during grantee convenings. These interactions were paramount to (1) building trust, (2) uncovering objectionable prior evaluation experiences, (3) establishing a bottom-up ethos in the development of evaluation methods and tools, and (4) using the culture cube to discern the cultural dimensions of PYD approaches.

Youth-Positive Development among Youth of Color • 161

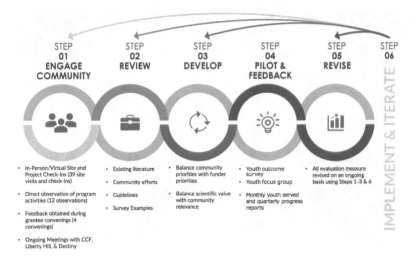

FIGURE 14.2 Outcome tool development.

With this deeper understanding of the cultural and contextual experiences of grantees, we *reviewed and synthesized* (CBPP Step 2) existing research and evaluation literature to *develop* meaningful cross-site evaluation tools (CBPP Step 3). The community suggested relational ties and networks of social support as focal items as they codesigned the questions and data collection strategies for the youth-impact findings in the R2R evaluation. We then *piloted* these measures, soliciting *feedback* during the process (CBPP Step 4).

In CBPP Step 5 (*revise*), based on grantee objectives, we were able to identify core PYD approaches that highlighted youth strengths and opportunities (rather than deficits). Last, to *implement and iterate* (CBPP Step 6), grantees privileged contextualized PYD approaches to meet the needs of their underserved, marginalized, low-income youth of color (Catalano, 2019; García-Poole et al., 2019). Each grantee's intervention was uniquely tailored to align with the culture and needs of the youth and communities in which they lived. Each of these steps as applied to R2R is outlined in Figure 14.2.

Youth Served

R2R is unique among youth PEI initiatives, as indexed by unprecedented youth participation numbers. Over three years, forty-nine grantees served 25,594 unique youth across 950,688 touchpoints (i.e., amount of participation in program activities). That the rates of participation increased during the COVID-19 pandemic is a testament to the responsiveness of the community organizations to community needs. Figure 14.3 illustrates the diverse cross-section of youth served.

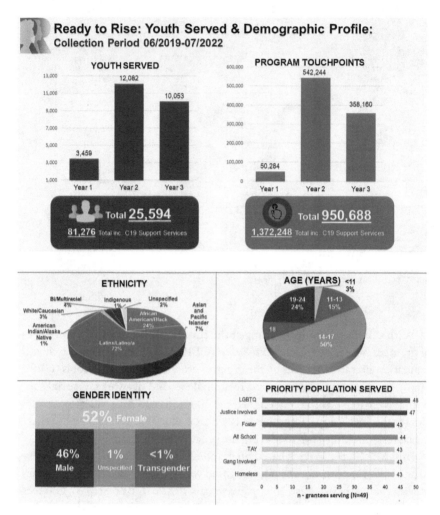

FIGURE 14.3 R2R youth's demographic profile.

These elevated youth service counts suggest that community-based approaches resonate with youth of color, particularly when compared to EBP interventions. The continuity of youth participation is also notable, as each youth averaged thirty-seven touchpoints. Grantee comments in Figure 14.4 illustrate the intersection of intervention type, culture, context, and community perspective.

Youth Outcomes

Because African American, Asian American, Native Hawaiian and Pacific Islander, and Latinx youth come from communal rather than individualistic

Youth-Positive Development among Youth of Color • 163

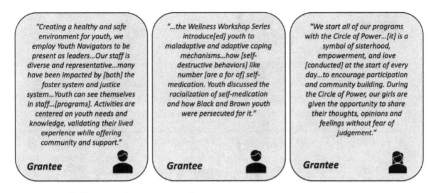

FIGURE 14.4 R2R grantee's voices.

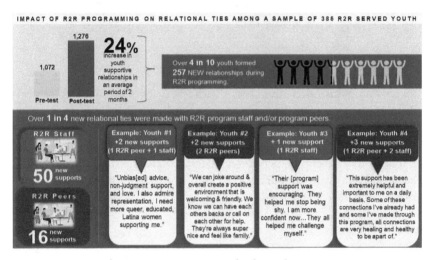

FIGURE 14.5 Impact of R2R programming on youth relational ties.

cultures, an important cultural factor identified by R2R grantees was the importance of a communal ethos. Relational ties were identified as a foundational outcome variable and cultural principle in positive youth development. This is in line with previous research wherein relational ties protect youth from local environmental risks, support them and their families, and foster healthy identity development (Gardner & Brooks-Gunn, 2009; Henderson et al., 2016; Henderson & Greene, 2014; Holleran & Waller, 2003; Theron et al., 2011).

A cross-site outcome measure of progress was developed to capture the "heart and soul" of short-term youth outcomes. These were (1) relational ties (recognizing that strong social supports and deep relational ties are foundational to PYD) and (2) self-defined goals (recognizing the value of youth defining their

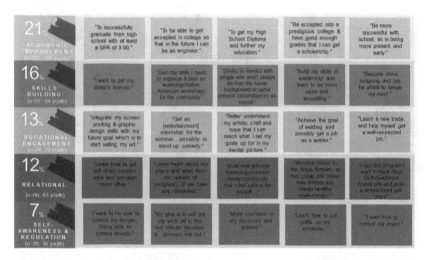

FIGURE 14.6 Top five prevalent PYD themes for youth program–related goals.

own needs, motivations, and outcomes). In total, 386 youth participated in pre- and post-program outcome surveys with these two variables as central outcomes.

Relational Ties

Figure 14.5 illustrates that, per survey findings, R2R improved the quality of relationships through supportive staff and peer relationships. Focus group results corroborated these findings.

Self-Defined Goals

Youths' needs, motivations, and outcomes will vary. At pretest, youth were asked, "From this program I want...." Nearly all 386 respondents (90 percent, $n = 349$) identified at least one personally generated goal. Figure 14.6 provides some examples of youth-defined goals across the five most prevalent PYD project themes.

From pretest ($M = 4.29$, $SD = 2.26$) to posttest ($M = 6.41$, $SD = 2.26$), youth made significant progress ($t = 14.16$, $p < .0001$) on their self-defined goal(s).[1] Youth were more cautious in their aspirational ratings. The average rating for future goal attainment was 7.82 ($SD = 2.63$) at pretest and 7.97 ($SD = 2.44$) at posttest. These findings suggest that youth made realistic appraisals of both their current goal status and their future goal status.

The new goals youth described at posttest were qualitatively coded using the same PYD themes. Primary theme frequencies are presented in Figure 14.7.[2] Skills and stability were particularly prominent in the new posttest goals,

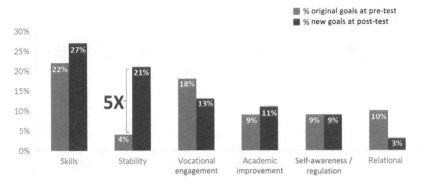

FIGURE 14.7 Shifts in youth goals from pre- to posttest.

signaling a shift in emphasis from relational ties toward pursuit of goals related to quality of life and having a future. These efforts laid the groundwork for youth to secure housing, complete their university degrees, and become financially self-sufficient as they worked to break the intergenerational cycle of violence, poverty, and disparity.

PYD allows young people to develop skills, confidence, and relational ties that support change in other areas including intentional self-regulation and disrupting violence. Skills include racial and cultural socialization, critical consciousness, civic engagement, strengthened relational ties, and other cultural tools. Doing so, PYD challenges dominant narratives of what YVP (and its youth) look like.

Where Are We Going?

While our CDEPs and CBPPs have been effective in California, we caution against overgeneralizing these practices to other states. We advise employing the six steps of the framework, coupled with the culture cube, to determine which approaches will best meet the unique needs of youth in each community. Rather than study communities from a place of detachment, we propose that researchers learn about their focal populations by attending community activities, school meetings, faith-based services, and civic events.

We also recommend disseminating information using language that community members use and understand, whether via newsletters, online posts, infographics, or community meetings. Radio and podcasts are also powerful communication platforms that can sidestep issues of literacy and reach a larger share of the population. Finally, assume that valuable knowledge will be gleaned from any engagement with the community. Prioritize ways to collaborate in a co-owned process of understanding and change.

Acknowledgments

A special thank-you to Devin Barney for his comments on an earlier version of this chapter.

Notes

1 Student's pairwise t-tests were used to examine whether there were differences from pre- to posttest on the average progress toward goal attainment. The strength of the result $(p = 2.91 \times 10^{-37})$, even after adjusting for type I error using the Bonferroni correction, strongly suggests a robust difference and that results will be maintained if not strengthened for youth continuing in the program.
2 Due to missing data only 70 of the 90 new goals were coded.

References

Abe, J., Grills, C., Ghavami, N., Xiong, G., Davis, C., & Johnson, C. (2018). Making the invisible visible: Identifying and articulating culture in practice-based evidence. *American Journal of Community Psychology, 62*(1–2), 121–134. https://doi.org/10.1002/ajcp.12266

Bermúdez, J. M., & Bérmudez, S. (2002). Altar-making with Latino families: A narrative therapy perspective. *Journal of Family Psychotherapy, 13*(3–4), 329–347. https://doi.org/10.1300/J085v13n03_06

Branson, C. E., Baetz, C. L., Horwitz, S. M., & Hoagwood, K. E. (2017). Trauma-informed juvenile justice systems: A systematic review of definitions and core components. *Psychological Trauma: Theory, Research, Practice and Policy, 9*(6), 635–646. https://doi.org/10.1037/tra0000255

Bronfenbrenner, U. (1979). *The ecology of human development: Experiments by nature and design.* Harvard University Press.

Brown, P., Morello-Frosch, R., Brody, J. G., Altman, R. G., Rudel, R. A., Senier, L., Pérez, C., & Simpson, R. (2010). Institutional review board challenges related to community-based participatory research on human exposure to environmental toxins: A case study. *Environmental Health, 9*(1), 39. https://doi.org/10.1186/1476-069X-9-39

Bunston, W., Franich-Ray, C., & Tatlow, S. (2017). A diagnosis of denial: How mental health classification systems have struggled to recognise family violence as a serious risk factor in the development of mental health issues for infants, children, adolescents and adults. *Brain Sciences, 7*(10), 133. https://doi.org/10.3390/brainsci7100133

Carlos Chavez, F. L., Gonzales-Backen, M. A., & Grzywacz, J. G. (2021). Work, stressors, and psychosocial adjustment of undocumented Guatemalan adolescents in United States agriculture: A mixed-methods approach. *Journal of Research on Adolescence, 31*(4), 1218–1234. https://doi.org/10.1111/jora.12640

Carlos Chavez, F. L., Gonzales-Backen, M. A., & Perez Rueda, A. M. (2022). International migration, work, and cultural values: A mixed-method exploration among Latino adolescents in US agriculture. *Family Relations, 71*(1), 325–351. https://doi.org/10.1111/fare.12603

Catalano, R. F., Skinner, M. L., Alvarado, G., Kapungu, C., Reavley, N., Patton, G. C., Jeseee, C., Plaut, D., Moss, C., Bennett, K., Sawyer, S. M., Sebany, M., Sexton, M., Olenik, C., & Petroni, S. (2019). Positive youth development programs in low- and middle-income countries: A conceptual framework and systematic review of efficacy. *Journal of Adolescent Health*, *65*, 15–31. https://doi.org/10.1016/j.jadohealth .2019.01.024

DeVance Taliaferro, J., Casstevens, W. J., & DeCuir Gunby, J. T. (2013). Working with African American clients using narrative therapy: An operational citizenship and critical race theory framework. *International Journal of Narrative Therapy & Community Work*, *1*, 34–45.

Dodge, K. A., & Pettit, G. S. (2003). A biopsychosocial model of the development of chronic conduct problems in adolescence. *Developmental Psychology*, *39*(2), 349–371. https://doi.org/10.1037//0012-1649.39.2.349

Dwyer, S. C., & Buckle, J. L. (2009). The space between: On being an insider-outsider in qualitative research. *International Journal of Qualitative Methods*, *8*(1), 54–63. https://doi.org/10.1177/160940690900800105

Epstein, J. L., Sanders, M. G., Sheldon, S. B., Simon, B. S., Salinas, K. C., Jansorn, N. R., Van Voorhis, F. L., Martin, C. S., Thomas, B. G., Greenfeld, M. D., Hutchins, D. J., & Williams, K. J. (2018). *School, family, and community partnerships: Your handbook for action* (4th ed.). Corwin Press.

Espelage, D. L., Merrin, G. J., & Hatchel, T. (2018). Peer victimization and dating violence among LGBTQ youth: The impact of school violence and crime on mental health outcomes. *Youth Violence and Juvenile Justice*, *16*(2), 156–173. https://doi.org /10.1177/1541204016680408

Foronda, C., Baptiste, D. L., Reinholdt, M. M., & Ousman, K. (2016). Cultural humility: A concept analysis. *Journal of Transcultural Nursing*, *27*(3), 210–217.

Foucault, M. (2000). The subject and power. In R. Hurley, J. D. Faubion, P. Rabinow, & C. Gordon (Eds.), *Power: Essential works of Foucault 1954–1984* (Vol. 3, pp. 326–348). New Press.

García-Poole, C., Byrne, S., & Rodrigo, M.-J. (2019). Implementation factors that predict positive outcomes in a community-based intervention program for at-risk adolescents. *Psychosocial Intervention*, *28*(2), 57–65. https://doi.org/10.5093/pi2019a4

Gardner, J. (2011). Placed blame: Narratives of youth culpability. *Urban Education*, *46*(4), 588–610. https://doi.org/10.1177/0042085911399792

Gardner, M., & Brooks-Gunn, J. (2009). Adolescents' exposure to community violence: Are neighborhood youth organizations promotive? *Journal of Community Psychology*, *37*, 505–525. doi:10.1002/jcop.20310

Gottfredson, D. C. (1997). School-based crime prevention. In L. W. Sherman et al. (Eds.), *Preventing crime: What works, what doesn't, what's promising* (pp. 5-1–5-74). U.S. Department of Justice, Office of Justice Programs. https://www.ojp.gov /pdffiles1/Digitization/165366NCJRS.pdf

Grills, C., Carlos Chavez, F. L., Saw, A., Walters, K. L., Burlew, K., Randolph Cunningham, S. M., Rosario, C. C., Samoa, R., & Jackson-Lowman, H. (2023). Applying culturalist methodologies to discern COVID-19's impact on communities of color. *Journal of Community Psychology*, *51*, 2331–2354. https://doi.org/10 .1002/jcop.22802

Grills, C., Cooke, D., Douglas, J., Subica, A., & Villaneuva, S. (2015). Culture, racial socialization, and positive youth development. *Journal of Black Psychology*, *42*(4), 343–373.

Grills, C., Hill, C. D., Cooke, D., & Walker, A. (2018). *California Reducing Disparities Project (CRDP) phase 2 statewide evaluation: Best practices in community based participatory practice.* Psychology Applied Research Center. https://www .purposefulagingla.com/sites/default/files/Best%20Practices%20in%20Community%20Based%20Participatory%20Practice%202018.pdf

Hartwig, K., Calleson, D., & Williams, M. (2006). *Unit 1: CBPR—Getting grounded. Examining community-institutional partnerships for prevention research group. Developing and sustaining community-based participatory research partnerships: A skill-building curriculum.* http://www.cbprcurriculum.info/

Henderson, D.X., DeCuir-Gunby, J. & Gill, V. (2016). "It *really* takes a village": A socio-ecological model of resilience for prevention among economically disadvantaged ethnic minority youth. *Journal of Primary Prevention, 37,* 469–485. https://doi.org/10.1007/s10935-016-0446-3

Henderson, D. X., & Greene, J. (2014). Using mixed methods to explore resilience, social connectedness, and re-suspension among youth in a community-based alternative-to suspension program. *International Journal of Child, Youth, and Family Studies, 5*(3), 423–446. https://doi.org/10.18357/ijcyfs.hendersondx.532014

Holleran, L. K., & Waller, M. A. (2003). Sources of resilience among Chicano/a youth: Forging identities in the borderlands. *Child and Adolescent Social Work Journal, 20*(5), 335–350. https://doi.org/10.1023/A:1026043828866

Kaya, Y. B., Maass, K. L., Dimas, G. L., Konrad, R., Trapp, A. C., & Dank, M. (2022). Improving access to housing and supportive services for runaway and homeless youth: Reducing vulnerability to human trafficking in New York City. *IISE Transactions.* https://doi.org/10.1080/24725854.2022.2120223

Kosciw, J. G., Greytak, E. A., Palmer, N. A., & Boesen, M. J. (2014). *The 2013 National School Climate Survey: The experiences of lesbian, gay, bisexual and transgender youth in our nation's schools.* GLSEN. https://www.glsen.org/sites /default/files/2020-03/GLSEN-2013-National-School-Climate-Survey-Full -Report.pdf

Lawrence, T. (2022). Family violence, depressive symptoms, school bonding, and bullying perpetration: An intergenerational transmission of violence perspective. *Journal of School Violence, 21*(4), 517–529. https://doi.org/10.1080/15388220.2022 .2114490

Minkler, M., & Wallerstein, N. (2008). *Community based participatory research for health: Process to outcomes* (2nd ed.). Jossey-Bass.

Payne, C. M. (2008). *So much reform, so little change: The persistence of failure in urban schools.* Harvard Education Press.

Pittman, K. J. (1991). *A new vision: Promoting youth development* (Testimony before the House Select Committee on Children, Youth and Families). Center for Youth Development and Policy Research.

Prince, D. M., Vidal, S., Okpych, N., & Connell, C. M. (2019). Effects of individual risk and state housing factors on adverse outcomes in a national sample of youth transitioning out of foster care. *Journal of Adolescence, 74,* 33–44. https://doi.org/10 .1016/j.adolescence.2019.05.004

Serrant-Green, L. (2002). Black on Black: Methodological issues for Black researchers working in minority ethnic. *Nurse Researcher, 9*(4), 30–44. https://doi.org/10.7748 /nr2002.07.9.4.30.c6196

Smith, L. T. (2021). *Decolonizing methodologies: Research and indigenous peoples* (3rd ed.). Zed.

Stevens, P. E., & Hall, J. M. (1998). Participatory action research for sustaining individual and community change: A model of HIV prevention education. *AIDS Education and Prevention, 10*(5), 387–402.

Sugimoto-Matsuda, J. J., & Braun, K. L. (2014). The role of collaboration in facilitating policy change in youth violence prevention: A review of the literature. *Prevention Science, 15*(2), 194–204. https://psycnet.apa.org/doi/10.1007/s11121-013-0369-7

Theron, L., Cameron, C., Didkowsky, N., Lau, C., Liebenberg, L., & Ungar, M. (2011). A "day in the lives" of four resilient youths: A study of cultural roots of resilience. *Youth and Society, 43*, 799–818. https://doi.org/10.1177/0044118X11402853

Umemoto, K., Baker, C., Helm, S., Miao, T., Goebert, D., & Hishinuma, E. (2009). Moving toward comprehensiveness and sustainability in a social ecological approach to youth violence prevention: Lessons from the Asian/Pacific Islander Youth Violence Prevention Center. *American Journal of Community Psychology, 44*, 221–232. https://doi.org/10.1007/s10464-009-9271-7

Van Leeuwen, J. M., Hopfer, C., Hooks, S., White, R., Petersen, J., & Pirkopf, J. (2004). A snapshot of substance abuse among homeless and runaway youth in Denver, Colorado. *Journal of Community Health, 29*(3), 217–229. https://doi.org/10.1023/B:JOHE.0000022028.50989.aa

White, M. K., & Morgan, A. (2006). *Narrative therapy with children and their families*. Dulwich Centre.

Part 3

Extensions

● ● ● ● ● ● ● ● ● ● ● ● ● ●

Hospital-Based Violence Intervention Programs for Violently Injured Youth

• • • • • • • • • • • • •

STEPHANIE BONNE

Overview

"Someone should tell self-important, anti-gun doctors to stay in their lane."

This was a tweet sent out by the National Rifle Association in late 2018, in response to an article in *Annals of Internal Medicine*. It started a firestorm of doctors crying out, "This is our lane!" Indeed, doctors have been caring for those who are injured in acts of violence for decades, including the severe injuries associated with gun violence. Recently, however, physicians have become increasingly interested in the upstream causes of violence and injury.

The role of physicians in addressing the upstream causes has been somewhat limited. In a world of fee-for-service medicine, public health approaches are often small projects, often funded by grants, and reliant on the interest of the physician rather than real prioritization and investment from the health care system. As described below, Hospital-based Violence Intervention is one such approach. There are, however, many opportunities to use public health principles to address injury and violence in general, if we could only create real momentum to invest in these issues.

Importantly, injury in general is not prioritized as a health care problem. Injury and violence result in the same number of years of potential life lost as cancer in the United States yet receive less than 10 percent of federal research funding by comparison. Funding for violence prevention is currently on the rise. But this historical inequity in funding is, in my opinion, in part because injury and violence disproportionately affect disenfranchised communities, racial/ethnic minorities, and individuals of low socioeconomic status (Boeck et al., 2022).

My own interest in violence prevention came about long before the NRA tweeted about my alleged "self-importance." I am a trauma surgeon. My trauma center is filled on a daily basis with those who are injured by violence. The heartbreaking work of caring for these patients and repeatedly telling parents and families that their children have died was compelling for me to seek solutions to these problems. The sequelae of these injuries, when survived, are disfiguring, life-threatening, and life-altering and come at enormous expense to individuals, their families, and their communities. Rather than addressing violent injury, one of the well-described downstream health consequences of a number of upstream social determinants of health, I chose to build, learn, and implement programs to prevent injury and violence by addressing these social determinants. In an ideal world, I would put myself out of business.

Background

The injuries associated with violence are frequently seen in the emergency departments and trauma centers around the country. Injuries can be minor to severe or even deadly and can lead to life-altering and disfiguring consequences when there is a need for surgery, repair of lacerations, or more severe consequences such as amputations. The past century has seen the development of the U.S. trauma system from a loosely affiliated group of hospitals and doctors to a highly interconnected, evidence-based approach to the systemic evaluation and treatment of injured patients. As the care of trauma patients has improved and the system has refined itself, increasing attention is being paid to the role of the hospital as a touchpoint for the management of other patient issues, such as long-term care, attention to social support services, and social determinants of health.

Hospitals, by definition, are not spaces where primary prevention of injury can be performed. If violence is approached from the lens of a health issue, patients who present with violent injury have already been subject to the "disease" of violence. Whereas some hospitals and medical centers have made attempts or partnered with primary prevention efforts in the community, the primary role of the hospital is in secondary and tertiary prevention. It is from this framework that the field of Hospital Based Violence Intervention has grown over the past several decades.

Hospital-based violence intervention programs (HVIPs) started primarily in Baltimore and San Francisco in the early to mid-2000s. There are several models that will be described below, but all include the same basic framework. The first is an understanding that victims of violence are victims and are not to be blamed for the circumstances or events that led to their injury. The second is that individuals can change their modifiable risk factors for future violence, most of which are largely related to social determinants of health. Finally, more recently, the integration of a trauma-informed care perspective into HVIPs has been shown to be of paramount importance (Grossman et al., 2021).

HVIP Program Structure

Hospital-based programs must start with buy-in from the hospital system and with a champion for the program in the institution. Sometimes this is a physician, but in some programs it can be a nurse, social worker, program manager, or public health practitioner (Dicker et al., 2017). Once funding and hospital buy-in are established, the structure can vary depending on the needs of the program. In general, however, there is a coordinator of some kind, employed either part-time or full-time. In some hospitals, this individual is the injury prevention coordinator in the trauma center. In others, it may be a position hired specifically for this program. This person is typically responsible for personnel onboarding and oversight, managing relationships with key community stakeholders, and the maintenance of a record of patient visits and services provided. The coordinator and hospital stakeholder also typically work together to apply for and manage funding for the program.

HVIPs also recognize that the lived experience of community members is extraordinarily valuable to success in these programs. The program itself is a team that includes health care workers, support staff such as coordinators, social workers, and other resources (Dicker et al., 2009). However, the primary face of the program to the patients, from first contact, should be individuals who are relatable community members with an understanding of local culture and context of violence in the community. These individuals also have valuable relationships and knowledge of community partners that can be leveraged to improve patient outcomes. Therefore, the inclusion of locally competent case managers is critically important to program success (Fischer et al., 2020). These individuals will typically report to the program coordinator.

The hospital stakeholder, coordinator, and HVIP case managers are the minimum key components to a successful program. However, the program can be augmented by a number of other professionals and programs that help expand the capabilities of the program and the services offered. One of the most common is social workers, who help the case manager with complicated social issues that may be out of the case manager's scope. Mental health professionals may be able to provide services under the funding of the program, thereby removing the complicated processes of billable services for individual or group therapy. Community partners may be able to provide programs such as art therapy, yoga and mindfulness training, or faith-based services (Bonne, 2017). It is critical that these types of programming and services are also offered to the case managers, to mitigate the secondary traumatic stress they may experience as part of the nature of their work.

The day-to-day function of an HVIP might look something like the following: a list of patients who may be eligible for the HVIP is generated, from review of new inpatients on the trauma service, emergency department patients, or patients who have been treated in the past day. Programs may also accept referrals or additionally serve family members of individuals who have been victims of violence. Some programs use structured tools to identify individuals in the emergency department or hospital who are at high risk of reinjury (Kramer et al., 2017). Once the patient is identified, a case manager will approach the patient or, in the case of a minor, the child's parent or guardian, explain the goals and resources of the program, and gain consent for participation. The first approach by the case manager is crucial to gaining trust and providing continuity of care for the program. This case manager then establishes a relationship and rapport with the patient during the remainder of the hospitalization, usually with daily visits. During this time, case managers come to understand the patient's individual needs and individual goals. These may be relatively simple goals, such as obtaining government identification, or could be complex goals, such as applying for education opportunities or job training. Mental health is addressed through screenings and, if needed, services. The patient's goals should be reflective of their individual self-actualization, such as finishing schooling, obtaining work, caring for their family, and participating in their community. They should also, however, be goal directed to reducing further violent victimization, by limiting contact with potentially violent circumstances or gang activity. In many patients, this may require relocation within the community or at times to a new city or state. Once the patient is discharged, they remain in contact with their case worker for as long as necessary for the patient to achieve their goals. These contacts can last as little as a few weeks to months or even years in some cases.

The role of the case manager is not to provide services themselves but rather to serve as a highly available contact and as a conduit to services, a process referred to as a "warm handoff." This can take many forms, from accompanying patients to appointments or services, to helping fill out forms or applications, to simply calling and checking in. Although the case managers typically document their interactions with the patients in some sort of record, these records are usually kept distinct from the medical record to protect privacy, and in most places are not billable hospital services. When needed, social workers or case managers may provide billable services, as may mental health professionals involved in the patient's care. The services that patients are referred to may provide them pro bono or as part of a nonprofit or community service partner, or may charge for services. Navigation tools developed by the programs or by social service and health agencies, or regional health care information exchanges, may assist case managers in sifting through resources and matching patients to the best resource for their needs (Patel et al., 2020). Regardless of the type of service that is provided, it is critical that the case managers accompany patients to the services that are provided and help navigate the community service providers.

HVIP Outcomes

As HVIPs developed over the past two decades, academic institutions have researched and followed the outcomes of this model. Initial studies showed promise in the reduction of reinjury in patients enrolled in the programs, and additional studies focused on weapon carrying, criminal justice offenses, or retaliatory violence as outcome measures of program participation (Shibru et al., 2007; Zun et al., 2006). As far back as 2006, Cooper and colleagues were demonstrating decreased arrests and convictions for violent criminal offenses in program participants (Cooper et al., 2006). A significant amount of research demonstrated process evaluation, such as program enrollment and participation, but not patient-centered or outcome evaluation (Watkins et al., 2021). The highest quality academic literature demonstrated outcome evaluations that included decreased hospital costs, decreased readmissions for violent injury, and increased patient-centered outcomes such as community engagement, health care follow-up, employment, and mental health outcomes (Chong et al., 2015; Juillard et al., 2016; Purtle et al., 2013; Purtle et al., 2015). Bell et al. recently used a regional health care information exchange to show that violent reinjury is decreased when information is gathered from multiple area hospitals (Bell et al., 2018). More recently, focus has shifted away from outcomes related to reinjury and hospital costs toward meaningful patient-centered outcomes such as goal-directed care, improved mental health, and qualitative patient-reported outcomes (Gorman et al., 2022; Monopoli et al., 2021). Zwaiman and colleagues' recent scoping review of HVIPs is the most recent comprehensive evaluation of HVIP literature and suggests that more patient-centered outcomes studies are needed (Zwaiman et al., 2022).

Further studies, as programs evolved, took the form of improving programmatic structure and function, providing guidance to new programs about implementation, and describing patient populations that may benefit (Bonne et al., 2020). Many programs found that not only were their patients benefitting, but families, community organizations, and the case workers themselves were experiencing meaningful improvements in their social determinants of health. Further data demonstrate that when hospital systems work together across cities or regions, the collaboration may result in increased benefit (Mueller et al., 2022).

In spite of some meaningful data to support the programs, some studies do not find the programs efficacious or find the outcomes to be highly variable and nuanced, and therefore evidence-based reviews and meta-analyses were unable to report a benefit to these programs (Simske et al., 2021). Other research found that program replication is difficult, as programs themselves must be culturally competent to their communities (Smith et al., 2013). The Eastern Association for the Surgery of Trauma performed two evidence-based reviews. In these, they concluded that Hospital Based Violence Intervention cannot be recommended as a means for gun violence prevention, although a more recent review demonstrated that community-based programs, many of which are closely related to hospital-based programs, can be recommended (Affinati et al., 2016; Bonne et al., 2021). This has led to significant dispute in medical and public health circles about the value of these intensive, resource-heavy, and expensive programs.

The rebuttal to the arguments about program efficacy has largely centered around patient-centered outcomes, the value proposition of life-altering experiences, and qualitative research that is compelling in its outcomes (Dicker, 2016). Additionally, even if the science is not perfect, the humanity of the argument for helping victims of violence has become enmeshed with the conversation about gun violence specifically in the United States. HVIPs and their counterpart, *community-based violence interventions*, are well liked politically for their community-focused approaches and avoidance of the firearm itself as central to the policymaking. As such, support for this model of programming increased dramatically in the late 2010s, starting first with philanthropic and state funding, and moving on to federal funding.

The Development of a Network of HVIPs

As HVIPs were being born across the United States, the first leaders of HVIPs recognized that there was value in collaboration. Sharing ideas about funding, implementation, evaluation, and sustainability became a focus of a relatively small group of HVIP leaders throughout the 2000s and early 2010s. This group banded together to form the National Network of Hospital Based Violence Intervention Programs (NNHVIP), which later became the Health Alliance for Violence Intervention, the HAVI (http://www.havi.org). The HAVI continues to increase in membership as new programs are born throughout the United States and internationally and has also broadened its scope to include community-based programs that use a public health approach. A national conference provides training and technical assistance to programs, and the organization has a political arm that advocates on state and national levels for the implementation and funding of the hospital-based approach (Bonne et al., 2022).

In addition to the HAVI, other organizations have lent their support to the HVIP model. The American College of Surgeons Committee on Trauma, the verifying body for U.S. trauma centers, supports the implementation of programs in trauma centers and has focused significant effort on publications related to HVIPs (Dicker et al., 2017). The American College of Emergency Physicians has issued similar guidance and support to emergency medicine physicians who build programs in their emergency departments. The American Academy of Pediatrics also has issued statements in support of these programs. From the standpoint of physicians, there is significant support in the medical community for those who are interested implementing HVIPs. There are, however, no mandates or clear requirements for HVIPs in any community, meaning the implementation heavily relies on interested stakeholders, hospital champions, and global hospital buy-in. There are still communities that could significantly benefit from these programs that do not have them for lack of the above.

Future of Hospital-Based Intervention

There is no doubt that Hospital Based Violence Intervention will continue to be a significant part of the future of the violence intervention community. It is also clear, however, that these programs are not a catchall for violence reduction, nor can they operate in a vacuum. They remain one part of the approach of a broader and more comprehensive violence reduction strategy for communities. Complementary strategies include alterations in policing strategies, alternatives to incarceration, and community-based violence intervention and interruption programs. Furthermore, these strategies can be successful only insofar as they are able to provide resources for the individuals they serve. Without addressing poverty, inequity, structural racism, social justice, place-based community interventions, and easy access to firearms, even a comprehensive and multifaceted approach to violence reduction will fail. In addition to addressing individual risk factors, it is imperative to take a progressive approach to investment in communities where violence remains high or ubiquitous. Hospital Based Violence Intervention will always remain a secondary prevention strategy. As such, it plays a role, but focus should be on the mitigation of community factors that lead to violence in the first place and mitigating youth violence before it starts.

References

Affinati, S., Patton, D., Hansen, L., Ranney, M., Christmas, A. B., Violano, P., Sodhi, A., Robinson, B., Crandall, M., & Eastern Association for the Surgery of Trauma Injury Control and Violence Prevention Section and Guidelines Section. (2016). Hospital-based violence intervention programs targeting adult populations: An Eastern Association for the Surgery of Trauma evidence-based review. *Trauma Surgery & Acute Care Open, 1*(1), e000024. https://doi.org/10.1136/tsaco-2016 -000024

Bell, T. M., Gilyan, D., Moore, B. A., Martin, J., Ogbemudia, B., McLaughlin, B. E., Moore, R., Simons, C. J., & Zarzaur, B. L. (2018). Long-term evaluation of a hospital-based violence intervention program using a regional health information exchange. *Journal of Trauma and Acute Care Surgery, 84*(1), 175–182. https://doi.org /10.1097/TA.0000000000001671

Boeck, M. A., Wei, W., Robles, A. J., Nwabuo, A. I., Plevin, R. E., Juillard, C. J., Bibbins-Domingo, K., Hubbard, A., & Dicker, R. A. (2022). The structural violence trap: Disparities in homicide, chronic disease death, and social factors across San Francisco neighborhoods. *Journal of the American College of Surgeons, 234*(1), 32–46. https://doi.org/10.1016/j.jamcollsurg.2021.09.008

Bonne, S. (2017, October 1). Trauma surgeon uses traveling fellowship to learn about HVIPs. *Bulletin of the American College of Surgeons*.

Bonne, S., Hink, A., Violano, P., Allee, L., Duncan, T., Burke, P., Fein, J., Kozyckyj, T., Shapiro, D., Bakes, K., Kuhls, D., Bulger, E., & Dicker, R. (2022). Understanding the makeup of a growing field: A committee on trauma survey of the national network of hospital-based violence intervention programs. *American Journal of Surgery, 223*(1), 137–145. https://doi.org/10.1016/j.amjsurg.2021.07.032

Bonne, S., Tufariello, A., Coles, Z., Hohl, B., Ostermann, M., Boxer, P., Sloan-Power, E., Gusmano, M., Glass, N. E., Kunac, A., & Livingston, D. (2020). Identifying participants for inclusion in hospital-based violence intervention: An analysis of 18 years of urban firearm recidivism. *Journal of Trauma and Acute Care Surgery, 89*(1), 68–73. https://doi.org/10.1097/TA.0000000000002680

Bonne, S. L., Violano, P., Duncan, T. K., Pappas, P. A., Baltazar, G. A., Dultz, L. A., Schroeder, M. E., Capella, J., Hirsh, M., Conrad-Schnetz, K., Rattan, R., Como, J. J., Jewell, S., & Crandall, M. L. (2021). Prevention of firearm violence through specific types of community-based programming: An Eastern Association for the

Surgery of Trauma evidence-based review. *Annals of Surgery, 274*(2), 298–305. https://doi.org/10.1097/SLA.0000000000004837

Chong, V. E., Smith, R., Garcia, A., Lee, W. S., Ashley, L., Marks, A., Liu, T. H., & Victorino, G. P. (2015). Hospital-centered violence intervention programs: A cost-effectiveness analysis. *American Journal of Surgery, 209*(4), 597–603. https://doi.org/10.1016/j.amjsurg.2014.11.003

Cooper, C., Eslinger, D. M., & Stolley, P. D. (2006). Hospital-based violence intervention programs work. *Journal of Trauma, 61*(3), 534–540. https://doi.org/10.1097/01.ta.0000236576.81860.8c

Dicker, R. A. (2016). Hospital-based violence intervention: An emerging practice based on public health principles. *Trauma Surgery & Acute Care Open, 1*(1), e000050. https://doi.org/10.1136/tsaco-2016-000050

Dicker, R. A., Gaines, B., Bonne, S., Duncan, T., Violano, P., Aboutanos, M., Allee, L., Burke, P., Masiakos, P., Hink, A., Kuhls, D. A., Shapiro, D., & Stewart, R. M. (2017, October 1). Violence intervention programs: A primer for developing a comprehensive program for trauma centers. *Bulletin of the American College of Surgeons.*

Dicker, R. A., Jaeger, S., Knudson, M. M., Mackersie, R. C., Morabito, D. J., Antezana, J., & Texada, M. (2009). Where do we go from here? Interim analysis to forge ahead in violence prevention. *Journal of Trauma, 67*(6), 1169–1175. https://doi.org/10.1097/TA.0b013e3181bdb78a

Fischer, K. R., Cooper, C., Marks, A., & Slutkin, G. (2020). Prevention professional for violence intervention: A newly recognized health care provider for population health programs. *Journal of Health Care for the Poor and Underserved, 31*(1), 25–34. https://doi.org/10.1353/hpu.2020.0005

Gorman, E., Coles, Z., Baker, N., Tufariello, A., Edemba, D., Ordonez, M., Walling, P., Livingston, D. H., & Bonne, S. (2022). Beyond recidivism: Hospital-based violence intervention and early health and social outcomes. *Journal of the American College of Surgeons, 235*(6), 927–939. https://doi.org/10.1097/XCS.0000000000000409

Grossman, S., Cooper, Z., Buxton, H., Hendrickson, S., Lewis-O'Connor, A., Stevens, J., Wong, L. Y., & Bonne, S. (2021). Trauma-informed care: Recognizing and resisting re-traumatization in health care. *Trauma Surgery & Acute Care Open, 6*(1), e000815. https://doi.org/10.1136/tsaco-2021-000815

Juillard, C., Cooperman, L., Allen, I., Pirracchio, R., Henderson, T., Marquez, R., Orellana, J., Texada, M., & Dicker, R. A. (2016). A decade of hospital-based violence intervention: Benefits and shortcomings. *Journal of Trauma and Acute Care Surgery, 81*(6), 1156–1161. https://doi.org/10.1097/TA.0000000000001261

Kramer, E. J., Dodington, J., Hunt, A., Henderson, T., Nwabuo, A., Dicker, R., & Juillard, C. (2017). Violent Reinjury Risk Assessment Instrument (VRRAI) for hospital-based violence intervention programs. *Journal of Surgical Research, 217*, 177–186. https://doi.org/10.1016/j.jss.2017.05.023

Monopoli, W. J., Myers, R. K., Paskewich, B. S., Bevans, K. B., & Fein, J. A. (2021). Generating a core set of outcomes for hospital-based violence intervention programs. *Journal of Interpersonal Violence, 36*(9–10), 4771–4786. https://doi.org/10.1177/0886260518792988

Mueller, K. L., Moran, V., Anwuri, V., Foraker, R. E., & Mancini, M. A. (2022). An exploration of factors impacting implementation of a multisystem hospital-based violence intervention program. *Health & Social Care in the Community, 30*(6), e6577–e6585. https://doi.org/10.1111/hsc.14107

Patel, D., Sarlati, S., Martin-Tuite, P., Feler, J., Chehab, L., Texada, M., Marquez, R., Orellana, F. J., Henderson, T. L., Nwabuo, A., Plevin, R., Dicker, R. A., Juillard, C., & Sammann, A. (2020). Designing an information and communications technology tool with and for victims of violence and their case managers in San Francisco: Human-centered design study. *JMIR mHealth and uHealth, 8*(8), e15866. https://doi.org/10.2196/15866

Purtle, J., Dicker, R., Cooper, C., Corbin, T., Greene, M. B., Marks, A., Creaser, D., Topp, D., & Moreland, D. (2013). Hospital-based violence intervention programs save lives and money. *Journal of Trauma and Acute Care Surgery, 75*(2), 331–333. https://doi.org/10.1097/TA.0b013e318294f518

Purtle, J., Rich, L. J., Bloom, S. L., Rich, J. A., & Corbin, T. J. (2015). Cost-benefit analysis simulation of a hospital-based violence intervention program. *American Journal of Preventive Medicine, 48*(2), 162–169. https://doi.org/10.1016/j.amepre.2014.08.030

Shibru, D., Zahnd, E., Becker, M., Bekaert, N., Calhoun, D., & Victorino, G. P. (2007). Benefits of a hospital-based peer intervention program for violently injured youth. *Journal of the American College of Surgeons, 205*(5), 684–689. https://doi.org/10.1016/j.jamcollsurg.2007.05.029

Simske, N. M., Rivera, T., Ren, B. O., Benedick, A., Simpson, M., Kalina, M., Hendrickson, S. B., & Vallier, H. A. (2021). Implementation of programming for survivors of violence-related trauma at a level 1 trauma center. *Trauma Surgery & Acute Care Open, 6*(1), e000739. https://doi.org/10.1136/tsaco-2021-000739

Smith, R., Evans, A., Adams, C., Cocanour, C., & Dicker, R. (2013). Passing the torch: Evaluating exportability of a violence intervention program. *American Journal of Surgery, 206*(2), 223–228. https://doi.org/10.1016/j.amjsurg.2012.11.025

Watkins, J., Scoggins, N., Cheaton, B. M., Nimmer, M., Levas, M. N., Baumer-Mouradian, S. H., & Melzer-Lange, M. D. (2021). Assessing improvements in emergency department referrals to a hospital-based violence intervention program. *Injury Epidemiology, 8*(Suppl. 1), 44. https://doi.org/10.1186/s40621-021-00333-x

Zun, L. S., Downey, L., & Rosen, J. (2006). The effectiveness of an ED-based violence prevention program. *American Journal of Emergency Medicine, 24*(1), 8–13. https://doi.org/10.1016/j.ajem.2005.05.009

Zwaiman, A., da Luz, L. T., Perrier, L., Hacker Teper, M., Strauss, R., Harth, T., Haas, B., Nathens, A. B., & Gotlib Conn, L. (2022). The involvement of trauma survivors in hospital-based injury prevention, violence intervention and peer support programs: A scoping review. *Injury, 53*(8), 2704–2716. https://doi.org/10.1016/j.injury.2022.06.032

Violence Prevention and Safety Promotion in the LGBTQ+ Community

• • • • • • • • • • • • •

COREY PRACHNIAK

Overview

Imagine a secret society so occult that even its own members take years to learn they are part of it, piecing clues together as they come of age. Some are excited, but many are horrified, as much of the public labels them heretics. Some outsiders offer supernatural "cures." Some just want them dead. Talking about the society is, thus, dangerous, and it may take years to find others who are in it.

At least for me, this is how it felt discovering that I was queer and, later, nonbinary. As I slowly came to accept who I was, I created my own space in the lesbian, gay, bisexual, transgender, and queer (LGBTQ+) community. But it was not easy then, and it is even more complicated for youth today. Why? While legal, political, and cultural progress has been sufficient to draw youth out of the closet, there is not yet adequate support available, creating a mirage of acceptance that dissipates as youth approach it. While much has changed since I entered LGBTQ+ activism as a student in 2008, the need to build a more inclusive society has not. LGBTQ+ youth today live in a complicated world with both personal ups and downs and both progress and backlash in politics and society.

To advance violence prevention among LGBTQ+ youth, we must acknowledge the full range of their identities, particularly of those facing intersectional discrimination, as well as the myriad sources of both violence and strengths that they experience. And because LGBTQ+ youth will also face risk and need support, we must bolster efforts to proactively create safe spaces in their schools, communities, homes, and even their own hearts.

Summary and Highlights

The first step in understanding LGBTQ+ youth violence prevention is identifying the broad range of experiences considered violent, which is often not intuitive to outsiders. LGBTQ+ people are at greater risk for violence than the general population, and it is usually committed by someone they know (McKay et al., 2019). At some point, most LGBTQ+ youth will experience abusive language from peers, professionals, family members, and strangers. Some will face physical or sexual violence as well as scientifically discredited attempts to change their sexual orientation or gender identity. This helps explain why gay-identified girls and boys were 1.9 and 3.7 times more likely (respectively) than their heterosexual peers to feel unsafe at or en route to school (Johns et al., 2018). Intimate partner violence is an issue and is exacerbated and complicated by stigma. Violence can even come in the form of self-harm, with sexual minority youth more than three times as likely as others to attempt suicide (Johns et al., 2018). Despite their differences, these forms of violence can all be addressed through creating safe and inclusive spaces and support systems that build agency and resilience. This broad approach is also useful because of the dearth of research on interventions framed explicitly as LGBTQ+ youth violence prevention, with a review of research from 2000 to 2019 finding only one study (Coulter et al., 2019).

LGBTQ+ youth violence prevention work often involves creating (physical or virtual) safe, supportive, and inclusive spaces, which function on several levels. First, they provide a safe place where youth can avoid violent experiences. Second, they provide resources for addressing histories of violence—for example, support groups addressing trauma. Third, they help build resiliency as a protective factor against future violence. Finally, on a macro level, the existence of these spaces sends a signal to the broader social community that LGBTQ+ youth are accepted, and they often provide outreach and education. For example, LGBTQ+ and ally student groups often advocate for more supportive school climates and features such as gender-neutral bathrooms that are associated with reduced suicidality (Eisenberg et al., 2021).

Before delving into specific types of interventions, there are a few pervasive, overarching issues to consider. First, LGBTQ+ initiatives frequently face objections from people who are hostile toward the community and/or who claim no personal hostility but express concern that others find the topic offensive. Ironically, this means that because LGBTQ+ people are disfavored, programming should not be implemented to address their needs, despite that being the very reason that intervention is needed. Second, LGBTQ+ initiatives are often characterized as being improper for government involvement. While public schools are ideal sites for interventions, opponents argue this improperly uses government resources to help youth "question" their identities. Making progress in youths' homes is even more challenging, given the long-standing concept of the home as a private sphere free of state interference (used historically to defend the "rights" of men to assault and control their spouses; Acikalin, 2000). Finally, while the world of LGBTQ+ advocacy has made progress over the years, it remains disproportionately driven by white and/or cisgender perspectives, with Black and Latinx LGBTQ+ folks' intersectional needs ignored and contributions minimized; this provides an important lens from which to critically evaluate the existing literature and interventions.

With these overarching themes in mind, we can examine initiatives for LGBTQ+ youth violence prevention in four roughly cut categories: school-based interventions for youth, community-based interventions for youth, interventions for families, and interventions for professionals.

First, *school-based interventions for youth* are the most widely established and very often the only game in town and are of growing importance as more states ban access to bathrooms and locker rooms for transgender students and censor LGBTQ+ topics. Their necessity is underscored by the fact that LGBTQ+ youth are far more likely than peers to experience issues such as bullying, physical threats or assaults, suicidality, and feeling unsafe attending school (Johns et al., 2018; Johns et al., 2019). When I was a high school student in a small town in the early 2000s, there were no fully "out" students in my class; today, it is not uncommon for even middle schools to have robust LGBTQ+ and allied student groups. These initiatives were widely known as gay-straight alliances, or GSAs, an acronym that today means genders and sexualities alliances, which include non-LGBTQ+ allies who wish to advocate for LGBTQ+ rights. Research has found that involvement in GSAs was associated with greater advocacy and awareness raising and that those skills contributed to agency, a critical factor in addressing violence (Poteat et al., 2018). Involvement in GSA-related advocacy is associated with increased interest in health topics such as substance use and mental and sexual health (Poteat et al., 2017), and the advocacy can yield changes such as gender-neutral bathrooms that are themselves protective factors (Eisenberg et al., 2021). Together, this indicates that GSA-based advocacy improves the well-being of individual students and the entire school.

Second, there are many forms of *community-based programs for youth* that advance violence prevention and safety promotion. While there are some stand-alone programs for LGBTQ+ youth, many are housed within organizations serving LGBTQ+ people of all ages (principally, LGBTQ+ centers) or organizations serving youth generally. Community-based programs include drop-in centers, groups, and one-to-one services. While some receive grants specifically for violence prevention, others receive funds to address issues such as HIV, which disproportionately impacts LGBTQ+ communities. My research has found that HIV organizations are often the leaders in LGBTQ+ issues in their communities, whether because they are the only ones with funding or because they are the only ones interested (Prachniak-Rincón et al., 2021). Reliance on this funding could bias services toward LGBTQ+ youth who are more at risk for HIV, which could unfortunately exclude young women, who make up only 19 percent of new HIV cases (Centers for Disease Control and Prevention, 2022) but who are just as in need of LGBTQ+ services. Building LGBTQ+ services around HIV funding could also repress interest due to lingering HIV-related stigma, but this funding source remains critical. There is comparably little funding available to simply provide a safe space for LGBTQ+ youth without it being tied to particular health outcomes (which, beyond HIV, includes topics like mental health and suicide prevention). Non-health-linked funding would allow for less siloed and more resilient services, so it is critical to consider the entire funding ecosystem when advocating for programs. Even in my state of Massachusetts, where state funding for "at-risk" LGBTQ+ youth in the community has been earmarked, the network of LGBTQ+-serving youth organizations would nonetheless be damaged by major HIV funding cuts (e.g., as has been unfolding in Tennessee; Ryan, 2023). Such cuts could happen with little media fanfare compared to specifically anti-LGBTQ+ laws, but the impact could be just as costly, underscoring the need for vigilant advocacy.

Third, *interventions aimed at families* exist both as stand-alone programs and as components of youth-facing initiatives. As noted above, the "role of the state" issue is a powerful barrier; most parents and caregivers of LGBTQ+ youth cannot be mandated to participate in programs, and those most in need of this education tend not to voluntarily participate. Nevertheless, these programs are vital for caregivers who want to learn how to be supportive, and they produce informal parent "ambassadors" who share their knowledge and resources with others. Local chapters of PFLAG (formerly Parents and Friends of Lesbians and Gays) and similar organizations are the most well-known such programs. Some schools and libraries also offer family assemblies on LGBTQ+ youth issues, which can draw far more adults (and can also produce controversy). Advocates should be creative in seeking to reach as many caregivers as possible. For example, during my work with the Massachusetts government, we fought to have required education for prospective foster and adoptive parents to include information on supporting LGBTQ+ youth. Foster and adoptive parents already undergo training that is considered well within the authority of the state, so this is much more feasible than is educating parents generally.

Finally, there are many *interventions for professionals* that advance violence prevention for LGBTQ+ youth. For example, training initiatives for school personnel on LGBTQ+ identities usually include content on addressing violence and at a minimum make professionals less likely to victimize LGBTQ+ youth. However, anti-bullying laws are set by the state and only half explicitly include LGBTQ+ students (Movement Advancement Project, n.d.), which naturally affects anti-bullying training and outcomes. Additionally, we found in Massachusetts that while the law included LGBTQ+ students and training was supposed to cover this topic, the lack of specific requirements for anti-bullying training meant that the quality and content varied greatly by school. Beyond schools, education for health and social service providers is key to supporting LGBTQ+ youth. Individual universities, certification programs, and employers can implement training requirements, but governments can also play a role. For example, Massachusetts passed a law requiring older adult service providers to have some LGBTQ+ training, and I worked with the state to develop a training prospectively for all state employees, contractors, and grantees. State agencies overseeing youth in group homes, foster care, and the juvenile justice system are responsible for the safety of all youth in their care. Our state's Department of Youth Services, which oversees the juvenile justice system, trained all employees—from its highly supportive commissioner on down—on LGBTQ+ youth and found that framing things as a matter of "youth safety" resonated with staff of all personal beliefs. Law enforcement and first responders also have the potential to either address or contribute to victimization of LGBTQ+ young people, particularly Black and Latinx youth. Finally, pediatricians and primary care providers can be an excellent source of support for both LGBTQ+ young people and their caregivers, but many lack knowledge on the subject as LGBTQ+ content in medical and other health profession schools is very limited (Cooper et al., 2022). In Massachusetts, my efforts to have the Board of Registration in Medicine work to establish standards for LGBTQ+ cultural competency within violence-related required trainings were not met with interest. Gender-affirming care improves mental health of gender-minority youth and so must also be included as a means of violence prevention (Chen et al., 2023).

Best Practices

To be successful and equitable, violence prevention interventions for LGBTQ+ youth should (1) be youth-led, (2) employ an intersectional approach, (3) build advocacy skills, (4) be cross-sectoral and collaborative, and (5) be driven but not limited by data.

First, LGBTQ+ youth initiatives should be youth-led or at least youth-informed. The concept of "nothing about us without us" rejects programs designed for LGBTQ+ youth without so much as their consultation. The needs of youth vary based on their local community and its resources; the needs of urban youth with multiple local LGBTQ+ organizations are different from the needs of rural youth in "resource deserts." When we do this work without youth at the center, we also miss a critical opportunity to foster leadership and agency among a population for whom those skills can save lives.

Second, programs must employ an intersectional approach (Crenshaw, 2015). Black, Latinx, and Indigenous LGBTQ+ youth are often found to have health and socioeconomic inequities compared to their white peers. The health of youth of color is heavily affected by systemic racism (Yusuf et al., 2022). One such impact is mistrust in the governmental, educational, and health institutions in which violence prevention programs are based. Trust must be built by prioritizing these youth and their unique needs. This issue also underscores the importance of supporting community-based programs led by institutions trusted by communities of color.

Third, initiatives should include building advocacy skills, which helps produce systemic change that will have a lasting impact for LGBTQ+ people throughout the community. Additionally, as noted above, building advocacy skills is a protective factor for LGBTQ+ youth, meaning there are both micro and macro benefits to this approach. Advocacy can include the political when appropriate, but also simply advocating for a more inclusive school or community and even self-advocacy (Poteat et al., 2020). This is not to say that all LGBTQ+ youth wish to be advocates or that programs should not also provide safe spaces to simply relax and be youth, but these options can be balanced.

Fourth, initiatives should be cross-sectoral and collaborative. Virtually all LGBTQ+ youth programming relates to violence prevention and safety promotion in some form, and funding comes from a variety of sources. Since LGBTQ+ programs are often limited, seeking partnerships and building capacity with non-LGBTQ+ services is key; guides and policies can ensure that whichever door LGBTQ+ youth enter seeking services, they are connected to all other types of services that are LGBTQ+ inclusive if not specific. Those wishing to engage in this work should practice what we preach and build inclusive and collaborative networks, even when limited funding and bad actors may pit us against each other.

Finally, LGBTQ+ youth violence prevention must be data-driven but not data-limited. "Lack of data" is often thrown in our faces by decision makers who themselves control data collection. We do not always need large-scale

Violence Prevention in the LGBTQ+ Community • 189

quantitative data to tell us what youth need; where formal research is not available, we can rely on youth themselves to tell us what they need. However, where there is advanced research, we should certainly use it to inform our work as not all approaches are created equal. Additionally, programs can improve data themselves; partnering with (though not being co-opted by) local research institutions is a great way to expand the literature and prove our case.

Where Are We Going?

LGBTQ+ rights remain in a tenuous position. There is an increasing divide between states seeking to advance and states seeking to curtail LGBTQ+ rights, and the majority of anti-LGBTQ+ legislation is aimed at youth. In recent years, forty-two states have considered legislation that would make school less inclusive by banning LGBTQ+ discussions, discriminating in school sports, and so forth (Movement Advancement Project, 2022). In addition, with the U.S. Supreme Court recently negating other rights, there is little guarantee that judicial progress will continue or that current victories will survive. Following are recommendations to advance LGBTQ+ youth violence prevention through practice, research, and policy:

1 While I have written much herein about quality, we also need quantity. Perhaps the biggest problem with LGBTQ+ youth programming is that there is simply not enough, especially for youth in areas where transportation is limited. Where LGBTQ+-specific organizations are not present, other entities can offer LGBTQ+ initiatives. Where even that is not possible, existing programs can at least ensure that they are inclusive. Including LGBTQ+ people in outreach materials, hanging an LGBTQ+ flag in the office, and so on encourage LGBTQ+ youth to come in for services and come out to their service provider. LGBTQ+ youth who are most in need of services face multiple forms of marginalization, so those of us concerned with LGBTQ+ youth should also support programs serving youth of color, system-involved youth, and others.

2 We need to explore both political and apolitical approaches. Sadly, extremism is growing worldwide and the idea of "working across the aisle" on LGBTQ+ youth issues is increasingly fantastical, with many politicians actively seeking to harm LGBTQ+ youth. We must elect leaders who support human rights and believe in science, whatever their specific political philosophy. On the other hand, even in politically favorable settings, an activist approach is often not effective when working on the ground with professionals and institutions. We can

focus on the science and frame our work as a matter not of changing people's religious, political, or moral views but of advancing youth safety. Professionals should, at a minimum, know how to respectfully interact with LGBTQ+ youth; ideally, they should also recognize and intervene against violence and refer youth to appropriate resources.

3 Where the political will exists, we can advance policies that require LGBTQ+ training for professionals working with youth; guarantee the right for students to form GSAs, change their name and gender marker in schools, access facilities matching their gender identity, and so on; earmark funding for a variety of purposes (e.g., HIV, mental health, violence prevention) to go specifically to programs serving LGBTQ+ youth; require all government-funded youth programs to implement nondiscrimination policies and conduct training; ensure all government-funded data collection includes sexual orientation and gender identity questions; and ban conversion therapy while guaranteeing access to legitimate health services. Such policies can often be achieved through administrative action, especially when there is leadership from the top, although I have seen progress made with and without interest from agency heads and governors.

4 We have entered a new stage in the Information Age in which an abundance of information, including misinformation, is consuming society. Advocates (and Big Tech) must combat the lies and hysteria surrounding LGBTQ+ youth issues or we will swiftly fail the current generation. We also need more professionals who can connect youth and their caregivers to correct information; larger issues, such as a dearth of mental health providers, are contributing to this problem.

While we face many challenges, we must remain optimistic. LGBTQ+ communities are our own strongest resource and biggest strength. We have supported ourselves and built a vibrant and resilient culture despite violence and marginalization. We must thank the older generation of LGBTQ+ people who protested, marched, and paraded and foster leadership in the next generation as they lead us onward in our fight for justice. Discovering, understanding, and disclosing one's sexual orientation and gender identity may always feel a bit like the "secret society" that I felt I was entered into, but finding a welcoming and supportive community can be a much easier road for today's and tomorrow's youth if we empower them to lead.

References

Acikalin, T. D. (2000). Debunking the dichotomy of nonintervention: The role of the state in regulating domestic violence. *Tulane Law Review, 74*(3), 1045–1066.

Centers for Disease Control and Prevention. (2022). *HIV and women*. https://www
.cdc.gov/hiv/pdf/group/gender/women/cdc-hiv-women.pdf

Chen, D., Berona, J., Chan, Y.-M., Ehrensaft, D., Garofalo, R., Hidalgo, M. A.,
Rosenthal, S. M., Tishelman, A. C., & Olson-Kennedy, J. (2023). Psychosocial
functioning in transgender youth after 2 years of hormones. *The New England
Journal of Medicine, 388*(3), 240–250.

Cooper, R. L., Ramesh, A., Radix, A. E., Reuben, J. S., Juarez, P. D., Holder, C. L.,
Belton, A. S., Brown, K. Y., Mena, L. A., & Matthews-Juarez, P. (2022). Affirming
and inclusive care training for medical students and residents to reducing health
disparities experienced by sexual and gender minorities: A systematic
review. *Transgender Health, 8*(4), 307–327. https://doi.org/10.1089/trgh.2021.0148

Coulter, R., Egan, J. E., Kinsky, S., Friedman, M. R., Eckstrand, K. L., Frankeberger,
J., Folb, B. L., Mair, C., Markovic, N., Silvestre, A., Stall, R., & Miller, E. (2019).
Mental health, drug, and violence interventions for sexual/gender minorities: A
systematic review. *Pediatrics, 144*(3), e20183367. https://doi.org/10.1542/peds.2018
-3367

Crenshaw, K. (2015, September 24). Why intersectionality can't wait. *Washington Post.*
https://www.washingtonpost.com/news/in-theory/wp/2015/09/24/why
-intersectionality-cant-wait/

Eisenberg, M. E., Wood, B. A., Erickson, D. J., Gower, A. L., Kessel Schneider, S., &
Corliss, H. L. (2021). Associations between LGBTQ+-supportive school and
community resources and suicide attempts among adolescents in Massachusetts.
American Journal of Orthopsychiatry, 91(6), 800–811. https://doi.org/10.1037/
ort0000574

Johns, M. M., Lowry, R., Andrzejewski, J., Barrios, L. C., Demissie, Z., McManus, T.,
Rasberry, C. N., Robin, L., & Underwood, J. M. (2019). Transgender identity and
experiences of violence victimization, substance use, suicide risk, and sexual risk
behaviors among high school students—19 states and large urban school districts,
2017. *Morbidity and Mortality Weekly Report, 68*(3), 67–71. https://doi.org/10.15585
/mmwr.mm6803a3

Johns, M. M., Lowry, R., Rasberry, C. N., Dunville, R., Robin, L., Pampati, S., Stone,
D. M., & Mercer Kollar, L. M. (2018). Violence victimization, substance use, and
suicide risk among sexual minority high school students—United States, 2015–
2017. *Morbidity and Mortality Weekly Report, 67*(43), 1211–1215. https://doi.org/10
.15585/mmwr.mm6743a4

McKay, T., Lindquist, C. H., & Misra, S. (2019). Understanding (and acting on)
20 years of research on violence and LGBTQ+ communities. *Trauma, Violence &
Abuse, 20*(5), 665–678. https://doi.org/10.1177/1524838017728708

Movement Advancement Project. (2022). *Policy spotlight: Curriculum censorship &
hostile school climate bills*. https://www.lgbtmap.org/2022-spotlight-school-bills
-report

Movement Advancement Project. (n.d.). *Equality maps: Safe schools laws*. https://www
.lgbtmap.org/equality-maps/safe_school_laws

Poteat, V. P., Calzo, J. P., & Yoshikawa, H. (2018). Gay-straight alliance involvement
and youths' participation in civic engagement, advocacy, and awareness-raising.
Journal of Applied Developmental Psychology, 56, 13–20. https://doi.org/10.1016/j
.appdev.2018.01.001

Poteat, V. P., Godfrey, E. B., Brion-Meisels, G., & Calzo, J. P. (2020). Development of
youth advocacy and sociopolitical efficacy as dimensions of critical consciousness

within gender-sexuality alliances. *Developmental Psychology, 56*(6), 1207–1219. https://doi.org/10.1037/dev0000927

Poteat, V. P., Heck, N. C., Yoshikawa, H., & Calzo, J. P. (2017). Gay-straight alliances as settings to discuss health topics: Individual and group factors associated with substance use, mental health, and sexual health discussions. *Health Education Research, 32*(3), 258–268. https://doi.org/10.1093/her/cyx044

Prachniak-Rincón, C., Mimiaga, M., & Zuniga, J. M. (2021). *LGBTI+ health equity: A global report of 50 fast-track cities.* International Association of Providers of AIDS Care. https://www.iapac.org/files/2021/08/LGBTQ-Health-Report-medium -081721.pdf

Ryan, Benjamin. (2023, February 2). How Tennessee axed millions in HIV funds amid scrutiny from far-right provocateurs. *NBC News.* https://www.nbcnews.com/nbc -out/out-news/tennessee-axed-millions-hiv-funds-scrutiny-far-right-provocateurs -rcna67769

Yusuf, H. E., Copeland-Linder, N., Young, A. S., Matson, P. A., & Trent, M. (2022). The impact of racism on the health and wellbeing of Black Indigenous and other youth of color (BIPOC youth). *Child and Adolescent Psychiatric Clinics of North America, 31*(2), 261–275. https://doi.org/10.1016/j.chc.2021.11.005

Disrupting the Crossover

• • • • • • • • • • • • •

Using and Improving Child Welfare Practice as Youth Violence Prevention

CLAIRE TERREBONNE

Overview: Full Disclosure

I am a child welfare lawyer who represents the best interests of kids navigating the foster care system. As we have lost too many kids to the juvenile and criminal justice systems or as victims of youth violence themselves, I recognize my role in youth violence and "crossover" prevention. When at least *half* of the juvenile justice population first touched the child welfare system and nearly *80 percent* of the juvenile justice population *could* touch the system having experienced some form of childhood maltreatment, my colleagues and I have an opportunity and obligation to disrupt that path. By definition child welfare professionals are in the business of crossover and violence prevention.

So Who Are These Kids?

"Crossover youth" refers to children (yes, adolescents are still children) who have both (1) experienced maltreatment by a parent or primary caregiver and (2) engaged in delinquent acts. This population can be further categorized by their pathways to crossover, defined by the timing, type, depth, and order of contact with the child welfare and juvenile justice systems.

Children in foster care have a much higher risk of juvenile justice involvement than their non-system-involved peers. Even without formal child welfare system involvement, youth who have experienced maltreatment are 47 percent more likely to enter the juvenile justice system than those in the general youth population. In fact, nearly 80 percent of youth in the juvenile justice system self-report having experienced some form of maltreatment even though never formally involved in the child welfare system. According to a 2021 study funded by the Office of Juvenile Justice and Delinquency Prevention, at least *half* of young people entering the juvenile justice system had current or past involvement in the child welfare system. Of these crossover youth, *95* percent are *first* involved in the child welfare system—by far the most common pathway to crossover (Tatem Kelley & Haskins, 2021). Based on these numbers alone, child welfare professionals have an opportunity to prevent nearly *half or more* of all entries into the juvenile justice system. What's more, shifting prevention efforts upstream prior to system involvement could potentially disrupt the vast majority of juvenile justice involvement.

Beyond factors associated with maltreatment and foster care, some groups are at even higher risk of crossing over. For example, African American youth are disproportionately overrepresented in both systems, and even more so in the crossover youth population. Making up only 14 percent of the general youth population, 23 percent of the foster care population, and 41 percent of the juvenile justice population, African American constitute 56 percent of crossover youth. This crossover overrepresentation is more than twice the rate than that in each system independently. Girls are also significantly overrepresented in the crossover population, making up only 27 percent of the overall juvenile justice population but 40 percent of crossover youth. LGBTQ+ youth are likewise overrepresented in both systems (Tatem Kelley & Haskins, 2021). These young people experience removal and out-of-home placement in foster and group homes at higher rates, up to seven times in some studies, than their straight and cisgender counterparts.

Of all demographic indicators relating to system involvement, the most consistent is poverty. The vast majority of youth involved in both the child welfare and juvenile justice systems are experiencing conditions of poverty, and in many cases these conditions are extreme and concentrated. While the correlation between poverty and child maltreatment or youth violence is the subject of much research (but note that poverty does not equal neglect), it's easy to see how children experiencing poverty are overrepresented when their counterparts with more financial means can often manage matters of maltreatment or delinquency privately.

When you can't avoid system involvement, the order and timing of that involvement impact the outcomes of your system experience. Concurrent system involvement (involvement with both systems at the same time) is associated with higher risks for longer and deeper stays in both systems. These youth are at higher risk for placement instability (i.e., a higher likelihood of multiple out-of-home and nonrelative placements), more and longer stays in congregate care facilities like residential treatment centers and group homes, and poorer permanency outcomes overall. Placement instability also leads to school instability, so these youth tend to struggle in traditional school settings, have poor attendance, have higher need for special education services, and exhibit challenging behaviors that teachers and administrators are often unprepared to handle—creating a crossover referral point. The longer these youth are system involved, the greater the likelihood there will be significant disruption in social and emotional developmental; and the deeper they are involved, the farther away they get from their family and community and less likely they are to have connections to positive and *consistent* relationships with caring adults—a perfect storm linked to higher rates of mental health, behavioral, and substance abuse problems. No surprise that studies suggest that up to 83 percent of crossover youth experience challenges with mental health or substance abuse.

The Common Denominator—Childhood Adversities and Complex Trauma

This relationship between maltreatment and delinquent behaviors is sadly unsurprising given what we know about childhood adversities and trauma. The disproportionality among groups also becomes predictable in light of historical and ongoing trauma associated with systemic racism and oppression, the impacts of generational poverty, and other deep-seated social and familial prejudices (especially against girls and LGBTQ+ youth). By definition, crossover youth have experienced at least some form of childhood adversity. These are circumstances or events that pose a serious threat to a child's physical or psychological well-being—things like physical, emotional, or sexual abuse; exposure to domestic violence; or being cared for by someone with a mental illness or substance use disorder. Some youth are more vulnerable to negative impacts of these experiences based on environmental or social conditions like community violence, concentrated poverty, or being members of a historically oppressed group. Similarly, children in the child welfare system experience uniquely complex adversities directly related to their foster care experience—removal from their parents and loss of relationships with family, friends, and community; loss of control over their own autonomy; placement disruptions and exposure to congregate care settings; and an overall discontinuity of care from frequent turnover of caseworkers and other providers who are underpaid and overworked.

We know that these experiences, especially when they occur early in life or are chronic or severe, can result in toxic stress (or prolonged and excessive activation of the body's stress response systems), which literally disrupts the normal development of brain architecture and other organ systems in young children and can even alter the physical structure of a person's DNA. This developmental disruption can lead to wide-ranging effects including physical and mental health problems and even early death. Kaiser Permanente and the Centers for Disease Control and Prevention's landmark study on adverse childhood experiences (ACEs) beginning in the 1990s found a significant relationship between the number of ACEs (a specific subset of childhood adversities) a person has experienced and various negative outcomes in adulthood. The more ACEs one has, the greater the likelihood of poor outcomes. Compared to the general population, children in the child welfare system are more than twice as likely to have experienced at least four ACEs. Therefore, we know the effects of these adverse experiences will show up in our foster youth population (and their families), some of which present as delinquent behaviors that lead to crossover.

Consequently, child welfare professionals must understand the impact of complex trauma and toxic stress. These effects range anywhere from physical, cognitive, and mental health issues to social, emotional, and behavioral problems and typically manifest in seemingly irrational, disproportionate, or counterproductive responses to triggering events and circumstances. Physical effects can include acute symptoms like stomachaches, headaches, and bedwetting, but can also become more general or chronic. When individuals are in constant survival mode, the areas of the brain responsible for executive functioning may not develop normally, leading to difficulty with thinking, learning, problem solving, and self-regulating. These kids struggle with language and reasoning and may also struggle to maintain attention and digest new information.

Effects also include challenges with identifying, expressing, and managing emotions and often result in depression, anxiety, or anger. Because of their overburdened stress response systems, even the mildest stressful event (like a menial school task or a household chore) may trigger an intense and disproportionate emotional response that a child cannot easily regulate. This can look like oppositional, volatile, defensive, and aggressive behavior. Children may also "shut down" or dissociate in response to a triggering event, which may look like inattention to an otherwise important event or instruction, or even "black out," having no memory of certain events. Behavioral responses may also look like overcompliance or "keeping the peace" to their own detriment or apathy to the simplest decision-making situations.

Children who experience maltreatment also learn that adults are unreliable, resulting in difficulty developing healthy attachments to safe caregivers. To "protect" themselves from harm or disappointment, they may respond inappropriately or even aggressively to relationship building efforts. This self-protection may interfere with friendships, "respecting" authority figures (like teachers, school administrators, employers, and law enforcement), and even romantic relationships. Shame, guilt, low self-esteem, and a poor self-image are also common among these children, resulting in negative expectations of themselves, often leading to risk-taking behaviors, like self-harm, early and unsafe sexual activity, general recklessness, alcohol and substance use and abuse, running away, and delinquent behaviors.

When we understand the effects of childhood adversities and how they show up in behaviors, we can better respond to reduce further harm and their long-term negative impacts, including crossover.

Trauma-Informed Child Welfare Best Practices Can Disrupt Crossover

We know that even when maltreatment has occurred, children do best (across all domains) when they can safely remain in their homes or, if removal is necessary, return to safer and healthier homes as quickly as possible. So then, after safety, the primary goal of the child welfare system is family preservation. Federal and state child welfare legislation and policy, at least theoretically, have long prioritized maltreatment prevention, family preservation planning and services, and timely permanency to achieve that goal. This legal framework actually is a useful tool in crossover prevention. With child-centered and trauma-informed best practices and skills, practitioners can use this legal framework to address and mitigate nearly every risk factor associated with crossover and can interrupt it simply by doing what they should be trained to do.

Legal Framework

Federal law requires state child welfare agencies to make "reasonable efforts" to prevent removal and, if removal is necessary, to develop and work a case plan to reunify children with parents. When children are removed from their homes, the law requires these agencies to place children in the least-restrictive, most family-like setting, preferably with grandparents, other relatives, or familiar people, and emphasizes the importance of keeping siblings together. Agencies' reasonable efforts to keep children safely in their homes with intensive in-home services or with relatives through kinship navigator programs will avoid common crossover points and other risk factors. When parents or relatives are not an option, traditional foster homes are preferred over group homes and other congregate care settings that are associated with higher risk of crossover.

The law also requires, throughout the entire foster care case, that the state agency coordinate with education providers to maintain educational stability, provide timely and adequate access to physical, dental, and mental health care, and provide access to age-appropriate prosocial, extracurricular, enrichment, and cultural activities. These services help reduce the negative impact of maltreatment and help youth heal from their adverse experiences, which reduces the problem behaviors that lead to crossover.

Where reunification with a parent is not possible within a reasonable time frame, the state agency must make "reasonable efforts" to find alternative permanency options for children through adoption, guardianship, or another alternative. This ensures that children will remain connected to caring adults and maintain a sense of belonging to family. Moreover, recognizing the significant risk factors associated with entering adulthood without family-based permanency, the law requires special care be given to these transition-aged youth by providing resources around housing, education, employment, and health care as well as maintaining connections with positive adults and peers, to empower them to be self-sufficient and reduce the likelihood of having future system involvement as adults.

Skills and Practice

This framework alone, however, does not prevent crossover. It's the skilled, trauma-informed practice within the framework that prevents crossover when done well and with adequate resources. Making effective use of the legal framework begins with *really* listening to and engaging with our children and families to develop a complete understanding about the child and their lives. By understanding how they experience their circumstances, we can build trusting relationships with the child and their family—the foundation of effective child advocacy. Seeing things through the child's and family's perspective helps in assessing physical and emotional safety without overreacting because of personal bias. If safety cannot be ensured in the home, this approach will help identify the most natural alternative placement. Safety out of the home must also be regularly assessed given how commonly youth report harm in out-of-home care, including foster homes and especially residential settings.

Needs assessments and case planning should prioritize the child's voice and choice as the experts in their own lives, recognizing how privilege, power, and inequalities impact how voice and choice are used. This process should empower families to identify their own strengths to build upon and share meaningful decision-making responsibility, and should also encourage self-efficacy in finding paths to learn, grow, and heal from their adverse experiences to prevent further maltreatment or deeper/longer system involvement.

Case planning should be an iterative process, developed early and regularly reviewed and updated. A successful case plan requires multidisciplinary collaboration, information sharing, and decision making with the child, family, and other supports to ensure appropriate services are being provided and evaluated. To promote placement stability in foster or relative homes, it must support caregivers in understanding a child's trauma history and provide tools to respond to difficult, trauma-based behaviors. To promote educational stability, the plan must include collaboration and information sharing with schools to ensure educators and administrators are equipped with appropriate tools and techniques to handle a child's educational challenges and behaviors and maximize time spent in the classroom. The case plan should include regular communication and collaboration among other providers beyond placement and school (e.g., therapists, health care providers, parent educators, case managers, treatment counselors, mentors, other family members, and natural supports) to ensure all have access to the same information and tools to support the child and family, even when they are still making mistakes. It's the support through the bad times that can often be the difference between success and failure.

The case plan should include evidence-based services when available. Relevant services include (1) family preservation, visitation, and locator services to keep children connected to their families, communities, and identities; (2) meaningful and effective mental and physical health care services tailored to address and mitigate the impact of trauma but without pathologizing typical childhood behaviors; (3) early childhood and education services, including school stability advocacy during placement changes, special education services, and school discipline protections to keep kids in classrooms and prevent adultification and crossover opportunities; (4) normative childhood extracurricular, enrichment, prosocial, and cultural activities; and, for older youth, (5) transition-related services like assistance with housing, employment, and developing independent living skills.

The case plan must also include services for parents, acknowledging that they are struggling with their own trauma histories, the effects of which are directly impacting their ability to parent. These services include assistance with meeting their family's basic needs like housing and employment, but also family-strengthening services like parenting education, mental health treatment, domestic violence counseling and intervention, and substance abuse treatment.

So Why Are We Still Failing Some Kids?

We know who these kids and families are and the poor outcomes they face without effective intervention. We know the supports and services that can address many or all of the contributing factors that lead to child welfare, juvenile justice, and dual system involvement. Guided by this knowledge, recent federal and state legislation and public policy, like the Family First Prevention Services Act, while not perfect, incentivize both the child welfare and juvenile justice systems to invest in preventative and community-based services. But our child welfare systems have not quite kept up with this broader view of prevention and instead continue to approach the work as finite interventions with scarce resources.

Now, instead of relying solely on the overburdened frontline workers to pull kids out of the proverbial river in a current moving too quickly to reach them all, we need to sufficiently invest in these systems and a collaborative network to build enough capacity to reach every person in the river *and* prevent people from falling in upstream. We need adequate system-level support and infrastructure that promotes collaboration, information and resource sharing, and workforce training and support so practitioners can truly activate best practices instead of the constant triage based on the crisis of the day.

Luckily, states and local jurisdictions don't need to develop a broader approach to prevention from scratch—models and guidance for these reforms already exist. The most relevant roadmap in this crossover space is Georgetown's Center for Juvenile Justice Reform's (CJJR) Crossover Youth Practice Model (CYPM). Launched in 2010 and now operating in over a hundred jurisdictions in twenty-three states, CYPM addresses the unique and complex needs of crossover youth, with goals of reducing youth crossover, out-of-home placement, the use of congregate care, and disproportionate representation of youth of color and other groups in systems. Based on more than a decade of learning, CJJR has compiled a set of prevention recommendations and strategies along the prevention continuum for jurisdictions to consider and implement.

Some of these strategies are already in place in systems and best practice models. Others could be easily implemented on the ground with adequate resources and support (e.g., mental health crisis response teams instead of using law enforcement, and ending zero tolerance policies in schools). So what these recommendations really highlight for me is the need for fearless, vocal, and servant leadership.

The single most effective stakeholder to fill that leadership role necessary to garner the system-level (and legislative and policy) support required to make real change is the juvenile court—we need judicial leadership. Their authority, their decision-making responsibility impacting children and families in crisis, and their overall community influence put juvenile court judges in a perfect position to convene stakeholders from all systems that touch children and families both when *and before* they appear in a court—including not only the child welfare, juvenile justice, and behavioral and mental health systems but also schools, hospitals, and other family- and community-serving systems. Judicial leadership can start meaningful conversations among stakeholders about this broader approach to prevention work—how systems intersect, overlap, and can work together to keep kids safely in their homes and communities; ways we can share information and resources across systems (and identify barriers currently preventing that exchange); and the importance of cross-system training and continuing education.

Real justice happens when children and families can thrive without ever touching the child welfare or juvenile justice systems or, if system involvement is necessary, when it is a positive experience. As stewards of justice, juvenile court judges can lead the way to finding the political will to operationalize a robust cross-system prevention network.

References

Centers for Disease Control and Prevention. (2019). *Preventing adverse childhood experiences (ACEs): Leveraging the best available evidence.* https://www.cdc.gov/violenceprevention/pdf/preventingACEs.pdf

Felix, S. (2016, June 1). Improving multisystem collaboration for crossover youth. *Advocates' Forum.* https://crownschool.uchicago.edu/student-life/advocates-forum/improving-multisystem-collaboration-crossover-youth

Herz, D. C., Dierkhising, C. B., Raithel, J., Schretzman, M., Guiltinan, S., George, R. M., Cho, Y., Coulton, C., & Abbott, S. (2019, August 5). Dual system youth and their pathways: A comparison of incidence, characteristics, and systems experiences using linked administrative data. *Journal of Youth and Adolescence, 48,* 2432–2450. https://doi.org/10.1007/s10964-019-01090-3

Miller, A., & Pilnik, L. (2021, July). *Never too early: Moving upstream to prevent juvenile justice, child welfare, and dual system involvement.* Georgetown University, McCourt School for Public Policy, Center for Juvenile Justice Reform. https://cjjr.georgetown.edu/resources/publications/

National Association of Counsel for Children. (2022). *Recommendations for legal representation of children and youth in neglect and abuse proceedings.* https://naccchildlaw.app.box.com/s/vsg6w5g2i8je6jrut3aeozjt2fvgltsn

Tatem Kelley, B., & Haskins, P. A., (2021, October). Dual system youth: At the intersection of child maltreatment and delinquency. *National Institute of Justice Journal, 283.* https://nij.ojp.gov/topics/articles/dual-system-youth-intersection-child-maltreatment-and-delinquency

Following the Lead of Child Survivors of Domestic Violence

●●●●●●●●●●●●●

Toward Peace, Equity, and Wholeness

SHENNA MORRIS AND
CASEY KEENE

Overview

It was a warm night in 1989 when a mother and her child fled from their home seeking reassured safety for the night. Despite the parents being separated since their child was five, the mother and child found themselves in what appeared to be an annual cycle of having to leave their home after the father's visits. The child's father would become violent in a matter of moments as visits with the child would come to an end. Though the mother and child lived in housing separate from the father, which was supposed to be the safe haven that liberated them from the violence, they still found themselves needing to leave their home and seek refuge at the home of a friend—lean on community—in these times of crisis.

It was the support of family, friends, and community that would carry them through the years as the child grew into adulthood and the repetitive cycle of violence ended. These supportive networks launched into a system of support, providing child care, financial assistance, and emergency shelter long before there was the strong network that we've come to know as the domestic violence movement. It has always been vital to ensure that family and friends, as critical players in the resilience of children exposed to violence, have the knowledge and resources needed to transform from bystanders to critical masses of collective care.

It was a cold winter morning just before dawn in 1991 when a mother and her three children, aged eleven, seven, and twelve months, arrived at the door of their local domestic violence shelter. Over the preceding years, she had navigated increasing isolation and loss of connection to her family, community, neighborhood, and place of employment. There had been several attempts to seek help from health care, law enforcement, church, and school along the way—all pleas ignored or rejected, or simply not enough. Now, this mother and her children were starting over with their collective strength in survival, the support of advocates, and their belief in the possibility of a life free of violence. Families can experience this kind of liberation when there is community connectedness, economic justice, and trauma-informed systems of care and support. When we invest in ensuring equitable access to the social and environmental conditions that are necessary for people to thrive, we create a world where liberation is possible.

While these are the stories of the authors, they are certainly not unique to them. According to the National Survey of Children's Exposure to Violence (NatSCEV), approximately 1 child in 12 witnessed family violence in the past year (8.2 percent), with lifetime rates of exposure to violence at 7 in 10 (71.5 percent) for youth ages 14 to 17 and 2 in 5 (39.2 percent) for all children and youth. Children who experience domestic violence are also likely to be exposed to other types of violence, described as *polyvictimization*, with nearly one-half (48.4 percent) reporting six or more types of direct or witnessed victimization and 1 in 20 (4.9 percent) reporting ten or more types (Finkelhor et al., 2015). While these numbers demonstrate that childhood trauma is common, the stories behind them illustrate the transformative potential of social networks and institutions that nurture the health and well-being of children and families.

Survivors of violence are the experts in their lived experiences. They are well positioned to offer insights about the dynamics and impacts of the abuse they experienced as well as important reflections on key factors that either helped to mitigate or compounded the harm. Children exposed to domestic violence have lived in a home with a person who used various abusive tactics to exert power and control over their primary caregiver. They have firsthand knowledge of various protective strategies that support survival and how communities, institutions, and systems can alleviate, complicate, or compound their trauma. This wisdom must guide our approach to addressing and preventing violence in the lives of children.

Refreshing Our Beliefs and Practices

The Adult Children Exposed to Domestic Violence (ACE-DV) Leadership Forum of the National Resource Center on Domestic Violence was established in 2014 to amplify the voices and experiences of ACE-DV to enhance efforts to end domestic violence. This project, led by advocates in the movement to end gender-based violence who identify as having experienced domestic violence in childhood, strives to build a movement that includes the perspectives and priorities of children exposed to domestic violence in the provision of services, the development of policy, the direction of research, and the general approach to effectively address and prevent domestic violence. The project advances its goals through training, technical assistance, resource development, and policy advocacy to create pathways to healing and justice and build the capacity of those who support children and families. These activities are in service to the project's larger purpose: *to center humanity as healing.*

The ACE-DV Leadership Forum is grounded in and guided by six core beliefs, crafted by ACE-DV members, that reflect the shared perspectives that emerged from their common experiences. Described throughout this chapter, each offers unique opportunities for best practice that is centered on the lived experiences and expertise of survivors.

1 Children exposed to domestic violence can heal and thrive.

The stories of children exposed to domestic violence are much more than tales of adversity. They are stories rich in assets and strengths rooted in family, culture, spirituality, and community that foster posttraumatic growth and resilience. Adverse childhood experiences lead to specialized skills for adaptation that can and do result in healthy, well-adjusted adult lives. The deficit model that informs our understanding of childhood domestic violence dwells on negative outcomes, impairment, and loss. This, in turn, traps survivors with expectations that they are doomed to repeat intergenerational cycles of violence and abuse. These assumed expectations can be particularly harmful and stigmatizing for children of color, particularly Black children, and can contribute to school-to-prison pipeline culture. But the fact is that most American children who experience domestic violence grow up to make a different choice.

The positive impacts of trauma are well documented in research (Michenbaum, 2011; Peterson et al., 2008; Tedeschi & Calhoun, 1996), and ACE-DV members have identified several assets gained through their experiences of trauma:

- enhanced awareness of red flags
- advanced protective capacity
- high tolerance for stress
- creative, high-level problem-solving skills
- greater flexibility and acceptance in relationships
- positive parenting choices
- increased empathy

A paradigm shift in which we amplify strengths, foster hope, and expect resilience can have a transformative effect on the well-being and growth of those who have experienced adversity. Experiences of trauma are complex and result in both losses and gains, but must always be approached through their potential for healing and thriving.

RECOMMENDATIONS INCLUDE THE FOLLOWING:

- Advance conversations that explicitly name the context and impact of racial oppression and center the lived experiences of communities of color and that promote or reinforce survivors' resilience as an equal part of their healing and journey.
- Explore points of posttraumatic growth with young people who experience harm, including the use of tools to measure strengths, assets, hope, and resilience (Keene, 2017).
- Amplify the cultural assets of young people who experience harm, including extended kin and social networks, faith and spirituality, hope and optimism, and familial role flexibility (Lloyd et al., 2022).

2 Each of us should be allowed and encouraged to name our own experience.

Trauma is a common human experience. It is something that happens to each of us in our lives and helps to shape who we are. Cultural norms that reject and devalue victimhood contribute to a harmful stigma that perpetuates the isolation and secrecy in which violence thrives.

Our prevention efforts must actively promote a cultural shift that allows survivors to bring their experiences into the light without fear or shame. Their lived experiences are critical to advance social change. Survivor identity is innately valuable in all spheres, and their stories and the lessons we glean from them are important to creating the future we want to see. This is *survivor-centered prevention*.

RECOMMENDATIONS INCLUDE THE FOLLOWING:

- Shift from framing survivor experiences in one-dimensional, deficit ways (the dangerous "Single Story")[1] to multilayered, complex stories with depth and value for the unique nuances of and intersections in their stories (Ngozi Adichie, 2009).
- Include survivors with lived experience in the planning of prevention programming, from inception to implementation (Vassell et al., 2021).

3 There is a difference between loving a person who uses violence and condoning their behavior.

One dynamic that can be challenging to understand for people who have not experienced domestic violence is the complex relationship between a person who uses violence and the family members they abuse. Children exposed to domestic violence may both love and hate or want and reject the person who is choosing to use violence in their home. These feelings can occur simultaneously. This is often an ongoing journey and can change at various points of a survivor's life cycle.

Those who use violence are inherently multidimensional people with various aspects to their personality that may be appealing, fun, or even loving. Additionally, the causes of their violent behavior are varied, although certainly reinforced by cultural norms and values. They are not one-dimensional monsters, and describing them in this way can be particularly problematic for children as they grow, form their own identities, and navigate what their relationships are or will be to the person who caused harm. The reality is that many children must remain in contact with those who abuse, and there can be value and developmental significance in these relationships despite the inherent harm.

In many cases, especially for victims in contact with those who abuse, true "safety" from violence may not be possible. This is often the case for families with children for whom ongoing contact is court mandated, for survivor parents who do not have the financial means to separate and support children on their own, or for those whose deeply held beliefs or values are to remain in the relationship. As Jill Davies notes in *Victim-Defined Advocacy Beyond Leaving: Safer through Strategies to Reduce Violent Behavior* (2019), "Even when the relationship ends, familial connections and parenting can mean a person subjected to violence will be in continued contact with a person who has hurt them." In these cases, we must support survivors in navigating and reducing the violence, through "safer" strategies that decrease harm, increase economic stability, and strengthen well-being. Limiting or severing ongoing contact can be an especially complex and harmful reality for survivors from culturally specific communities such as Indigenous or Native Alaskan communities. Survivors in these communities are often faced with the realities of being unable to physically relocate due to geographical barriers or incapable of disassociating because doing so removes them from the only family, culture, and community they may have.

People who choose to abuse are human, and our prevention efforts must recognize and embrace the full humanity of those who cause harm. Centering the humanity of those who cause harm sees them in the context of their whole lives—past and present. It is a practice that allows people to live in authentic relationships, embracing discomfort, imperfection, and humility. Embracing humanity means rejecting a culture of individualism and disconnection that is a breeding ground for violence and oppression, and nurturing connection, interdependence, and wholeness.

RECOMMENDATIONS INCLUDE THE FOLLOWING:
- Find ways to support survivors in each phase of their healing and journey in navigating the relationship to those who have caused them harm.
- Promote "safer" strategies with those for whom "safety" is not possible, especially those who remain in relationship with those who cause harm (Davies, 2019).
- Acknowledge and explore the humanity of those who cause harm in conversations with survivors.
- Reinforce narratives that hold the truths that (1) each of us may cause harm, (2) each of us is deserving of love, and (3) we are all more than the harm we have caused.

4 Violence is learned and reinforced by societal norms, yet accountability and commitment to change can create a new path.

Hurt people hurt people. Rooted in oppressive social ideals, violence is a learned behavior that is culturally enforced and internalized in many ways. This means that the belief systems contributing to the creation of an acceptable culture of violence can be unlearned. Prevention strategies that help to shift from a culture of individual to collective care and responsibility, and from punishment to accountability, can create new possibilities for a nonviolent future.

Traditional mainstream responses to harm are punitive and carceral in nature, involving the removal of resources, caring, and compassion. These responses are focused on individual-level change and often replicate violence and oppression. Our historical overreliance on these solutions has also caused community harm and thus has become a contributing factor to the continuous cycles of violence communities experience.

By shifting to approaches that seek to heal and restore, opportunities arise where individuals and communities are thriving rather than simply surviving. Transformative justice approaches focus on understanding and addressing the conditions that allowed harm to occur in the first place (Chow Reeve, 2020). These conditions stem from a variety of factors at all levels of the social environment—society, community, relationship, and individual—that increase the risk of domestic violence occurring (Centers for Disease Control and Prevention [CDC], 2021). Identifying and nurturing protective factors at each level helps to create conditions, instead, where people can thrive.

Transformative justice approaches are focused on systemic-level, collective change that is the very nature of prevention work. These responses center equity and justice for those who are disproportionately impacted by violence and oppression, creating pathways for access to resources that support well-being, such as advocating for policies that allow for a thriving wage, clean water, and quality health care. In the video *What Is Transformative Justice?* from the Barnard Center for Research on Women (2020), Mia Mingus says that transformative justice "most importantly, helps to create and cultivate the very things we know help to prevent violence. Things like resilience, safety, healing, connection, all of those things."

RECOMMENDATIONS INCLUDE THE FOLLOWING:

- Resist narratives that reinforce negative stereotypes of those who have caused harm and promote those that see them in the fullness of their humanity. For example, describing a person who has caused harm as a "bad person" versus focusing on the person's behavior can reinforce social norms of focusing on the individual instead of the various social factors that contribute to people's use of violence.
- Leverage learnings from holistic and community-driven frameworks in violence prevention efforts (CDC, 2022), such as looking across all levels of the social-ecological model to identify and promote protective factors and opportunities for norms change (CDC, 2022).
- Explore, embrace, and infuse transformative justice values and frameworks into primary prevention efforts. For example, implement community-informed and -led efforts rather

than prioritizing engagement and leadership of systemic interventions.

5 Our survivor parent was faced with limited and complex choices.

We do not often pause to consider and appreciate the survival of parents who navigate violence. Parenting within the context of violence is uniquely difficult, as the very nature of abuse is the removal of the victim's personal agency and autonomy. But within the controlling and oppressive limitations of abuse, and under the stress that these conditions create, studies have consistently shown that survivor parents possess similar or higher quality parenting strengths compared to parents in nonviolent homes. In fact, research shows that survivor parents can play a major role in mitigating the impact of their children's exposure to violence and often attempt to compensate for the violence through demonstrations of maternal warmth (Safe & Together Institute, 2017).

There is power in survival at the intersections of trauma and oppression. As the experts of their experiences, survivors have a keen awareness of what they and their families need to live free from violence. This can be a difficult concept for helping systems to embrace, particularly as mainstream responses and practices have not historically centered inclusion of the voices and lived experiences of those harmed. Embracing survivors as experts shifts our perceptions of who survivors are and helps us to see them in the fullness of their humanity.

Prevention strategies can focus on creating conditions where survivors have safer options. For example, economic insecurity is often cited as the primary or most significant barrier to safety for survivors of intimate partner violence (Wider Opportunities for Women, 2013). Advocacy efforts have often shown that survivors are keenly aware of the needed economic supports that will aid them in remaining safe. Removing economic barriers creates a pathway for living free of violence.

Additionally, strategies focused on enhancing the social determinants of health can create more equitable conditions where liberation and freedom from violence are much more possible. These include economic stability, access to quality education and health, healthy and safe neighborhoods, and social and community support (CDC, 2021).

RECOMMENDATIONS INCLUDE THE FOLLOWING:

- Value, elevate, and celebrate survivorship and its positive impact on families, communities, organizations, and institutions.

- Center or recenter programmatic goals, directions, and priorities based on the direct input, guidance, and primary leadership of survivors most impacted, including mechanisms for ongoing accountability to survivors.
- Invest in prevention strategies that are focused on creating or enhancing equity and access to increase options and support agency for those navigating abuse.

6 Our unique experiences bring added value to social change movements and human service sectors.

Individuals who experienced domestic violence in childhood are in your family, your neighborhood, your workplace, and your place of worship. They are in communities leading efforts to create meaningful change. Many are driven to social change work because of their personal experiences with trauma. In our organizations, social service settings, and community organizing work, it is important that we not ask survivors to separate their lived experience from their professional expertise, as they are one and the same. Liberation is possible only when each of us can live into our full humanity.

RECOMMENDATIONS INCLUDE THE FOLLOWING:
- Create trauma-informed workplaces that acknowledge and respond to employees' experiences of harm and support survivors in bringing their whole selves to their work, if they choose to do so.
- Value the expertise and contributions of survivors in all spaces, demonstrated tangibly through the provision of, at minimum, thoughtful accommodations and fair compensation.

Conclusion

When we refresh our beliefs and practices, we call forth the opportunity to create a just society where communities and individuals can live free from violence, grow, and thrive with all that they need and as the best versions of themselves. As survivors of childhood domestic violence, we offer a shared vision of hope and possibility for a peaceful and equitable society:

In this society, punitive responses are not the immediate response, and community does not turn away from what is occurring or pass judgement. This society is one where a family can call upon their community at first sight of changing dynamics, where both partners are embraced, and flaws are used to bring forth their collective strengths. In this society the children are certain that they are safe in their homes, will witness the modeling of respect and regard for humanity through the interactions of their parents and community members, and will know that there is always room for all the unique complexities that make them who they are.

This becomes possible when we work in service of the purpose of the ACE-DV Leadership Forum: *to center humanity as healing.*

Note

1 Author Chimamanda Ngozi Adichie (2009) uses the phrase "single stories" to describe the overly simplistic and sometimes false perceptions we form about individuals, groups, and countries. She says, "The single story creates stereotypes, and the problem with stereotypes is not that they are untrue, but that they are incomplete. They make one story become the only story."

References

Barnard Center for Research on Women. (2020, March). *What is transformative justice?* https://www.youtube.com/watch?v=U-_BOFz5TXo&t=156s

Centers for Disease Control and Prevention. (2021, November). *Risk and protective factors for perpetration.* National Center for Injury Prevention and Control, Division of Violence Prevention. https://www.cdc.gov/violenceprevention /intimatepartnerviolence/riskprotectivefactors.html

Centers for Disease Control and Prevention. (2022). *The social-ecological model: A framework for prevention.* National Center for Injury Prevention and Control, Division of Violence Prevention. https://www.cdc.gov/violenceprevention/about /social-ecologicalmodel.html

Chow Reeve, L. (2020, June). *How can advocates better understand transformative justice and its connection to gender-based violence intervention and prevention work?* National Resource Center on Domestic Violence. https://vawnet.org/news/how -can-advocates-better-understand-transformative-justice-and-its-connection -gender-based

Davies, J. (2019). *Victim-defined advocacy beyond leaving: Safer through strategies to reduce violent behavior.* Building Comprehensive Solutions to Domestic Violence, National Resource Center on Domestic Violence. https://vawnet.org/sites/default /files/assets/files/2020-05/NRCDV_VictimDefinedAdvocacyBeyondLeaving -Oct2019.pdf

Finkelhor, D., Turner, H., Shattuck, A., Hamby, S., & Kracke, K. (2015, September). Children's exposure to violence, Crime, and abuse: an update. In *Juvenile justice bulletin: National Survey of Children's Exposure to Violence.* U.S. Department of Justice, Office of Justice Programs, Office of Juvenile Justice and Delinquency Prevention. https://www.unh.edu/ccrc/sites/default/files/media/2022-02 /-childrens-exposure-to-violence-crime-and-abuse-an-update.pdf

Keene, C. (2017, January). *How can victim advocates utilize self-assessment tools as an empowerment strategy in practice?* National Resource Center on Domestic

Violence. https://vawnet.org/news/how-can-victim-advocates-utilize-self
-assessment-tools-empowerment-strategy-practice

Lloyd, C., Shaw, S., Sanders, M., Abdul-Masih, M., Schaefer, C. (2022, February). *Reimagining Black families' cultural assets can inform policies and practices that enhance their well-being.* Child Trends. https://www.childtrends.org/publications /reimagining-black-families-cultural-assets-can-inform-policies-and-practices-that -enhance-their-well-being

Michenbaum, D. (2011). *Important facts about resilience: A consideration of research findings about resilience and implications for assessment and treatment.* Melissa Institute. https://www.melissainstitute.org/documents/facts_resilience.pdfNgozi Adichie, C. (2009). The danger of a single story [Video]. TED/YouTube. https:// www.youtube.com/watch?v=D9Ihs241zeg

Office of Disease Prevention and Health Promotion. (2022). *Healthy People 2030: Social determinants of health.* Office of the Assistant Secretary for Health, Office of the Secretary, U.S. Department of Health and Human Services. https://health.gov /healthypeople/priority-areas/social-determinants-health

Peterson, C., Park, N., Pole, N., D'Andrea, W., Seligman, M. E. (2008). Strengths of character and posttraumatic growth. *Journal of Trauma Stress, 21*(2), 214–217. https://doi.org/10.1002/jts.20332

Safe & Together Institute. (2017, August). *Domestic violence-informed research briefing: Domestic violence survivors' parenting strengths.* https://safeandtogetherinstitute .com/

Tedeschi, R. G., & Calhoun, L. G. (1996). The Posttraumatic Growth Inventory: Measuring the positive legacy of trauma. *Journal of Trauma Stress, 9*(3), 455–471. https://doi.org/10.1007/BF02103658

Vassell, A., Corley-Funchess, S., & Morgan, V. (2021, October). *Survivor-centered prevention: Listening to survivors of color / Apertura, clausura y plenaria— Prevención centrada en les sobrevivientes: escuchemos a les sobrevivientes de color.* National Resource Center on Domestic Violence. https://vawnet.org/material /national-prevention-town-hall-2021-day-1-opening-closing-plenary-survivor -centered

Wider Opportunities for Women (WOW). (2013). *Fact sheet: Economic abuse.* https://safehousingpartnerships.org/sites/default/files/2017-01/ESS-Economic -Abuses-Fact-Sheet-2013.pdf

Current Issues and Emerging Needs in Teen Dating Violence Prevention

• • • • • • • • • • • • •

KATRINA J. DEBNAM

Overview

Each day in the United States, three women are murdered by a current or former intimate partner (Catalano, 2013). One woman in four and one man in seven will experience intimate partner violence (IPV) in their lifetime (Walters et al., 2013). More than 81 million women and men have experienced psychological aggression by an intimate partner (Niolon & Centers for Disease Control and Prevention [CDC], 2017). Among people from communities that have been marginalized (e.g., African American, sexual minority) rates of IPV are even higher, ranging from 45 to 54 percent (Niolon & CDC, 2017). For IPV survivors who attempt to leave their abuser, data show that it takes an average of seven attempts for a survivor to leave their abuser and stay separated for good. This time of leaving and attempted separation is the most dangerous time in an abusive relationship and is often when homicides occur. These heartbreaking statistics coupled with the stories of those close to me and my own personal experiences with sexual assault compelled me to do this work.

Through my initial research, I learned that IPV often begins early in life. Sixteen million women and men who reported experiencing sexual violence, physical violence, or stalking by an intimate partner in their lifetime also reported that they first experienced these forms of violence before the age of eighteen (Niolon & CDC, 2017). To me, this was evidence that we needed to start the prevention of IPV during early adolescence. Early adolescence (i.e., ages ten to fourteen) is a challenging time for a myriad of developmental reasons, but historically practitioners and researchers have been hesitant to explicitly discuss partner violence with adolescents at this early age. Yet research shows adolescents are actively engaging in healthy and unhealthy relationship behaviors during this time. Thus, I began to invest my time and energy into understanding the factors that put adolescents at risk for or protect them from this form of violence. I am compelled by a personally driven belief that prevention of IPV is possible. If we can, as a society, promote healthy, respectful, and nonviolent romantic relationships in our homes and communities then we will succeed at reducing the occurrence of IPV and homicides committed by intimate partners.

Summary and Highlights

The CDC uses the term "teen dating violence" (TDV) to describe a version of IPV that affects at least one in ten adolescents in the United States each year (CDC, 2021). TDV can occur in person, online, or through technology (e.g., cell phone) and includes the following subtypes:

- physical—hitting, kicking, or using another type of physical force (e.g., choking) to hurt or try to hurt a partner
- sexual—forcing or attempting to force a partner to take part in a sex act, sexual touching, or a nonphysical sexual event (e.g., sexting) when the partner does not or cannot consent
- psychological/emotional—using verbal and nonverbal communication with the intent to harm another person mentally or emotionally and/or exert control over another person
- stalking—pattern of repeated, unwanted attention and contact by a partner that causes fear or concern for one's own safety or the safety of someone close to the victim

Ecological Influences on TDV

It is critical to consider how the levels of our social ecology (i.e., societal, community, relational, individual) increase challenges and risk for TDV (CDC, n.d.). At the societal level, traditional gender norms, structural racism, and weak health and educational policies have a tremendous trickle-down effect on TDV. For example, traditional masculine norms center around expectations that boys and men should be tough, strong, dominant, fearless, sexually promiscuous, emotionally stoic, homophobic, and aggressive and should take risks. Some research shows that boys and men who strongly adhere to these views are more likely to perpetrate sexually related partner violence than individuals who are not high in these attitudes (McCauley et al., 2014; Reed et al., 2011; Reidy et al., 2014; Reidy et al., 2015; Vagi et al., 2013). For youth who contend with intersecting identities, like young Black women, sexualized marginalization has resulted in pejorative gendered and racialized stereotypes that affect their self-image and experiences of TDV victimization (Blackmon et al., 2017; Debnam et al., 2021).

At the community level, systematic reviews of TDV literature indicate that several neighborhood factors might increase perpetration of TDV: alcohol outlet density, perceived neighborhood disorder, social disorganization, and lack of connectedness (Johnson et al., 2015; Offenhauer & Buchalter, 2011). These studies suggest that community violence (e.g., having seen someone assaulted and witnessing a murder or shooting) may also desensitize adolescents to violence, which may lead to them seeing violence as acceptable in a relationship (Copp et al., 2015; Voith, 2019). However, collective efficacy, defined as the community's cohesiveness and residents' willingness to intervene for the common good, was found to lower the risk of dating violence perpetration by male youth aged thirteen to nineteen (Jain et al., 2010). There is limited evidence that neighborhood factors are associated with TDV victimization.

Family, friends, and social networks, or the interpersonal level of the social ecology, account for much of the existing research on risk and protective factors for TDV victimization and perpetration. In general, exposure to violence in one's family, either through witnessing parental violence or being the victim of violence/abuse from a parent (i.e., child maltreatment), places children at risk for dating violence perpetration during adolescence (Glass et al., 2003; Vezina & Hebert, 2007). Some studies also suggest growing up in a home environment characterized by a lack of parental affection, support, supervision, or excessive discipline can increase the risk of dating violence victimization for adolescents (Ehrensaft et al., 2003; Glass et al., 2003; Howard & Wang, 2003; Vezina & Hebert, 2007). Finally, beliefs about aggression within romantic and sexual relationships are often developed within friend groups and peer social circles

Adolescents with friends who normalize relational and sexual violence have increased odds of experiencing dating violence themselves (Collins et al., 2009).

At the individual level, though youth identifying with marginalized gender, racial, ethnic, socioeconomic, and sexual orientation groups hold higher rates of TDV victimization and perpetration when compared to other groups, these elevated rates are a by-product of the above societal, community, and relational factors that they are more likely to experience. Yet a number of individual-level factors are associated with TDV victimization. Internalizing symptoms, like feelings of depression and suicidal ideation, place adolescents at increased risk for dating violence victimization (Ehrensaft et al., 2003). Adolescents with histories of suicide attempts and those who exhibit disordered eating are also at higher risk for experiencing TDV victimization (Spencer et al., 2020). Externalizing behaviors and attendant negative interactions, such as school disciplinary action, aggressive retaliation, and negative peer responses, have been strongly associated with TDV perpetration (Fix et al., 2021).

In summary, TDV perpetration and victimization is associated with depression, disordered eating, and acquiring sexually transmitted infections as well as experiencing unplanned pregnancy, substance use, suicidal ideation, injury, and death (Ackard et al., 2007; Exner-Cortens et al., 2013). However, it is important to recognize that there is often a reciprocal association between the risk factors for TDV and the consequences of TDV, such that a behavior might both increase a teen's risk for experiencing TDV and be a result of TDV experience. Unfortunately, while much research has been devoted to factors associated with TDV, there is less known about root causes of TDV.

Prevention Programs for TDV

Effective and comprehensive prevention programming is needed to reduce TDV. Prevention programming generally occurs at the primary or secondary levels of prevention; primary prevention refers to universal approaches to preventing victimization and perpetration before it occurs. Primary prevention programming seeks to address the underlying attitudes, norms, and behaviors that support TDV. These programs target prominent risk factors of TDV (e.g., acceptance of violence, conflict-management skills, bystander norms) or promote protective factors like healthy relationship characteristics (Coker et al., 2011; Foshee et al., 1998; Wolfe et al., 2009). Secondary prevention targets individuals or groups of individuals that are at higher than average risk of experiencing or perpetrating TDV. These prevention programs often focus on males, youth with previous exposure to violence, and youth with involvement with child protective services (Exner-Cortens et al., 2019; Exner-Cortens et al., 2020; Miller et al., 2012).

How Is the Best Work Getting Done?

A number of prevention programs have shown effectiveness at preventing TDV perpetration and victimization. The majority of these programs are delivered in schools and take a primary prevention focusing on both TDV perpetration and victimization; they use educational curriculum to target middle- and high-school-aged adolescent attitudes, beliefs, and behaviors. For example, the Fourth R curriculum targets the interpersonal level of the social ecology using twenty-one lessons delivered to students by their teachers regarding negotiation, problem solving, and navigating peer conflicts (Wolfe et al., 2009). The initial evaluation trial of Fourth R found significantly reduced physical dating violence perpetration by boys compared with a control group at the 2.5-year follow-up as well as increased condom use and small effects on sexual assault victimization in a later study (Cissner & Ayoub, 2014; Wolfe et al., 2009). Another school-based TDV prevention program, Safe Dates, also primarily targeted interpersonal and individual factors among middle and high school students but also included activities for parents. Four years after the program, youth reported less physical, serious physical, and sexual perpetration and physical abuse victimization when compared to the control group (Foshee et al., 2004).

More recent programs, like the CDC's Dating Matters, have broadened the focus of primary prevention programs to include the community ecology and have seen similar positive effects (Taylor et al., 2013; Tharp, 2012; Tharp et al., 2011). The Dating Matters program incorporates training for parents of sixth to eighth graders, educator training, a youth communications program, and local health department activities to assess capacity and track TDV-related policy and data. Trial results revealed lower TDV perpetration, lower TDV victimization, and lower use of negative conflict resolution strategies (DeGue et al., 2021; Niolon et al., 2019). While the programs described above targeted perpetration *and* victimization, an innovative program with coaches and high school male athletes focused solely on reducing TDV perpetration through social norms in the community. The Coaching Boys into Men program trained athletic coaches to talk with their adolescent male athletes about respect, nonviolence, healthy relationships, and positive bystander behaviors. Research findings showed that the program increased high school male athletes' intentions to intervene and actual bystander intervention behaviors.

Across these programs, teaching safe and healthy relationship skills, creating safe and protective environments (i.e., schools and neighborhoods), and engaging peers and influential adults (i.e., parents and teachers) emerge as core elements of successful prevention programs (Niolon & CDC, 2017). While the success of these programs is to be celebrated, overall, we have yet to see substantial change in the nationwide prevalence of TDV victimization reporting and perpetration of TDV is not currently assessed in nationwide surveys (CDC,

2019). Unfortunately, the long-term effects of prevention programs are often limited to those youth who directly participated in the curriculum and are rarely monitored longitudinally. The lasting success of these programs is likely dependent on how sustained the programs become to the school environment. How many schools are able to continue implementing the program once research funding has ended? Sustained implementation of TDV prevention programs like these in schools and communities would impact interpersonal and individual risk factors for TDV.

Where Are We Going?

There are many gaps in existing research on TDV that urgently need to be addressed. One large gap is the lack of attention, programs, and resources designed for marginalized groups in the United States. The vast majority of existing evidence-based TDV programs were developed with and for cisgender, heterosexual, white youth (Crooks et al., 2019). Very few prevention programs have been developed with Black and Indigenous populations who, based on national data, have the highest prevalence of TDV among racial and ethnic groups. For example, the Fourth R program has been modified, through partnership with Indigenous communities, to become the Fourth R: Uniting Our Nations initiative. This program is distinct from the original Fourth R in its use of culturally relevant teaching methods, inclusion of community members (i.e., elders), and focus on mentorship and youth voice (Crooks et al., 2015). Emerging research shows similarly high rates among LGBTQ+ youth. Research is underway to develop prevention programming that would meet the needs of LGBTQ+ youth (Crooks et al., 2019). Furthermore, very rarely do we discuss TDV prevention among youth with (dis)abilities, unhoused or precariously housed youth, or youth in contact with child welfare and criminal justice institutions. Research by Emily Rothman at Boston University is currently exploring the challenges that youth on the autism spectrum face when maintaining healthy relationships with dating partners (Rothman et al., 2015; Rothman et al., 2022). Youth whose identity intersects with more than one of these marginalized groups are at even greater risk of repeated exposure to TDV. We have the data that show these groups are experiencing elevated levels of perpetration and victimization, and now it is time to work *with* these youth to develop prevention programs that consider their specific cultures, situations, and challenges.

Bridging Siloed Violence Prevention Efforts

In addition to a new focus on marginalized groups, research in the area of violence prevention for youth is still fragmented and disparate. It is important to not treat relationship abuse as a singular experience that youth undergo.

Experience with TDV happens within the context of other important exposures, like bullying, child maltreatment, and sex trafficking. More research, both theoretical and empirical, to understand how these experiences relate to one another, could drive the creation of more effective and comprehensive violence prevention programming. A study by Hamby and colleagues found that child maltreatment was associated with physical TDV. In their study more than half of physical TDV victims had a history of some form of child maltreatment (Hamby et al., 2012). Numerous studies have found that bullying and TDV tend to cooccur with bullying experiences preceding TDV developmentally (Debnam et al., 2016; Wincentak et al., 2017). And though not all bullies or victims of bullying go on to perpetrate or become victims of TDV, studies have shown that bullying may predict TDV perpetration longitudinally (Espelage et al., 2021; Espelage & Holt, 2007 Foshee et al., 2016). Furthermore, there is some evidence that a common pathway to commercial sexual exploitation (e.g., sex trafficking) for minors is through their dating partners, who agree to engage in sex work out of loyalty and devotion to their dating partners (Rothman et al., 2015). Last, recent studies have found associations between viewing violent pornography, sexually aggressive behavior, and TDV (Rothman & Adhia, 2015; Ybarra et al., 2011). These are all research areas with established relationships with TDV that need to be considered in the overall developmental trajectory of youth.

A Stronger Focus on Protective Factors

Finally, much research has focused on identifying the risk factors and consequences of TDV victimization and perpetration to the detriment of investigating protective factors. Even on the CDC website you can view a list of thirty or more specific risk factors for IPV compared to a vague list of six protective factors for IPV perpetration (https://www.cdc.gov/intimate-partner-violence/risk-factors/index.html#cdc_risk_factors_protect_factor-protective-factors-for-perpetration). Prevention science has historically taken a deficit-based approach to understanding violence, but what would happen if we refocused on strengths-based approaches? It is possible that primary prevention efforts would be more impactful if they targeted specific *modifiable* positive factors that protect youth. To this end, a recent technical package of IPV prevention programs developed by CDC emphasizes positive conditions at various levels of the social ecology, like teaching relationship skills and creating protective school and neighborhood environments, that help to prevent TDV (Niolon & CDC, 2017). Many of the positive conditions in the technical package are already built into effective dating violence prevention programs.

Research is currently underway to uncover and promote other, more specific modifiable protective factors (Smith-Darden et al., 2017). For example, a recent study by Espelage and colleagues (2020) found that empathy, social support, parental monitoring, and school belonging in middle school were protective against various forms of TDV perpetration. There is also evidence that some protective factors may be culturally bound or cultural assets. Emerging research shows cultural assets, like racial identity and communalism, may enable African American and Indigenous youth to obtain and maintain healthy relationships (Filbert & Flynn, 2010; Wallace et al., 2018; Woods-Jaeger et al., 2021). Greater knowledge about and support for the protective factors related to healthy romantic relationship development among youth may be just as impactful as or more impactful than our current attempts to reduce ecological risk factors of TDV.

References

Ackard, D. M., Eisenberg, M. E., & Neumark-Sztainer, D. (2007). Long-term impact of adolescent dating violence on the behavioral and psychological health of male and female youth. *Journal of Pediatrics, 151*(5), 476–481.

Banyard, V. L., Cross, C., & Modecki, K. L. (2006). Interpersonal violence in adolescence: Ecological correlates of self-reported perpetration. *Journal of Interpersonal Violence, 21*(10), 1314–1332.

Blackmon, S. M., Owens, A., Geiss, M. L., Laskowsky, V., Donahue, S., & Ingram, C. (2017). Am I my sister's keeper? Linking domestic violence attitudes to Black racial identity. *Journal of Black Psychology, 43*(3), 230–258.

Catalano, S. M. (2013). *Intimate partner violence—Attributes of victimization, 1993–2011.* U.S. Department of Justice, Office of Justice Programs, Bureau of Justice Statistics.

Centers for Disease Control and Prevention. (2019). *Youth Risk Behavior Survey (YRBS).*

Centers for Disease Control and Prevention. (2021). *Preventing teen dating violence.* https://www.cdc.gov/violenceprevention/pdf/ipv/TDV-factsheet_508.pdf

Centers for Disease Control and Prevention. (n.d.). *The social-ecological model: A framework for prevention.* https://www.cdc.gov/violenceprevention /publichealthissue/social-ecologicalmodel.html

Cissner, A. B., & Ayoub, L. H. (2014). *Building healthy teen relationships.* Center for Court Intervention.

Coker, A. L., Cook-Craig, P. G., Williams, C. M., Fisher, B. S., Clear, E. R., Garcia, L. S., & Hegge, L. M. (2011). Evaluation of Green Dot: An active bystander intervention to reduce sexual violence on college campuses. *Violence Against Women, 17.* https://doi.org/10.1177/1077801211410264

Collins, W. A., Welsh, D. P., & Furman, W. (2009). Adolescent romantic relationships. *Annual Review of Psychology, 60*(1), 631–652.

Copp, J. E., Kuhl, D. C., Giordano, P. C., Longmore, M. A., & Manning, W. D. (2015). Intimate partner violence in neighborhood context: The roles of structural disadvantage, subjective disorder, and emotional distress. *Social Science Research, 53,* 59–72.

Crooks, C. V., Burleigh, D., Snowshoe, A., Lapp, A., Hughes, R., & Sisco, A. (2015). A case study of culturally relevant school-based programming for First Nations youth: Improved relationships, confidence and leadership, and school success. *Advances in School Mental Health Promotion, 8*(4), 216–230.

Crooks, C. V., Jaffe, P., Dunlop, C., Kerry, A., & Exner-Cortens, D. (2019). Preventing gender-based violence among adolescents and young adults: Lessons from 25 years of program development and evaluation. *Violence Against Women, 25*(1), 29–55.

Debnam, K. J., Milam, A. J., & Finigan-Carr, N. (2021). Superwoman, racial identity, and teen dating violence victimization among young Black women. *Journal of Interpersonal Violence, 37.* https://doi.org/10.1177/08862605211021984

Debnam, K. J., Waasdorp, T. E., & Bradshaw, C. P. (2016). Examining the contemporaneous occurrence of bullying and teen dating violence victimization. *School Psychology Quarterly, 31*(1). https://doi.org/10.1037/spq0000124

DeGue, S., Niolon, P. H., Estefan, L. F., Tracy, A. J., Le, V. D., Vivolo-Kantor, A. M., Little, T. D., Latzman, N. E., Tharp, A., & Lang, K. M. (2021). Effects of Dating Matters® on sexual violence and sexual harassment outcomes among middle school youth: A cluster-randomized controlled trial. *Prevention Science, 22*(2), 175–185.

Ehrensaft, M. K., Cohen, P., Brown, J., Smailes, E., Chen, H., & Johnson, J. G. (2003). Intergenerational transmission of partner violence: A 20-year prospective study. *Journal of Consulting and Clinical Psychology, 71*(4), 741–753.

Espelage, D. L., & Holt, M. K. (2007). Dating violence and sexual harassment across the bully-victim continuum among middle and high school students. *Journal of Youth and Adolescence, 36,* 799–811. https://doi.org/10.1007/s10964-006-9109-7

Espelage, D. L., Ingram, K. M., Hong, J. S., & Merrin, G. J. (2021). Bullying as a developmental precursor to sexual and dating violence across adolescence: Decade in review. *Trauma, Violence, & Abuse, 23*(4), 1358–1370.

Espelage, D. L., Leemis, R. W., Niolon, P. H., Kearns, M., Basile, K. C., & Davis, J. P. (2020). Teen dating violence perpetration: Protective factor trajectories from middle to high school among adolescents. *Journal of Research on Adolescence, 30*(1), 170–188.

Exner-Cortens, D., Eckenrode, J., & Rothman, E. (2013). Longitudinal associations between teen dating violence victimization and adverse health outcomes. *Pediatrics, 131,* 71–78. https://doi.org/10.1542/peds.2012-1029

Exner-Cortens, D., Hurlock, D., Wright, A., Carter, R., & Krause, P. (2020). Preliminary evaluation of a gender-transformative healthy relationships program for adolescent boys. *Psychology of Men & Masculinities, 21*(1), 168–175.

Exner-Cortens, D., Wright, A., Hurlock, D., Carter, R., Krause, P., & Crooks, C. (2019). Preventing adolescent dating violence: An outcomes protocol for evaluating a gender-transformative healthy relationships promotion program. *Contemporary Clinical Trials Communications, 16,* 100484.

Filbert, K. M., & Flynn, R. J. (2010). Developmental and cultural assets and resilient outcomes in First Nations young people in care: An initial test of an explanatory model. *Children and Youth Services Review, 32*(4), 560–564.

Fix, R. L., Aaron, J., & Greenberg, S. (2021). Experience is not enough: Self-identified training needs of police working with adolescents. *Policing, 15,* 2252–2268. https://doi.org/10.1093/police/paab039

Foshee, V. A., Bauman, K. E., Arriaga, X. B., Helms, R. W., Koch, G. G., & Linder, G. F. (1998). An evaluation of Safe Dates, an adolescent dating violence prevention program. *American Journal of Public Health, 88*(1), 45–50.

Foshee, V. A., Benefield, T. S., Ennett, S. T., Bauman, K. E., & Suchindran, C. (2004). Longitudinal predictors of serious physical and sexual dating violence victimization during adolescence. *Preventive Medicine, 39*(5), 1007–1016.

Foshee, V. A., Benefield, T. S., McNaughton Reyes, H. L., Eastman, M., Vivolo-Kantor, A. M., Basile, K. C., Ennett, S. T., & Faris, R. (2016). Examining explanations for the link between bullying perpetration and physical dating violence perpetration: Do they vary by bullying victimization? *Aggressive Behavior, 42*(1), 66–81.

Glass, N., Fredland, N., Campbell, J., Yonas, M., Sharps, P., & Kub, J. (2003). Adolescent dating violence: Prevalence, risk factors, health outcomes, and implications for clinical practice. *Journal of Obstetric, Gynecologic & Neonatal Nursing, 32*, 227–238. https://doi.org/10.1177/0884217503252033

Hamby, S., Finkelhor, D., & Turner, H. (2012). Teen dating violence: Co-occurrence with other victimizations in the National Survey of Children's Exposure to Violence (NatSCEV). *Psychology of Violence, 2*(2), 111–124.

Howard, D. E., & Wang, M. Q. (2003). Risk profiles of adolescent girls who were victims of dating violence. *Adolescence, 38*(149), 1–14.

Jain, S., Buka, S. L., Subramanian, S. V., & Molnar, B. E. (2010). Neighborhood predictors of dating violence victimization and perpetration in young adulthood: A multilevel study. *American Journal of Public Health, 100*(9), 1737–1744. https://doi.org/10.2105/AJPH.2009

Johnson, R. M., Parker, E. M., Rinehart, J., Nail, J., & Rothman, E. F. (2015). Neighborhood factors and dating violence among youth: A systematic review. *American Journal of Preventive Medicine, 49*(3), 458–466.

Maas, C. D., Fleming, C. B., Herrenkohl, T. I., & Catalano, R. F. (2010). Childhood predictors of teen dating violence victimization. *Violence and Victims, 25*(2), 131–149.

McCauley, H. L., Jaime, M. C. D., Tancredi, D. J., Silverman, J. G., Decker, M. R., Austin, S. B., Jones, K., & Miller, E. (2014). Differences in adolescent relationship abuse perpetration and gender-inequitable attitudes by sport among male high school athletes. *Journal of Adolescent Health, 54*(6), 742–744.

Miller, E., Tancredi, D. J., McCauley, H. L., Decker, M. R., Virata, M. C. D., Anderson, H. A., Stetkevich, N., Brown, E. W., Moideen, F., & Silverman, J. G. (2012). "Coaching boys into men": A cluster-randomized controlled trial of a dating violence prevention program. *Journal of Adolescent Health, 51*(5), 431–438. https://doi.org/10.1016/j.jadohealth.2012.01.018

Niolon, P. H., & Centers for Disease Control and Prevention. (2017). *Preventing intimate partner violence across the lifespan: A technical package of programs, policies, and practices.* Government Printing Office.

Niolon, P. H., Vivolo-Kantor, A. M., Tracy, A. J., Latzman, N. E., Little, T. D., DeGue, S., Lang, K. M., Estefan, L. F., Ghazarian, S. R., & McIntosh, W. L. K. (2019). An RCT of Dating Matters: Effects on teen dating violence and relationship behaviors. *American Journal of Preventive Medicine, 57*(1), 13–23.

Offenhauer, P., & Buchalter, A. (2011). *Teen dating violence: A literature review and annotated bibliography.* National Criminal Justice Reference Service.

Reed, E., Silverman, J. G., Raj, A., Decker, M. R., & Miller, E. (2011). Male perpetration of teen dating violence: Associations with neighborhood violence involvement, gender attitudes, and perceived peer and neighborhood norms. *Journal of Urban Health, 88*(2), 226–239.

Reidy, D. E., Berke, D. S., Gentile, B., & Zeichner, A. (2014). Man enough? Masculine discrepancy stress and intimate partner violence. *Personality and Individual Differences, 68*, 160–164.

Reidy, D. E., Smith-Darden, J. P., Cortina, K. S., Kernsmith, R. M., & Kernsmith, P. D. (2015). Masculine discrepancy stress, teen dating violence, and sexual violence perpetration among adolescent boys. *Journal of Adolescent Health, 56*(6), 619–624.

Rothman, E. F., & Adhia, A. (2015). Adolescent pornography use and dating violence among a sample of primarily Black and Hispanic, urban-residing, underage youth. *Behavioral Sciences, 6*(1), 1.

Rothman, E. F., Bazzi, A. R., & Bair-Merritt, M. (2015). "I'll do whatever as long as you keep telling me that I'm important": A case study illustrating the link between adolescent dating violence and sex trafficking victimization. *Journal of Applied Research on Children, 6*(1), 8.

Rothman, E. F., Graham Holmes, L., Caplan, R., Chiang, M., Haberer, B., Gallop, N., Kadel, R., Person, M., Sanchez, A., & Quinn, E. (2022). Healthy Relationships on the Autism Spectrum (HEARTS): A feasibility test of an online class co-designed and co-taught with autistic people. *Autism, 26*(3), 690–702.

Rothman, E. F., Johnson, R. M., Young, R., Weinberg, J., Azrael, D., & Molnar, B. E. (2011). Neighborhood-level factors associated with physical dating violence perpetration: Results of a representative survey conducted in Boston, MA. *Journal of Urban Health, 88*(2), 201–213.

Smith-Darden, J. P., Kernsmith, P. D., Reidy, D. E., & Cortina, K. S. (2017). In search of modifiable risk and protective factors for teen dating violence. *Journal of Research on Adolescence, 27*(2), 423–435.

Spencer, C. M., Anders, K. M., Toews, M. L., & Emanuels, S. K. (2020). Risk markers for physical teen dating violence victimization in the United States: A meta-analysis. *Journal of Youth and Adolescence, 49*(3), 575–589.

Taylor, B. G., Stein, N. D., Mumford, E. A., & Woods, D. (2013). Shifting boundaries: An experimental evaluation of a dating violence prevention program in middle schools. *Prevention Science, 14*(1), 64–76.

Tharp, A. T. (2012). Dating Matters: The next generation of teen dating violence prevention. *Prevention Science, 13*(4), 398–401.

Tharp, A. T., Burton, T., Freire, K., Hall, D. M., Harrier, S., Latzman, N. E., Luo, F., Niolon, P. H., Ramirez, M., & Vagi, K. J. (2011). Dating Matters: Strategies to promote healthy teen relationships. *Journal of Women's Health, 20*(12), 1761–1765.

Vagi, K. J., Rothman, E. F., Latzman, N. E., Tharp, A. T., Hall, D. M., & Breiding, M. J. (2013). Beyond correlates: A review of risk and protective factors for adolescent dating violence perpetration. *Journal of Youth and Adolescence, 42*, 633–649. https://doi.org/10.1007/s10964-013-9907-7

Vezina, J., & Hebert, M. (2007). Risk factors for victimization in romantic relationships of young women: A review of empirical studies and implications for prevention. *Trauma, Violence, & Abuse, 8*(1), 33–66.

Voith, L. A. (2019). Understanding the relation between neighborhoods and intimate partner violence: An integrative review. *Trauma, Violence, & Abuse, 20*(3), 385–397.

Wallace, C. M., McGee, Z. T., Malone-Colon, L., & Boykin, A. W. (2018). The impact of culture-based protective factors on reducing rates of violence among African American adolescent and young adult males. *Journal of Social Issues, 74*(3), 635–651.

Walters, M. L., Chen, J., & Breiding, M. J. (2013). *The National Intimate Partner and Sexual Violence Survey (NISVS): 2010 findings on victimization by sexual orientation*. National Center for Injury Prevention and Control, Centers for Disease Control and Prevention.

Wincentak, K., Connolly, J., & Card, N. (2017). Teen dating violence: A meta-analytic review of prevalence rates. *Psychology of Violence, 7*(2), 224–241.

Wolfe, D. A., Crooks, C., Jaffe, P., Chiodo, D., Hughes, R., Ellis, W., Stitt, L., & Donner, A. (2009). A school-based program to prevent adolescent dating violence: A cluster randomized trial. *Archives of Pediatrics & Adolescent Medicine, 163*(8), 692–699.

Woods-Jaeger, B., Briggs, E. C., Gaylord-Harden, N., Cho, B., & Lemon, E. (2021). Translating cultural assets research into action to mitigate adverse childhood experience–related health disparities among African American youth. *American Psychologist, 76*(2), 326–336.

Ybarra, M. L., Mitchell, K. J., Hamburger, M., Diener-West, M., & Leaf, P. J. (2011). X-rated material and perpetration of sexually aggressive behavior among children and adolescents: Is there a link? *Aggressive Behavior, 37*(1), 1–18.

20

Spiritual and Faith-Based Approaches to Preventing Youth Violence

• • • • • • • • • • • • •

KRISTA R. MEHARI AND
DEMETRIUS R. SMITH

Overview

Youth violence is an urgent concern for many communities that have been hit hard by violence and are actively working to reduce youth violence through grassroots strategies. These grassroots strategies likely include faith-based approaches—the majority of people in the United States have spiritual or religious beliefs, and about half belong to a local house of worship, like a church, synagogue, or mosque (Pew Research Center, 2016). Spiritual or faith-based youth violence prevention approaches could have a far-reaching impact on youth violence. But there is a disconnect between violence prevention research in public health and the practice of faith, religion, or spirituality. Because of this disconnect, there is very little scientific evidence about the impact of faith-based or spiritually integrated approaches to youth violence prevention.

One possible reason for this disconnect is the history of science versus religion, winner-take-all battles (e.g., Captari et al., 2022). Another reason for the disconnect is that religion has been used to justify violence and oppression against members of marginalized groups. Every major global religion has at some point supported the oppression of and violence against minoritized groups. As evidence of this, the United Nation's Human Rights Council tracks how religion is currently being used to incite violence and other human rights violations (United Nations, 2022). In the United States, for example, the Christian church played a major role in the artificial creation of subhuman status for Black people in order to justify enslavement and other forms of violence and oppression (for a brief review, see Bahler, 2020).

Despite the science-faith disconnect, much violence prevention work may be motivated by a sense of meaning and purpose. Faith communities often have a sense of purpose in working toward creating a better world. As practitioners and applied researchers, many of us believe youth have a fundamental human right to be safe, to be protected from violent acts, and to be free to pursue good lives. At a systems level, religious institutions like churches and mosques can promote safety and wellness by serving as a source of public health information, providing access to resources, creating social support and community, and catalyzing collective action to address social injustice. This is especially true for people who are members of marginalized racial or ethnic groups such as African Americans. Classic examples of this include Nat Turner's rebellion, which was driven by Black Christianity, and collective action organized through faith leaders such as the Reverend Dr. Martin Luther King Jr. (e.g., Gates, 2021). Locally, there are organizations such as Faith in Action Alabama, which is an interfaith organization with a goal of creating systemic change to allow pathways to opportunity for everyone, including by protecting voting rights and preventing violence. There are also countless examples of religious institutions leading prayer walks and vigils and organizing rallies and protests, all with the goal of moving toward safety. Anecdotally, religious buildings can sometimes provide safe places or neutral ground in ongoing neighborhood or gang-associated conflict. Overall, religious institutions have served as major pillars in promoting wellness, safety, and justice in their communities, and much of the motivation for doing so has been based in faith and spirituality.

Our journey to spiritually conscious violence prevention began in community-based participatory action research as part of Project THRIVE, a citywide effort in Mobile, Alabama, to reduce youth violence and promote resilience following trauma. We led a needs assessment in a community burdened with high rates of violence. We engaged in a series of conversations in schools and community centers, including interviews and focus groups, youth advisory board meetings, and community advisory board meetings. The most pressing concern, universally expressed by all respondents, was youth violence and the need for safety. The murders of children, youth, and young adults have created deep wounds in the community. We heard grief for the loss of each life, rage for the seemingly endless killings, and hopelessness about the future. In contrast, strengths that were identified included a sense of community and historical pride (especially related to civil rights action) as well as active churches and faith-based community centers.

This sparked a larger intervention development project, in which the authors and others collaborated in a participatory action research approach to build and test a culturally grounded violence prevention program for youth, taking a strengths-based or positive youth development approach (see Mehari, Jeffrey, Chastang, Blanton, et al., 2023). Our community partners emphasized the need for a sense of purpose and hope in order to thrive or to obtain a good life. The themes that emerged were as follows: being others-focused, maintaining integrity and acting consistently with one's values, having an awareness of right and wrong, and living life with purpose. In other words, youth need to see that they are part of something greater than themselves and to have values, purpose, and meaning that provide guidance and direction (Mehari et al., n.d.).

Through this participatory action process, we decided to build Empowered, a youth violence prevention strategy focused on developing youths' sense of transcendent meaning and hope, peace, wisdom, and forgiveness. The intervention also included skills building for problem solving, emotion regulation, and assertive communication within the context of youths' transcendent meaning and character strengths. To build the intervention, we pulled components of existing best-practice violence interventions (e.g., Responding in Peaceful and Positive Ways; Farrell et al., 2001) and positive psychology interventions (e.g., REACH Forgiveness; Worthington, 2003), wove in meaning and purpose, and developed new components based on our participatory action process (cf. Mehari, Jeffrey, Chastang, & Schnitker, 2023). We also developed a site-level strategy to reinforce and scaffold youths' positive development.

Summary and Highlights

Meaning and purpose are important parts of people's lives and may even be fundamental to humanity (Frankl, 1959). We use the words "meaning" and "purpose" to include the meaning systems of people who identify as agnostic or atheistic (see Table 20.1). Meaning systems play a major role in how people see themselves and the world and in their behavioral choices. Meaning systems and purpose can also be strengths that can be promoted for the good of the individuals as well as for communities and society. Purpose is particularly relevant for youth development.

Adolescence is a period of rapid change, including biological change (such as puberty), cognitive change (including brain development), social change

Table 20.1

Terms in the research literature about meaning, purpose, spirituality, and religion

Term	Definition
Meaning system	A system of beliefs, goals, and sense of purpose and/or significance that connects individuals to something that is greater than (or that transcends) themselves
Purpose	A stable intention to work toward outcomes that are meaningful to the individual and that contribute to the world beyond the individual
Spirituality	A pursuit of the sacred that includes searching for the sacred, maintaining a relationship with the sacred, and growing in understanding of the sacred
Religious spirituality	A pursuit of, closeness to, or connection with the divine, higher power, or worship tradition, based on a specific religion
Humanistic spirituality	A pursuit of, closeness to, or connection with other humans and humanity, including compassion and prosocial behaviors
Nature spirituality	A pursuit of, closeness to, or connection with nature
Cosmos spirituality	A pursuit of, closeness to, or connection with the universe
Religion	A pursuit of the sacred and search for significance that takes place within institutions that were established for the purpose of facilitating that pursuit

(increasing importance of peers, friends, and dating), and structural change (moving from primary to secondary schools). One major task of adolescence is identity development, which includes identity related to ideology (including faith/spirituality and meaning systems; e.g., Ebstyne King, 2003; Erikson, 1968). Although people can develop a sense of purpose throughout the lifespan, adolescence is a key sensitive period for exploring identity, meaning, and purpose (Damon et al., 2003).

One way that adolescents form their sense of identity is through observing themselves. For example, an adolescent who regularly chooses to comfort friends who are upset may conclude, "I am a good friend," and subsequently, "Being a good friend is important to me." If other friends or teachers show approval of this behavior (e.g., smiling, giving compliments), that adolescent also learns that being a good friend is valued in their community. Through others' reactions and patterns of behavior, adolescents learn what their communities find valuable.

Adolescents' behaviors and identity influence each other: adolescents interpret their stable patterns of behaviors to create an emergent sense of identity;

at the same time, they use their emergent sense of identity to make choices (Spencer et al., 2003). For example, if the "good friend" adolescent gets hurt by a friend, they might try to let it go or talk it out rather than fight because that is what a good friend might do. Over time, adolescents' behavioral patterns can stabilize into a values-based identity as they make deliberate choices to act in a way that is consistent with their meaning and purpose. Importantly, youth with a sense of purpose are less likely to engage in aggression (Damon et al., 2003). Integrating youths' developing sense of purpose into violence prevention programming may help to increase the effectiveness of programs.

Best Practices

There are no current best practices around how to integrate meaning systems into violence prevention. However, the existing research on positive youth development and spiritually integrated care, along with the pilot work on our program, Empowered, can help to inform decision making. In a pilot test of Empowered, implemented at community centers among middle school youth, we found that youth who participated in the program showed greater increases in effective nonviolent behavior compared to youth who did not, according to their teachers' report (Mehari, Jeffrey, Chastang, Blanton, et al., 2023). This section outlines our thoughts about "key ingredients" in leveraging meaning and purpose to help youth make decisions that are good for them and good for the people around them.

1 Create space for youth to explore their values. Practitioners need to meet youth where they are and walk with them through the process of exploring what is important to them and who they want to be. One major caution is that adults must not impose their values on youth; the goal here is to create opportunities for youth to explore their values.

2 Build hope and purpose. Practitioners should create opportunities for youth to imagine positive future possibilities. They should also nurture youths' sense of agency to move toward the future they want. They can do this by showing the larger world (e.g., novel activities, field trips) and creating space for youth to explore what they want their futures to look like (e.g., vision boards).

3 Use youths' values and transcendent meaning to create motivation for behavior change. Social-emotional learning skills, such as emotion regulation, empathy, and conflict resolution skills, are foundational to youth-focused violence prevention. However, youth may not believe that those skills are important if those skills are not directly connected to who they want to be and what they want to do with their lives. All

skills should be connected to youths' self-identified transcendent meaning or purpose.

4 Serve as positive role models. Teenagers see hypocrisy, and they will shut adults out if the adults are not practicing what they preach. For example, in other work, we addressed gender bias in a high school curriculum. In a focus group afterward, the students told us, "You can talk about how stereotypes are bad, but when you walk out of the room, that's all teachers do to us all day long." If we want to help youth make positive change, we have to build environments that align with those changes.

5 Provide scaffolding and reinforcement for youth. One community member described this as "see the spark and call it out." We see the spark by noticing youths' strengths and call it out by labeling it using our shared language. For example, an adult could say, "I love how you were honest there. I know honesty is really important to you," or "Look how you are getting mad about injustice that's happening to other people."

6 Invest in relationships. It is not fair to expect that any youth would trust any adult quickly; in fact, unearned trust in adults could potentially be not only unwise but also unsafe for youth. Adults show that they are trustworthy by being present, authentic, honest, reliable, predictable, and kind over months of time.

7 Be aware of culture, history, and context. Youth are under a lot of stress. At times, youth being served in our programs have been jumped, shot, or killed. Historical and ongoing race-based injustices, both nationally and locally, present an ongoing danger to communities. We argue that any positive youth development strategies must occur alongside fighting against the systems and structures that have deliberately created high burden in communities and robbed them of resources. This action may look many different ways, including youth activism, collective community action, conventional civic engagement like voting, and protest.

8 Stand on the shoulders of giants. There is a large body of research on what works in youth violence prevention and positive youth development (see, for example, the Centers for Disease Control and Prevention's guide [David-Ferdon et al., 2016] or Durlak and colleagues' [2007] review). Any spiritually integrative or faith-based intervention should include the key active ingredients identified in the large body of research showing violence prevention effectiveness. For example, sessions should be sequenced, active, focused, and explicit. Facilitators should be enthusiastic and engaged. Youth need opportunities to practice and generalize skills. At the systems level, administration must be invested and change policies and practices so the focus is on

helping youth to develop positive behaviors rather than on punishing youth.

9 Evaluate. It is important to evaluate whether an intervention is doing what it is intended and to maintain humility that sometimes the best intentions just do not work out. The history of intervention is littered with programs that made things worse instead of better, such as D.A.R.E., Scared Straight, and zero tolerance policies. In addition to youth surveys and teacher reports, we found debriefing interviews to be helpful because the participating youth could tell us how they thought the program worked (and many of these tips are based on the things that youth have told us).

Where Are We Going?

Spiritually integrative or faith-based violence prevention is a new area. On the ground, we need true cross-agency, academic-private-public collaborations to move toward the shared goal of community safety and well-being. From a research perspective, we need to have systems-level research on how to promote an environment that facilitates and reinforces acting in value-congruent ways. Part of the work that needs to happen is to develop better ways to assess the strengths of social environments as well as inner strengths such as purpose and hope so that we can evaluate whether or not these interventions are working.

From a policy perspective, we need to emphasize investing in communities. Local and state governments, businesses, and nonprofits can play a key role in investing in communities, including in the physical environment (green spaces, sidewalks, abandoned buildings); transportation infrastructure; employment opportunities that provide living wages and benefits and are accessible; and opportunities for youth recreational activities. The core components of hope are to envision a good future and to have a sense of agency in moving toward that future; being part of a vibrant community and having opportunities to experience good things and explore possibilities can build hope. In addition, being part of a society that values justice and community, as evidenced by patterns of investment, may also positively impact youths' self-worth and values-based identity formation.

To the adults who choose to work with youth: we are grateful for you. The work is hard, and it sometimes feels like a battle. We encourage you to hold onto the purpose that guides you and the hope that motivates you. We hold onto what a wise friend once told us: "If we were working on problems that could be solved in our lifetimes, they wouldn't be problems worth working on." Tapping into our own purpose makes it possible to keep going under difficult circumstances. We are glad to be part of a global community working toward a shared goal: that generations of youth can be safe to pursue good lives.

Acknowledgments

This work was supported by a John Templeton Foundation grant awarded to Baylor University (PI: Schnitker) via a subaward to the University of South Alabama (Project Lead: Mehari).

References

Bahler, B. (2020). *Religion, race, and racism: A (very) brief introduction*. University of Pittsburgh, Department of Religious Studies. https://www.religiousstudies .pitt.edu/resources-social-action/religion-race-and-racism-very-brief -introduction

Captari, L. E., Sandage, S. J., & Vandiver, R. A. (2022). Spiritually integrated psychotherapies in real-world clinical practice: Synthesizing the literature to identify best practices and future research directions. Psychotherapy, *59*, 307–320. http://dx.doi.org/10.1037/pst0000407

Damon, W., Menon, J., & Cotton Brook, K. (2003). The development of purpose during adolescence. Applied Developmental Science, 7, 119–128.

David-Ferdon, C., Vivolo-Kantor, A. M., Dahlberg, L. L., Marshall, K. J., Rainford, N., & Hall, J. E. (2016). *A comprehensive technical package for the prevention of youth violence and associated risk behaviors*. National Center for Injury Prevention and Control, Centers for Disease Control and Prevention.

Durlak, J. A., Taylor, R. D., Kawashima, K., Pachan, M. K., DuPre, E. P., Celio, C. I., Berger, S. R., Dymnicki, A. B., & Weissberg, R. P. (2007). Effects of positive youth development programs on school, family, and community systems. American Journal of Community Psychology, *39*, 269–286. https://doi.org/10.1007/s10464 -007-9112-5

Ebstyne King, P. (2003). Religion and identity: The role of ideological, social, and spiritual contexts. Applied Developmental Science, *7*(3), 197–204.

Ellison, C. G., & McFarland, M. J. (2013). The social context of religion and spirituality in the United States. In K. I. Pargament (Ed.), *APA handbook of psychology, religion, and spirituality (vol. 1): Context, theory, and research* (pp. 21–50). American Psychological Association.

Erikson, E. H. (1968). *Identity: Youth and crisis*. Norton.

Farrell, A. D., Meyer, A. L., & White, K. S. (2001). Evaluation of Responding in Peaceful and Positive Ways (RIPP): A school-based prevention program for reducing violence among urban adolescents. Journal of Clinical Child Psychology, *30*(4), 451–463.

Frankl, V. E. (1959). *Man's search for meaning: An introduction to logotherapy*. Beacon.

Gates, H. L., Jr. (2021). *The Black church: This is our story, this is our song*. Penguin.

Marcia, J. E. (1966). Development and validation of ego-identity status. Journal of Personality and Social Psychology, *3*(5), 551–558. https://doi.org/10.1037/h0023281

Mehari, K. R., Jeffrey, A., Chastang, C. M., Blanton, M. A., & Currier, J. M. (2023). Impact of a participatory action approach to virtue promotion among early adolescence. Journal of Positive Psychology. https://doi.org/10.1080/17439760.2023 .2169628

Mehari, K. R., Jeffrey, A., Chastang, C. M., Currier, J. M., & Empowered Team. (n.d.). *Empowered qualitative interviews*. Unpublished NVivo project.

Mehari, K. R., Jeffrey, A., Chastang, C. M., & Schnitker, S. A. (2023). Transdisciplinary participatory action research: How philosophers, psychologists, and practitioners can work (well) together to promote adolescent character development within context. *Journal of Positive Psychology.* https://doi.org/10.1080/17439760.2023.2179933

Pew Research Center. (2016). *Religion in Everyday Life.* Washington, DC: Pew Research Center.

Spencer, M. B., Fegley, S. G., & Harpalani, V. (2003). A theoretical and empirical examination of identity as coping: Linking coping resources to the self processes of African American youth. Applied Developmental Science, *7*(3), 181–188.

United Nations. (2022). *Rights of persons belonging to religious or belief minorities in situations of conflict or insecurity: Report of the Special Rapporteur on freedom of religion or belief.* 49th Session of the Human Rights Council. https://www.ohchr.org/en/documents/thematic-reports/ahrc4944-rights-persons-belonging-religious-or-belief-minorities

Worthington, E. L., Jr. (2003). *Forgiving and reconciling: Bridges to wholeness and hope.* InterVarsity Press.

Reimagining Violence Prevention within Youth Sport

• • • • • • • • • • • • •

A Social Justice Approach to Youth Development through Sport

JILL KOCHANEK

Overview

Sport can contribute to a young person's development in ways that benefit them and society. These benefits are not an automatic part of sport participation, however. Sport can perpetuate violence inflicted both *by* and *on* youth. Sport participation can lead to aggressive or violent behavior, and young people can experience discrimination due to forms of social identity oppression (e.g., racism, cissexism) in/through sport. Newman et al. (2021) conducted a scoping review on the link between youth sport participation and violent or aggressive behaviors. While they found some evidence that sport enhanced youth social-emotional skills to serve as a protective factor against aggression/violence, results also evidenced a possible causal relationship between sport participation and violent behavior given contextual and individual youth characteristics. Among other social risk factors, sport put younger male youth of color living in urban communities at greater risk for engaging in violent behaviors. Researchers posited that intentionally designed and facilitated sport-based activities are needed to ensure that sport serves as a protective and adaptive developmental experience. An approach to youth development through sport that accounts for identity, privilege/power, and oppression is vital to mitigate the violence inflicted *on* youth in sport and proactively equip youth and adult leaders with the knowledge and skills to flourish.

Youth sport researchers have made efforts to identify what conditions allow youth sport participants to thrive (e.g., Fraser-Thomas et al., 2005). These scholarly works are oriented toward a strength-based approach that regards young people as agents who are capable of acquiring capacities to fully function in society and draws on positive youth development (PYD) frameworks (Weiss, 2016). A PYD approach puts forth that positive development is most likely to occur when youth participate in a chosen sport with supportive adult mentors in a developmentally appropriate context. While a strength-based PYD approach has laudably sought to embrace and build off the assets that young people possess, it falls short of viewing a young person's developmental process within the context of systems of oppression (Coakley, 2016). Mainstream perspectives do not account for how youth, given their multiple and intersectional social identities, may have different developmental experiences in sport. Prevalent approaches typically define development in status quo or functional ways.

Functional views of development can (dis)advantage youth based on their social identity because such an understanding can uphold oppressive systems (e.g., racism, cissexism) and pressure minority youth (e.g., Black, transgender sport participants) to conform to and endure discriminatory sport practices (e.g., unpaid labor of [majority] Black athletes who drive revenue in big-time college athletics, restrictions on locker room access for transgender athletes; Kochanek & Erickson, 2019a). A lack of emphasis on critical capacity building is also a missed developmental opportunity for youth sport participants with privileged identities (e.g., white, cisgender). Critical capacity building refers to knowledge, attitudes, and skills that individuals can develop to challenge discrimination and injustice (Gonzales et al., 2020). Youth with social advantages may internalize false beliefs about their superiority that prevent them from (1) honoring the humanity of peers with different lived and contextual experiences and (2) developing the attitudes/skills to use their privilege to contribute to positive social change through sport. When youth with social advantages do not develop critical capacities to treat others with dignity and standup for injustice, disadvantaged youth may likely endure social/emotional harm caused by social discrimination and unfairly shoulder all responsibility of creating change.

My Background

As a youth sport coach and critical sport scholar, I learned firsthand that it is vital to account for identity, power/privilege, and oppression to ensure that sport is an empowering context for all. I identify as a white, cisgender, queer woman. I grew up in an upper-middle-class, predominately white community. My first coaching job led me to more sharply examine my privilege in working with athletes who had different lived experiences. I soon realized that in order to support my soccer players' development, I needed to listen and learn from them. This became clear to me when one of my Black student athletes came to practice with unusually low energy; she was not excelling at the level I knew she was capable of and—at face—*seemed* to be unmotivated. After training she bravely shared with me that police had assaulted her pregnant older sister. In that moment, I learned that I could not "walk in her shoes." However, I could walk alongside her by honoring their experiences, showing up in the ways they want to be supported, and creating opportunities for youth to learn to be caring teammates. As sport scholars and practitioners, a strength-based *and* social justice perspective is needed to ensure *all* youth athletes can develop as skilled performers, supportive teammates, and inclusive leaders.

Chapter Purpose

In this chapter I address this empirical and practical gap in youth development through sport research and practice. I adopt a strength-based approach to violence prevention. I characterize violence as the harm that systems of oppression inflict on individuals with minoritized identities in various forms (i.e., intrapersonal/interpersonal and institutional/systemic; Gonzales et al., 2020). I argue that a nondominant PYD approach is needed to mitigate the violence inflicted on youth in/through sport and proactively equip youth and adult leaders with the critical capacities to contest rather than reinforce oppressive systems. Youth development scholars have called for integrating social justice principles outside of sport (e.g., Ginwright & Cammarota, 2002; Gonzales et al., 2020). Thus, I overview one prevalent non-sport-specific framework as a guide to highlight key assets as part of a young person's critical capacity-building process. I then describe a promising approach to equip youth and adult leaders in sport with critical capacities: intergroup dialogue. I provide key findings from initial research on the effectiveness of one initiative, Dialogue in Athletics. I conclude with implications for future research and practice to adopt a social justice perspective of youth development through sport.

Summary and Highlights

Gonzales et al. (2020) recently put forth a social-justice-oriented model of youth development, *critical positive youth development* (CPYD), that can help guide youth sport scholars and practitioners. Gonzales et al. (2020) posit *critical consciousness* (i.e., an individual's ability to identify and reflect upon and take action to change oppressive social conditions) as a key developmental outcome. Critical consciousness has three aspects: critical reflection, political efficacy, and critical action. Youth engagement in *critical reflection* (i.e., an understanding of the ways in which systems of power create and sustain oppression) paired with *political efficacy* (i.e., a person's belief in their capacity to enact social change) in a supportive environment builds a young person's confidence and competence to effectively engage in social change, nurtures connection and solidarity among social groups, and reinforces cultures of care and support. Such a developmental context allows for open, respectful dialogue and diverse perspectives to pave the way for youth to engage in critical action. *Critical action* regards forms of social contribution that allow youth to challenge oppressive social conditions (e.g., peer mentoring in minority affinity groups). This definition of social action diverges from traditional notions of social contribution (e.g., donating), which may fall short of actually changing systemic inequities.

Critical Scholarship on Youth Development Through Sport

Despite the lack of practical frameworks and research to guide a social justice approach to youth development through sport, some scholars have critiqued mainstream PYD perspectives (e.g., Coakley, 2016; Kochanek & Erickson, 2019a; Rauscher & Cooky, 2016). More recently, Camiré and colleagues (2022) implored researchers and practitioners to consider how youth sport can more boldly serve as a context for social justice life skills development. My colleagues and I have made efforts to carry out research in this vein (Kochanek & Erickson, 2019b, 2021). We have explored how high school sport coaches and administrators navigate broader social issues (e.g., racism) in the service of youth development. We found that adult leaders' critical awareness and action varied along a continuum and attempted to identify harmful assumptions (e.g., race/racial protest as irrelevant in predominately white spaces) that adults made concerning coach effectiveness and athlete development. Sport administrators expressed that they would benefit from initiatives to help them and their coaches to better address social issues. Initiatives that help youth and adult leaders build their critical capacities need to be explored to ensure that sport is empowering for all.

Best Practices for Capacity Building: Intergroup Dialogue

One promising technique to social justice education applicable to sport is *intergroup dialogue*. Intergroup dialogue is a research-informed approach that teaches individuals to deepen their understanding of identity, power/privilege, and oppression and develop competencies to engage across different social identity groups (Gurin et al., 2013). Intergroup dialogue has three key features: engaged learning, facilitated learning environment, and structured interaction (Nagda et al., 2009). Trained facilitators guide participants through experiential activities to examine their own and consider others' lived (and socialized) experiences before proceeding to think critically about power and systems of oppression and foster alliance building. The curriculum covers a range of concepts (e.g., privilege, stereotypes) and helps participants develop practical skills (e.g., perspective taking) to promote inclusion, equity, and justice.

A traditional intergroup dialogue encounter brings together members of two or more social identity groups (e.g., race) with equal representation in order to balance power. While balanced representation is ideal, using a traditional intergroup structure may not always possible (e.g., when a community does not have the diversity required; Frantell et al., 2019). Intercultural dialogue refers to when the group structure is less balanced in composition. Practitioners have largely used intergroup dialogue in higher education (Kaplowitz et al., 2019; Nagda et al., 2003). Research has shown that intergroup dialogue facilitates critical thought about social-identity- and justice-related issues among undergraduate students (Gurin et al., 2011; Gurin et al., 2013; Nagda, 2006). Intergroup dialogue has been less often applied to youth and/or sport settings. Some practitioners have engaged high school students in dialogue-based pedagogy and shown its efficacy (e.g., Aldana et al., 2012; Kaplowitz et al., 2019). Given the unique cultural value that sport has in society and way that this activity context can bring people together, sport presents a fruitful opportunity to help individuals (under conditions of psychological safety) engage across differences to create a more inclusive and equitable participation context and society.

Intergroup Dialogue in Athletics

Given the efficacy of this technique, my colleagues and I carried out an evaluation of a sport-specific program (Dialogue in Athletics) that used an intergroup (race) dialogue approach. A mixed-methods evaluation assessed the impact of Dialogue in Athletics among coaches/administrators (group 1) and student athletes (group 2) within one high school sport community. An outline of the six-session program curriculum and full results from the utilization-focused evaluation study are provided in Kochanek et al. (2023).

Programming followed a sequential design where participants first became familiar with their own identities and personal/interpersonal levels of oppression in sport (e.g., context-specific stereotypes). Later sessions built off this foundation to explore institutional/systemic levels of oppression in sport (e.g., context-specific inequities and policies and links to other social institutions such as media). Dialogue in Athletics was delivered virtually and did not take place during a regular competitive season due to the COVID-19 pandemic. However, dialogue-based activities adopted a sport-specific approach. For example, participants explored sport-specific stereotypes, microaggressions, myths about sport being a level playing field where social identities/privilege do not matter, practices that undermine team cohesion and inclusive leadership, and ways to better promote inclusive, equitable team dynamics and sport environments.

Overall, evaluation results suggest that adult leaders and youth strengthened their critical awareness (of racism and other forms of oppression) along with their confidence to take and intentions to engage in social justice action. The program—at least partially—helped participants develop skills (e.g., interrupting derogatory comments) for social justice promotion and transfer them to other aspects of their life, including the classroom, dorm, sport/recreational spaces, and home. Processes that emerged as salient to participants' learning included their deep engagement with one another. Coaches and student athletes described that the psychologically safe group climate helped them work through their initial discomfort sharing personal information and considering other perspectives. They attributed feelings of psychological safety to the small-group, interactive setting and supportive peer/facilitator behaviors (e.g., listening without judgment).

Discussion of Findings

One unique finding that emerged from this formative evaluation that may have implications for future dialogue-based or similar educational initiatives regards differences in critical awareness development between youth and adult groups. Results indicated that while student athletes expressed some understanding of racial/social privilege, they less sharply probed aspects of structural oppression and their relationship to those systems relative to coaches/administrators. Reasons that may explain why Dialogue in Athletics less optimally supported improvements in youths' critical awareness levels may be due to their unique developmental needs and dialogue context. Youth more often verbalized an understanding of racial/social oppression at the individual level (e.g., sport stereotypes as harmful) but seemed to less immediately grasp structural dynamics. And because of the more racially/ethnically balanced composition of the student athlete group, the dialogue that organically emerged less exclusively centered on interrogating whiteness. Distinctly, most adult participants identified as white and were—differently (though no less) challenged by—coming to terms with their white racial identity and had rich lived experiences on which to draw. As such, while adults may need unique forms of programmatic support to fully unpack their socialization, youth participants may need added help via curriculum content to deepen their understanding of institutional inequities and more guided questions from facilitators to link (inter)personal experiences to those systems (Griffin et al., 2012). With greater awareness adults and youth will be better able to prevent and minimize violence inflicted both by and on youth.

The Dialogue in Athletics project served as a first step to address the lack of research on social justice education initiatives within youth sport. Given the program's room for improvement in equipping all sport leaders with the capacity to take meaningful action, more extensive empirical and programmatic efforts are needed.

Where Are We Going?

There are several future directions for *youth development through sport research* to minimize the violence inflicted on youth in/through sport and proactively equip all leaders with the critical capacities for all to flourish. First, sport scholars need to integrate critical rather than functional views of youth development to extend theory. Leaning on non-sport-specific social justice frameworks (e.g., Gonzales et al., 2020) that define critical developmental assets, scholars can better clarify what these assets look like in youth sport practice and offer evidence-based guidance on how to support youth and adult leaders' critical skill building through sport.

Researchers can also add to the literature by carrying out studies guided by theories of behavior change. Two frameworks applicable to sport are the *theory of planned behavior* and *transtheoretical model* (e.g., Lee et al., 2020; Mac Intosh et al., 2020). Using these *conscious* approaches has strengthened our understanding of the individual variation and barriers to taking social justice action in sport. Given that *unconscious* biases have a strong influence on action, researchers might consider integrating other implicit approaches to behavior change such as nudge theory (see *inclusion nudges*; Nielsen & Kepinski, 2016) applicable to youth development (Whitley, 2022).

Researchers can also build the knowledge base through evaluation studies of social justice education initiatives. Evaluation research can include assessing programs that adopt a dialogue-based or other educational approach in varied sport contexts. Impact and process evaluations of programming in different sport organization and community spaces can provide contextually relevant information on social justice education. Varying demographics and contextual norms may uniquely impact how programming is received and its impact on various stakeholders (e.g., athletes, coaches, parents). Related research can explore how participants with varying levels of critical awareness, attitudes, and action may be differently affected by an educational experience such as comparing the impact of programming across clusters of individuals relative to their baseline score on learning outcomes. Assessment of how programming can cater to youth given their unique developmental needs and backgrounds (e.g., adverse or traumatic experiences) is also key. Longitudinal approaches can be taken to examine how ongoing programming might further support participants' learning and growth.

There are individual and programmatic steps that practitioners and decision makers can take to center athletes' multiple identities and account for systems of oppression to help lessen the harm that minoritized youth may experience within sport. At the individual level, coaches and administrators must adopt a more critical PYD approach that attends to identity, power/privilege, and oppression. Adult leaders can first reflect on their identities. They can consider how their social identities and past experiences inform their leadership style (e.g., a male coach recognizing that they don't show empathy or vulnerability because of harmful social beliefs about masculinity and toughness). Leaders can check their blind spots on certain social issues by critically considering what assumptions underline their approach by asking, *do my practices optimally support youth sport participants with identities/experiences different from my own?*

Adult leaders can also benefit from critically reflecting on how the community and sport context may make certain social issues *seem* less relevant. For example, while racism might be perceived as less relevant within a predominately white community, (white) adult leaders may actually fall short of considering how their personal biases and community structures uphold racism (e.g., color-blind statements that equate individual hard work with success). Moreover, a sport context (e.g., football) may discourage discussion of some issues (e.g., mental health) given dominant norms (e.g., behaviors associated with masculinity). To make visible these biases, adult leaders can ask, *how might the culture of my sport prevent social issues from being considered?*

Adult sport leaders need to have the ability to center identity in their work with youth. Coaches and administrators can account for the lived experiences of youth participants rather than avoiding conversations around aspects of who our athletes are and discussions about related social injustices. Instead of presuming that such matters are not developmentally salient or relevant to youth, we can invite youth to reflect on and share information about their identities and experiences on their own terms. We can create space for youth sport participants to listen generously and learn about the different experiences/identities of peers. Building critical awareness and relatedness through dialogue can support youth athletes' performance, development, well-being—and by extension prevent violence inflicted both by and on youth.

Sport program leaders also need to create opportunities for youth and adults to develop knowledge and skills to contribute to inclusive sport climates free of violence. Sport administrators can devote resources to support coaches' and young people's critical capacity development. Pursuing collaborations with organizations doing social justice education work can be beneficial to equip youth and adult leadership with the critical capacities needed to ensure that sport is empowering for all (e.g., Ross Initiative in Sports for Equality [RISE]; Mac Intosh & Martin, 2018). And given the prevalence of dialogue programs at U.S. universities/colleges, opportunities for partnerships and established resources may be more accessible than sport decision makers realize.

Conclusion

While sport can be an empowering context for youth, social and emotional harm is often perpetuated in sport. Young people can experience discrimination due to forms of social identity oppression through their sport participation. A nondominant approach to PYD through sport is vital in order to mitigate this violence and allow sport to deliver on its developmental potential.

References

Aldana, A., Rowley, S., Checkoway, B., & Richards-Shuster, K. (2012). Raising racial-ethnic consciousness: The relationship between intergroup dialogues and adolescents' ethnic racial identity and racial awareness. *Equity & Excellence in Education, 36*, 120–137.

Camiré, M., Newman, T. J., Bean, C., & Strachan, L. (2022). Reimaging positive youth development and life skills in sport through a social justice lens. *Journal of Applied Sport Psychology, 34*, 1058–1076. https://doi.org/10.1080/10413200.2021 .1958954

Coakley, J. (2016). Positive youth development through sport: Myths, beliefs, and realities. In N. L. Holt (Ed.), *Positive youth development through sport* (2nd ed., pp. 21–33). Routledge.

Frantell, K. A., Miles, J. R., & Ruwe, A. (2019). Intergroup dialogue: A review of recent empirical research and its implications for research and practice. *Small Group Research, 50*, 654–695. https://doi.org/10.1177/1046496419835923

Fraser-Thomas, J. L., Côté, J., & Deakin, J. (2005). Youth sport programs: An avenue to foster positive development. *Physical Education and Sport Pedagogy, 10*, 19–40.

Ginwright, S., & Cammarota, J. (2002). New terrain in youth development: The promise of a social justice approach. *Social Justice, 29*, 82–95.

Gonzales, M., Kokozos, M., Byrd, C., & McKee, K. (2020). Critical positive youth development: A framework for centering critical consciousness. *Journal of Youth Development, 15*, 24–43.

Griffin, S. R., Brown, M., & Warren, N. (2012). Critical education in high schools: The promise and challenges of intergroup dialogue. *Equity & Excellence, 45*, 159–180.

Gurin, P., Nagda, B. A., & Sorensen, N. (2011). Intergroup dialogue: Education for a broad conception of civic engagement. *Liberal Education, 97*(2), 46–51.

Gurin, P., Nagda, B. A., & Zùñiga, X. (2013). *Dialogue across difference. Practice, theory, and research on intergroup dialogue*. Russell Sage Foundation.

Kaplowitz, D. R., Griffin, S. R., & Seyka, S. (2019). *Race dialogues: A facilitator's guide to tackling the elephant in the classroom.* Teachers College Press.

Kochanek, J., & Erickson, K. (2019a). Interrogating positive youth development through sport using critical race theory. *Quest, 72,* 224–240.

Kochanek, J., & Erickson, K. (2019b). Outside the lines: An exploratory study of high school sport head coaches' critical praxis. *Psychology of Sport & Exercise, 45.* https://doi.org/10.1016/j.psychsport.2019.101580

Kochanek, J., & Erickson, K. (2021). What counts as educational athletics? An exploration of high school athletic directors' critical praxis. *Psychology of Sport and Exercise Journal, 53.* https://doi.org/10.1016/j.psychsport.2020.101871

Kochanek, J., Erickson, K., & Secaras, L. (2023). *Dialogue in athletics*: A program evaluation of a social justice education initiative in high school sports. *Journal of Applied Sport Psychology, 35*(4), 680–709. https://doi.org/10.1080/10413200.2022.2084181

Lee, A., Singh, G., & Wright, M. E. (2020). Using the transtheoretical model to promote behavior change for social justice in kinesiology. *Journal of Sport Psychology in Action, 12,* 181–195.

Mac Intosh, A., & Martin, E. (2018). Creating athletic activists: Using sport as a vehicle to combat racism. *Journal of Sport Psychology in Action, 9,* 159–171.

Mac Intosh, A., Martin, E., & Kluch, Y. (2020). To act or not to act? Student-athletes' perceptions of social justice activism. *Psychology of Sport & Exercise, 51,* 101766.

Messner, M., & Musto, M. (2016). *Child's play: Sport in kids' worlds.* Rutgers University Press.

Nagda, B. A. (2006). Breaking barriers, crossing boundaries, building bridges: Communication processes in intergroup dialogues. *Journal of Social Issues, 62,* 553–576.

Nagda, B. A., Gurin, P., & Lopez, G. E. (2003). Transformative pedagogy for democracy and social justice. *Race, Ethnicity, and Education, 6,* 165–191.

Nagda, B. A., Gurin, P., Sorensen, N., & Zúñiga, X. (2009). Evaluating intergroup dialogue: Engaging diversity for personal and social responsibility. *Diversity & democracy, 12*(1), 4-6.

Newman, T., Magier, E., Kimiecik, C., & Burns, M. (2021). The relationship between youth sport participation and aggressive and violent behaviors: A scoping review of the literature. *Journal of the Society for Social Work and Research, 12,* 371–389.

Nielsen, T. C., & Kepinski, L. (2016). *Inclusion nudges guidebook: Practical techniques for changing behaviour, culture & systems to mitigate unconscious bias and create inclusive organizations* (2nd ed.). CreateSpace.

Rauscher, L., & Cooky, C. (2016). Ready for anything the world gives her? A critical look at sports-based positive youth development for girls. *Sex Roles, 74,* 288–298.

Weiss, M. R. (2016). Old wine in a new bottle: Historical reflections on sport as a context for youth development. In N. L. Holt (Ed.), *Positive youth development through sport* (2nd ed., pp. 7–20). Routledge.

Whitley, M. A. (2022). Using behavioral economics to promote positive youth development through sport. *Journal of Sport Psychology in Action, 13,* 78–88. https://doi.org/10.1080/21520704.2021.1883783

Part 4

Vistas

● ● ● ● ● ● ● ● ● ● ● ● ●

Understanding the Roles of Structural, Interpersonal, and Intrapersonal Violence in the Lives of Black Girls

● ● ● ● ● ● ● ● ● ● ● ● ●

JANICE JOHNSON DIAS

Overview

Between 2003 and 2019, suicides among Black girls ages fifteen to twenty-four rose by nearly 59 percent (Caron, 2021). During that same period, Black femicide, the homicide of Black women, became the leading cause of death among young Black girls and women ages fifteen to thirty-four and one of the leading causes of premature death among Black women overall (Langley & Sugarmann, 2014)—and if that was not enough, roughly one Black woman in five was living in poverty (U.S. Census Bureau, 2020). These statistics paint a gloomy outlook of the lives of Black girls and women.

250 • Janice Johnson Dias

Despite the overwhelming evidence of structural influences in shaping these outcomes, answers to why these social issues pervade Black life typically infer that there is something wrong in the ideas and/or actions of Black folk. The logic usually follows that the failings of Black families or communities contributed to these realities. An overwhelming number of analyses recapitulate old tropes that by and large blame the victims (Harris-Lacewell, 2001).

In this chapter, I challenge these notions and present a framework for examining and responding to the sociocultural and institutional issues that obstruct Black girls from reaching their fullest human potential. My argument is simple: Black girls are subject to a set of co-occurring structurally violent conditions that play out as interpersonal or intrapersonal violence. More poignantly, Black girls consistently face racially gendered violence that is often unrecognized or disregarded. These diverse manifestations of structural violence are unique in Black girls' lives, though we often observe only the individual outcomes that we more readily see. In sum, I argue that the challenges facing Black girls all have institutional foundations; therefore, the needed solutions must locate and address these hidden structural factors that shape and influence the interpersonal and intrapersonal violence we observe in Black girls' lives.

This chapter considers the linkages among three levels of violence—structural, interpersonal, and intrapersonal—in the lives of Black girls. For Black girls, structural violence has a transactional relationship with other types of violence, such as interpersonal (i.e., domestic violence and childhood sexual abuse) and intrapersonal (i.e., suicide attempts and drug overdose) violence. I draw connections among the structural factors that present themselves as institutional rules, the hostilities exacted on Black girls within these organizational spaces, and the detrimental self-harm that is prevalent among Black girls. I show how harmful actions by social and governmental institutions and their various organizational units such as schools obstruct the human potential of Black girls. In several instances, I will rearticulate my core theme: though the source of violence may be subtle, indirect, and covert, the challenges we observe in Black girls' lives can be traced to structural causes.

To make this case, I highlight the work of the GrassROOTS Community Foundation (GCF), a New Jersey–based public health and social justice organization whose Black girls' leadership development work can be a model for interrupting this cycle of violence. GCF helps girls and their families learn and identify structural antecedents that lead to interpersonal conflict and self-harm. Its educational and social justice training offers a promising example for preventing or ameliorating these forces of institutional, community, and individual violence.

Understanding Structural Violence

"Structural violence refers to the avoidable limitations that society places on groups of people that constrain them from meeting their basic needs and achieving the quality of life that would otherwise be possible" (Lee, 2019, 123–142). This violence is often embedded in social structures that operate normatively, making it more likely that people will overlook such violence as nothing more than ordinary or commonplace difficulties that some groups of people encounter during their daily lives. For example, one girl in four will miss school due to the absence of menstrual supplies. Such gender-based inequities are rarely factored into conversations about school completion rates. Yet studies show that the same girls who receive free and reduced-price lunch are also the girls not likely to afford menstruation products (Rapp & Kilpatrick, 2020; Rueckert, 2018). We know that these environments are also stigmatizing because girls who soil their clothing while on their periods are likely to be made fun of and therefore less likely to attend school during their menstrual cycle. Missing nine weeks of school (one week for every month of the school year due to their period) impedes girls' educational success. Equally likely is that these hostile structural environments may lead to increased interpersonal challenges. Girls who are harangued because of period mishaps may become emotionally agitated and engage in altercations and fights. Such actions can frustrate the situation and lead to girls missing school due to suspensions. But without a structural analysis of how the lack of resources and policies of the school shape these experiences, we are likely to misread girls' individual actions like absenteeism, underperformance, and interpersonal conflicts as personal failings. But it is the structurally unjust school environment that sets the context for these outcomes.

This chapter reminds us that structural violence, though often subtle, invisible, and accepted as a matter of fact, is the most potent underlying cause of other forms of violence. Because even more difficult than detecting structural violence is assigning culpability for it. Its sources are often concealed and obscured within social institutions and practices. Structurally violent ideologies are now normalized in our social institutions and practices. The case of menstrual inequity provides a good case of how this happens. For example, we expect all public institutions to provide toilet paper but not menstrual products, but defecation, urination, and menstruation are natural bodily occurrences. Yet little thought is given to how these gendered inequities in allocation of resources promote violence toward girls and women, especially those who are Black and low income.

Structural, interpersonal, and intrapersonal violences mutually impact and support each other in ways that are especially challenging individually and collectively for Black girls and women. One way structural violence manifests is through *misogynoir*. Misogynoir refers to specific forms of anti-Blackness that Black girls and women experience. According to Bailey and Trudy (2018), who coined the term, misogynoir is the combination of racism sprinkled with heterosexual desires and normative expressions of gender. Evidence of this type of violence can be found in a host of policies and within institutions, even those specifically crafted to increase equity. Affirmative action is one example. Steinbugler et al. (2006) analyze how gender/racial stereotypes about African Americans affect whites' attitudes about two types of affirmative action programs: (1) job training and education and (2) hiring and promotion. The researchers found that prejudice toward Black women has a larger effect on whites' policy preferences than does prejudice toward Black men or Blacks in general.

Similarly, while governmental child welfare agencies are created to protect children, they often fragment Black families and harm Black girls. According to a 2017 report by the National Women's Law Center, more than one-third of Black girls who are placed in foster care are sent to between ten and an astounding ninety-nine residential homes. While in foster care, Black girls are more likely than white girls in foster care to experience sexual abuse, exposure to violence, and other forms of maltreatment. These organizing structural forces lead to institutional violence.

Interpersonal Violence in Schools

Child welfare is one place to understand the interplay between structural and interpersonal violence, but schools provide a more apt location of study. As a legal requirement for youth under sixteen years old, schools provide an ideal site to examine the transactional relationship between structural and interpersonal violence in the lives of Black girls. The cumulative evidence shows that Black adolescents in the United States commonly experience racially discriminatory experiences within school contexts (Gale & Dorsey, 2020; Mims & Williams, 2020; Seaton et al., 2014). A Seaton et al. (2014) study using a nationally representative sample of Black American adolescents shows that approximately 97 percent of Black students reported experiencing at least one discriminatory event over two weeks. Though the violence may be expressed as reactive physical, sexual, or psychological violence (also called emotional violence), its roots are institutional.

Nowhere is the nested association between structural violence and interpersonal violence clearer than in the disciplinary actions taken against Black girls. While scholars and practitioners have long supported discipline policies under the pretense that they help to manage interpersonal violence between and among youth (Arum, 2003), Black feminists have offered alternative theories (Crenshaw et al., 2014). They argue that individuals living at the intersections of vulnerable racial and gender identities are subject to multiple forms of violence. Their framework provides plausible explanations for understanding why Black girls are overrepresented in school discipline data (Crenshaw et al., 2014) and why Black girls experience disproportionate school-based violence.

Investigations into how this operates illustrate that Black girls are viewed as less innocent and more adult-like than their white peers, even at young ages. According to the U.S. Department of Education, Office for Civil Rights (2014), from 2011 to 2012 Black girls in public elementary and secondary schools across the nation were suspended at a rate of 12 percent, compared to a rate of 2 percent for white girls. Black girls were suspended more than girls of any other race or ethnicity and more than white or Asian boys.

The interpersonal violence Black girls are experiencing in schools is not so much among the student body but rather from those in power: teachers, guidance counselors, and principals. In some cases, these inequities show up as microaggressions—everyday exchanges that send denigrating messages to certain individuals because of their group membership. Black girls' educational experiences are marred by such microaggressive exchanges. A body of research (Gadson & Lewis, 2022; Kohli et al., 2019; Nunn, 2018) documents the unfair ways in which these types of interpersonal violence pervade Black girls' school life. Such harm is both an outgrowth and a reflection of structural conditions that shape Black girls' realities in schools.

More recent studies also confirmed these findings. The Georgetown Law Center on Poverty and Inequality's Initiative on Gender Justice & Opportunity and the RISE Research team at New York University analyzed the U.S. Department of Education's Office for Civil Rights Civil Rights data collection for the 2017–2018 academic year to examine the patterns in discipline in K–12 public schools. They found that, compared to all other groups, Black girls have the highest rate of overrepresentation in receiving out-of-school suspensions, expulsions, arrests at school, restraints, and other disciplinary actions.

There is also a growing body of evidence establishing that many of Black girls' school-related challenges with teachers and school leaders involve discriminatory practices at the intersection of racism and sexism (Andrews et al., 2019; Bailey and Trudy, 2018; Davis, 2020; Morris, 2016; Neal-Jackson, 2018; Watson, 2016). In particular, Black girls are likely to be disciplined for failing to meet and perform dominant cisgender expectations of femininity (Sharma, 2010). They are also likely to be disciplined for "talking back" (Henry, 1998) and being "unladylike" (Morris, 2007). Worse, Black girls more so than any other group are also likely to be arrested for being "disrespectful" and "uncontrollable" (Morris, 2012).

According to a study conducted by the African American Policy Forum and the Center for Intersectionality and Social Policy Studies at Columbia

254 • Janice Johnson Dias

University (Crenshaw et al., 2015), which examined Black girls' experiences with school discipline in Boston and New York, 12 percent of Black girls across the cities' public schools had been suspended in 2013, compared to 2 percent of their white peers. The study also found that 90 percent of girls expelled from New York Schools in 2011–2012 were Black, while *none* of the girls expelled were white. Between 2009 and 2010, Black teenage girls represented 17 percent of female students but were 31 percent of girls referred to law enforcement and 43 percent of girls subjected to a school-related arrest (DuMonthier et al., 2017). The policy brief titled *Black Girls Matter: Pushed Out, Overpoliced, and Underprotected* showed that even within their own racial group, Black girls face greater risks of suspension and expulsion than Black boys and their non-Black peers (Crenshaw et al., 2015). This inequity is ubiquitous across the United States. Research conducted by Smith and Harper (2015) reveals that between 2011 and 2012 Black girls represented 45 percent of girls suspended across southern states and 42 percent of girls expelled from K–12 public schools nationally.

Researchers have found that racial and gender discrimination from teachers toward Black girls was associated with higher levels of depressive symptomatology (Butler-Barnes et al., 2022), which makes it even more crucial to understand how structural conditions of interpersonal violence are linked to intrapersonal violence.

Intrapersonal Violence: The Harm to Self

Structural violence is at work in the intrapersonal violence of Black girls. Ample evidence connects institutional harm that is structural in nature to interpersonal violence (observable violence between people). Likewise, it is important to make the connection between the violence we see take place between people and the way that impacts the way people treat themselves. Intrapersonal violence refers to the individual-level harm that often results from experiencing a host of structural and interpersonal violence. Intrapersonal violence may include but is not limited to psychological distress, destructive communication skills, drug abuse, and suicide (Foshee et al., 2008; James et al., 2003). It follows that intrapersonal violence (self-harm) is more likely to occur when there is widening and legitimizing of institutional violence. Said differently, the more we focus on individual outcomes alone, without a look at the role of the broader social contexts in producing those outcomes, the more likely we are to miss the way these larger forces are influencing individual health decision making and behaviors.

Decades of research confirm that health problems are not equally distributed across subgroups of adolescents (Foshee et al., 2008). Racialized minority youth at the bottom of the social strata will experience more health-related problems and higher rates of mental health challenges as compared to those at the top of the social hierarchy. Because of the transactional nature of structural violence, these young people are more likely to experience greater personal harm. Black girls whose race and gender are socially marginalized are at risk of experiencing high levels of intrapersonal violence, particularly negative health-related problems such as higher depressive symptoms and greater suicidal ideation (Ivey-Stephenson et al., 2020; Williams, 2018). Reports have found that Black girls are consistently more likely than Black boys to report multiple instances of suicidal ideation (Hooper et al., 2015; Joe et al., 2009; Miller & Taylor, 2012; Tomek et al., 2015). Institutional marginalization due to their unique gendered and racial group membership increases intrapersonal violence and exacerbates Black girls' psychological distress, anxiety, and depression (Perry, Harp, et al., 2013; Perry, Stevens-Watkins, et al., 2013).

Solutions Are Possible

Despite these current conditions, there is hope. Violence is created and is the result of social arrangements (Farmer, 2003). Therefore, we, as members of society, can undo it and create new infrastructures to support Black girls to help them achieve their fullest potential. We can end structural violence and interrupt its transactional relationships with interpersonal and intrapersonal violence. We can create safe spaces for Black girls, where we protect Black girls from being overly exposed to punitive, unfair, and unresponsive systems of harm. We can support their physical and emotional well-being.

One place to start is with schools. Schools play a vital role in the American democracy. Even with their challenges, schools continue to prepare young people for work and life. The struggle lies with achieving their essential goals of helping to enhance democracy and facilitate full participation in society. Our school systems could choose to demonstrate that Black girls matter through curriculum, hiring practices, availability of resources, relationship with community members, and treatment of students because mattering is one of the most universal needs and Black girls do indeed matter.

To pursue an agenda that pushes schools toward fulfilling their purpose of providing more just and humanizing socialization and educational processes, inclusive of Black girls, we must reconsider our data collection process so that we can distinguish whether things are occurring by chance or through ordered or deliberate systematic neglect. To assess and discern the areas of structural violence, we need granular data so we can better understand if, how, and in what ways violence is shaping the lives of Black girls.

The work that is being done by the Center on Poverty and Inequality at Georgetown Law is a good example of how we can better use data to understand and document structural and interpersonal violence of Black girls in public systems. Their *Girlhood Interrupted: The Erasure of Black Girls' Childhood* report provides empirical evidence of why we must eliminate the discriminatory use and overuse of exclusionary disciplinary practices based on actual or perceived race, ethnicity, color, national origin, sex/gender, and sexuality (Epstein, Blake, and Gonzalez, 2017). Their work confirmed disparities in school discipline, specifically harsher punishment for Black girls compared to other groups by educators and school resource officers. Within schools, Black girls were viewed as needing less nurturing, protection, and support, which translated to fewer leadership and mentorship opportunities in schools. This type of evidence is central to creating deliberate and more equitable policies and programs for Black girls.

The work of GCF is another place to look for hope. Having recognized this challenge, GCF has set out to interrupt violence toward Black girls and their communities. Using a multilevel systems approach, GCF designs and implements programs that consider the uniqueness of Black girls' intersectional identities, gifts, and challenges. GCF programming centers around Black girls from elementary to high school. The organization works with cohorts of girls and their families to develop social action programs that rethink, expand, and create new pathways for solving social issues. Its programming is individual (offering individual and group therapy and self-affirmation workshops), family-centered (parental engagement is required daily), and community-based (voluntarism is a condition for continued participation).

Working individually and in cohorts, Black girls conceptualize and develop social action projects—inquiry-based learning campaigns that assess girls' leadership development skills through a social justice framework. Girls create projects based on their passions and social frustrations—things they see happening in their communities that they wish they could change. The process of supporting and collaborating with Black girls on social action projects provides an opportunity for Black girls to understand the interplay between individual action and large, society-wide issues.

One example is Marley Dias's #1000BlackGirlBooks, a GCF-supported initiative aimed at collecting and donating a thousand books where Black girls are the main characters. This work led to the collection of over fourteen thousand books with Black girl protagonists and the development of an online database of Black girl books, curricula, and legislation for greater inclusion of Black girl stories in school districts in the United States and around the globe. It is not an accident that this project also implicates what occurs in schools.

By arming Black girls with knowledge of themselves, their communities, and the world, by teaching them reasons and demonstrating for them that passions and talents can be used to address social issues, and by ensuring that they see value in connections, GCF is providing a foundation for assessing and responding to the interrelationships among structural, interpersonal, and intrapersonal violence.

References

Andrews, D. J. C., Brown, T., Castro, E., & Id-Deen, E. (2019). The impossibility of being "perfect and white": Black girls' racialized and gendered schooling experiences. *American Educational Research Journal, 56*(6), 2531–2572.

Annan, J., & Brier, M. (2010). The risk of return: Intimate partner violence in northern Uganda's armed conflict. *Social Science & Medicine, 70*(1), 152–159.

Arum, R. (2003). *Judging school discipline: The crisis of moral authority.* Harvard University Press.

Bailey, M., and Trudy. (2018) On misogynoir: Citation, erasure, and plagiarism. *Feminist Media Studies, 18*(4), 762–768. DOI: 10.1080/14680777.2018.1447395

Bronfenbrenner, U. (1992). *Ecological systems theory.* Jessica Kingsley.

Butler-Barnes, S. T., & Inniss-Thompson, M. N. (2020). "My teacher doesn't like me": Perceptions of teacher discrimination and school discipline among African-American and Caribbean Black adolescent girls. *Education Sciences, 10*(2), 44.

Butler-Barnes, S. T., Leath, S., Inniss-Thompson, M. N., Allen, P. C., D'Almeida, M. E. D. A., & Boyd, D. T. (2022). Racial and gender discrimination by teachers: Risks for Black girls' depressive symptomatology and suicidal ideation. *Cultural Diversity & Ethnic Minority Psychology, 28*(4), 469–482.

Caron, C. (2021, November 23). Why are more Black kids suicidal? A search for answers. *New York Times.* https://www.nytimes.com/2021/11/18/well/mind/suicide-black-kids.html

Crenshaw, K., Ocen, P., & Nanda, J. (2015). *Black girls matter: Pushed out, overpoliced, and underprotected.* African American Policy Forum and Columbia Law School's Center for Intersectionality and Social Policy Studies.

Davis, S. (2020). Socially toxic environments: A YPAR project exposes issues affecting urban Black girls' educational pathway to STEM careers and their racial identity development. *Urban Review, 52*(2), 215–237.

DuMonthier, A., Childers, C. E., & Milli, J. (2017). *The status of Black women in the United States.* Institute for Women's Policy Research.

Epstein, R., and Blake, J., and González, T. (2017). Girlhood interrupted: The erasure of Black girls' childhood. SSRN: https://ssrn.com/abstract=3000695 or http://dx.doi.org/10.2139/ssrn.3000695

Farmer, P. (2003). *Pathologies of power: Health, human rights, and the new war on the poor* (1st ed., Vol. 4). University of California Press.

Fins, A. (2020, December). *National snapshot: Poverty among women & families, 2020.* National Women's Law Center. https://nwlc.org/wp-content/uploads/2020/12/PovertySnapshot2020.pdf

Foshee, V. A., Karriker-Jaffe, K. J., Reyes, H. L. M., Ennett, S. T., Suchindran, C., Bauman, K. E., & Benefield, T. S. (2008). What accounts for demographic differences in trajectories of adolescent dating violence? An examination of intrapersonal and contextual mediators. *Journal of Adolescent Health, 42*(6), 596–604.

Gadson, C. A., & Lewis, J. A. (2022). Devalued, overdisciplined, and stereotyped: An exploration of gendered racial microaggressions among Black adolescent girls. *Journal of Counseling Psychology, 69*(1), 14–26.

Gale, A., & Dorsey, M. (2020). Does the context of racial discrimination matter for adolescent school outcomes? The impact of in-school racial discrimination and general racial discrimination on Black adolescents' outcomes. *Race and Social Problems, 12*(2), 171–175.

Harris-Lacewell, M. (2001). No place to rest. *Women & Politics, 23*(3), 1–33.

Henry, A. (1998). *Taking back control: African Canadian women teachers' lives and practice.* Suny Press.

Hooper, L. M., Tomek, S., Bolland, K. A., Church, W. T., Wilcox, K., & Bolland, J. M. (2015). The impact of previous suicide ideations, traumatic stress, and gender on future suicide ideation trajectories among Black American adolescents: A longitudinal investigation. *Journal of Loss and Trauma, 20*(4), 354–373.

Hunt, M. (2022, March). A new podcast speaks to Black girls' experience in foster care. *Imprint.* https://imprintnews.org/foster-care/podcast-speaks-to-black-girls-experience-in-foster-care/63417

Ivey-Stephenson, A. Z., Demissie, Z., Crosby, A. E., Stone, D. M., Gaylor, E., Wilkins, N., Lowry, R., & Brown, M. (2020). Suicidal ideation and behaviors among high school students—Youth Risk Behavior Survey, United States, 2019. *MMWR Supplements, 69*(1), 47.

James, S. E., Johnson, J., Raghavan, C., Lemos, T., Barakett, M., & Woolis, D. (2003). The violent matrix: A study of structural, interpersonal, and intrapersonal violence among a sample of poor women. *American Journal of Community Psychology, 31*(1–2), 129–141.

Joe, S., Baser, R. S., Neighbors, H. W., Caldwell, C. H., & Jackson, J. S. (2009). 12-month and lifetime prevalence of suicide attempts among Black adolescents in the National Survey of American Life. *Journal of the American Academy of Child and Adolescent Psychiatry, 48*(3), 271–282.

Joseph, N. M., Viesca, K. M., & Bianco, M. (2016). Black female adolescents and racism in schools: Experiences in a colorblind society. *High School Journal, 100*(1), 4–25.

Kohli, R., Arteaga, N., & McGovern, E. R. (2019). "Compliments" and "jokes": Unpacking racial microaggressions in the K–12 classroom. In C. M. Capodilupo, K. L. Nadal, D. P. Rivera, D. W. Sue, & G. C. Torino (Eds.), *Microaggression theory: Influence and implications* (pp. 276–290). John Wiley.

Langley, M., & Sugarmann, J. (2014, January). *Black homicide victimization in the United States: An analysis of 2011 homicide data.* Violence Poverty Center. https://search.issuelab.org/resource/black-homicide-victimization-in-the-united-states-an-analysis-of-2011-homicide-data.html

Leath, S., Ware, N., Seward, M. D., McCoy, W. N., Ball, P., & Pfister, T. A. (2021). A qualitative study of Black college women's experiences of misogynoir and anti-racism with high school educators. *Social Sciences, 10*(1), 29.

Lee, B. X. (2019). *Violence: An interdisciplinary approach to causes, consequences, and cures.* John Wiley.

Miller, B., and Taylor, J. (2012). Racial and socioeconomic status differences in depressive symptoms among black and white youth: An examination of the mediating effects of family structure, stress and support. *Journal of Youth and Adolescence, 41*(4), 426–437. 10.1007/s10964-011-9672-4

Mims, L. C., & Williams, J. L. (2020). "They told me what I was before I could tell them what I was": Black girls' ethnic-racial identity development within multiple worlds. *Journal of Adolescent Research, 35*(6), 754–779.

Morris, E. W. (2007). "Ladies" or "loudies"? Perceptions and experiences of Black girls in classrooms. *Youth & Society, 38*(4), 490–515.

Morris, M. W. (2012). *Race, gender and the school-to-prison pipeline: Expanding our discussion to include Black girls.* African American Policy Forum.

Morris, M. W. (2016). *Pushout: The criminalization of Black girls in schools.* New Press.

Neal-Jackson, A. (2018). A meta-ethnographic review of the experiences of African American girls and young women in K–12 education. *Review of Educational Research, 88*(4), 508–546.

Nunn, N. (2018). Super-girl: Strength and sadness in Black girlhood. *Gender and Education, 30*(2), 239–258.

Osbourne, A. (2020). On a walking tour to no man's land: Brokering and shifting narratives of violence in Trench Town, Jamaica. *Space and Culture, 23*(1), 48–60. https://doi.org/10.1177/1206331219871892

Patrick, K., & Chaudhry, C. (2017). *Let her learn: Stopping school pushout for girls in foster care.* National Women's Law Center. https://nwlc.org/wp-content/uploads/2017/04/Final_nwlc_Gates_FosterCare.pdf

Perry, B. L., Harp, K. L., & Oser, C. B. (2013). Racial and gender discrimination in the stress process: Implications for African American women's health and well-being. *Sociological Perspectives, 56*(1), 25–48.

Perry, B. L., Stevens-Watkins, D., & Oser, C. B. (2013). The moderating effects of skin color and ethnic identity affirmation on suicide risk among low-SES African American women. *Race and Social Problems, 5*(1), 1–14.

Rapp, A., & Kilpatrick, S. (2020, February). *Changing the cycle: Period poverty as a public health crisis.* University of Michigan School of Public Health. https://sph.umich.edu/pursuit/2020posts/period-poverty.html

Rueckert, P. (2018, May). *Period poverty, stigma are keeping girls out of schools.* Global Citizen. https://www.globalcitizen.org/en/content/menstrual-hygiene-day-education/

Seaton, E. L., Upton, R., Gilbert, A., & Volpe, V. (2014). A moderated mediation model: Racial discrimination, coping strategies, and racial identity among Black adolescents. *Child Development, 85*(3), 882–890.

Sharma, S. (2010). Contesting institutional discourse to create new possibilities for understanding lived experience: Life-stories of young women in detention, rehabilitation, and education. *Race Ethnicity and Education, 13*(3), 327–347.

Smith, E. J., & Harper, S. R. (2015). *Disproportionate impact of K–12 school suspension and expulsion on Black students in southern states.* University of Pennsylvania, Center for the Study of Race and Equity in Education.

Steinbugler, A. C., Press, J. E., & Dias, J. J. (2006). Gender, race, and affirmative action: Operationalizing intersectionality in survey research. *Gender & Society, 20*(6), 805–825.

Tomek, S., Hooper, L. M., Church, W. T., Bolland, K. A., Bolland, J. M., & Wilcox, K. (2015). Relations among suicidality, recent/frequent alcohol use, and gender in a Black American adolescent sample: A longitudinal investigation. *Journal of Clinical Psychology, 71*(6), 544–560.

U.S. Census Bureau. (2020). *Current Population Survey, 2020 annual social and economic supplement.* https://www.census.gov/data/datasets/time-series/demo/cps/cps-asec.2020.html#list-tab-165711867

U.S. Department of Education, Office for Civil Rights. (2014). *Civil rights data collection: Data snapshot (school discipline).* https://ocrdata.ed.gov/assets/downloads/CRDC-School-Discipline-Snapshot.pdf

Watson, T. N. (2016). "Talking back": The perceptions and experiences of Black girls who attend city high school. *Journal of Negro Education, 85*(3), 239–249.

Williams, D. R. (2018). Stress and the mental health of populations of color: Advancing our understanding of race-related stressors. *Journal of Health and Social Behavior, 59*(4), 466–485.

Wun, C. (2016). Against captivity: Black girls and school discipline policies in the afterlife of slavery. *Educational Policy, 30*(1), 171–196.

23

Broadening the Scope of Hospital-Based Programs to Prevent Youth Gun Violence

• • • • • • • • • • • • •

WILLIAM WICAL AND JOSEPH
RICHARDSON JR.

Overview

Since 2018, the leading cause of death for children and adolescents in the United States has been gun violence. While Black youth compose just 14 percent of all youth in America, they account for 43 percent of firearm-related deaths in their age group. According to the Centers for Disease Control and Prevention (CDC, 2020b), Black boys and adolescents are approximately eighteen times more likely than are their white peers to be killed with a gun.

In order to make sense of these marked differences in levels of gun violence, researchers, practitioners, and policymakers interested in violence prevention must consider the continuum of trauma Black youth experience throughout their lives—often beginning at an early age. There are significant psychological, physical, and social consequences of adverse childhood experiences (ACEs), including higher likelihoods of violent victimization and perpetration, depression, anxiety, heart disease, substance abuse, and difficulty in school (see CDC, 2020a; Felitti et al., 1998; Vasan et al., 2021). While initial research on early exposure to trauma focused on abuse, neglect, and family problems, additional research has demonstrated the need to consider potentially traumatizing experiences at the community level. These events include witnessing violence, experiencing racial discrimination, feeling unsafe in one's neighborhood, enduring bullying, and encountering the impacts of mass incarceration, hypersurveillance, and police brutality (Geller, 2021; Pachter et al., 2017). The consequences of these adverse experiences are exacerbated by the fact that many Black youth experience poor access to quality education, have early engagement with the criminal justice system, and lack meaningful access to adequate mental health services (Assari, 2018).

The frequency and severity of ACEs and limited access to vital resources point to a significant need for comprehensive wraparound services for those at the highest risk of injury—both in childhood and as they become adults. Hospital-based violence intervention programs (HVIPs) have emerged as one such service provider for victims of violent injury. The national network of HVIPs—the Health Alliance for Violence Intervention (HAVI)—has underscored the importance of "multidisciplinary programs that identify patients at risk of repeat violent injury and link them with hospital- and community-based resources aimed at addressing underlying risk factors for violence" (HAVI, 2020). These programs correctly note that those individuals who are shot are at an elevated risk of being reinjured (Evans & Vega, 2018; Richardson et al., 2020). Unfortunately, many HVIPs do not provide services to youth since programs have minimum age requirements and lack age-appropriate programming. These barriers limit the ability to engage individuals under the age of eighteen years old in violence prevention efforts.

The HVIP intervention strategy relies on the fact that nearly all victims of violent injury seek medical care at an emergency department or trauma service. Because people who are violently injured are often significantly socially marginalized, HVIPs attempt in varying degrees to address social determinants of health (specifically education, food insecurity, employment, and criminal justice involvement) to improve health outcomes and reduce the likelihood of repeat injury and retaliatory violence. However, these programs do not emphasize the significance of relationships of power that marginalize program participants, engender traumatic experience and responses, and cause social inequity. This limited perspective results in a narrow understanding of what constitutes gun violence prevention and how hospital-based efforts may be able to best contribute to it.

Based on the authors' ethnographic research that examines the emotional experiences of Black men who receive services at an HVIP and the findings of the D.C. Violence Fatality Review Committee (DC VFRC), it is unequivocally clear that many Black men who are injured or killed later in life were failed by the educational, juvenile justice, and health care systems throughout their adolescence. We argue that any attempt to substantively reduce gun-violence-related disparities rests on the ability to address the unique forms of social marginalization experienced by Black boys and adolescents. Efforts to improve youth violence prevention will require collaboration across multiple institutions. HVIPs are uniquely positioned to partner with other agencies to facilitate "upstream" prevention—including participating in preventative work in schools, working in family court and the juvenile justice system to provide additional support for violently injured youth with histories of criminal justice involvement, and engaging with the court system and department of probation for youth offenders charged with gun possession.

Insight from the Narratives of Those Most Impacted by Gun Violence

Case Examples of the Special Five and HVIP Participants

A closer look at how social institutions impact the lives of Black youth who are at the highest risk for gun violence injury reveals multiple opportunities for intervention and prevention. We draw on the narratives of those who have lost their lives or survived gun violence to identify and recommend efficacious youth gun violence prevention strategies. These data offer unique insights into the failures of institutions to support Black youth and the long-term consequences of these shortcomings.

In collaboration with the interim deputy mayor of public safety and justice, the DC VFRC conducted an in-depth case review of five adolescents—referred to as the "Special Five"—who were under supervision from the D.C. Department of Youth Rehabilitation Services. All five were Black adolescents ages seventeen to eighteen who were victims of fatal gun violence. This assessment found that despite their numerous interactions with different institutions, these agencies did not collaborate with each other and that, related to this, youth still lacked adequate access to vital resources. We heard about these same problems in our ethnographic research with Black men who survived gunshot wounds and received services from either of the two HVIPs associated with the busiest trauma centers in the state of Maryland (one program also provides services to Washington, D.C.). The communities near these two programs experience some of the highest levels of gun violence in the country. Participants' perspectives on meaningful intervention, safety, and healing underpin our analysis of youth gun violence prevention and the roles that HVIPs may play in efforts to decrease violence. These men—some not much older than the Special Five—argue that it is only through structural change that serious improvements in community safety can be made.

Support with Schooling—Truancy, Performance, and Criminalization

All of the Special Five had extended histories of truancy—issues of chronic absenteeism were first identified during elementary school. Similarly, HVIP participants indicated they had difficulties in school and did not receive adequate support in their attempts to stay engaged with their education. They noted that the transition to adolescence coincided with increased exposure to community violence and an inability to focus on their classwork. This was particularly significant for those individuals who had friends murdered while they were in middle or high school. In all of these cases, they received no mental health support from their school. As one participant explained: "Just imagine that, we were fifteen, sixteen . . . and we losing homies, you got five dead men already. We only in tenth grade, like damn, that shit f-cks you up . . . what is the point [in focusing on school]? Especially like, D.C. is small, there is only but so many schools you are going to go to. So the person who killed your friend is in your school or they are right there (living in close proximity)."

The consequences of having limited psychosocial support in school were compounded by being criminalized at an early age—even for behavior in school. For those youth who described being "put out" of school, there were often limited options for future education and stable employment. They explained that this increased psychological stress and the likelihood of being in the street for economic survival. Unsurprisingly, they noted that being in the street placed them at higher risk of being shot or incarcerated. When asked what kinds of intervention strategies would most significantly decrease gun violence, participants were emphatic about improving programs for youth and alternatives to expulsion. They suggested that these programs should be designed to keep children in school, provide opportunities for exploring interests, and offer avenues for youth-led social change. Participants emphasized that these programs could divert children away from violence in school and, in turn, keep them engaged in their education. The importance of creating alternatives for expulsion is supported by Barnes and Motz's (2018) evaluation of the unequal suspension/expulsion practices for Black youth compared to their white peers. They found that Black youth were suspended or expelled at approximately 1.75 times the rate of their white peers for the same behavior and that eliminating these differences would likely result in a 16 percent reduction in risk for later arrest. According to HVIP participants, addressing this component of the school-to-prison pipeline must be coupled with additional support for students who are at the highest risk for expulsion or suspension—including mentoring, peer support, and access to mental health services.

Although HVIP participants had a wide range of perspectives about the best ways to prevent violence in their neighborhoods, they were unanimous in their belief that investing time and resources into the lives of youth is one of the most effective strategies to decrease injuries both early and later in life. HVIPs may contribute to the upstream preventative work needed to decrease gun violence by leveraging their resources and community partnerships to support socially marginalized children and adolescents who live in high-risk neighborhoods nearest to the program. Collaborations between schools and HVIPs may be uniquely suited to support marginalized youth as these partnerships can build on the expertise and lived experience of HVIP participants to engage with youth. Strategies may include mentoring relationships connecting students and program participants, workshops on conflict mediation, credible messengers working in schools, and student-led awareness campaigns of the impacts of community violence.

Repeat Juvenile Justice Involvement

Of the Special Five, three had been involved with Child and Family Services from an early age; this involvement contributed to future juvenile justice involvement (as early as nine years old). Child and Family Services records show that these three families were unable to provide an environment needed to address behavioral issues and keep the youth from repeated arrest. The review committee also noted that families were not mentally, emotionally, or physically prepared for their youth to return home after being in custody of the Department of Youth Rehabilitation Services. The committee agreed that this lack of preparedness and the adolescents' return into an unstable environment partially contributed to their death. Similarly, HVIP participants recounted how their early experiences with incarceration shaped their lives, mental health, and perceived safety. As one participant explained,

> You are supposed to be in a rehabilitation center. You're not being rehabilitated. You're in a place where you literally learn how to do worse crimes. You're gonna meet worse, criminals, everybody, [they'll] teach you what to do, where to do, how to do, it's not what it's supposed to be. You're supposed to be helping people. You really do the exact opposite to people. If the longer you survive in a jail is a mentality . . . the worse you get. And that's why I always tell people my scariest part about jail is not that I'm scared or something gonna happen to me, it's I'm scared that I could get used to it.

Access to community-based mental or behavioral health services for marginalized Black youth is limited or nonexistent. As Richardson and Van Brakle

(2011) noted, this dearth of services has resulted in the juvenile justice system being used as a stopgap measure for children and adolescents who need social services and mental health treatment. In some cases, parents may place their children in state or local juvenile justice systems with the hope of getting help for their mental health and behavioral issues. However, these efforts often have harmful effects on youth, as they receive inappropriate care and are exposed to violence while being detained.

Since some HVIPs offer services to violently injured patients who are under eighteen years old, it is essential that they identify those participants who have been or are involved in the juvenile justice system to offer additional supportive services. Program participants' descriptions of early engagement with the criminal justice system as a traumatizing experience warrant the development and implementation of age-appropriate intervention strategies in the hospital since the majority of current HVIP programming is tailored for adults. Additionally, HVIPs may foster collaborative relationships with probation officers to strategize alternative solutions to detention or incarceration, thus providing more meaningful access to social and behavioral services for violently injured youth.

Monitoring, Probation, and Gun Possession

All members of the Special Five were subjected to multiple community-based juvenile justice programs, including monitoring through Global Positioning System (GPS) hardware. This kind of surveillance is common for individuals with gun possession cases. However, the DC VFRC noted that the effectiveness of this invasive approach to monitoring youth is not well understood. Participants at the HVIP recounted how they or their peers' (often repeated) involvement with the juvenile justice system removed them from meaningful social relationships. They explained that these experiences with confinement and early criminalization profoundly impacted their self-identities and feelings of safety in their neighborhood. Rather than simply placing youth on probation and monitoring, it is essential to connect those individuals who have early gun possession charges with additional comprehensive wraparound services. While HVIPs are underequipped and insufficiently funded to provide all of the wraparound services needed for this support, they can play an important part by fostering meaningful supportive relationships. As one survivor noted, "When you connect with certain people [who have had similar experiences], they bring out things in you that you don't know about." These newfound appreciations included alternative ways of addressing trauma, conflict resolution strategies, and enjoyable experiences.

We know that many youth are carrying firearms due to a lack of trust in law enforcement, fear, and the need for protection in response to pervasive community violence. As one participant explained,

It's a scary thing to have to carry [a firearm] to feel safe. A lot of the gangster stuff goes out the window when you're being real, right? It's scary. Being a young Black man walking out, you have to be on defense every day. It's scary, man. You have to be a wolf, you might not even be a wolf, but you have to have this persona about yourself that you are willing to take a life for your life because the next man would do that to you. We got youngsters that's fourteen years old killing out here. So it's a scary life out here really, just to survive every day and think we gonna make it back home.

HVIP participants emphasized that the best way to decrease youth carrying weapons is to enhance their feelings of safety. They also noted that it is necessary to develop alternative methods of dealing with early gun possession charges that do not criminalize youth for attempting to feel safe. These insights are supported by Richardson et al.'s (2016) analysis of the most significant risk factors for repeat violent injury—which include both a history of using a weapon and a history of incarceration.

In addition to other social services, both HVIPs in this study previously included working closely with probation and parole officers and youth at high risk for firearm violence. However, these efforts were abandoned (without any information as to their success or failure) in favor of strictly focusing on educational, employment, and housing support. A recommitment to engaging the ways in which the criminal justice system is closely linked to the health outcomes of Black youth remains a critical avenue for violence prevention. Youth-led, trauma-informed, and restorative-justice-focused approaches to youth engagement have been shown to be successful in beginning to address problems associated with community violence exposure (Harden et al., 2015). These findings align with HVIP participants' opinion that their ability to share their life experiences, time, and concern with youth offered a more viable violence prevention strategy than anything the hospital program could offer.

Directions for Youth Gun Violence Prevention

The narratives of the Special Five and HVIP participants emphasize that we need to significantly expand our definitions of what youth gun violence prevention looks like. For HVIPs, this expansion must include the development of age-appropriate resources that are sensitive to traumas occurring over the life course, robust program staff including those with shared lived experience, services tailored for youth, and strong interinstitutional collaborations. These partnerships must specifically seek to address how the educational and criminal justice systems fail and harm Black youth. This broader approach to violence prevention acknowledges that simply assisting patients after they are shot is an inadequate prevention strategy. HVIPs have a significant role to play in this expanded vision of violence prevention. Their participation rests on the ability to move beyond the prevailing—and limited—notion that repeat injury for participants is primarily related to instances of violent retaliation.

In an attempt to better understand the root causes of health inequalities, the fields of public health, medical anthropology, and sociology have highlighted the significance of structural racism. This emphasis is necessary when considering the possible role HVIPs can play in youth-focused gun violence prevention as it rejects the notion that violence is best understood by concentrating on individual crime, behavior, and risk. We argue that substantial decreases in the number of youth injured and killed by gun violence will remain an elusive goal until there is a serious movement toward changing the structural conditions that harm them. Based on the narratives of the Special Five and HVIP participants, we acknowledge the importance of the educational and criminal justice systems in producing health disparities for marginalized youth. Supporting youth and their families in achieving success in school, working to provide meaningful alternatives for youth who are at risk for involvement in the juvenile justice system, and addressing the root causes of gun carrying are vital starting places for decreasing gun violence. These efforts may have additional positive benefits for socially marginalized youth—including disrupting the school-to-prison pipeline.

While HVIPs are underequipped and insufficiently funded to provide all of the wraparound services needed to effectively decrease youth gun violence, the trauma centers and emergency departments that house HVIPs are often affiliated with large research-focused universities with access to substantial social and human capital. These resources must be leveraged toward building partnerships capable of offering the comprehensive services needed to support people who are injured and their families. In coupling these efforts with a commitment to grounding violence prevention in the perspectives of those most impacted by gun violence, HVIPs may begin to advocate for social change to address the structural causes of gun violence. This collaborative approach serves as an invaluable challenge to the narrow ways in which violence is typically understood and, in turn, how preventative work is often done. We see drawing on the lived experience and expertise of Black men who participate in HVIPs to support marginalized youth as a vital way to decrease youth gun violence. While this method of engagement addresses common barriers to effective violence prevention work—including the justifiable mistrust of institutions by marginalized communities—it must be coupled with increased institutional buy-in and governmental fiscal support. In doing so, these efforts present a viable means to offer increased social support to those children and adolescents who are at the highest risk of injury or death at the present moment or in the future.

Acknowledgments

The collection of ethnographic data by William Wical was supported by a National Science Foundation, Doctoral Dissertation Research Improvement Grant (award 2117054) and a Wenner-Gren Foundation, Dissertation Fieldwork Grant (award 5383152402).

References

Assari, S. (2018). Health disparities due to diminished return among Black Americans: Public policy solutions. *Social Issues and Policy Review, 12*(1), 112–145.

Barnes, J. C., & Motz, R. T. (2018). Reducing racial inequalities in adulthood arrest by reducing inequalities in school discipline: Evidence from the school-to-prison pipeline. *Developmental Psychology, 54*(12), 2328–2340.

Centers for Disease Control and Prevention. 2020a. *Injury center.* https://www.cdc .gov/injury/

Centers for Disease Control and Prevention. 2020b. *Web-Based Injury Statistics Query and Reporting System (WISQARS). Injury mortality reports.* https://wisqars.cdc .gov

Evans, D., & Vega, A. (2018). Critical care: The important role of hospital-based violence intervention programs. In *Denormalizing violence: A series of reports from the John Jay College evaluation of cure violence programs in New York City.* Research and Evaluation Center, John Jay College of Criminal Justice, City University of New York.

Felitti, V. J., Anda, R. F., Nordenberg, D., Williamson, D. F., Spitz, A. M., Edwards, V., & Marks, J. S. (1998). Relationship of childhood abuse and household dysfunction to many of the leading causes of death in adults: The Adverse Childhood Experiences (ACE) study. *American Journal of Preventive Medicine, 14*(4), 245–258.

Geller, A. (2021). Youth-police contact: Burdens and inequities in an adverse childhood experience, 2014-2017. *American Journal of Public Health, 111*(7), 1300–1308.

Harden, T., Kenemore, T., Mann, K., Edwards, M., List, C., & Martinson, K. J. (2015). The Truth n' Trauma Project: Addressing community violence through a youth-led, trauma-informed and restorative framework. *Child and Adolescent Social Work Journal, 32*(1), 65–79.

Health Alliance for Violence Intervention (HAVI). 2020. "The Health Alliance for Violence Prevention—what is an HVIP?" https://www.thehavi.org/what-is-an -hvip

Office of the Chief Medical Examiner, Washington D.C. (2022). *2020 Violence Fatality Review Committee.* https://ocme.dc.gov/page/2020-violence-fatality -review-committee

Pachter, L. M., Lieberman, L., Bloom, S. L., & Fein, J. A. (2017). Developing a community-wide initiative to address childhood adversity and toxic stress: A case study of the Philadelphia ACE task force. *Academic Pediatrics, 17*(7), S130–S135.

Richardson, J. B., Jr., & Van Brakle, M. (2011). A qualitative study of relationships among parenting strategies, social capital, the juvenile justice system, and mental health care for at risk African American male youth. *Journal of Correctional Health Care, 17*(4), 319–328.

Richardson, J. B., Vil, C. S., Sharpe, T., Wagner, M., & Cooper, C. (2016). Risk factors for recurrent violent injury among Black men. *Journal of Surgical Research*, *204*(1), 261–266.

Richardson, J. B., Jr., Wical, W., Kottage, N., & Bullock, C. (2020). Shook ones: Understanding the intersection of nonfatal violent firearm injury, incarceration, and traumatic stress among young Black men. *American Journal of Men's Health*, *14*(6). https://doi.org/10.1177/1557988320982181

Vasan, A., Mitchell, H. K., Fein, J. A., Buckler, D. G., Wiebe, D. J., & South, E. C. (2021). Association of neighborhood gun violence with mental health–related pediatric emergency department utilization. *JAMA Pediatrics*, *175*(12), 1244–1251.

The Law Alone Cannot Fix it

• • • • • • • • • • • • •

MARSHA LEVICK

Overview

In 2014, J. S., a thirteen-year-old girl from a white, middle-class family in a small town in Pennsylvania, became involved with a twenty-year-old man who at the time was enlisted in the military. While apparently living a normal middle school life and possessed of extremely high intelligence, J. S. carried emotional and physical scars that left her particularly vulnerable to the romantic overtures of this older man. They began a relationship, carried out initially in secret, that spanned about six months. At some point, she disclosed the relationship to her mother but lied about his age. Because they did not live in the same community, the relationship relied on endless text messaging, often into the late hours of the night, filled with typical teenage angst and longing and unsurprising exploration of this young woman's emerging sexuality. The relationship was also emotionally, physically, and sexually abusive.

Eventually, J. S.'s mother learned that her boyfriend was seven years older than J. S. She told her daughter the relationship would have to end. For an emotionally and psychologically fragile thirteen-year-old who had become completely dependent on this man's attention, the demand was intolerable. The two began plotting over text messages about how they might "kill" her mother.

Shortly after J. S. turned fourteen, and after her mother had taken her and the twenty-year-old to a concert as their "last date," the twenty-year-old killed her mother in the mother's car while her daughter was in the back seat. J. S. and her adult boyfriend then purchased cleaning and other supplies at a local store to cover up the crime and bury the mother's body.

This was not a perfect crime. The mother's absence was noted and investigated, and both J. S. and her boyfriend were quickly brought in for questioning and ultimately charged with first degree murder.

What happened next is a story of the failings of our legal system, which treated this young girl as a premeditated murderer, a mastermind of criminal planning, and utterly beyond rehabilitation. The judge who heard her request to be tried in juvenile court denied it, characterizing this fourteen-year-old as a manipulative liar whose actions were responsible not only for the death of her mother but for the arrest and prosecution of her now twenty-one-year-old boyfriend. Her lawyer likewise considered her to be a liar and unfortunately limited his representation accordingly. A guilty plea was negotiated literally behind closed doors among her lawyer, the district attorney, and the judge, completely without her knowledge or participation. On the advice of her counsel and with no other options, she plead guilty to first degree murder and was sentenced to serve thirty-five years to life in prison. Prior to this incident, J. S. was an accomplished student who had never been in any kind of trouble before— let alone trouble involving the juvenile or criminal justice system.

On appeal, the decision denying her petition to transfer her case to juvenile court was affirmed. Postconviction proceedings challenging her lawyer's ineffective representation and other trial errors were initiated and are in process. Since her incarceration began, J. S. has earned her high school diploma and is currently taking college classes in prison.

Seven years earlier, in 2007, in another small town in Pennsylvania, H. T., a fifteen-year-old tenth grade student, was arrested and charged with harassment for creating a social media post that mocked her high school vice-principal. Other students were invited to post on the site as well. Following the arrest, her mother was discouraged by local law enforcement officials from obtaining counsel, given the trivial nature of the offense, and specifically encouraged to sign a waiver of her daughter's right to counsel when they appeared in court for her daughter's adjudicatory hearing. While the charge and conduct itself were not only trivial but hardly criminal, the consequences were serious. After a perfunctory hearing that lasted no more than a few minutes, unrepresented H. T. was adjudicated delinquent, immediately handcuffed, and transported to a juvenile correctional facility for an initial period of ninety days.

This aggressive response to normal adolescent behavior by our juvenile justice system was the opening act of the now-notorious Luzerne County, Pennsylvania, "Kids for Cash" scandal. The scandal involved courtroom violations of youths' most fundamental constitutional rights in combination with a vast corruption scheme that netted two judges in Luzerne County, including the juvenile court judge, nearly three million dollars in alleged unreported kickbacks from the developer and former co-owner of a private for-profit juvenile detention center—the construction of which the judges facilitated through misuse of their official positions and to which the juvenile court judge routinely committed youth who appeared before him. The two judges were convicted on federal criminal charges and sentenced to significant prison terms; the children and their parents also received substantial monetary awards arising out of several settlements of civil lawsuits filed on their behalf. Even so, many of the youth impacted by this scandal still retain vestiges of that trauma (Scribner, 2022).

While seemingly at opposite ends of the spectrum of criminal conduct committed by children, each of these cases illustrates how our justice system—whether we are talking about the juvenile or criminal justice system—overreaches in its treatment of children. In J. S.'s case, it shows how a particular act of violence committed by a child—even a tragic and heinous act like homicide—does not necessarily warrant condemning that child to several decades in prison. While the refusal to treat this child as a child and the imposition of this very harsh, adult sentence was undoubtedly viewed by those who made those decisions as having something to do with violence prevention, the system actually tossed aside a young teen with enormous promise because they could assess her only through the lens of the killing of her mother by her twenty-year-old boyfriend and her participation in that crime. This myopic view of her was further warped by her gender: like Eve, she was seen as the temptress pulling the strings of her military boyfriend who not only was substantially older but also had a documented history of violence and fascination with knives.

In H. T.'s case, we see a different kind of overreach: thousands of children were pulled into the juvenile justice system in Luzerne County for trivial instances of misconduct and often incarcerated because the juvenile court judge there believed official discipline for any misconduct, especially school-based misconduct, was in the child's best interest and a necessary substitute for the parents' failures to discipline their children themselves. The financial gains that animated the judge's conduct are undoubtedly central to the Luzerne County story—but it cannot be ignored that the youth who were targeted were low-risk, nonthreatening youth who all too often were guilty of nothing more than normative adolescent acting out. Yet they were brought before a "law-and-order" judge who often humiliated and verbally abused them before adjudicating them delinquent.

As a civil rights lawyer who has advocated on behalf of youth involved in our juvenile and criminal justice systems for several decades, I understand that these examples of overreach are all too common. Indeed, at the same time that J. S.'s and H. T.'s cases were going on, another legal story was unfolding across the country, involving children who had been convicted of both murder and non-murder crimes years or decades earlier and who had received extreme sentences in criminal court for their conduct, from the death penalty to sentences of life without parole. In a series of rulings between 2005 and 2016, the U.S. Supreme Court struck the juvenile death penalty (*Roper v. Simmons*, 2005), life without parole sentences for children convicted of non-homicide crimes (*Graham v. Florida*, 2010), and mandatory life without parole sentences for children convicted of homicide (*Miller v. Alabama*, 2012; *Montgomery v. Louisiana*, 2016). In each of these cases, the Supreme Court relied on both social science and emerging neuroscience to identify key developmental differences between children and adults that diminished youths' culpability for their crimes and thus disqualified them, in accordance with the Eighth Amendment's ban on cruel and unusual punishment, from the death penalty and life without parole sentences that otherwise remain in play—and remain constitutional—for adult offenders. Specifically, the Court held that three particular research findings distinguished youth for sentencing purposes under the Constitution:

1 their immature judgment means that they are more likely to make impulsive and impetuous decisions, without regard for long-term consequences
2 they are particularly susceptible to peer influences, and especially negative peer influences
3 because adolescence is a transitory developmental stage through which youth pass, youth have a unique capacity for change and rehabilitation

These characteristics of youth were already widely recognized by developmental psychologists. Yet the increased utilization of brain scans by neuroscientists since the *Roper* decision (banning the juvenile death penalty) in 2005 to map and record, among other things, the growth and maturation of different areas of the brain showed a correlation between these developmental traits and the delayed development of the frontal lobe of the brain during adolescence, which is key to mature decision making.

While there were just over 70 former youth awaiting execution at the time *Roper* came down in 2005 and approximately 160 former youth serving life without parole sentences for non-homicide crimes in 2010 when the Court banned these sentences in *Graham*, there were over 2,000 former youth serving mandatory life without parole sentences in 2012 when the Court banned these sentences in *Miller*. Pursuant to *Miller* and *Montgomery* (which ruled *Miller* retroactive), the members of this extremely large cohort were all entitled to resentencing hearings, and over the course of the next ten years, as a result of those resentencing hearings and new opportunities for parole, hundreds of men and women were released from prison and returned to their communities.

Remarkably, and relevant to the question of how the American legal system either promotes or impedes violence prevention, all but a tiny fraction of these individuals have reintegrated successfully into their communities. They have reconnected with family, made new social connections, entered the workforce, married, and are raising children. Many are working with advocacy or other community organizations, determined to give back and mentor young people. This incredibly positive outcome is significant. I was involved in all of these extreme sentencing cases before the U.S. Supreme Court, where I and others fought for a chance at freedom for these men and women who were all sentenced to die in prison decades ago, deemed unworthy of ever being released from prison because of the serious and heinous nature of their crimes. But again our system guessed wrong—a lifetime of incarceration was not necessary to keep our communities safe. The initial decision to lock these people up for life was simply trading one lost life for another, with little thought to the efficacy of this response. Today, I count many of these men and women among my colleagues and friends, my partners in the fight for a more humane justice system.

History of the Juvenile Court in the United States

How did we get here? Well over a century ago, in 1899, the first juvenile court in the country was established in Cook County, Illinois. Prior to the creation of this court, children accused or found guilty of criminal conduct were treated for the most part like adults. Over the course of the next twenty-five years, every state passed legislation to establish a separate a juvenile justice system. Key hallmarks of this separate system were privacy, confidentiality, and procedural informality. Privacy and confidentiality were intended to protect children from public disclosure of their criminal offending and spare them the consequences of that disclosure; procedural informality meant that the court proceedings lacked the most basic features of due process, such as the right to counsel, the right to notice, protection against self-incrimination, and the right to confront witnesses. The juvenile court was premised on an intuitive understanding that children were different from adults and should be treated as such; it would be over a hundred years before research provided the scientific vocabulary we routinely use today to justify treating children differently under the Constitution as well as under state laws and policies (Steinberg & Scott, 2003). Central to this idea that children should be treated differently was the elevation of rehabilitation over punishment and retribution.

Of course, when a system operates behind closed doors it may take time to understand how well or poorly the system is functioning. In the case of juvenile court, it wasn't until a few cases made their way to the U.S. Supreme Court in the 1960s that cracks in the juvenile justice system were exposed. Peering behind the curtain of these proceedings cast a bright but ill light on this secret system.

Rehabilitation and treatment, it turned out, often took the form of years of incarceration in prisonlike settings for trivial offending. Such punitive confinement was imposed without even rudimentary due process. Children could be transferred to criminal court for prosecution with no evidentiary record or stated reasons supporting their removal from juvenile court, despite the substantially worse penalties imposed by criminal court. Even in juvenile court, a civil standard of proof governed the determination of delinquency, counsel was not required, witness testimony was scant—despite the dire consequences many youth faced once adjudicated.

These procedural lapses were addressed in several landmark cases decided by the Supreme Court in the sixties and seventies. In the first of these cases, involving the transfer of children to criminal court for prosecution, the Supreme Court ruled that the removal of children from the jurisdiction of juvenile court was so consequential that such proceedings must comport with due process, including a clear statement of reasons justifying the decision (*Kent v. United States*, 1966). Children were guaranteed the right to counsel in delinquency proceedings (*In re Gault*, 1967) as well as the right to notice of charges and hearings, the right to confront witnesses, and the right against self-incrimination. They were entitled to have the state prove the delinquent charges against them on proof beyond a reasonable doubt (*In re Winship*, 1970) and also entitled to the Constitution's protection against double jeopardy (*Breed v. Jones*, 1975). While these constitutional safeguards appeared to remake the juvenile court, at least with respect to the imposition of procedural safeguards in the adjudication of the youth it sanctioned, the original rehabilitative goals of the juvenile justice system remained essentially intact.

But in the late 1980s the country witnessed a substantial rise in violent crime among juveniles and adults alike. This crime surge led to the now infamous but ultimately renounced declaration that we were facing a generation of teen "superpredators" whose violent, criminal behavior would place all of our communities at risk as we turned the corner into the twenty-first century. "Adult time for adult crime" became the impetus for a nationwide scramble to change existing state laws to push ever greater numbers of children into the criminal justice system. By the time the crime wave abated in the early 1990s, the damage was done; every state had overhauled their juvenile justice system by shrinking its jurisdictional boundaries and upping the punishment for juvenile offending, in juvenile court or criminal court. Emblematic of this era was the case of the Central Park Five, a group of five Black and Latino youth charged with the aggravated assault and rape of a white woman in Central Park in 1989. Although the Central Park Five were eventually exonerated in 2003, the case initially sparked discussion about crime, criminal behavior by youths, and violence toward women. After the exonerations, the case came to represent systemic racial profiling, discrimination, and inequality in the legal system (History.com Editors, 2019).

The historic, structural racism that permeates our justice system as reflected in the Central Park Five case contributes to the ambiguous role the legal system plays in combatting youth violence. This racism has led to a system that primarily surveils and infiltrates communities of color, creating an unacceptable imbalance in who is targeted by law enforcement and other actors in the justice system generally. The legal system has likewise proven ill-equipped to address and correct this. Black and Brown youth are disproportionately characterized as—and thus mistakenly perceived to be—the perpetrators of youth violence. But historic, systemic racism perpetuates myths and suppositions that lack true factual grounding. We cannot effectively and successfully address youth violence in America until we recalibrate how we dispatch law enforcement or how we allocate discretion across all aspects of the justice system (Birckhead, 2016).

From Retribution to Rehabilitation to Uncertainty

The rush to once again emphasize retribution over rehabilitation for young offenders in the nineties—a return to a nineteenth-century view of children—was itself reversed yet again with the U.S. Supreme Court sentencing cases discussed above, which led to the release of so many men and women otherwise condemned to die in prison. The Court's reliance on scientific research to mandate a more treatment-oriented approach to youth who commit even the most serious crimes reverberated across the country. Just as the nineties were marked by a demand for adult time for adult crime, the first two decades of the twenty-first century adopted the mantra that "kids are different" and demanded that children be treated accordingly by our justice systems—juvenile or criminal. This period was also marked by declining crime and arrest rates and substantial reductions in youth incarceration and transfer rates. The average daily number of youth in custody has plummeted 60 percent since 2000, to approximately 48,000 more recently (Sawyer, 2019). Similarly, more than 250,000 youth were transferred to adult court annually on average in the mid-nineties; today that number is closer to 53,000 (Kelly, 2021). Scores of both pretrial detention centers and juvenile secure care and correctional facilities closed nationwide.

Today, we face yet another period of uncertainty, as a new Supreme Court majority is unlikely to view the rights and circumstances of young offenders as favorably as their predecessors. In the only case involving youthful offenders to come before it, the Court narrowed the scope of its ruling prohibiting mandatory life without parole sentences for children convicted of homicide by giving judges broad discretion to still impose such sentences in individual cases. (*Jones v. Mississippi*, 2021).

This historic ping-pong approach to our treatment of young offenders makes it difficult to assess what role the legal system itself has in violence prevention. More often than not the legal system appears to be playing catch-up, adapting or adopting laws, policies, and practices as societal demands, scientific research, and other influences dictate change. And as the vignettes shared above illustrate, the actual operation of the legal system in children's lives frequently creates more harm than good and consistently perpetuates racist patterns. Current research supports not only treating children like children and keeping them out of the adult criminal justice system but also substantially streamlining custody and confinement generally. Kids do no worse in their communities with limited interventions than when placed in custodial settings, and often do better. The challenge for the legal system is to support the transformation of a system away from confinement to investments in kids and their communities. Nor can we tolerate a justice system that is itself grounded in centuries of racism and hate.

References

Birckhead, T. R. (2016). The racialization of juvenile justice and the role of the defense attorney. *Boston College Law Review, 58*, 379–462.

Breed v. Jones, 421 U.S. 519 (1975).

Graham v. Florida, 560 U.S. 48 (2010).

History.com Editors. (2019, September 23). *The Central Park Five*. https://www.history .com/topics/1980s/central-park-five

In re Gault, 387 U.S. 1 (1967).

In re Winship, 397 U.S. 358 (1970).

Jones v. Mississippi, 593 U.S. ____, 141 S. Ct. 1307 (2021).

Kelly, J. (2021, November 9). Estimate shows adult court is increasingly rare destination for youth. *Imprint*. https://imprintnews.org/youth-services-insider/estimate-shows -adult-court-is-increasingly-rare-destination-for-youth/60281#.Y_j5YWkIYmg .mailto

Kent v. United States, 383 U.S. 541 (1966).

Miller v. Alabama, 567 U.S. 460 (2012).

Montgomery v. Louisiana, 557 U.S. ____, 136 S. Ct. 718 (2016).

Roper v. Simmons, 543 U.S. 551 (2005).

Sawyer, W. (2019, December 19). *Youth confinement: The whole pie 2019*. https://www .prisonpolicy.org/reports/youth2019.html

Scribner, H. (2022, August 17). Judges behind "kids-for-cash" scandal ordered to pay more than $200M. *Axios*. https://www.axios.com/2022/08/17/judges-kids-for-cash -scandal

Steinberg, L., & Scott, E. S. (2003). Less guilty by reason of adolescence: Developmental immaturity, diminished responsibility, and the juvenile death penalty. *American Psychologist, 58*(12), 1009–1018.

Hip Hop Culture and a New Paradigm for Preventing Violent Experiences among Youth

● ● ● ● ● ● ● ● ● ● ● ● ●

RAPHAEL TRAVIS JR. AND
SIERRA MULLAN

Overview

"At this point, these kids don't just need a hug, they need to be held accountable," stated Prince George's County executive Angela Alsobrooks responding to the announcement of a countywide curfew to keep teenagers off of the streets at night (Associated Press, 2022). "I know it's not a popular thing to say, but it's a fair question: Where are their parents? Where are the aunties, where are the uncles and other family members who are responsible for them?" As we have seen throughout this volume, we as a society have the requisite knowledge and a variety of ways to prevent youth violence, to promote protective factors and inhibit what is risky.

Best Practices: A New Hip Hop and Empowerment Integrated Paradigm

A bold new vision forward for youth violence prevention requires us to understand evidence-based approaches incorporating what we know about the life course, complex interactions between person and environment, and the potential for change and growth at any point in a person's life. Six strategies highlighted by the Centers for Disease Control and Prevention (CDC) align with these ideas and help guide research and practice: (1) promoting family environments that support healthy development, (2) ensuring quality education in early life, (3) strengthening youth skills, (4) maintaining connections to caring adults and activities, (5) creating protective community environments, and (6) intervening to lessen harms and prevent future risk (CDC, 2022; David-Ferdon et al., 2016). These micro and macro efforts can help prevent problematic behaviors, lessen impacts of violence exposure, and avoid continuation or escalation of violence. They can also help to build skills and strengthen protective factors, through more engaging, creative, and culturally responsive approaches.

Meanwhile, a separate movement to promote community well-being has continued to evolve, grounded in Hip Hop culture, and with similar attention to investing in individuals as much as the environment. Hip Hop culture, like the CDC recommendations, has continually insisted that we address missed developmental opportunities from a life course perspective. As such, applied researchers along with educational, therapeutic, and other youth work practitioners have built upon these cultural roots to meet the needs of youth (Abdul-Adil, 2014; Alvarez, 2012; DeCarlo & Hockman, 2004; Elligan, 2000; Gann, 2010; Hadley & Yancy, 2012; Harper et al., 2007; Levy, 2012; Levy & Travis, 2020; Travis, 2016; Travis et al., 2019; Tyson, 2004; Viega, 2016, 2018; Washington, 2018).

Specific to violence prevention, within early Hip Hop culture, even before the song "Self-Destruction" and the 1989 Stop the Violence Movement (started by Nelson George and led by KRS-One and Boogie Down Productions), there were similar within-culture efforts toward unity and community. Afrika Bambaataa, the United Zulu Nation, and others drew inspiration from prior community health and social justice efforts within Black and Brown communities in the sixties, like the Black Panther Party for Self Defense and the Brown Berets (Chang, 2005; Travis, 2016). Further, at this time was the oft-discussed phrase "Peace, Love, Unity, and Having Fun," linked to different gangs/crews, artists, and people from all over coming together in the spirit of joy, self-expression, and community through elements of Hip Hop culture. Fast forward to the present and culture-based narratives and strategies within Hip Hop culture continue to speak to personal, collective, *and* societal responsibilities for personal and community betterment.

Hip Hop-Integrated Practices for Health Promotion

Existing research and youth work strategies that integrate Hip Hop culture have offered opportunities to critically reflect on, advocate for, and assess their effectiveness on mental health and broader community concerns (Travis et al., 2021). Thus, both research and practice guide us in conceptualizing a paradigm linking the most empowering elements of Hip Hop culture with CDC priority areas for youth violence prevention.

We see four broad but essential directions that can allow research-based Hip Hop models to be used within CDC evidence-based strategies or as standalone practices: (1) healthy home environments, (2) quality educational experiences, (3) positive role modeling and prosocial experiences, and (4) inhibited trauma-inducing experiences and environments. *But, within these four areas* are critical features to help reimagine a new era of innovative Hip Hop-integrated prevention practices. These practices must be *healing-centered, active, and engaging; identity and trauma contextualized; empowerment-focused;* and *life course and intergenerational* (see Figure 25.1).

Healing-Centered, Active, and Engaging

Hip Hop provides alternative means of healing across a spectrum of strategies, from self-care to prevention, treatment, and community engagement, through cultural values of empowerment, alongside the use of expressive art tools such

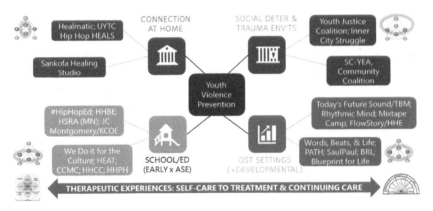

FIGURE 25.1 A map of opportunities for Hip Hop-oriented program integration within a developmentally rich system of youth violence prevention experiences. The map includes academic, social, and emotional goals across settings (i.e., home, school, and community) to impact individuals and communities.

as writing, music, visual arts, drama, dance, and imaginative play. Malchiodi (2022) highlights how expressive arts therapy differs from traditional forms of talk-based therapy by letting the senses tell the story, self-soothing the mind and body, engaging the body, enhancing nonverbal communication, recovering self-efficacy, rescripting the dominant narrative, making meaning, and restoring aliveness.

Recent research describes music-based strategies to address trauma as along a spectrum from bottom-up to top-down approaches, moving from stabilizing to entrainment, exploratory (expressive), and performative approaches (McFerran et al., 2020). A recent systematic review builds on these ideas and similarly aligns with Perry's (2006) neurosequential model (regulate, relate, reason). In this review, Rodwin et al. (2022) emphasized the effectiveness of combined and overlapping somatosensory, social-emotional, and cognitive-reflective music experiences, helping us to better understand how music-based strategies can be used in interventions.

Hip Hop culture, embedded with expressive arts, has afforded promising tools for engaging young people academically and for social and emotional development (Adjapong & Levy, 2021). We can conceptualize Hip Hop's core elements of emceeing, deejaying, breaking, graffiti, and knowledge of self from an artistic and expressive perspective. Using arts, the typical youth setting can be transformed into an interactive music and art makerspace where youth are given opportunities to tell their own stories, challenge ideas, learn, and have fun in a safe space, individually or among peers. With boundless creativity and an assist from digital technology, youth can collaborate in a healing process that validates their voice, culture, knowledge, and experiences.

Identity and Trauma Contextualized

Hip Hop also prioritizes, validates, and celebrates youths' unique cultural contexts. It speaks to cultural realities and personal narratives shaped within these realities. KOTA The Friend offers a mentoring perspective as he speaks to the complexity of youth negotiating harsh experiences and coping with trauma inducing environments in his track titled "For Troubled Boys." The Brooklyn bred emcee says, "You was born out of trauma, and you was put in the lion's den with no weapon or armor. Your coping mechanisms helped, now they makin' it harder; and you was handin' out revenge, wasn't thinkin' 'bout karma." *Esteem* narratives in lyrics continually revisit the existential question of "Who am I?" and the self-regulatory and reflexive question of "How am I?" Traumatic experiences can promote self-defeating thoughts that are an assault on personal identity and create triggers for dysregulation and unhealthy reactionary thoughts, attitudes, and behaviors (Fischer et al., 2022; Menakem, 2017). Developmental narratives in Hip Hop lyrics validate traumatic experiences, reinforce the cultural significance of knowledge of self, and model self and social awareness, healing, and the importance of creating strengths-based counternarratives. Thus, Hip Hop narratives are always specific to multiple and overlapping identities.

In other Hip Hop narratives, attention is toward one's lived experience and social reality. Narratives answer the questions "What is my story?" (*resilience* narratives) and "What is our story?" (*community* narratives). Kendrick Lamar's "Mother I Sober" and Jon Connor's "Let Go" are prime examples. Telling, retelling, and validating social realities and lived experiences are essential. Trauma experiences linked to these identities can be from the present or the past and be intergenerational. At the same time, traumatic experiences are often forced to be reconciled with cultural misconceptions, stereotypes, discrimination, inequities, and injustices.

Hip Hop narratives can also shift from present-oriented to future-focused and lead to imagining how things can be, asking the questions "How can I do or be better?" (*growth* narratives), "How can we do or be better?" (*change* narratives). Because trauma experiences have been linked to historical assaults on groups' social identities through experiences like institutional racism and other long-standing injustices, narratives often focus on better conditions, asking "What changes do I or we need to see?"

Empowerment Focused

In a popular culture example of Hip Hop's potential in healing, Logic's song "1-800-273-8255" was associated with more people reaching out to the National Suicide Prevention Lifeline and fewer reports of suicide when social media discussion of the song was highest (Niederkrotenthaler et al., 2021). Hip Hop lyrics, dance, music and beats, and visual arts are part of organic, culturally grounded healing processes that continue to be used in self-care and also to design effective strategies to promote well-being (Travis et al., 2022). Logic's song is an example of these more direct validations of emotional struggling and affirmations of the importance of healthy coping can be empowering. KOTA The Friend speaks to this, again with lyrics from "For Troubled Boys." He continues with, "And you don't trust nobody, you got beef with your mom and your dad. All your brother do is shit on you like nobody gon' want your ass. You always lookin' for home, you always lookin' for love. Nobody to meet your needs, I'm fittin' to set you free, bruh."

However, there is also potential for risky attitudes and behaviors amid empowerment, and these risks are often reflected in narratives. Questions about glorification of violence, misogyny, and substance use in Hip Hop are a constant. Alongside these concerns are sobering trends that show that violence is a leading cause of death and nonfatal injuries among adolescents in the United

States (CDC, 2020) and that violence in the media can yield untoward impacts on feelings and behaviors in the short term and cumulatively over time (Anderson et al., 2015). As concerning are the extreme disparities shown across all categories of violence victimization (e.g., excess risk for Black youth, for women, and for youth identifying as LGBTQI+) and for worsening trends for negative mental health and suicide indicators (CDC, 2020).

More subtle, less overt aspects of empowerment can also be risky. For example, youth may be empowered and learn to feel better, emotionally or about themselves, through materialism, by the victimization of others, or through a reliance on external validation. Each of these potentially empowering and risky strategies in pursuit of feeling better can contribute directly or indirectly to a youth violence scenario. Similarly, in situations of resilience, risks exist in how people learn to cope with everyday challenges (e.g., use of weapons for self-defense, revenge/violence in response to disrespect or victimization, illegal income-generating activity to buffer the effects of poverty, and risky substance use as self-medication for emotional distress).

Life Course and Intergenerational

Hip Hop culture is now firmly grounded in regions and communities around the world, allowing for deep connections across populations and generations. The modern era of Hip Hop culture (ca. 1973) began as a platform for Black and Brown self-expression where youth could share their narratives and counternarratives through their own unique voices, bodies, and creations. Today, marginalized populations around the globe have narratives that speak to past and present injustices and oppression and to historical traumas, but also to shared strengths and resiliency (Gulbay, 2021; Levy & Wong, 2022). BJ The Chicago Kid and Coast Contra exemplify this collective resiliency and strength that can be empowering with lyrics from their track "Queen and Slim." They say, "Blood of a thousand hearts coursing through our veins. This Black pride, don't shuck and jive to entertain. Soul of a lion. . . . Suited to triumph all of our days and reign."

Empowerment, as the core value in Hip Hop, transcends race, ethnicity, gender, culture, geography, and nation. But distinct cultural narratives and counternarratives exist that can strengthen within-group solidarity by celebrating historical and collective strengths unique to each community. Each neighborhood, town, city, and region, across states, across countries, across continents, has a story to tell and a context that influences the well-being of their children, youth, and families.

Hip Hop's consistent calls for social change (i.e., within culture and social determinants) can inspire and motivate investments in improved health trajectories. The more we can create Hip Hop-based pathways that organically touch on features of empowerment-based positive youth development (Travis & Leech, 2013), the more we are investing in strengths-based pathways for youth to continuously learn and grow (Travis et al., 2021).

To complement younger artists providing contemporary adolescent and young adult narratives, artists like Nas and Jay-Z, once chart-topping adolescents and now in their forties and fifties, are in positions to help shed light on life course influences—how early life events manifest throughout and later in life (Schor, 2021), in new and powerful ways. In other life course examples, Hip Hop narratives speak about fatherhood. The potential role of the father, through presence, absence, and actions, is consistently explored as a critical factor in young lives and family systems (Travis, 2016), as a factor intergenerationally, and as a life course concept (Russ et al., 2022). By using these narratives to help illuminate inequities and injustices often at the heart of trauma-inducing environments and violence, it is possible to highlight opportunities and create pathways for personal change (reducing risky behaviors), but also upstream social change (better structural conditions for an entire community; Barbero et al., 2022).

Where Are We Going? Practices within a New Hip Hop and Empowerment Paradigm

Healthy Home Environments

Research-based Hip Hop models can be used directly *within CDC evidence-based strategies or as standalone practices* for youth violence prevention. Strategies, such as the Finding Fatherhood Hip Hop and Empowerment Toolkit, use songs, lyrics, videos, focused inquiry, and opportunities for reflection and discussion to focus on a wide range of issues related to parenting, relationships, and strengthening the quality of the home environment, especially within the context of the most difficult and challenging social environments (FlowStory, 2013). Advocating for more time and opportunities for positive relational experiences or "connection" as a family system is vital to raise awareness about healthy development. Families can be supported in providing high-quality relational environments, reinforcing young people's moral identity, and providing a strong foundation for learning and development that contributes to a better long-term health trajectory (Hambrick et al., 2019).

In another example, as part of the Urban Youth Trauma Center (UYTC), Hip-Hop H.E.A.L.S.! added to the STRONG Families program, a family systems intervention for youth coping with traumatic stress, by adding critical consciousness, media literacy, and culturally engaging content. As part of a prevention-to-intervention continuum of care, it uses Hip Hop culture and media as motivation and a doorway to addressing complex topics and issues relevant to violence prevention (Abdul-Adil & Suárez, 2022).

Quality Education and Positive Experiences

School-based activities, drop-ins, workshops, and programs often creatively expand knowledge and enhance content for youth relevant to their specific cultural and environmental contexts. Programs such as We Do It for the Culture (2022) enhance academic, social, and emotional learning by helping students feel affirmed in their identities and cultural realities through Hip Hop songs, lyrics, and culture. #HipHopEd and other Hip Hop-based education initiatives explore ways of using Hip Hop culture in pedagogy and practice within school-related domains for STEM, English, counseling, school leadership, and wellness (HipHopEd, 2022).

We can eliminate gaps in education and school-related skill-building programs by promoting more inclusive, strengths-based pedagogies that validate current school realities and also redress disparities in educational practices (Levy et al., 2021) that create school environments that increase the risk of violence, involvement with the juvenile justice system (Appleseed Network, 2020), and depression (Choi et al., 2022; Perryman et al., 2022). Encouraging Hip Hop-integrated approaches to learning such as Hip Hop Based Education (Adjapong & Levy, 2021; Evans, 2019), Hip Hop Development (Harper & Offiong, 2020), Reality Pedagogy (Emdin, 2020), and Hip Hop Spoken Word Therapy (Levy et al., 2021) at a programming level is essential. Further, the Hip Hop Expressive Arts Therapy (HEAT) Model (Hall & Tyson, 2018) and the High School for Recording Arts (Seidel et al., 2022) at an institutional and community-building level can allow for more strategies, practices, and programming that view youth violence prevention through unique cultural lenses.

Out-of-school-time activities also provide youth with more opportunities for creativity-driven development and bring attention to summer strain and other context-specific mental health needs (Travis et al., 2021). Hip Hop-driven mentorship and modeling, in-person and in digital spaces (Evans, 2019), can connect youth with supportive adults and safe settings for social and emotional support and allow self-expression and reinforce critical thinking. Group contexts also help build positive social networks and belonging. Further, being "in" the community provides opportunities to renegotiate relationships with physical and digital spaces and people (positive experiences and positive relationships), while affirming community strengths.

Many programs provide a blueprint to using Hip Hop culture in out-of-school contexts or in hybrid in-school / out-of-school / alternative school formats including Words, Beats and Life (D.C.), Preserving, Archiving, and Teaching Hip Hop (PATH Inc.; Florida), Rhythmic Mind (California), Beats Rhymes and Life/BRL Inc. (California), and programming at the JC Montgomery School / Kings County Juvenile Detention Center (California). Some programs like Today's Future Sound (California) have a "home" community

Hip Hop Culture • 287

for programming but reach populations around the United States and the globe through mobile in-person or digital/streaming practices.

Trauma Environments

Practitioners and community leaders help youth feel empowered to embrace leadership roles, use their voice and sense of agency, and act on behalf of positive change by participating in outreach and social change opportunities (Youth Justice Coalition, 2022). Youth are provided opportunities through youth-adult partnerships, youth advisory boards, and support of youth-led organizing and activism/social action groups. Programs like SC-YEA of the Community Coalition (California) provide opportunities for youth who are actively engaged, youth who are less engaged but want to redress social disparities and contribute to positive change, and also youth who have yet to discover their value in helping to shape their community's well-being (Community Coalition and UCLA Black Male Institute, 2021). Youth-adult partnerships for change are instrumental because only through collaboration and curiosity can we properly define youth violence, consider youth perspectives on youth violence, and contribute to innovative solutions specific to their social and generational realities (Funders' Collaborative on Youth Organizing, 2021).

Practitioners and stakeholders must validate the lived experiences of youth in the context of trauma-inducing environments, such as the effects of racism, to help facilitate personal and community change (Bañales et al., 2021). Culturally responsive and trauma-responsive practitioners who validate the utility of Hip Hop culture in individual and family therapeutic and healing practices such as Brittani Williams (Healmatic) and Jacqui Johnson (Sankofa Healing Studio) and interventions like the Young Warrior's Model—a precursor to Hip Hop H.E.A.L.S.! (Abdul-Adil, 2014, p. 161)—are pioneers and exemplars for practice. Systemic inequities and injustices must also be identified and challenged for their contributions to complex trauma experiences. Advocates must focus on real-time and evolving risks and challenges as well as disparities that have negative effects across developmental settings (e.g., schools, community, juvenile justice, health, employment; Wildeman & Wang, 2017).

Conclusion

We can save lives. We can prevent youth violence. We have a chance to integrate practices within existing youth violence prevention efforts that are healing-focused, holistically integrated, culturally responsive, trauma-informed, attentive to intergenerational needs and realities, kinesthetic and flow-inducing, expressive arts-integrated and intermodal, drawing upon individual and community strengths, validating lived experiences, and encouraging of self-care. These practices are grounded in all core elements of Hip Hop culture and in empowerment at the individual and community levels.

Imagine a future with more empowered, engaged, and connected kids, teens, young adults; imagine a system that highlights individual strengths and sees them not only in terms of academics but also in terms of empathy, creativity, positive relationships, and leadership; imagine a reshaping of how we see conflict and manage this together as a society. Tupac Shakur, emcee, cultural icon, and oftentimes voice of the voiceless regarding issues impacting the Black community, helped usher in a new interpretation of the concept of "thug" through the acronym THUG LIFE. At one point he stated that it meant The Hate U Give Little Infants, F-cks Everybody—more specifically, that the way society is set up is THUG LIFE. By focusing on the "THUG" or The Hate U Give our children, we actually have some opportunity to reorganize our investments in youth and create a new narrative for "The HUG," literally and figuratively.

References

Abdul-Adil, J. K. (2014). From voiceless to victorious: Street sounds and social skills for gang-involved urban youth. In B. Porfilio, D. Roychoudhury, & L. M. Gardner (Eds.), *See you at the crossroads: Hip hop scholarship at the intersections—Dialectical harmony, ethics, aesthetics, and panoply of voices* (pp. 149–168). Sense.

Abdul-Adil, J., & Suárez, L. M. (2022). The Urban Youth Trauma Center: A trauma-informed continuum for addressing community violence among youth. *Community Mental Health Journal, 58*(2), 334–342. https://doi.org/10.1007/s10597-021-00827-4

Adjapong, E., & Levy, I. (2021). Hip Hop can heal: Addressing mental health through Hip Hop in the urban classroom. *New Educator, 17*, 242–263. https://doi.org/10.1080/1547688X.2020.1849884

Alvarez, T. T. (2012). Beats, rhymes, and life: Rap therapy in an urban setting. In S. Hadley & G. Yancy (Eds.), *Therapeutic uses of rap and Hip Hop* (pp. 117–128). Routledge.

Anderson, C. A., Bushman, B. J., Donnerstein, E., Hummer, T. A., & Warburton, W. (2015). SPSSI research summary on media violence. *Analyses of Social Issues and Public Policy, 15*(1), 4–19. https://doi.org/10.1111/asap.12093

Appleseed Network. (2020). *Protecting girls of color from the school-to-prison pipeline.* http://www.appleseednetwork.org/uploads/1/2/4/6/124678621/appleseed_network_-_protecting_girls_of_color_2020.pdf

Associated Press. (2022, September 6). Maryland county to enforce youth curfew amid rise in violence. *NBC News.* https://www.nbcnews.com/news/us-news/maryland-county-enforce-youth-curfew-rise-violence-rcna46379

Bañales, J., Aldana, A., Richards, S. K., Flanagan, C. A., Diemer, M. A., & Rowley, S. J. (2021). Youth anti-racism action: Contributions of youth perceptions of school racial messages and critical consciousness. *Journal of Community Psychology, 49*(8), 3079–3100. https://doi.org/10.1002/jcop.22266

Barbero, C., Hafeedh Bin Abdullah, A., Wiggins, N., Garrettson, M., Jones, D. S., Guinn, A., Girod, C., Bradford, J., & Wennerstrom, A. (2022). Community health worker activities in public health programs to prevent violence: Coding roles and scope. *American Journal of Public Health, 112*(8), 1191–1201. https://doi.org/10.2105/ajph.2022.306865

Centers for Disease Control and Prevention. (2020, October 28). *Youth Risk Behavior Survey: Data summary & trends report.* https://www.cdc.gov/healthyyouth/data/yrbs/pdf/YRBSDataSummaryTrendsReport2019-508.pdf

Centers for Disease Control and Prevention. (2022). *Preventing youth violence* [Fact sheet]. https://www.cdc.gov/violenceprevention/pdf/yv/YV-factsheet_2022.pdf

Chang, J. (2005). *Can't stop, won't stop: A history of the Hip Hop generation.* St. Martin's.

Choi, M., Hong, J., Travis, R., & Kim, J. (2022). Effects of school environment on depression among Black and white adolescents. *Journal of Community Psychology.* https://doi.org/10.1002/jcop.22969

Community Coalition and UCLA Black Male Institute. (2021). *Community Coalition: South Central Youth Empowered thru Action (SCYEA): Youth poll survey findings.*

David-Ferdon, C., Vivolo-Kantor, A. M., Dahlberg, L. L., Marshall, K. J., Rainford, N., & Hall, J. E. (2016). *A comprehensive technical package for the prevention of youth violence and associated risk behaviors.* National Center for Injury Prevention and Control, Centers for Disease Control and Prevention.

DeCarlo, A., & Hockman, E. (2004). RAP therapy: A group work intervention method for urban adolescents. *Social Work with Groups, 26*(3), 45–59. https://doi.org/10.1300/J009v26n03_06

Elligan, D. (2000). Rap therapy: A culturally sensitive approach to psychotherapy with young African American men. *Journal of African American Men, 5*(3), 27–36. https://www.jstor.org/stable/41819404

Emdin, C. (2020). A ratchetdemic reality pedagogy and/as cultural freedom in urban education. *Educational Philosophy and Theory, 52*(9), 947–960. https://doi.org/10.1080/00131857.2019.1669446

Evans, J. (2019). "Deeper than rap": Cultivating racial identity and critical voices through Hip Hop recording practices in the music classroom. *Journal of Media Literacy Education, 11*(3), 20–36. https://doi.org/10.23860/JMLE-2019-11-3-3

Fischer, A., Fosner, R., Renneberg, B., & Steil, R. (2022). Suicidal ideation, self-injury, aggressive behavior and substance use during intensive trauma-focused treatment with exposure-based components in adolescent and young adult PTSD patients. *Borderline Personality Disorder and Emotion Dysregulation, 9*(1), 1–13. https://doi.org/10.1186/s40479-021-00172-8

FlowStory. (2013). *Finding fatherhood 2.0: The official hip hop and empowerment tool kit.* https://www.fatherhood.gov/sites/default/files/resource_files/e000002983.pdf

Funders' Collaborative on Youth Organizing (FCYO). (2021). *20 years of youth power: The 2020 national youth organizing field scan.* https://fcyo.org/uploads/resources/20-years-of-youth-power-the-2020-national-youth-organizing-field-scan_resource_609d4a85ebe152ee0283274e.pdf

Gann, E. (2010). *The effects of therapeutic Hip Hop activity groups on perception of self and social supports in at-risk urban adolescents.* Doctoral dissertation, Wright Institute.

Gulbay, S. (2021). Exploring the use of hip hop-based music therapy to address trauma in asylum seeker and unaccompanied minor migrant youth. *Voices: A World Forum for Music Therapy, 21*(3), 1–16. https://doi.org/10.15845/voices.v21i3.3192

Hadley, S., & Yancy, G. (2012). *Therapeutic uses of rap and Hip Hop*. Routledge.

Hall, J. C., & Tyson, E. (2018). *Hip hop therapy*. https://www.hiphoptherapy.com/about-Hip Hop-therapy

Hambrick, E. P., Brawner, T. W., Perry, B. D., Brandt, K., Hofmeister, C., & Collins, J. O. (2019). Beyond the ACE score: Examining relationships between timing of developmental adversity, relational health and developmental outcomes in children. *Archives of Psychiatric Nursing, 33*(3), 238–247. https://doi.org/10.1016/j.apnu.2018.11.001

Harper, P.T.H., & Offiong, A. (2020). Hip Hop development: The roots 4 positive youth development and engagement in education and health prevention. In E. Adjapong & I. Levy (Eds.), *#HipHopEd: The compilation on Hip Hop education* (Vol. 2, pp. 69–82). Peter Lang.

Harper, P.T.H., Rhodes, W.A., Thomas, D.E., Leary, G., & Quinton, S.L. (2007). Hip Hop development bridging the generational divide for youth development. *Journal of Youth Development, 2*, 42-55.

HipHopEd. (2022). *Facilitating innovative educational programming*. https://hiphoped.com/

Levy, I. P. (2012). Hip hop and spoken word therapy with urban youth. *Journal of Poetry Therapy, 25*(4), 219–224. https://doi.org/10.1080/08893675.2012.736182

Levy, I., Harper, P.T.H., Spellman, Q., & Emdin, C. (2021). The roots beneath the rose: Hip Hop, counselling, and development. *Journal of Critical Psychology, Counselling and Psychotherapy, 21*(2), 41–53.

Levy, I. P., & Travis, R. (2020). The critical cycle of mixtape creation: Reducing stress via three different group counseling styles. *Journal for Specialists in Group Work, 45*(4), 307–330. https://doi.org/10.1080/01933922.2020.1826614

Levy, I., & Wong, C. (2022). Processing a white supremacist insurrection through hip hop mixtape making: A school counseling intervention. *Equity & Excellence in Education, 55*, 395–407. https://doi.org/10.1080/10665684.2022.2158398

Malchiodi, C. A. (2022). *Handbook of expressive arts therapy*. Guilford.

McFerran, K. S., Lai, H. I. C., Chang, W.-H., Acquaro, D., Chin, T. C., Stokes, H., & Crooke, A. H. D. (2020). Music, rhythm and trauma: A critical interpretive synthesis of research literature. *Frontiers in Psychology, 11*(324), 1–12. https://doi.org/10.3389/fpsyg.2020.00324

Menakem, R. (2017). *My grandmother's hands: Racialized trauma and the pathway to mending our hearts and bodies*. Penguin.

Niederkrotenthaler, T., Tran, U. S., Gould, M., Sinyor, M., Sumner, S., Strauss, M. J., Voracek, M., Till, B., Murphy, S., Gonzalez, F., Spittal, M. J., & Draper, J. (2021). Association of Logic's hip hop song "1-800-273-8255" with Lifeline calls and suicides in the United States: Interrupted time series analysis. *BMJ, 375*, e067726. https://doi.org/10.1136/bmj-2021-067726

Perry, B. D. (2006). Applying principles of neurodevelopment to clinical work with maltreated and traumatized children: The neurosequential model of therapeutics. In N. B. Webb (Ed.), *Working with traumatized youth in child welfare* (pp. 27–52). Guilford.

Perryman, C., Platt, S., & Montiel Ishino, F. (2022). Identifying the mental health profiles of Black adolescents who experience school policing and school discipline: A person-centered approach. *Journal of the American Academy of Child and Adolescent Psychiatry, 61*(8), 1034–1040.

Rodwin, A. H., Shimizu, R., Travis, R., James, K. J., Banya, M., & Munson, M. R. (2022). A systematic review of music-based interventions to improve treatment engagement and mental health outcomes for adolescents and young adults. *Child and Adolescent Social Work Journal, 40*, 537–566. https://doi.org/10.1007/s10560-022-00893-x

Russ, S. A., Hotez, E., Berghaus, M., Verbiest, S., Hoover, C., Schor, E. L., & Halfon, N. (2022). What makes an intervention a life course intervention? *Pediatrics, 149*, S1–S11. https://doi.org/10.1542/peds.2021-053509D

Schor, E. L. (2021). Life course health development in pediatric practice. *Pediatrics, 147*(1), 1–6. https://doi.org/10.1542/peds.2020-009308

Seidel, S., Simmons, T., & Lipset, M. (2022). *Hip hop genius 2.0: Remixing high school education.* Rowman & Littlefield.

Travis, R. (2013). Rap music and the empowerment of today's youth: Evidence in everyday music listening, music therapy, and commercial rap music. *Child & Adolescent Social Work Journal, 30*(2), 139–167. https://doi.org/10.1007/s10560-012-0285-x

Travis, R. (2016). *The healing power of hip hop.* Praeger.

Travis, R., Gann, E., Crooke, A. H. D., & Jenkins, S. M. (2021). Using therapeutic beat making and lyrics for empowerment. *Journal of Social Work, 21*(3), 551–574. https://doi.org/10.1177/1468017320911346

Travis, R., & Leech, T. G. J. (2013). Empowerment-based positive youth development: A new understanding of healthy development for African American youth. *Journal of Research on Adolescence, 24*(1), 93–116. https://doi.org/10.1111/jora.12062

Travis, R., Levy, I. P., & Morphew, A. C. (2022). "Now we're all family": Exploring social and emotional development in a summer hip hop mixtape camp. *Child and Adolescent Social Work Journal, 41*, 43–60. https://doi.org/10.1007/s10560-022-00821-z

Travis, R., Rodwin, A. H., & Allcorn, A. (2019). Hip hop, empowerment, and clinical practice for homeless adults with severe mental illness. *Social Work with Groups, 42*(2), 83–100. https://doi.org/10.1080/01609513.2018.1486776

Tyson, E. H. (2004). Rap music in social work practice with African-American and Latino youth: A conceptual model with practical applications. *Journal of Human Behavior in the Social Environment, 8*(4), 1–21. https://doi.org/10.1300/J137v08n04_01

Viega, M. (2016). Exploring the discourse in hip hop and implications for music therapy practice. *Music Therapy Perspectives, 34*(2), 138–146. https://doi.org/10.1093/mtp/miv035

Viega, M. (2018). A humanistic understanding of the use of digital technology in therapeutic songwriting. *Music Therapy Perspectives, 36*(2), 152–160. https://doi.org/10.1093/mtp/miy014

Washington, A. R. (2018). Integrating Hip Hop culture and rap music into social justice counseling with Black males. *Journal of Counseling & Development, 96*(1), 97–105. https://doi.org/10.1002/jcad.12181

We Do It for the Culture. (2022). *Our program.* https://wedoit4theculture.com/our-program/

Wildeman, C., & Wang, E. A. (2017). Mass incarceration, public health, and widening inequality in the USA. *Lancet, 389*(10077), 1464–1474. https://doi.org/10.1016/S0140-6736(17)30259-3

Youth Justice Coalition. (2022). *Youth Justice Coalition.* https://youthjusticela.org/

26

Rooted Solutions

● ● ● ● ● ● ● ● ● ● ● ● ●

A Critical Race Perspective on Violence Prevention for Black Youth

NONI K. GAYLORD-HARDEN AND
ROBYN D. DOUGLAS

Overview

Violence during adolescence has numerous health and economic consequences, increasing risk for life-threatening injuries and early death and placing a staggering financial burden of over $17 billion per year on the health care system (David-Ferdon & Simon, 2014). For Black youth, violent injury is responsible for more than 600,000 emergency department visits annually (David-Ferdon et al., 2016). Homicide is the leading cause of death for Black boys from age fifteen to age thirty and the second leading cause of deaths for Black girls ages fifteen to nineteen (Currie, 2020). Over half of young Black men who survive a violent penetrative injury return to the hospital for a similar penetrative injury within five years, and 20 percent of these men will die within the same time period (Rich, 2009; Richardson et al., 2016). Moreover, violence exposure places youth on a trajectory to greater risk of incarceration, underemployment, and mental health symptoms and physical illness into adulthood. Collectively, this staggering evidence suggests that violence during adolescence is a critical public health issue, and there is a robust body of research dedicated to violence prevention during adolescence. We argue, however, that there is a substantial disconnect between current violence prevention strategies and the unique needs of Black youth growing up in a society deeply rooted in racism and oppression (Wendel et al., 2021). Consistent with critical race theory, a valid and informative understanding of violence prevention rests on recognizing how institutions, social norms, political and economic inequities, racism and prejudice, discrimination and oppression, and legacies of ongoing segregation have substantial and pervasive influence on violence impacting Black youth and underscore the need for a more progressive approach to violence prevention.

Limitations of Existing Violence Prevention Efforts

Across multiple frameworks for violence prevention, violence prevention strategies that are considered "best practices" often include efforts to change youths' intrapersonal skills, connect them to caring adults (e.g., parents, mentors, teachers, etc.), and/or enhance community programs that create more protective community environments (David-Ferdon et al., 2016; Fagan & Catalano, 2013; Thornton et al., 2000). While there are violence prevention programs that have shown effectiveness at reducing violence by enhancing youth skills and interpersonal relationships, these programs are targeting symptoms of violence and not root causes of violence. For example, social-cognitive interventions aim to reduce violence through improving the social-cognitive skills of youth, such as increasing positive attitudes toward nonviolence and teaching conflict resolution skills (Zettler, 2021).

Despite effectiveness, these programs assume that skills deficits in youth (e.g., attitudes toward violence, misperception of social cues) are the drivers of violence, and this perspective ignores or minimizes the structural conditions that create conditions of violence among marginalized groups (Gaylord-Harden et al., 2018; Wendel et al., 2021). As a result, best practices for violence prevention give youth better tools to cope with the presence of systemic barriers but fail to focus on structural reforms to remove those systemic barriers (Wendel et al., 2021). Even primary or universal prevention programs that are supposed to focus "upstream" to address root causes of violence rarely extend prevention efforts beyond the individual level or interpersonal relationships. As such, there will always be a need for violence prevention efforts. Instead, we challenge the field to work toward a future in which systemic racism is eradicated and violence prevention efforts for youth are no longer needed.

A More Progressive Approach: Application of Critical Race Theory to Violence Prevention

How can violence prevention researchers play a more prominent role in eliminating root causes of inequities? We believe that efforts can begin with the application of critical race scholarship to violence prevention research. Critical race theory is the integration of methodologies that seek to illuminate and combat root causes of structural and institutional racism in the pursuit of racial equity (Ford & Airhihenbuwa, 2010). Despite the recent explosion of the term in public discourse, critical race theory is not a new or emerging construct. In fact, it has a long history in the field of law, having been developed by various legal scholars in the late 1980s (Ford & Airhihenbuwa, 2010, 2018). Over the years, critical race theory has moved beyond its discipline-specific application in the legal realm to other fields. Critical race theory provides a blueprint for understanding how systemic racism creates the necessary conditions for violence (Sheats et al., 2018), and we believe that when researchers acknowledge the ways that structural, systemic, and historical trauma impact violence, their prevention efforts will be more effective and equitable.

First, prevention scientists must acknowledge the influence of both forms of systemic racism—institutional racism and structural racism—on violence impacting Black youth. The World Health Organization's Social Determinants of Health Framework (Solar & Irwin, 2010) identifies historically oppressive factors, such as poverty, racism, disparate access to health care and education, polluted air and water, and unsafe housing and neighborhoods, as the root causes of health problems, such as violence. Current violence prevention efforts fall short of operationalizing violence outside of interpersonal interactions, and the focus on "fixing" youth is inadequate for violence prevention (Wendel et al., 2021). When designing preventive interventions, researchers must measure the effect of structural indicators (e.g., punitive policing practices, access to quality health care, and systematic incarceration of Black youth) on violence (Nation et al., 2021) and include metrics to assess the policies and practices that maintain social and structural inequities and access to resources (Nation et al., 2021).

For example, researchers designing and implementing school-based violence interventions should acknowledge the disparities in how Black youth are viewed and treated by the educational system. Specifically, teachers view Black students as more aggressive and disruptive than white students, and Black youth receive harsher punishment within schools (Bates & Glick, 2013; Stevenson, 2016). This disproportionate treatment of Black youth calls into question the use of teachers' reports of "aggressive" behavior among youth or school discipline records as measures of treatment outcomes or eligibility for interventions. Further, researchers should assess the impact of the school discipline policies of their partner schools on violence among students, and violence intervention programs in schools should go beyond working at the individual level to change youth behavior and work at the organization level to create changes in the system.

Second, prevention scientists can begin to use both humanizing and anti-oppressive language in their research and preventive intervention designs. We often hear the term "violent communities," but communities are not violent. Communities with high rates of violence are experiencing structural and institutional racism, economic disinvestment and exclusion, state-sanctioned violence, lack of affordable housing, mass incarceration, and limited health care access (Jacoby et al., 2018; Spievack & Okeke, 2020). Any term that combines a "deficit" and a "geography" (e.g., high-crime communities, low-income communities) is dehumanizing (Vey & Love, 2020). Related, the phrase "youth violence prevention" is stigmatizing for marginalized and minoritized youth as it centers "youth" as the causes of violence. To combat these harmful narratives, we suggest that researchers use more responsive framing, such as "structural violence prevention," to shift the focus of prevention to structural reform and community empowerment (Nation et al., 2010). We recommend that researchers utilize The Dart Center Style Guide for Trauma-Informed Journalism, the Philadelphia Center for Gun Violence Reporting, and other similar resources (e.g., Henry et al., 2021) for guidance on antioppressive language.

Third, prevention scientists should utilize community-based participatory research methods when designing and implementing preventive interventions for violence. Youth-led participatory action research is a form of community-based participatory research in which youth are trained to identify and analyze systemic problems relevant to their lives, conduct research, and advocate for change based on research findings (Ozer, 2017). For violence prevention, youth-led participatory action research should identify and analyze racialized policies and institutional oppression that create conditions for violence (Nation et al., 2021; Wendel et al., 2021). Youth-led participatory action research empowers youth (Sprague Martinez et al., 2018) and allows Black youth to reclaim the process of knowledge production by ensuring that the data that are generated about their experiences with violence are relevant, humanizing, and asset-driven.

Fourth, researchers should avoid the use of between-group research designs (i.e., comparing two or more racial-ethnic groups) in violence prevention work. While race-comparative research can provide descriptive information on disparities in violence and violence-related outcomes, it is the interpretation of findings from this research that can be harmful to Black youth and counterproductive to violence prevention efforts. When researchers collect, interpret, and apply race-comparative data without acknowledging that race/ethnicity is not the cause for disparities but rather a proxy for the structural inequities that marginalize Black youth, they are perpetuating racist ideals (Volpe et al., 2022).

When researchers use white youth as the standard for normative behavior in race-comparative research and position Black youth as deficient, they are advancing detrimental and erroneous narratives about Black youth (Volpe et al., 2022). When researchers "explain" racial/ethnic disparities in violence by asserting that "being Black" is a risk factor for violence, they are pathologizing Blackness. Narratives are critical to violence prevention, and dominant narratives of Black youth as delinquent, aggressors, predators, and criminals not only minimize their humanity but also lead to violence prevention efforts that frame violence as genetically or culturally based rather than systemically and structurally based (Metzler et al., 2021; Wendel et al., 2021).

Finally, prevention scientists must consider the importance of intersectionality (Collins, 2015; Crenshaw, 1989) in violence prevention work with Black youth. According to critical race theory, social categories (e.g., race, gender, class) and the corresponding forms of social stratification that maintain them (e.g., racism, sexism, classism) intersect to multiply oppress youth (Ford & Airhihenbuwa, 2010). Black youth hold many identities in addition to their racial/ethnic identity (Volpe et al., 2022), and these identities interact with oppression in ways that have implications for their experience of violence (Ford & Airhihenbuwa, 2010). For example, within samples of Black adolescents, experiences of violence show gendered patterns of development and gender disparities (Belgrave et al., 2011; Finigan-Carr et al., 2016; Waasdorp et al., 2013; Yonas et al., 2005). Further, Black sexual and gender minoritized adolescents, particularly those who are transgender and nonbinary, experience heightened rates of violence exposure (McBride, 2021; Toomey et al., 2017). Violence is also inextricably tied to socioeconomic status among Black youth, with violence rates much higher in economically disinvested neighborhoods (Browning & Loeber, 1999; DuRant et al., 1995) than in more resourced communities (Childs & Ray, 2017; Goings et al., 2022). Further, immigration status impacts the ability of youth to feel safe joining violence prevention programs or research (Garcia & Birman, 2020). To avoid one-size-fits-all models for violence prevention and truly minimize disparities in violence, researchers must tailor interventions to the unique experiences of vulnerable, underserved subpopulations of Black youth (immigrant, girls, LGBTQI+ youth).

Conclusion

Applying tenets of critical race theory to violence prevention efforts represents a radical shift in prevention science methods, but a shift that is necessary to create long-lasting healing for Black youth and communities impacted by violence. Leveraging the power of critical race theory will offer an opportunity for prevention scientists to decenter the voices of researchers and center the voices of youth, dismantle barriers between researchers and participants, and create systemic change that builds health equity. Violence prevention efforts that focus on enhancing youth skills should focus on raising Black youths' critical consciousness regarding the role of systemic and structural racism on violence, increasing critical efficacy to empower youth to advocate for change, and supporting critical action to challenge systems of inequality (Douglas, 2022). An example of a violence prevention approach that highlights structural violence as a root cause of violence, engages youth as active research partners, and works to challenge harmful narratives is the University of Louisville Youth Violence Prevention Research Center (YVPRC). Using a social justice lens, the YVPRC implements strategies at multiple levels of proximity to youth (Wendel et al., 2021; YVPRC, 2016). At the individual level, the intervention aimed to cultivate positive racial identity among Black youth by elevating accurate history and corresponding counternarratives and supported youth to engage in social change efforts. At the organizational level, the YVPRC worked with youth-serving organizations in the community to help them identify policies and practices in their organizations that may perpetuate institutional violence and help change them. At the community level, the YVPRC worked to impact public dialogue related to structural racism and its harmful effects on Black youth. By influencing how different community structures approach, include, and engage youth, the program showed measurable promise in curbing increases in violence impacting youth (YVPRC, 2019). The YVPRC represents a promising example of how to shift the narrative of violence prevention, and it is our hope that future research in this area will seek to inform similar efforts to target the root causes of violence. With the increased calls for changes to the prevailing Eurocentric research approaches (e.g., Buchanan et al., 2021), the time is ripe for new approaches to prevention science that work to create a world in which violence prevention for Black youth is no longer necessary.

References

Bates, L. A., & Glick, J. E. (2013). Does it matter if teachers and schools match the student? Racial and ethnic disparities in problem behaviors. *Social Science Research, 42*(5), 1180–1190. https://doi.org/10.1016/j.ssresearch.2013.04.005

Belgrave, F. Z., Nguyen, A. B., Johnson, J. L., & Hood, K. (2011). Who is likely to help and hurt? Profiles of African American adolescents with prosocial and aggressive behavior. *Journal of Youth and Adolescence, 40*(8), 1012–1024. https://doi.org/10.1007/s10964-010-9608-4

Browning, K., & Loeber, R. (1999). *Highlights of findings from the Pittsburgh Youth Study.* U.S. Department of Justice, Office of Justice Programs, Office of Juvenile Justice and Delinquency Prevention.

Buchanan, N. T., Perez, M., Prinstein, M. J., & Thurston, I. B. (2021). Upending racism in psychological science: Strategies to change how science is conducted, reported, reviewed, and disseminated. *American Psychologist, 76*(7), 1097–1112.

Childs, K. K., & Ray, J. V. (2017). Race differences in patterns of risky behavior and associated risk factors in adolescence. *International Journal of Offender Therapy and Comparative Criminology, 61*(7), 773–794. https://doi.org/10.1177/0306624X15599401

Collins, P. H. (2015). Intersectionality's definitional dilemmas. *Annual Review of Sociology, 41*(1), 1–20.

Crenshaw, K. (1989). Demarginalizing the intersection of race and sex: A black feminist critique of antidiscrimination doctrine, feminist theory and antiracist politics. *University of Chicago Legal Forum, 1989* (1 Article 8), 139–167.

Currie, E. (2020). *A peculiar indifference: The neglected toll of violence on Black America*. Metropolitan Books.

David-Ferdon, C., & Simon, T. (2014). *Preventing youth violence: Opportunities for action*. Centers for Disease Control and Prevention, National Center for Injury Prevention and Controls.

David-Ferdon, C., Vivolo-Kantor, A. M., Dahlberg, L. L., Marshall, K. J., Rainford, N., & Hall, J. E. (2016). *A comprehensive technical package for the prevention of youth violence and associated risk behaviors*. National Center for Injury Prevention and Control, Centers for Disease Control and Prevention.

Douglas, R. (2022, November 15). The healing nature of critical consciousness development and community care for Black youth exposed to community violence. *Search Institute Blog*. https://blog.searchinstitute.org/the-healing-nature-of-critical-consciousness-development-and-community-care-for-black-youth-exposed-to-community-violence

DuRant, R. H., Getts, A., Cadenhead, C., Emans, S. J., & Woods, E. R. (1995). Exposure to violence and victimization and depression, hopelessness, and purpose in life among adolescents living in and around public housing. *Journal of Developmental and Behavioral Pediatrics, 16*(4), 233–237.

Fagan, A. A., & Catalano, R. F. (2013). What works in youth violence prevention: A review of the literature. *Research on Social Work Practice, 23*(2), 141–156.

Finigan-Carr, N. M., Gielen, A., Haynie, D. L., & Cheng, T. L. (2016). Youth violence: How gender matters in aggression among urban early adolescents. *Journal of Interpersonal Violence, 31*(19), 3257–3281. https://doi.org/10.1177/0886260515584348

Ford, C. L., & Airhihenbuwa, C. O. (2010). Critical race theory, race equity, and public health: Toward antiracism praxis. *American Journal of Public Health, 100*(Suppl. 1), S30–S35.

Ford, C. L., & Airhihenbuwa, C. O. (2018). Commentary: Just what is critical race theory and what's it doing in a progressive field like public health? *Ethnicity & Disease, 28*(Suppl. 1), 223.

Garcia, M. F., & Birman, D. (2020). Ethical issues in research with late-arriving and unaccompanied immigrant youth. *Translational Issues in Psychological Science, 6*(3), 207–213.

Gaylord-Harden, N. K., Barbarin, O., Tolan, P. H., & Murry, V. M. (2018). Understanding development of African American boys and young men: Moving from risks to positive youth development. *American Psychologist, 73*(6), 753–767.

Goings, T. C., Salas-Wright, C. P., Legette, K., Belgrave, F. Z., & Vaughn, M. G. (2022). Far from a monolith: A typology of externalizing behavior among African American youth. *Social Psychiatry and Psychiatric Epidemiology, 57*(1), 111–125.

Henry, M., Wallace, L. R., & Ritchie, A. R. (2021). *Don't be a copagandist!* Interrupting Criminalization.

Jacoby, S. F., Dong, B., Beard, J. H., Wiebe, D. J., & Morrison, C. N. (2018). The enduring impact of historical and structural racism on urban violence in Philadelphia. *Social Science & Medicine*, *199*, 87–95. https://doi.org/10.1016/j.socscimed.2017.05.038

McBride, R. S. (2021). A literature review of the secondary school experiences of trans youth. *Journal of LGBT Youth*, *18*(2), 103–134.

Metzler, M., Jackson, T., & Trudeau, A. (2021). Youths and violence: Changing the narrative. *American Journal of Public Health*, *111*(S1), S35–S37.

Nation, M., Chapman, D. A., Edmonds, T., Cosey-Gay, F. N., Jackson, T., Marshall, K. J., . . . Trudeau, A. R. T. (2021). Social and structural determinants of health and youth violence: Shifting the paradigm of youth violence prevention. *American Journal of Public Health*, *111*(S1), S28–S31.

Nation, M., Collins, L., Nixon, C., Bess, K., Rogers, S., Williams, N., . . . Juarez, P. (2010). A community-based participatory approach to youth development and school climate change: The Alignment Enhanced Services Project. *Progress in Community Health Partnerships: Research, Education, and Action*, *4*(3), 197–205.

Ozer, E. J. (2017). Youth-led participatory action research: Overview and potential for enhancing adolescent development. *Child Development Perspectives*, *11*(3), 173–177.

Rich, J. A. (2009). *Wrong place, wrong time: Trauma and violence in the lives of young Black men*. Johns Hopkins University Press.

Richardson, J. B., St Vil, C., Sharpe, T., Wagner, M., & Cooper, C. (2016). Risk factors for recurrent violent injury among Black men. *Journal of Surgical Research*, *204*(1), 261–266.

Sheats, K. J., Irving, S. M., Mercy, J. A., Simon, T. R., Crosby, A. E., Ford, D. C., . . . Morgan, R. E. (2018). Violence-related disparities experienced by Black youth and young adults: Opportunities for prevention. *American Journal of Preventive Medicine*, *55*(4), 462–469.

Solar, O., & Irwin, A. A. (2010). *A conceptual framework for action on the social determinants of health*. World Health Organization.

Spievack, N., & Okeke, C. (2020, February 26). How we should talk about racial disparities. *Urban Wire*. https://www.urban.org/urban-wire/how-we-should-talk-about-racial-disparities

Sprague Martinez, L., Richards-Schuster, K., Teixeira, S., & Augsberger, A. (2018). The power of prevention and youth voice: A strategy for social work to ensure youths' healthy development. *Social Work*, *63*(2), 135–143.

Stevenson, H. C. (2016). Dueling narratives: Racial socialization and literacy as triggers for re-humanizing African American boys, young men, and their families. In L. Burton, D. Burton, S. M. McHale, V. King, & J. Van Hook (Eds.), *Boys and men in African American families, national symposium on family issues 7* (pp. 55–84). New York, NY: Springer. http://dx.doi.org/10.1007/978-3-319-43847-4_5

Thornton, T. N., Craft, C. A., Dahlberg, L. L., Lynch, B. S., & Baer, K. (2000). *Best practices of youth violence prevention: A sourcebook for community action*. Centers for Disease Control and Prevention, National Center for Injury Prevention and Control, Division of Violence Prevention.

Toomey, R. B., Huynh, V. W., Jones, S. K., Lee, S., & Revels-Macalinao, M. (2017). Sexual minority youth of color: A content analysis and critical review of the literature. *Journal of Gay & Lesbian Mental Health*, *21*(1), 3–31.

Vey, J., & Love, H. (2020, July 13). Recognizing that words have the power to harm, we commit to using more just language to describe places. *The Avenue*. https://www

.brookings.edu/blog/the-avenue/2020/07/13/recognizing-that-words-have-the-power-to-harm-we-commit-to-using-more-just-language-to-describe-places/

Volpe, V. V., Smith, N. A., Skinner, O. D., Lozada, F. T., Hope, E. C., & Del Toro, J. (2022). Centering the heterogeneity of Black adolescents' experiences: Guidance for within-group designs among African diasporic communities. *Journal of Research on Adolescence, 32*, 1298–1311.

Waasdorp, T. E., Baker, C. N., Paskewich, B. S., & Leff, S. S. (2013). The association between forms of aggression, leadership, and social status among urban youth. *Journal of Youth and Adolescence, 42*(2), 263–274.

Wendel, M. L., Nation, M., Williams, M., Jackson, T., Jones, G., Debreaux, M., & Ford, N. (2021). The structural violence of white supremacy: Addressing root causes to prevent youth violence. *Archives of Psychiatric Nursing, 35*(1), 127–128.

Yonas, M. A., O'Campo, P., Burke, J. G., Peak, G., & Gielen, A. C. (2005). Urban youth violence: Do definitions and reasons for violence vary by gender? *Journal of Urban Health, 82*(4), 543–551.

Youth.Gov. (n.d.). *Collaborative efforts to address youth violence.* https://youth.gov/feature-article/collaborative-efforts-address-youth-violence

Youth Violence Prevention Research Center. (2016). *Power by practicing pride, peace, and prevention.* https://pridepeaceprevention.org

Youth Violence Prevention Research Center. (2019). *Technical report: Youth data, 2017–2018.* University of Louisville School of Public Health & Information Sciences.

Zettler, H. R. (2021). Much to do about trauma: A systematic review of existing trauma-informed treatments on youth violence and recidivism. *Youth Violence and Juvenile Justice, 19*(1), 113–134.

Conclusion

• •

Transcending the Silos:
The Mixtape in Theory
and Practice

RAPHAEL TRAVIS JR.

AND PAUL BOXER

The first whisperings of ideas for this book began two decades ago when we met at what was affectionately nicknamed "Violence Camp." We were both predoctoral fellows at a summer training institute on youth violence prevention sponsored by the Centers for Disease Control–funded Southern California Center for Excellence in Youth Violence Prevention. We were part of a diverse and multidisciplinary group of very early career scholars—representing public health and social work (RT) and clinical child psychology (PB); we joined students of sociology, developmental and family science, criminology, and education to hear from experts about current thinking in the science and practice of youth violence prevention. We shared our deep appreciation for music, humor, and cold beverages along with a commitment to unlocking some of society's biggest mysteries around youth violence. While our own scholarship might appear to have moved in different directions since then— understanding and managing aggressive behavior especially among those at greatest risk (PB) versus Hip Hop culture as a pathway to positive youth development along with individual and community health (RT)—a closer look shows a common thread. We both explore how both policy and practice can be intentionally developed and implemented to best support and promote the well-being of youth in the short term and the long term. Our conversations continued but really hit a turning point during the COVID-19 lockdowns. The global pandemic was a time of transition across many disciplines, particularly those connected to social and racial justice as we all watched in real time the struggles to keep vulnerable communities, and particularly youth of color, safe—safe from rising gun violence, safe from rapidly spreading illness, safe from the persistent strains of underinvestment and systemic racism.

We felt compelled to act—to leverage and combine our interests and push the conversation around preventing youth violence forward. We knew there were many ways to "do" youth violence prevention, with many different and disparate voices calling for more and better efforts. We wanted to hear all of those voices in the same room. This volume is for children, for partners, for friends, for mentors and students, for mothers, for fathers, for families, for schools, for community programs and services—for all those devastated by the impacts of youth violence and for all those committed to ending it. And as importantly, for those instigating, aiding, and turning a blind eye to the causes of youth violence. So here we are.

Now that you've "heard" our mixtape in all its variety and splendor, from theory to action, from policy to practice, from basic to applied research, from visions for change to how these visions manifested, how can we collectively instigate meaningful advances in youth violence prevention? What can we do now? How can we ensure that this information and these promising practices get into the hands of the people that need it most? We now see that the levers of meaningful change intersect with every youth-serving setting. These are levers that both promote and inhibit violence. And this appreciation for the multiple ways in which positive development can be promoted and violence prevented can come together to support the emergence and training of a new interdisciplinary workforce and perhaps even a new category of professional: the youth violence prevention specialist.

Through the chapters in this volume we moved from abstract to concrete examples and real-world scenarios and back again, beginning with the theoretical and empirical underpinnings of long-standing best practices in part I, moving to novel or more recent applications of those basic ideas in part II, then considering the implementation of approaches addressing critical and emergent issues in part III, and finally approaching some of the biggest picture and most urgent frameworks surrounding this work in part IV. We felt the pain of those ensnared in the net of youth violence, from those directly impacted and in crisis to the vicarious trauma of those witnessing and in service to those in crisis. We were also inspired by the many voices committed to being agents of change for youth violence prevention, effectively moving the needle for youth violence in a positive direction.

We saw a bright through line of developmental considerations and an insistence that investing in the overall well-being of youth is a nonnegotiable necessity—from a dizzying array of voices. We heard repeatedly how all strategies must be developmentally appropriate and attentive to both person and environment. Efforts at youth violence prevention must recognize youth contexts as sources both of risk and of opportunity. Social environments can have features that are risky or protective. In short, it is critical to invest in positive relationships and positive settings, early and often. We must move away from the unearned stigmas often attributed to adolescents, youth of color, youth and families impacted by juvenile justice, child welfare, poverty, and a range of other stigma-inducing -isms. We read how instead asset-based, strengths-driven, and social-emotional strategies that are early and enduring can anchor investments in well-being and be a foundation for youth violence prevention. Mentorship and modeling of healthy relationships, whenever possible by credible messengers, can be the scaffolding for youth violence prevention strategies throughout the life course.

What we have seen throughout this volume is that beyond clinicians and caseworkers, parents, partners, teachers, physicians, coaches, mentors, and more all can act impactfully in the service of preventing youth violence. Efforts can emanate from homes, hospitals, juvenile and criminal justice settings, child welfare settings, ball fields and basketball courts, schools, after-school programs, clinic rooms, spiritual and faith-based communities and their houses of worship, and of course the broader community (e.g., the streets). Physically and psychologically safe environments are necessary but not sufficient—even those cutting-edge strategies that carefully and effectively intervene in physical infrastructure and conditions require the critical work of personal relationships for full implementation.

We saw across chapters the significant value placed on culturally responsive initiatives that are attentive to race, gender, and class, but also to intersectional identities, and how these identities might exacerbate both risk and opportunities. We saw recommendations to affirm and create conditions that can be empowering for these identities, highlighting and amplifying cultural resilience. At the same time, we heard about how it is essential to invest in strategies that inhibit risk based on disparate conditions and outcomes impacting certain populations (e.g., Black youth, women and girls of color, LGBTQIA+ identified).

We also read about the tragic role of trauma experiences and how youth violence prevention must be trauma responsive and consider early childhood adversity as much as the impacts of ongoing toxic stress and complex trauma throughout life. Survivorship must be valued and leveraged. We heard how these trauma challenges, like other issues and areas, may compound with the realities of intersectional identities. Both victims and victimizers are impacted.

We also saw that healing through and with trauma is as important for individuals as it is for communities, which are the contexts within which subsequent developmental experiences or youth violence scenarios will occur.

Within these chapters, we witnessed how discussions of trauma and youth violence prevention inevitably included interpersonal violence as well as structural violence as components of trauma-inducing environments. Systemic violence, denied opportunity, and a range of -isms, including racism, were identified for their deleterious and trauma-inducing impacts. Threats to equity and justice were recognized for their influences on stress, mental health, poverty, and distribution of risk for violence exposure. Finally, we saw the necessity for organized and ongoing opportunities for voice and agency among those most deeply impacted by violence. A collaborative seat at the table for policy and service stakeholders, and for youth and families with a vested interest in preventing violence, can ensure that the beliefs about causes of, effects of, and solutions for youth violence are always prominent and prioritized.

Alongside our foundational knowledge about youth violence prevention were innovative practice models that challenge us to think in bold new ways. These new models integrate and amplify unique components within strategies with assistance from sports, music, arts, technology, culture, and more. These new approaches are collaborative and cross-sector efforts that link normally independent, siloed efforts.

A mixtape makes the ordinary extraordinary, whether we are talking about the first party mixtapes bringing the earliest live Hip Hop events from the Bronx to the rest of the Tri-State area, DJ mixtapes bringing the newest blends and remixes, private mixtapes with a compilation of favorite songs of any genre from the radio or your collection to a cassette tape, or the modern-day playlist on your preferred streaming service. At its best, a mixtape can take something that was accessible to only a limited few and breathe life into it so that many far and wide can experience the magic in their own place in time. It can take something considered classic and enduring and reimagine it in an entirely new way. It can bring together previously separate strands of knowledge, and experience(s) never considered together, to create something special and new. Or a mixtape can simply elevate something already powerful and impactful to even greater heights. What we have witnessed in these chapters has this same level of respect for the classics and foundational knowledge, but also the innovation, dynamism, recontextualizing, and reimagining of what is and can be around preventing violence. This information really is accessible to us all. It transcends siloed disciplines and professions. It is universally applicable and urgently needed.

Please use, reuse, and share.

Acknowledgments

Paul Boxer

At one point during my clinical training I was assigned to work with a young adolescent who had been shipped from the other side of the state to the residential care facility where I was interning. He had already been removed from multiple other short-term placements, including juvenile detention facilities and inpatient psychiatric wards, for persistent oppositional and aggressive behavior. Nothing seemed to have helped him—and he seemed rapidly to be understanding that he was running out of adults who were looking out for him. I brought a summary of his case to my supervisor, Eric Dubow—who has since become my longtime friend and colleague. Eric took a look at the paperwork and said, without hesitation, "We have to get this kid some coping skills." I definitely tried—but the youth was exceedingly difficult to engage. He had a tough time sitting still or even listening patiently as I tried to employ with him standard cognitive behavioral techniques, adapted for the most minimal approach. After a couple of weeks of going nowhere, and routinely getting punished by his staff for severe and aggressive outbursts with them and with his peers, I finally asked him, "What's it going to take to get you to stop with all the fighting and screaming?" He looked right at me and said, "Take me to lunch." We quickly worked out a contract whereby I would take him out to a nearby deli for lunch if he made it through a whole week without incidents. His outbursts ceased immediately, and we enjoyed a few weeks' worth of lunches until his team from home decided to relocate him to another facility. Throughout my career I have seen and heard about numerous cases like this—where the traditional methods of engagements fail and nontraditional methods that still hang on basic theoretical ideas can be leveraged for positive change. So in my first acknowledgment I want to recognize the children and adolescents with whom I have worked over the years, who have inspired my commitment to pressing on in our prevention and intervention science to do better, to expand, to consider modes of helping that might be off the beaten path, and to recognize the core, foundational theories that allow us to bring change.

Across over twenty years of research and practice in the arena of youth violence prevention I have learned a lot of things from a lot of people—not just facts and ideas but ways of thinking about and doing this work in a manner that can elevate and sustain. These are the people whom I never actually felt like I worked with—that instead we shared deep and abiding interests in trying to make things better for kids managing adverse experiences and environments, trying to get a handle on difficult emotions, and struggling to make it through one challenge after another. So, thank you to Eric Dubow, Joel Fiedler, and Jim Bow, for your thoughtful and patient supervision; and thanks again to Eric as well as Rowell Huesmann, Laurie Heatherington, Marie Tisak, Nancy Guerra, and Annette Mahoney for your guidance in shaping the direction of my scholarship.

Rutgers University–Newark has been a supportive and exciting place to spend the bulk of my career so far, particularly over the past several years under the pathbreaking leadership of Nancy Cantor, whose commitment to scholarly engagement in community challenges included funding a variety of outreach programs that allowed me to connect meaningfully with colleagues in the arenas of juvenile justice, social services, community mental health, and local and state government. Those efforts have deeply informed my thinking about the universe of possibilities for preventing youth violence and promoting positive youth development. And it has been truly invigorating to work with the diverse and impressive array of colleagues in the Department of Psychology at Rutgers–Newark, along with collaborators in the Rutgers Schools of Social Work and Criminal Justice.

To my coeditor, former "violence camp"–mate, and now longtime friend and colleague, Raphael Travis Jr., I cannot even begin to describe what this experience has meant for me professionally and personally. To think that this all started with a KRS-One track and a handful of J.Period mixtapes is just wild! I have long admired your work, and I am grateful now to have taken part in some of it with you. Thank you also to Peter Mickulas and Rutgers University Press for allowing us to bring our shared vision forward.

Finally I will say that none of this would have been possible without the support and love of my brilliant and patient wife, Sara Goldstein, who over the years has also been my colleague and my collaborator. To her and also to our children Noah, Lilah, and Maya, and to my mother and the memory of my father, I say thank you for everything.

Raphael Travis Jr.

My interest in this work and my path to this collaboration can be described as a kind of mixtape of experiences. In this mix I want to acknowledge "the Park" across the street from our apartment at 171 Laurel Street. This includes the basketball courts, the handball court that doubled as a bean ball wall and stickball court, the tennis court that doubled as a baseball field and kickball field, the grass that doubled as a football field. I want to acknowledge "the Center" which was the ultimate training ground for ping-pong, pool, and talking junk, but also a place you knew was safe, welcoming, and fun. I want to acknowledge "Night Center" on Friday nights at Roslyn High School including the teachers and coaches who volunteered their time to make the space available. This includes opening up the indoor basketball courts, the weight room, and of course the milkshake maker! I want to acknowledge weekends in Hempstead with my father where we'd go watch Hempstead High basketball and football games, which to me felt like watching the NBA and NFL. We'd also hang out and watch the adult softball leagues at Lincoln and Kennedy Park—rooting for Henry Street and Larry's Taxi like they were the Yankees or Mets. Music, laughter, food, and fun filled these moments, and there simply was nothing better.

I want to acknowledge summers in Kinston, North Carolina, with my grandparents Romeo and Sybeleen. This includes big breakfasts, card games with my grandfather, helping my grandmother in her garden and with her trips to the dollar store, and late-night cantaloupe and ice cream (and ice cream floats). I want to acknowledge my K–12 teachers who were supportive and encouraging of me even when I did not bring 100 percent to the classroom or my homework; who engaged my potential instead of only what I presented with on any given day. I also want to acknowledge my mom and dad, Theano and Raphael Sr., who although they split when I was young were continual sources of unconditional love and the ultimate models for "hard work" (also interestingly enough the Hempstead High chant when breaking team huddles).

At the same time, I want to acknowledge the lean times, the hungry times, the times when the electricity was cut off, the times with eviction notices on the door, the times with no phone, and the ugly realities of violence and substance use and abuse that too many families had to cope with.

In this fiftieth anniversary year of its birth within modern history I want to acknowledge Hip Hop culture. To me it has been a fuel for life, a gift of a universe of outlets of expressivity within spaces and times that could be incredibly stressful, oppressive, and challenging. The ability to express visually with graffiti, the ability to express physically with breaking, the ability to immerse oneself in and create incredible soundscapes through DJing, the ability to embrace my love of words and lose myself in the lyricism of emceeing, and of course the ability to be reflexive and proactive in the most empowering ways through a knowledge of self. That was Hip Hop for me. The lions of the culture at the time were significant as well with groups like Public Enemy helping me recognize the significance of being strong, Black, intelligent, and positive in a time when the headlines and policies tried to push a mythical narrative of Black youth as superpredators. And a shoutout to the bus to Jamaica Avenue to get those Hip Hop tapes off of the street and gear from the Colosseum Mall. These experiences and settings and so many more were the foundation and fuel for my childhood and adolescent years. At the same time there was a tremendous amount of luck and grace at times that protected me from being ensnared in the tentacles of violence and the criminal justice system.

Fast-forward to today, I want to acknowledge my beautiful wife Dnika for being so supportive and my inspiration for being the best version of myself each day. To Morgan and Niko for being so brilliant, funny, caring, and talented; and ultimately true motivation for thinking about the importance of pathways to youth violence prevention. Thank you Abijah and Sanai, my goddaughters, for being the epitomes of Black Girl Magic. I am so proud of you both. Keep shining!

Thank you, Paul Boxer, for your similar love of music (including KRS-One and J.Period!), your commitment to violence prevention, and your continued attention to community well-being. We were curious as to what would be similar and what might be different across these many voices about this critically important issue. We did it! Thank you to each and every author for joining this journey and sharing not just your expertise but your personal experiences and your professional experiences, allowing us to learn from you and push our respective fields forward in service of more peaceful, equitable, and health-enhancing communities. Thank you Peter Mickulas and Rutgers University Press for your belief in the importance of bringing these voices to life. Thank you to the Texas State University community for your support of the research and pedagogy informing this work, with a special shoutout to Angela Ausbrooks, Scott Bowman, Ray Cordero (and TRIO), and Jesse Silva. Finally, I would like to acknowledge the many collaborators in research, practice, and thought leadership, including but not limited to Timothy Jones and the #HipHopEd community, and those who I like to refer to as Therapeutic Wu-Tang (Elliot, JC, Aaron, Brittani, Jacqui, Jonah, Max, Alex), and so many more. Thank you.

Notes on Contributors

JALEEL ABDUL-ADIL, PHD, is an associate professor of clinical psychology in psychiatry at the Institute for Juvenile Research in the Department of Psychiatry at the University of Illinois at Chicago (UIC). He is the codirector of the Urban Youth Trauma Center at UIC that is part of the National Child Traumatic Stress Network, and his current work involves culturally sensitive, evidence-based, and trauma-informed services for community-based prevention and clinic-based intervention with urban youth and families.

ELIZABETH BARNERT, MD, MPH, MS, is a pediatrician and associate professor of pediatrics at the University of California, Los Angeles. Her research, grounded in human rights and social action, examines children affected by violence, family separation, and incarceration.

KAREN L. BIERMAN, PHD, is the Evan Pugh University Professor of Psychology and Human Development and Family Studies and director of the Child Study Center, Pennsylvania State University. Her forty-year research career has focused on social-emotional development and children at risk, with an emphasis on the design and evaluation of school-based and family-focused prevention programs.

STEPHANIE BONNE, MD, is a trauma surgeon and chief of trauma and surgical critical care at Hackensack University Medical Center in New Jersey. She is a professor of surgery there and adjunct associate professor of surgery at Rutgers New Jersey Medical School. She focuses her work on the epidemiology of trauma and violence, with a specific focus on gun violence. She is nationally recognized in the trauma community for her work developing hospital-based violence intervention and community trauma recovery programs.

Notes on Contributors

PAUL BOXER, PHD, is a professor of psychology at Rutgers University–Newark. He holds faculty affiliate appointments in the Rutgers School of Criminal Justice and the Rutgers School of Social Work as well as the Institute for Social Research at the University of Michigan. He studies the development and management of youth aggression and violence as well as the impact of violent conditions on youth development. He also examines evidence-based practices for helping youth in the juvenile justice system.

JOEL M. CAPLAN, PHD, is professor of criminal justice, Rutgers University–Newark, director of the Rutgers Center on Public Security, and faculty advisor to the Newark Public Safety Collaborative. He is a criminologist focused on communities, crime, and prevention. He specializes in mapping and pattern analysis and is the coinventor (with Leslie Kennedy) of Risk Terrain Modeling.

FIORELLA L. CARLOS CHAVEZ, PHD, is a human development and family scientist, a community health researcher, and an assistant professor in the Edson College of Nursing and Health Innovation at Arizona State University. She is one of the pioneers in the study of the implications of work-life stressors on Latino migrant farmworker youths' health and development by using phenomenological and mixed methodologies.

LIZA CHOWDHURY, PHD, is director of the Paterson Healing Collective, a community-based violence intervention effort in Paterson, New Jersey. She is a scholar-activist and former probation officer who cofounded and leads Reimagining Justice, a nonprofit dedicated to justice system reform. Previously she served on the teaching faculties of Manhattan College/CUNY, Farleigh Dickinson University, and Rutgers University.

ISAIAS M. CONTRERAS is a doctoral student in the Department of Psychological Science at the University of California, Irvine. He majored in both psychology and criminology as an undergraduate and has worked on the study of anger, rumination, and aggression. His doctoral research focuses on job stress, anger, and burnout among law enforcement officers.

ZION CRICHLOW, MA, is a doctoral student in clinical-community psychology at the University of South Carolina. He received his MA in psychology at Rutgers University–Newark, where he studied the impact of violent perpetration on psychological adjustment. His interests include mental health in LGBTQ+ youth and young adults of color and the role of systemic racism in the mental health of Black youth.

KATRINA J. DEBNAM, PHD, MPH, is an associate professor with a joint appointment in the School of Education & Human Development and the School of Nursing at the University of Virginia. Her research focuses on adolescent development of healthy romantic relationships and the prevention of teen dating violence as well as the design and assessment of culturally responsive school-based interventions.

JANICE JOHNSON DIAS, PHD, is the president of GrassROOTS Community Foundation as well as interim dean of Student Academic Engagement and Retention and associate professor of sociology at John Jay College of Criminal Justice. She studies stratification and inequality focusing on women and girls, particularly mothers and Black folk, and she develops solutions to respond to those challenges. Her book, *Parent Like It Matters: How to Raise Joyful-Changemaking Girls*, summarizes her life experiences and offers practical tips of how caregivers can raise children who are devoted to social justice.

ROBYN D. DOUGLAS, MA, is a clinical psychology doctoral student, Department of Psychological and Brain Sciences, Texas A&M University. Her research, clinical, and advocacy work examines the experiences of Black youth and youth of color exposed to community violence, racial trauma, and neighborhood poverty. She is passionate about class-conscious and culturally informed mental health treatments, community-based healing practices, and the overall resiliency of disinvested communities.

NONI K. GAYLORD-HARDEN, PHD, is professor and director of the Youth Rising Lab in the Department of Psychological and Brain Sciences, Texas A&M University. She conducts research on the impact of exposure to community violence and traumatic loss on Black adolescents in disinvested, urban communities. An overarching goal of her work is to minimize the impact of violence exposure and promote healing by enhancing existing strengths and assets embedded in Black youth, families, and communities.

ALEJANDRO GIMENEZ-SANTANA, PHD, is assistant professor of professional practice, School of Criminal Justice, Rutgers University–Newark, deputy director, Rutgers Center on Public Security, and director, Newark Public Safety Collaborative. He is a criminologist focused on communities, geospatial analysis, and socioeconomic determinants of crime. He has worked extensively in developing community solutions to crime problems through the data-informed community engagement model.

CHERYL GRILLS, PHD, is a clinical psychologist with a current emphasis in community psychology. She is a professor in the Department of Psychological

Science at Loyola Marymount University, and founder and director of its Psychology Applied Research Center. A national past president of the Association of Black Psychologists, she provides action research and evaluation support to social justice and social service organizations. Her research focuses on African psychology, mental health disparities, and positive youth development.

MATTHEW HAGLER, PHD, is an assistant professor of psychology at Francis Marion University and a licensed clinical psychologist in South Carolina. His research examines processes and outcomes of intergenerational social support, especially mentoring interventions for marginalized youth. Clinically, he works with children, adolescents, and young adults, with particular interests in supporting recovery from complex trauma and mitigating risk for serious mental illness (SMI).

NEAL HALFON, MD, MPH, is a professor of pediatrics, public health, and public policy at the University of California, Los Angeles. He is the founding director of the UCLA Center for Healthier Children, Families, and Communities.

STANLEY J. HUEY JR., PHD, is an associate professor of psychology at the University of Southern California. His research focuses on reducing disparities in behavioral health by optimizing treatments for high-risk populations, with a particular focus on effectiveness of culturally tailored treatments. He teaches classes addressing mental health and diversity, and recent courses include culture and mental health, the psychology of African Americans, race and crime, and the psychology of racial bias.

JONATHAN JAY, DRPH, JD, is an assistant professor of community health sciences at the Boston University School of Public Health. He is a social epidemiologist who studies urban, especially youth exposure to firearm violence. His work combines computational analysis and community engagement with the goal of informing local intervention strategies.

CASEY KEENE, LMSW, believes that social change is both possible and necessary. She is director of programs & prevention at the National Resource Center on Domestic Violence (NRCDV), where she works to advance special projects and resource development initiatives. These include PreventIPV, VAWnet, the Domestic Violence Awareness Project, and the Adult Children Exposed to Domestic Violence (ACE-DV) Leadership Forum.

KATHERINE KELTON, PHD, MSPH, is a psychologist and advanced fellow with the VA Boston Healthcare System. Her research is heavily informed by her clinical practice and public health lens and examines how sociostructural, systemic inequities such as incarceration and homelessness impact posttraumatic stress and substance use disorders. She also focuses on translating research into practice through developing sustainable trauma-informed and culturally affirming interventions at the personal, therapeutic, supervisory, and systemic levels.

JILL KOCHANEK, PHD, is assistant professor and Athletic Leadership Master's Program director in the Department of Physical Education and Health Education at Springfield College. She is a sport scholar, coach, and practitioner whose work centers on promoting inclusion, equity, and social justice through sports. In research, she critically examines status quo sport dynamics and their marginalizing effects. In practice, she is a youth soccer coach and works as a sport psychology practitioner with youth and adult leaders to help them develop the knowledge and skills to render sport more inclusive and empowering for all.

JORJA LEAP, PHD, is an anthropologist and member of the faculty of the Department of Social Welfare in the UCLA Luskin School of Public Affairs and serves as the executive director of the UCLA Social Justice Research Partnership. She is the lead researcher for the White House Community Violence Intervention Collaborative and is engaged in a longitudinal evaluation of Homeboy Industries, the largest gang reentry program in the world. She is the cofounder of the UCLA Watts Leadership Institute, working closely with the community-based leaders of Watts as well as its nonprofit network. She is the author of *Jumped In: What Gangs Taught Me about Violence, Drugs, Love and Redemption*, *Project Fatherhood: A Story of Courage and Healing in One of America's Toughest Communities*, and *Entry Lessons: The Stories of Women Fighting for Their Place, Their Children, and Their Futures after Incarceration.*

JOYCE LEE, MPH, is a fourth-year medical student in the David Geffen School of Medicine at UCLA. She is passionate about the health of vulnerable populations. She hopes to integrate public health policy with clinical experience to bring health justice to vulnerable populations in her career.

MARSHA LEVICK, JD, is the chief legal officer and cofounder of the Juvenile Law Center, the first public interest law firm for children in the United States. She has spent her career challenging abusive and unconstitutional laws, policies, and practices harming children in the justice and child welfare systems through litigation and other legal advocacy in jurisdictions, and state and federal courts, across the country. She is also an adjunct professor at the University of Pennsylvania Carey Law School and Temple University Beasley School of law.

KRISTA R. MEHARI, PHD, LCP, is an assistant professor of psychology and human development at Vanderbilt University. Her research focuses on youth violence prevention, particularly by partnering with communities to implement systems-level strategies using participatory action research.

SHENNA MORRIS, MA, is director of policy in the National Resource Center on Domestic Violence (NRCDV). In this role she provides policy vision and expertise across NRCDV's areas of focus and social justice issues impacting survivors of domestic violence. Prior to joining NRCDV, she was the director of policy and community engagement at the Georgia Coalition Against Domestic Violence, where she advocated for responsive DV public policies, led capacity-building technical assistance efforts to culturally specific community-based organizations, worked with system partners to strengthen service provision and housing advocacy for survivors and people experiencing homelessness in HUD housing programs, and provided training and support to systems on addressing systemic racism and building equitable response systems.

SIERRA MULLAN, MSW, recently completed graduate training in social work at Texas State University. Youth empowerment is an area that she gravitated to early in her post-BSW career. It has continued through her interactions over the past eight years with youth involved in the juvenile justice system, residential placement, and teen support group settings. She will continue following this passion through advocacy, promoting the value of youth voice, ideas, and engagement in our communities.

RAYMOND W. NOVACO, PHD, is professor of psychological science, University of California, Irvine. He originated cognitive behavioral anger treatment and coined the term "anger management." He has extensive expertise on the assessment and treatment of anger with a variety of clinical populations having a history of violence, including those in forensic hospitals, the military, and juvenile detention facilities.

COREY PRACHNIAK, JD, MPH, is a lawyer and public health professional who is focused on policy solutions to address health and social inequities, with a particular focus on LGBTQ+ communities. They have served as principal investigator in international investigations on topics such as reproductive rights, HIV activism, and LGBTQ+ resilience, and are especially interested in the real-world, local impact of health policy and civil rights.

PETER REJ, PHD, is a biocultural anthropologist with a background in community-based participatory research and a commitment to understanding (and correcting) health, social, and structural inequalities. He serves as a research fellow at the Psychology Applied Research Center at Loyola Marymount

University and as a senior researcher with Imoyase Community Support Services.

JEAN RHODES, PHD, is the Frank L. Boyden Professor of Psychology and the founding director of the Center for Evidence-Based Mentoring at the University of Massachusetts Boston. She has devoted her career to understanding and advancing the role of intergenerational relationships in the intellectual, social-emotional, educational, and career development of marginalized youth. She has led the movement for integrating evidence-based practices into youth mentoring programs.

JOSEPH RICHARDSON JR., PHD, is the Joel and Kim Feller Professor of African-American Studies and Anthropology at the University of Maryland–College Park. His research investigates cycles of gun violence, trauma, and social marginalization. Using innovative research methods, including digital storytelling, his work explores the intersections of the criminal justice, educational, and health care systems in lives of young Black men and their communities by emphasizing the ways in which structural conditions routinely harm them.

EMILY N. SATINSKY, MSC, is a doctoral student in clinical psychology at the University of Southern California. Her research focuses on better understanding environmental and social influences on mental health and increasing access to mental health care for culturally diverse and historically oppressed communities. She is dedicated to community engagement and using qualitative methods to inform the development of culturally relevant interventions.

ASHLI J. SHEIDOW, PHD, is a senior research scientist in the Lighthouse Institute of Chestnut Health Systems. She researches treatments and services for adolescents and emerging adults, particularly those who have substance use problems and legal system involvement. She also focuses on effective implementation of evidence-based practices through improving training supports and task-shifting in low-resourced environments, as well as recovery support services and community-engaged research with and by people who have lived experience in recovery and the legal system.

REBECCA SLOTKIN, MS, is a doctoral candidate in child clinical psychology at Pennsylvania State University. Following undergraduate studies at Vassar College and two years as a research assistant at Duke University's Center for Child and Family Policy, she initiated doctoral studies in child clinical psychology at Penn State to pursue her research and clinical interests in peer relations, parent-child relationships, and social-emotional learning interventions.

318 • Notes on Contributors

DEMETRIUS R. SMITH, MS, LPC, serves as adjunct faculty in the Psychology Department of University of South Alabama. He is the owner of I.C.U. Counseling and Mental Health Support Services, LLC, a community-based agency for Black and impoverished communities. His work focuses on infusing innovative, evidence-based methods with culturally sensitive approaches in order to promote resilience and empowerment.

SAMSON STYLES is a filmmaker, actor, on-air personality, and content director. After being released from many years of incarceration, Styles produced a documentary called "Brooklyn Girls Fight Club" with the support of Black Entertainment Television (BET) and soon became a regular news correspondent for BET. He currently runs his own production company, JayCity Enterprises, producing the film "Killing Beef: Gun Violence in the Black Community" and serving as consulting producer for the Netflix documentary "Crack: Cocaine, Corruption, and Conspiracy."

CLAIRE TERREBONNE, JD, is the vice president of operations, formerly the director of legal services, at Jackson County CASA in Kansas City, Missouri. She first discovered child welfare through her pro bono work during her early days as a complex commercial litigator, eventually moving into the nonprofit sector to represent children full-time. She holds a Child Welfare Law Specialist certification from the National Association of Counsel for Children. She also teaches child welfare law as an adjunct professor to Child and Family Law Clinic students at the University of Missouri–Kansas City School of Law.

RAPHAEL TRAVIS JR., DRPH, MSW, is a professor at Texas State University in the School of Social Work. His research, practice, and consultancy work emphasize healthy development over the life course, resilience, and civic engagement. He also investigates creative arts, especially hip-hop culture, as a source of health and well-being for individuals and communities. He is author of *The Healing Power of Hip Hop*. His latest research, linking arts engagement and well-being, appears in a variety of academic journals and book chapters.

WILLIAM WICAL, MA, is a doctoral student in anthropology and a research assistant in the Translational Research and Applied Violence Intervention Lab (TRAVAIL) at the University of Maryland—College Park. His research examines the emotional experiences of Black men who survived a gunshot wound and received services from a hospital-based violence intervention program. In underscoring the political significance of those aspects of life that are not frequently registered within discourses of resistance and agency—including emotional experiences—his work contributes to abolitionist scholarship and efforts to achieve racial justice.

Index

adolescence, 216, 229, 263, 285; and adverse childhood experiences (ACEs), 82; and antisocial behavior, 37; and behavior, 272–73; and criminal behavior, 36; and development, 4, 274; female, 97; and friendship, 230–231; and identity development, 230; and intimate partner violence (IPV), 216; and male athletes, 219; and mental health, 95; phases of, 25; and teen dating violence (TDV), 219; and violence, 36, 217, 264, 293–294

Adult Children Exposed to Domestic Violence (ACE-DV), 205–26, 212

Adverse Childhood Experiences (ACEs), 14, 56, 58–59, 82, 196, 262

adverse health effects, 147

advocacy, 88–89, 127, 275; child, 198; LGBTQ+, 185–186, 188; medical, 126, 128; policy, 205; school stability, 199; skills, 188; and survivors, 210

Anti-Drug Abuse Act (1986), 59

antisocial behaviors, 36–37, 40, 70–71, 73, 77, 98

Bandura, Albert, 13–14

Beats Rhymes and Life (BRL Inc.), 286

behavioral health, 3, 62, 96, 265–266

Black community, 111, 118, 228, 280, 288; and athletes, 238–239; and community-based violence intervention (CVI), 127; and crack cocaine, 115, 119; and criminality, 60, 119; and empowerment, 98, 101; and gun violence, 116, 144; and hospital-based violence intervention programs (HVIPs), 262–263; and incarceration, 120; and intersectionality, 217; and LGBTQ+ needs, 185; and Newark (NJ), 134; and Paterson (NJ), 125–26; and Pink Houses, 116; and radio stations, 93; and Toledo (OH), 144; and Victims of Crime Compensation Office (VCCO), 128; and violence, 72, 119–120; and women, 249–51

Black Entertainment Television (BET), 121

Black girls, 251, 256; and characterization, 253–254; and discrimination, 254; and homicides, 249; and interpersonal violence, 252, 255; and intrapersonal violence, 255; and leadership development, 250; and misogynoir, 252; and self-harm, 250; and structural violence, 250, 254–256; and suicide, 249

Black Lives Matter movement, 101

Black Panther Party, 280

Black youth, 1–2, 59, 205, 262, 264–265, 276, 284, 297–298; and firearm homicide rates, 70, 261; and Functional Family Therapy (FFT), 72; and harm, 26; and high-violence neighborhoods, 73; and hospital-based violence intervention programs (HVIPs), 262–263, 267–268; and intersectionality, 188, 217; and

319

320 • Index

Black youth (cont.)
  multisystemic therapy (MST), 71; and
    risk, 305; as students, 59–60; and teen-
    dating violence (TDV), 220; and
    victimization, 187; and violence, 70,
    253–255, 277, 293–296
Board of State and Community Correc-
    tions (BSCC), 111
Boyle, Greg, 106
Boyle Heights, 106, 111
boys: Asian, 253; Black, 1, 26, 254–255, 261,
    263, 293; and juvenile detention, 120;
    LGBTQ+, 184; and masculinity, 217;
    and sexually related partner violence, 217;
    and violence prevention, 219; white, 253;
    young, 118
Bureau of Justice Statistics, 2

California, 47, 64, 112, 158, 165, 286–287;
    Center for Excellence in Youth
    Violence Prevention, 303; Fair Chance
    Act, 112
Canada, 27–28, 95
Caring School Community, 39
Center for Juvenile Justice reform (CJJR):
    Crossover Youth Practice Model
    (CYPM), 200
Centers for Disease Control and Preven-
    tion (CDC), 21, 96, 99–100, 209,
    215–216, 221, 261, 280–281, 285
Child and Family Services, 265
childhood, 23, 262; adversity, 21, 36, 83,
    195–197, 205, 305; and behavioral
    development, 36, 199; and domestic
    violence, 205, 211, 250; early, 21, 25;
    maltreatment, 193; and mental health,
    82; and sexual abuse, 250; and stress, 21;
    trauma, 123, 204
child welfare, 11, 199, 305; caseworkers, 85;
    costs, 64; and interpersonal violence,
    252; and policy, 156; and structural
    violence, 252; system, 20, 193–197,
    200–201, 220
civil rights, 60, 134, 229, 253, 273
clinical training, 85–86
Coaching Boys into Men, 219
cognitive behavioral therapy (CBT), 9, 49,
    52–53, 61, 87
Columbine High School, 48–49

communities, 149, 196, 204, 220, 250, 262,
    286–88, 304; and activism, 124–127, 134,
    148, 211–212, 232; Black, 111, 116; and
    businesses, 106; and cohesion, 29; and
    crime, 133–134, 140; and diversity, 40;
    and entrepreneurship, 110; faith, 158, 228,
    305; and funding, 64; and health, 280, 303;
    high-crime, 86; and Homeboy Industries
    (HBI), 107, 110; and intimate partner
    violence (IPV), 215–216; and kinship,
    107, 109–110; LGBTQ+, 158, 183–86, 188,
    190; marginalized, 27, 215, 268; nested,
    26; oppressed, 96; and poverty, 56; and
    research, 100, 106; and risks, 24, 94; and
    safety, 201; and skill development, 87;
    and sports, 243–244; and stakeholders,
    135–137, 156, 175–176; structures of, 229,
    244, 285, 298; and support, 101, 128, 161,
    178, 205, 208–211, 233; and teen dating
    violence (TDV), 220; underresourced,
    62–63, 118, 145; underserved, 119–121;
    and university partnerships, 88; and
    violence, 2, 28, 63, 94, 99, 111, 127, 130,
    147, 150, 195, 209, 217, 227, 263–267,
    275–276, 296; and violence prevention,
    109, 116, 124, 128, 130, 179–180;
    working-class, 123; and youth, 28, 99, 101,
    109, 113, 161, 165, 184, 188, 199, 205, 218,
    230, 232, 278, 297
communities of color, 125, 127, 174, 208,
    238, 256, 280; and cultural features, 158;
    and environmental conditions, 146;
    experiences of, 206; and institutions, 188;
    needs of, 126; and racism, 277; under-
    served, 121, 156; and violence, 26, 70; and
    violence prevention, 96
community-based activity linkages, 97
community-based intervention, 12, 76,
    126, 185
community-based juvenile justice
    programs, 266
community-based organizations, 62, 71,
    134–137, 139–140, 147, 150, 156–157, 161,
    200, 275
community-based participatory practice
    (CBPP), 156, 158–161, 228, 256
community-based participatory research
    (CBPR), 63, 100, 106–107, 156, 158,
    228, 296

community-based programs, 178–179, 186, 188

community-based public safety, 124, 126, 135, 264

community-based service, 98, 101, 162, 200, 255–256, 165

community-based settings, 29

community-based strategies, 72, 160, 162, 178

community-based support, 71, 125, 150

community-based violence intervention (CVI), 111, 124–127, 130, 178–179

community-based youth violence prevention, 109

community centers, 1, 10, 228–229, 231

community-defined evidence practices (CDEPs), 156–157, 160, 165

community ecology, 219

community engagement, 28, 134, 157–159, 165, 177, 281

community health, 280, 303

community intervention, 5, 12, 25, 41, 71–72, 76, 96, 124, 126, 129, 179–180, 185

community mental health centers, 88, 96, 265

community narratives, 283

community norms, 22

community policing, 118–119, 135, 140

community programs, 304

community representatives, 22

community safety, 294

community stakeholders, 20

community underinvestment, 21

community violence, 14, 23, 62, 96, 128–129, 178, 250; and adolescents, 217; conditions of, 99, 195; and gang leaders, 127; impacts of, 265, 267; indicators of, 2; and law enforcement, 147; and Portland (Oregon), 150; prevention of, 28, 63, 94, 266; and youth, 264

community workshops, 121

community youth centers, 29

conversion therapy, 190

Credible Messenger Justice Center, 126

credible messengers, 121, 124, 126–128, 265, 305

crime, 138, 147, 268, 272–273, 277; and Edward Byrne, 118–119; experiences of, 120; fear of, 146; neighborhood, 4; and

policing, 139–140; and violence, 119, 127, 276

crime analytics, 12, 137

crime arrests, 87

crime detection, 71

crime prevention, 135–137, 140

crime rates, 13, 56, 135–136, 276

crime reduction, 134–135

crime related-issues, 60

criminal justice systems, 263, 268, 272–273, 276, 305; and child welfare, 193, 200; and criminal offenses, 177; engagement with, 266; and involvement, 88; and racism, 277–278; and violence, 70; and youth of color, 70, 262, 267

criminal legal system, 27–28

critical consciousness, 97, 165, 240, 285, 298

critical race theory, 159, 294–95, 297

cultural tailoring, 70, 73–76

data-informed community engagement (DICE), 134–137, 139–140

Department of Justice (DOJ), 111, 134

Department of Juvenile Justice (CA), 64

Department of Youth Services, 187

domestic abuse, 36

domestic violence, 26, 46, 95, 99, 137, 195, 199, 204–205, 207, 209, 211, 250

economic conditions, 13, 26, 96, 99, 157, 264; and disinvestment, 296–297; and inequity, 294; and justice, 204; and opportunities, 125; and segregation, 149; and stability, 113, 207, 210; and sustainability, 129; and uncertainty, 21, 112, 210; and violence, 293

empowerment, 83, 98, 101, 281, 283–285, 288, 296

England, 95

entrepreneurship, 106, 108–113

ethnic disparities, 144, 297

ethnic groups, 26, 125, 156, 160, 174, 218, 220, 228, 296

ethnic minority youth, 70, 72–73, 75–76, 94, 96, 99–100

ethnic studies, 159

ethnography, 24, 107, 146, 263

evidence-based approaches, a, 10, 12, 97, 111, 126, 174, 243, 280–281, 285

322 • Index

evidence-based interventions, 73, 75
evidence-based practices (EBPs), 3, 5, 109, 124, 155
evidence-based programs, 40–41, 100, 199; and teen-dating violence programs, 220; and universal SEL programs, 38–39
evidence-based reviews, 178
evidence-based social skills, 96
evidence-based training, 85
evidence-based treatments, 64, 73
evidence-based violence prevention, 96, 98

faith-based community centers, 229
faith-based services, 165, 176, 232
faith-based violence interventions, 227, 233
families, 55, 111, 195, 205, 262, 287, 303; and Bandura's paradigm, 14; and caregiver skills, 12; and community, 204; and conflict resolution, 24; and criminal justice system, 70, 83, 263, 275; dynamics of, 22, 28–29, 74–75, 82, 96, 198, 280; and environments, 280; and family service agents, 4; and finances, 47, 64, 116; and gangs, 58–59, 108; and GrassROOTS Community Foundation (GCF), 256; and intervention, 71, 74; and LGBTQ+ youth, 184, 186, 196; and life course health development (LCHD), 25; and life course interventions, 19; middle-class, 271; and multisystemic therapy (MST), 75; preservation of, 197, 199; as systems, 285; and therapy, 61–62; and violence, 22, 45, 50, 129, 176, 204, 207–208, 211, 217; and violence prevention interventions, 26; and youth development, 26, 76, 157, 198–200; and youth violence, 19, 23
Family First Prevention Services Act, 200
"For Troubled Boys"; 282–283
Functional Family Therapy (FFT), 61–62, 72, 74

gender, 58, 60, 218, 255–256, 273, 305; affirmation, 96; affirming care, 187; bias, 232; discrimination, 254; empowerment, 284; expressions of, 252; and inequity, 251; markers, 190; minority youth, 187, 297; neutral bathrooms, 184–185; norms, 217; stereotypes, 252; and violence, 205, 253
gender identity, 96, 184, 190

Georgetown Law Center on Poverty and Inequality, 255; Gender Justice & Opportunity, 253
GrassROOTS Community Foundation (GCF), 250, 256
group therapy, 256
gun violence, 115, 146–147, 173, 304; and awareness, 129; and Black community, 116, 120; causes of, 268; experiences of, 121; and gangs, 101; and deaths, 100, 121, 124, 130, 261, 263; and environmental patterns, 148; and gun possession, 266–267; increases of, 120, 124; interpersonal, 144; and Paterson Healing Collective, 128; and Paterson (NJ), 125; prevention, 149–50, 178, 262–265, 267–268; retaliatory, 124; and Shape-Up, 150; and Toledo (OH), 144; youth, 72, 100, 124, 149, 264, 267

health care, 204, 287; access to, 198, 209, 296; and decision making, 254; institutions, 188; outcomes, 186, 217, 262, 267, 293; professionals, 187, 199; regional, 177; and social determinants of health, 174–175, 178, 210; and violence, 175
health care systems, 12, 29, 124–126, 145, 159, 174–175, 263
health development, 25–29, 163, 280, 285
health disparities, 94, 99–100, 156, 268, 295
health equity, 26–27, 298
health-promotion, 13
health-risk, 13
health trajectories, 21–23, 284
healthy relationships, 23, 218–220, 222, 305
high-crime communities, 86, 296
High School for Recording Arts, 286
high schools, 230, 240; and Black girls, 256; completion of, 108–109, 111, 272; curricula, 232; and entry, 23; and safety issues, 46, 49; and students, 10, 119, 185, 219, 241; transition to, 40; and violence, 264
Hip Hop culture, 3, 98, 280–282, 284; growth of, 101; and H.E.A.L.S., 95, 97; and narratives, 283; prosocial use of, 95; and service programs, 99; and strategies, 100; and violence, 99; and violence prevention, 101. *See also* rap

Hip Hop Development, 286
Hip Hop Expressive Arts Therapy (HEAT) Model, 286
HIV, 186, 190
Homeboy Industries (HBI), 106–113
homicides, 100, 145, 273, 278; of Black boys, 293; of Black women, 249; of children, 56; firearm, 26, 70, 72; rates of, 99; and risk factors, 69; and youth victims, 77
Hope Expressive Arts Therapy (HEAT) Model, 286
hospital-based intervention programs (HVIPs), 124, 126, 175–179, 262–268
Howard University, 93

Incredible Years Program, 28, 40, 71, 75–76
intimate partner violence (IPV), 215–16, 221

justice, 190, 263; and adolescents, 3, 10, 49, 53, 126, 160; and community, 233; economic, 204; and equity, 158, 209, 241, 306; and LGBTQ+ youth, 187; and policy advocacy, 205; and racism, 277; and religious institutions, 228; settings, 3, 76; system, 50, 160, 275
juvenile detention, 120, 273
juvenile justice, 11, 71, 156, 193, 200, 263, 265, 287, 305
juvenile justice systems, 49, 194, 201, 266, 268, 273; and adolescent behavior, 272; and intervention services, 3; and judges, 201; and population, 194; and problems, 275–276; and safety, 187; and violence, 286, 263, 286

Kaiser Permanente, 196
KOTA The Friend, 282–83

law enforcement, 12, 27, 46, 71, 112, 119, 126–127, 135, 140, 147, 157, 187, 197, 200, 204, 254, 266, 272, 277. See also policing
leadership, 106–107, 188, 190, 210–211, 244, 250, 256, 287–288; adult, 245; inclusive, 242; judicial, 200; programs, 28; school, 40, 266; shared, 159; youth, 110, 245
legal system, 59; and inequality, 277; juvenile, 10, 50, 61; and violence prevention, 275, 278; and youth violence, 277
LGBTQ+ activism, 183

LGBTQ+ communities, 111, 158, 160, 183, 190; and cultural competency, 187
LGBTQ+ rights, 189
LGBTQ+ youth, 160, 184, 189–190, 194–95; and abuse, 184; and advocacy, 185; and allies, 184; and initiatives, 185, 188–189; and services, 186, 220; violence, 184, 187–189
life course health development (LCHD), 20–22, 25–29, 111
Life Course Intervention Research Framework, 22, 25, 29
Life Course Intervention Research Network (LCIRN): Node on Youth Justice, 22

marginalized communities, 37, 41, 62–63, 94, 99; and firearms, 26; and gender, 218; and health services, 265; and intimate partner violence (IPV), 215; and intrapersonal violence, 255; and oppression, 228, 284; and police brutality, 27; socially, 262, 265; and teen-dating violence, 220; and violence, 294; and violence prevention, 220; and youth of color, 160–161, 265, 296
Marjory Stoneman Douglas High School (FL), 46
Massachusetts, 47, 88, 186–187
Massachusetts Juvenile Justice Pay for Success Initiative, 109
media, 14, 21, 60, 97, 99, 108, 159, 186, 242, 272, 284–85
mental health, 15, 40, 47, 50, 53, 62, 81, 83, 100, 128, 145, 244, 306; care, 72, 86, 156, 198, 200, 266, 286; experts, 41, 86, 176–177; and gender-affirming care, 187; problems, 195–196, 255, 294; programming, 41, 129, 135; providers, 95, 190; services, 74, 88, 94, 96, 107–108, 113, 124, 126, 199, 262, 265, 281; and suicide, 186, 284; systems, 70, 88; and youth, 82, 264
mentoring, 10, 128; adult, 72; and at-risk youth, 81–84, 88, 124; career, 85; and health care systems, 12; limits of, 86; peer, 240; perspectives, 282; practices of, 82–83, 86; relationships, 265; and skill building, 62; and trauma-informed practices, 84–85, 87–89; and youth development, 28

324 • Index

mentoring programs, 81, 86; expansion of, 82; limits of, 86; therapeutic, 89; and trauma exposure, 84–85, 88; and youth enrollment, 82–84

minorities, 94, 238, 240; and adolescents, 72, 75–76, 187, 238, 296; and adverse childhood experience, 56; low-income, 96, 99; and oppression, 94, 239, 244; and organizations, 127, 240; racial, 70, 72, 75, 83, 99–100, 125, 174, 254; sexual, 184, 215, 297; and violence, 26, 228; and violence prevention, 73

motor vehicle thefts (MVTs), 137, 139–140

multisystemic therapy (MST), 61–62, 71, 74–76

National Child Traumatic Stress Network (NCTSN), 96

Newark (NJ), 134, 137; International Film Festival, 121; Police Division (NPD), 134; public safety, 127, 135; Public Safety Collaborative (NPSC), 134–137, 139–140; youth residents, 139

Newark Community Street Team (NCST), 127, 135

New Jersey's Victims of Crime Compensation Office (VCCO), 128

NJ Violence Intervention and Prevention Coalition, 127

non-homicide crimes, 274

Nurse-Family Partnership (NFP), 25, 28

Office of Juvenile Justice and Delinquency Prevention, 2, 70, 194

Orange County Family Justice Center, 45

Oxford High School (MI), 46

Parent-Child Interaction Therapy (PCIT), 71

peer pressure, 121

peer relationships, 77, 164

peer-to-peer support, 97

police brutality, 27, 94, 99, 101, 121, 130, 262

policing, 120, 126, 140, 159, 179, 239, 295; and adverse health effects, 147; and community relations, 140; and community safety, 135; and crime problems, 139; and discrimination, 134, 145; and overpolicing, 130, 136; and

police officers, 47, 62, 109, 117–118; and police reforms, 130, 134; and policing models, 135; and problem-oriented policing, 136; and racial bias, 157; and risk-based policing, 136; and unlawful practices, 134

policy, 25, 84–85, 87, 200; child welfare, 197; and community investment, 233; development, 156, 205, 304; level strategies, 72; social, 42; and teendating violence, 219; and violence prevention, 189; and youth support, 303–304

policy advocacy, 205, 209

policymakers, 88, 111–112, 147, 159, 261

poverty, 119, 123, 129, 180, 284, 295, 305–306; and children, 10, 15, 58, 84, 194–195; indicators of, 2; intergenerational, 134, 165, 195; and race, 149; rates of, 56, 117, 125, 146, 249; and structural inequalities, 99; urban, 94; and welfare, 116

Preserving, Archiving, and Teaching Hip Hop (PATH Inc.), 286

primary prevention, 70, 72, 175, 209, 218–219, 221

prison, 83, 107, 116, 118, 120–121, 272–273, 275, 277

prison-industrial complex, 64

Promoting Alternative Thinking Strategies (PATHS), 38–40

prosocial activities, 62, 97–98, 107, 198–199

psychological development, 19, 56, 95, 274

psychological distress, 15–16, 47, 50, 195, 215, 241, 254–255, 262, 264, 271

psychological interventions, 25, 51, 89, 94, 229, 242, 305

psychology, 63, 82, 86, 274; clinical, 10, 45, 94, 303; and criminology, 45; and disorders, 49; and education, 49–50, 52, 61, 85; and psychosis, 53; school, 45; training, 10; and violence, 252; and youth programs, 95

psychosocial programs, 94–95

psychotherapy, 10–11, 49, 51

public health, 46, 69, 124–125, 130, 173–174, 228, 250, 268, 294, 303; emergencies, 100, 144; and programs, 178–179; and violence prevention, 227 public safety, 124, 127, 134–137, 139–140, 263; and community-based violence intervention (CVI), 126; funding, 64; sustaining, 113

race, 58, 125, 145, 240–241, 253, 255–256, 284, 296–297, 305; and injustice, 232; mixed, 160; and poverty, 149; relations, 134; and schools, 2
racial justice, 147, 304
racism, 2, 24, 95, 237–238, 240, 242, 244, 252, 278, 287, 306; and Black youth, 294; and carceral system, 27; and inequality, 21; institutional, 147, 283, 295–296; and sexism, 253; structural, 156, 180, 217, 268, 277, 296–298; systemic, 125, 133, 188, 195, 277, 294, 304; and violence, 28
rap, 94–95, 97–101. *See also* Hip Hop culture
recidivism, 72, 107, 111, 121
Reimagining Justice Inc. (RJ), 124
relationships, 24, 46–47, 58, 83, 88–89, 97, 195, 221; abusive, 216; and depression, 50; and domestic violence, 209; family, 28–29, 196, 285; formation of, 84–85, 126, 197, 207–208; healthy, 23, 36–37, 81–82, 164, 175, 218–220, 222, 286, 288, 305; improvement of, 12, 207–208, 221; interpersonal, 294; intimate, 84; parent, 39; peer, 77; and power, 262; romantic, 57, 197, 216, 222, 271; sexual, 217; social, 266; therapeutic, 52; and trust, 198; unhealthy, 22, 216; and violence, 217
restorative justice, 97, 267
Rhythmic Mind, 286
risk factors, 4, 14–16, 23, 36, 60–61, 83, 175, 198; environmental, 70; individual, 180; mitigation of, 156; multilevel, 50; social, 238; and teen-dating violence (TDV), 218, 220–222; and trauma, 84; and violence exposure, 21, 144, 262, 267
risky behavior, 146, 285

school-based violence interventions, 36–37, 253, 295
schools, 3, 36, 50–52, 59–60, 62, 71, 96, 139, 159, 204, 228, 250, 262, 268; and administrations, 37, 197; and after-school programs, 85, 97, 305; and attendance, 25,

145, 176; charter, 135; and climates, 3–4, 29, 116, 184, 195, 221, 286; and cognitive behavioral therapy (CBT), 87; and counselors, 39; and democracy, 255; and discipline, 2, 199, 218, 253–254, 256, 273; and discrimination, 253–256; elementary, 38, 56, 230, 264; and entry, 23; and funding, 42, 158; and hospital-based intervention programs (HVIPs), 265; and inclusivity, 188, 190, 251; and individualized treatment plans, 75; and interventions, 185; and mental health programs, 95, 200; and mentoring programs, 89; middle, 37, 45, 93, 117, 185, 222, 231, 271; and multisystemic therapy (MST), 61; and preschools, 99; and programming, 37, 41, 49, 165, 286, 296; and psychologists, 45; and remote schooling, 100; and safety, 29; and school shootings, 27, 49; and social-emotional learning (SEL), 36–42; and social gatekeepers, 47; and socialization of aggression, 35; and sports, 189; and staff, 38, 58, 187; and team structures, 40; and teen-dating violence (TDV), 219–220; underresourced, 157; and violence, 14, 46, 48, 56, 63, 69, 158, 252, 295; and violence prevention, 16, 28, 263. *See also* high schools
school-to-prison pipeline, 59, 99, 205, 264, 268
sexual abuse, 50, 56, 82, 195, 250, 252. *See also* sexual violence
sexual activity, 37, 197, 297
sexual health, 185
sexual minorities, 184, 215
sexual orientation, 190, 218
sexual violence, 58, 60, 145, 184, 216, 218–219, 221
social action, 240, 256, 287
social change, 20, 206, 211, 229, 264, 268, 284–285, 287, 298
social-cognitive programs, 36–38, 96, 294
social competence, 28, 39
social conditions, 134, 195, 204, 240
social development, 2
social disorder, 145
social disparities, 287
social ecologies, 2, 9, 13, 22, 75, 209, 217, 219, 221

326 • Index

social-emotional learning (SEL), 36–39, 59, 82, 231, 282, 305
social engagement, 146
social enterprises, 107, 109–111, 113
social environment, 14, 233, 285, 305
social experiences, 14
social hierarchies, 254–255, 297
social identity, 237–38, 241, 244–245, 283
social inclusion, 60
social inequity, 145, 262, 287, 295
social innovation, 20
social institutions, 242, 251, 263
social interactions, 4, 58
socialization, 36, 255; cultural, 165; of aggression, 35
social justice, 239–240, 250, 280, 298; and action, 242; and community-defined evidence practices (CDEPs), 156; and education, 241, 243, 245; frameworks, 256; and resources, 140; and training, 250; and violence prevention, 180; and youth development, 240
social learning, 58
social media, 48, 99, 139, 272, 283
social networks, 4, 58, 204, 206, 217, 286
social norms, 209, 219, 294
social organization, 28
social policy, 42
social problem solving, 39
social relationships, 47, 266
social safety net, 134, 157, 177
social services, 45, 126, 177, 187, 211, 266–267
social skills, 96
social structures, 26, 251
social support, 161, 163, 174, 222, 228, 268, 286
social turbulence, 21
social welfare, 71
social work, 106, 303; workers, 86, 113, 175–177
socioecology, 55–58, 60–64, 96
stress, 210, 264, 306; and adaptation, 26; and childhood, 21; and coping methods, 15, 22; inoculation, 52; job, 46; management, 39; persistent, 21; posttraumatic, 82, 123; of racism, 2; tolerance for, 206; toxic, 23, 28, 196, 305; and trauma, 14, 16, 176, 285; and youth, 13, 232

substance abuse, 36, 96, 107, 195, 199, 262
suicide, 48, 59, 70, 184, 218, 250, 254, 284
suicide prevention, 186, 283–84

talk-based therapy, 282
teachers, 52, 58, 158, 197, 230–232, 253–254, 294–295, 305; and administrators, 37, 195, 197; and clinical training, 85; and health care providers, 86; and lesson plans, 38; and parents, 39, 219; and peer pressure, 121; and peers, 36; and students, 36, 46
teen dating violence (TDV), 216–222
transformative justice, 209
trauma, 14, 24, 108, 205, 228, 273; and abuse, 51, 262; centers, 174–175, 178–179, 263, 268; and childhood events, 83, 123, 195, 199, 204; experiences of, 16, 82–83, 86, 129, 160, 196, 206, 211, 261, 281, 283, 305; history, 58, 84, 199, 295; inducing environments, 4, 285, 287, 306; and mentoring, 83, 89; and oppression, 210; persistent, 2; and risk, 58; screening, 88; and trauma-informed practices, 29, 64, 84–89, 96–97, 100, 111, 126, 175, 197–198, 204, 267, 287; treatment of, 88, 107, 121, 176, 184, 266; untreated, 89; vicarious, 304; and vulnerability, 16; and youth, 83, 85–87, 282

University of California, Los Angeles (UCLA), 22, 110, 287
Urban Youth Trauma Center (UYTC), 96–97, 285

victimization, 2, 13–14, 46, 48, 60, 129, 139, 144–145, 176, 187, 204, 217–221, 262, 284
violence prevention, 23–24, 89, 93, 98, 174, 184–85, 190, 227–228, 261, 280; and child welfare, 193; and collaboration, 135; and critical race theory, 297; effective, 3–4, 21, 70–72, 101, 113, 232, 239, 267, 296–298, 305–6; faith-based, 233; gun, 178, 262–264; interventions, 72–74, 76, 96, 100, 187; and legal system, 275, 278; and marginalized communities, 296; practice, 29, 287; professionals, 13, 304; programs, 4, 16, 95–96, 99–101, 109, 186–188, 221, 231, 286, 297; and research, 295; strategies, 42, 96–97, 144, 189, 209, 229, 263,

267–268, 285, 294; and trauma, 305; and vocational development, 110–112; youth, 2–3, 5, 10–12, 20–22, 25–29, 70–72, 74–75, 95–96, 106, 220, 231, 263, 273, 281, 306

Virginia, 47

vocational development, 106–113

women, 113, 117, 119, 121, 129, 275, 305; Black, 217, 249, 251–252; and murder, 215; violence against, 215–16, 277, 284; young, 186

Workforce Innovation and Opportunity Act, 111–112

World Health Organization (WHO), 46, 295

youth behavior, 60, 296

youth delinquency, 87

youth development, 2, 13, 63, 81, 157, 163, 229, 231–232, 238–240, 243, 285, 303

youth employment, 112

youth engagement, 101, 240, 267

youth justice, 20, 27–28, 76

youth population, 194, 196

youth programming, 98, 108, 188–189

youth rehabilitation, 263, 265

youth safety, 146, 187, 190

youth sports, 237–240, 243–244

Youth Uprising, 110, 112–13

"zero tolerance" policies, 58–60, 200, 233